Page

THE BPP STUDY TEXT

Aims of this Study Text

To provide you with the knowledge and understanding, skills and application techniques that you need if you are to be successful in your exams

This Study Text has been written around the **Financial Accounting Fundamentals** syllabus.

- It is **comprehensive**. It covers the syllabus content. No more, no less.
- It is written at the **right level**. Each chapter is written with CIMA's precise learning outcomes in mind.
- It is targeted to the **exam**. We have taken account of the pilot paper, questions put to the examiners at the recent CIMA conference and the assessment methodology.

To allow you to study in the way that best suits your learning style and the time you have available, by following your personal Study Plan (see page (x))

The BPP Study Test has a variety of features, highlighted by icons. You can use these features in different ways to suit your learning style. You may be studying at home on your own until the date of the exam, or you may be attending a full-time course. You may like to (and have time to) read every word, or you may prefer to (or only have time to) skim-read and devote the remainder of your time to question practice. Wherever you fall in the spectrum, you will find the BPP Study Text meets your needs in designing and following your personal Study Plan.

To tie in with the other components of the BPP Effective Study Package to ensure you have the best possible chance of passing the exam (see page (vi))

Recommended period of use	Elements of the BPP Effective Study Package
Three to twelve months before the exam	**Study Text** Use the Study Text to acquire knowledge, understanding, skills and the ability to use application techniques.
Throughout	**MCQ cards and i-Pass** Revise your knowledge and ability to use application techniques, as well as practising this key exam question format, with 150 multiple choice questions. **i-Pass**, our computer-based testing package, provides objective test questions in a variety of formats and is ideal for self-assessment.
One to six months before the exam	**Practice & Revision Kit** Try the numerous examination-format questions, for which there are realistic suggested solutions prepared by BPP's own authors. Then attempt the two mock exams.
From three months before the exam until the last minute	**Passcards** Work through these short, memorable notes which are focused on what is most likely to come up in the exam you will be sitting.
One to six months before the exam	**Success Tapes** These audio tapes cover the vital elements of your syllabus in less than 90 minutes per subject. Each tape also contains exam hints to help you fine tune your strategy.
Three to twelve months before the exam	**Breakthrough Videos** Use a Breakthrough Video to supplement your Study Text. They give you clear tuition on key exam subjects and allow you the luxury of being able to pause or repeat sections until you have fully grasped the topic.

HELP YOURSELF STUDY FOR YOUR CIMA EXAMS

Exams for professional bodies such as CIMA are very different from those you have taken at college or university. You will be under **greater time pressure before** the exam - as you may be combining your study with work. There are many different ways of learning and so the BPP Study Text offers you a number of different tools to help you through. Here are some hints and tips: they are not plucked out of the air, but **based on research and experience**. (You don't need to know that long-term memory is in the same part of the brain as emotions and feelings - but it's a fact anyway.)

The right approach

1 **The right attitude**

Believe in yourself	Yes, there is a lot to learn. Yes, it is a challenge. But thousands have succeeded before and you can too.
Remember why you're doing it	Studying might seem a grind at times, but you are doing it for a reason: to advance your career.

2 **The right focus**

Read through the Syllabus and learning outcomes	These tell you what you are expected to know and are supplemented by Exam Focus Points in the text.
Study the Exam Paper section	Take note of the form of assessment that will be used in the exam you will be facing.

3 **The right method**

The big picture	You need to grasp the detail - but keeping in mind how everything fits into the big picture will help you understand better. • The **Introduction** of each chapter puts the material in context. • The **Syllabus content, learning outcomes** and **Exam focus points** show you what you need to **grasp.** • **Mind Maps** show the links and key issues in key topics.
In your own words	To absorb the information (and to practise your written communication skills), it helps to **put it into your own words.** • **Take notes.** • Answer the **questions** in each chapter. As well as helping you absorb the information you will practise your question answering skills, which become increasingly important as you progress through your CIMA exams. • Draw **mind maps**. We have some examples. • Try 'teaching' a subject to a colleague or friend.

Give yourself cues to jog your memory	The BPP Study Text uses **bold** to **highlight key points** and **icons** to identify key features, such as **Exam focus points** and **Key terms.** • Try **colour coding** with a highlighter pen. • Write **key points** on cards.

4 **The right review**

Review, review, review	It is a **fact** that regularly reviewing a topic in summary form can **fix it in your memory**. Because **review** is so important, the BPP Study Text helps you to do so in many ways. • **Chapter roundups** summarise the key points in each chapter. Use them to recap each study session. • The **Quick quiz** is another review technique to ensure that you have grasped the essentials. • Go through the **Examples** in each chapter a second or third time.

Suggested study sequence

Tackle the chapters in the order you find them in the Study Text. Taking into account your individual learning style, you could follow this sequence.

Key study steps	Activity
Step 1 **Topic list**	Each numbered topic is a numbered section in the chapter.
Step 2 **Introduction**	This gives you the **big picture** in terms of the **context** of the chapter, the **content** you will cover, and the **learning outcomes** the chapter assesses - in other words, it sets your **objectives for study.**
Step 3 **Knowledge brought forward boxes**	In these we highlight information and techniques that it is assumed you have 'brought forward' with you from your earlier studies. If there are topics which have changed recently due to legislation for example, these topics are explained in more detail.
Step 4 **Explanations**	Proceed methodically through the chapter, reading each section thoroughly and making sure you understand. You should pay particular attention to these topics.
Step 5 **Key terms and Exam focus points**	• **Key terms** can often earn you *easy marks* if you state them clearly and correctly in an appropriate exam answer (and they are indexed at the back of the text). • **Exam focus points** give you a good idea of how we think the examiner intends to examine certain topics.
Step 6 **Note taking**	Take brief notes if you wish, avoiding the temptation to copy out too much.

Key study steps	Activity
Step 7 **Examples**	Follow each through to its solution very carefully.
Step 8 **Case examples**	Study each one, and try to add flesh to them from your own experience - they are designed to show how the topics you are studying come alive (and often come unstuck) in the real world.
Step 9 **Questions**	Make a very good attempt at each one.
Step 10 **Answers**	Check yours against ours, and make sure you understand any discrepancies.
Step 11 **Chapter roundup**	Work through it very carefully, to make sure you have grasped the major points it is highlighting.
Step 12 **Quick quiz**	When you are happy that you have covered the chapter, use the **Quick quiz** to check how much you have remembered of the topics covered and to practise questions in a variety of formats.
Step 13 **Question(s) in the Question bank**	Either at this point, or later when you are thinking about revising, make a full attempt at the **Question(s)** suggested at the very end of the chapter. You can find these at the end of the Study Text, along with the **Answers** so you can see how you did. We highlight those that are introductory, and those which are of the standard you would expect to find in an exam. Whether you are sitting the exam in November 2001 or May 2002, **attempt all the question formats provided**. If you have purchased **MCQ cards**, use these too.

Developing your personal Study Plan

Preparing a Study Plan (and sticking closely to it) is one of the key elements in learning success.

Step 1. How do you learn?

First you need to be aware of your style of learning. There are four typical learning styles. Consider yourself in the light of the following descriptions and work out which you fit most closely. You can then plan to follow the key study steps in the sequence suggested.

Learning styles	Characteristics	Sequence of key study steps in the BPP Study Text
Theorist	Seeks to understand principles before applying them in practice	1, 2, 3, 4, 7, 8, 5, 9/10, 11, 12, 13 (6 continuous)
Reflector	Seeks to observe phenomena, thinks about them and then chooses to act	
Activist	Prefers to deal with practical, active problems; does not have much patience with theory	1, 2, 9/10 (read through), 7, 8, 5, 11, 3, 4, 9/10 (full attempt), 12, 13 (6 continuous)
Pragmatist	Prefers to study only if a direct link to practical problems can be seen; not interested in theory for its own sake	9/10 (read through), 2, 5, 7, 8, 11, 1, 3, 4, 9/10 (full attempt), 12, 13 (6 continuous)

Step 2. How much time do you have?

Work out the time you have available per week, given the following.

- The standard you have set yourself
- The time you need to set aside later for work on the Practice & Revision Kit and Passcards
- The other exam(s) you are sitting
- Very importantly, practical matters such as work, travel, exercise, sleep and social life

		Hours
Note your time available in box A.	A	

Step 3. Allocate your time

• Take the time you have available per week for this Study Text shown in box A, multiply it by the number of weeks available and insert the result in box B.	B	
• Divide the figure in Box B by the number of chapters in this text and insert the result in box C.	C	

Step 4. Implement

Set about studying each chapter in the time shown in box C, following the key study steps in the order suggested by your particular learning style.

This is your personal **Study Plan**.

Short of time: *Skim study technique*?

You may find you simply do not have the time available to follow all the key study steps for each chapter, however you adapt them for your particular learning style. If this is the case, follow the **skim study** technique below (the icons in the Study Text will help you to do this).

- Study the chapters in the order you find them in the Study Text.
- For each chapter, follow the key study steps 1-3, and then skim-read through step 4. Jump to step 11, and then go back to step 5. Follow through steps 7 and 8, and prepare outline answers to questions (steps 9/10). Try the Quick quiz (step 12), following up any items you can't answer, then do a plan for the Question (step 13), comparing it against our answers. You should probably still follow step 6 (note-taking), although you may decide simply to rely on the BPP Passcards for this.

Moving on...

However you study, when you are ready to embark on the practice and revision phase of the BPP Effective Study Package, you should still refer back to this Study Text, both as a source of **reference** (you should find the list of key terms and the index particularly helpful for this) and as a **refresher** (the Chapter roundups and Quick quizzes help you here).

And remember to keep careful hold of this Study Text - you will find it invaluable in your work.

SYLLABUS AND LEARNING OUTCOMES

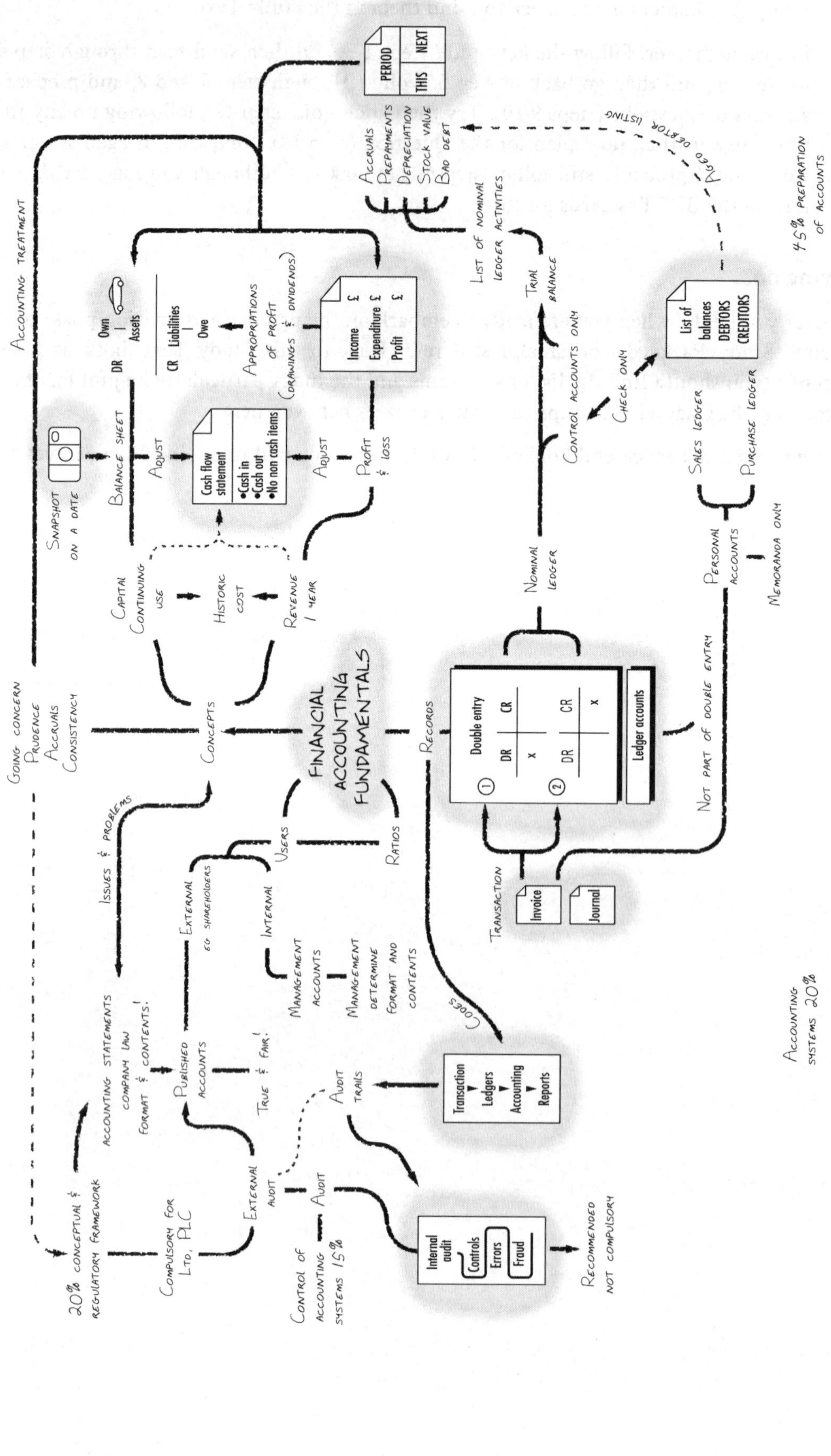

SYLLABUS AND LEARNING OUTCOMES

Syllabus overview

This is an introduction to financial accounting and assumes no prior knowledge of the subject. It deals with the recording of accounting transactions and the preparation of accounting statements for single entities. The basic concepts of accounting are dealt with and the student will be expected to understand the limitations of financial accounts in attempting to meet the needs of all users. An understanding of the different approaches to asset valuation and the resulting influence on profit management is required.

There is an introduction to the regulatory framework that determines published accounts requirements and a basic introduction to the role of accounting standards. An awareness of published accounts is required but students will not be asked to prepare accounts in a published accounts format. No knowledge of any specific accounting standard is required. There will be an introduction to accounting systems and their control.

Although the emphasis is on the basic methods and techniques of the subject, students will be expected to develop a critical approach by asking why the methods and techniques are used and in what circumstances they are appropriate.

This syllabus addresses the fundamentals of the subject and recognises that some terms and definitions vary from one area of the world to another. As a result students can use accepted alternative names to those that appear in this syllabus and be aware of alternative accounting formats. For example International Accounting Standard 1 (IAS 1) uses Income Statement instead of Profit and Loss Account and Non-current assets instead of Fixed Assets. Others include inventories, receivables and payables. All of these are acceptable for use in answers in this paper but it will be expected that they are applied consistently. Similarly, IAS 1 provides illustrations of accounting formats that are used widely in published accounts and are acceptable in this paper.

Aims

This syllabus aims to test the student's ability to:

- Explain the conceptual and regulatory framework of accounting
- Explain the nature of accounting systems and understand the control of such systems
- Prepare accounts for a single entity

Assessment

There will be a written paper of 3 hours in November 2001. Section A will use objective testing and will contain 50% of the marks. Section B will be compulsory for 30% of the marks and Section C will offer a choice of one question from two for 20% of the marks.

From May 2002 onwards the exam will be 100% objective testing style questions.

Learning outcomes and syllabus content

1(i) Conceptual and regulatory framework – 20%

Learning outcomes

On completion of their studies students should be able to:

- Identify the various user groups who need accounting information and the characteristics of such information necessary to meet their objectives
- Explain the function of and differences between financial and management accounting systems
- Identify and explain the fundamental accounting concepts, bases and policies
- Explain the concepts of capital and revenue, cash and profit, income and expenditure and assets and liabilities
- Explain the historical cost convention
- Identify the basic methods of valuing assets on current cost, market value and economic value bases and demonstrate their impact on profit measures and balance sheet values
- Explain the influence of legislation (eg Companies Acts) and accounting standards on the production of published accounting information for organisations

Syllabus content

		Covered in chapter
•	Users of accounts and the objectives of financial statements; functions of financial and management accounts; purpose of accounting statements; stewardship; the accounting equation	1, 3, 21
•	Fundamental accounting concepts, bases and policies; capital and revenue; cash and profit; income, expenditure, assets and liabilities	2, 3, 4
•	Historical cost convention	2
•	Methods of asset valuation and their implications for profit measurement and the balance sheet	2
•	The regulatory influence of company law and accounting standards; items in format for published accounts	2, 4, 19

1(ii) Accounting systems – 20%

Learning outcomes

On completion of their studies students should be able to:

- Explain the purpose of accounting records and their role in the accounting system
- Prepare cash and bank accounts; prepare bank reconciliation statements
- Prepare petty cash statements under an imprest system
- Prepare accounts for sales and purchases including personal accounts and control accounts
- Identify the necessity for financial accounting codes and construct a simple coding system
- Prepare nominal ledger accounts; prepare journal entries; prepare a trial balance
- Prepare accounts for indirect taxes (eg VAT)
- Prepare accounts for payroll

Syllabus content

		Covered in chapter
•	The accounting system and accounting records	5
•	Ledger accounts; double entry bookkeeping	6
•	Preparation of accounts for cash and bank; bank reconciliations; imprest system for petty cash	5, 6, 12
•	Accounting for sales and purchases including personal accounts and control accounts	5, 6, 9, 13
•	Financial accounting codes and their uses	5
•	Nominal ledger accounting; journal entries	6
•	Trial balance	7
•	Accounting for indirect taxes (eg VAT)	14
•	Accounting for payroll	15

1(iii) Control of accounting systems – 15%

Learning outcomes

On completion of their studies students should be able to:

- Identify the requirements for external audit and the basic processes undertaken
- Explain the purpose and basic procedures of internal audit
- Explain the meaning of true and fair view
- Explain the need for financial controls
- Explain the purpose of audit checks and audit trails
- Explain the nature of errors and to be able to make accounting entries for them
- Explain the nature of fraud and basic ideas of prevention

Syllabus content

		Covered in chapter
•	The purpose of external audit and the meaning of true and fair view	21
•	Internal audit	21
•	Financial controls; audit checks on financial controls; audit trails	21
•	Errors or fraud	16, 21

1(iv) Preparation of accounts – 45%

Learning outcomes

On completion of their studies students should be able to:

- Prepare accounts using accruals and prepayments
- Explain the difference between and prepare accounts for bad debts and provisions for doubtful debts
- Explain and calculate the methods of depreciation including straight line, reducing balance and revaluation and prepare accounts using each method
- Prepare a fixed asset register
- Explain, calculate and prepare accounts for stock
- Prepare trading accounts, profit and loss accounts, appropriations of profit and balance sheets from trial balance
- Prepare manufacturing accounts
- Prepare income and expenditure accounts
- Prepare accounts from incomplete records
- Calculate and explain basic ratios
- Prepare cash flow statements

Syllabus content

		Covered in chapter
•	Adjustments to the trial balance: accruals and prepayments	8, 16
•	Bad debts and provision for doubtful debts	9
•	Accounting treatment for depreciation (straight line, reducing balance and revaluation methods)	11
•	Fixed asset register	11
•	Accounting for stocks (excluding long term contract work-in-progress); methods of stock valuation (FIFO, LIFO and average cost)	8, 10
•	Trading, profit and loss accounts and balance sheets from trial balance: accounting for the appropriations of profit	7, 19
•	Manufacturing accounts	20
•	Income and expenditure accounts	17
•	Production of accounting statements from incomplete data	18
•	Ratios: return on capital employed; gross and net profit margins: asset turnover; debtors collection and creditors time to pay; current and quick ratios; stock turnover; gearing	22
•	Cash flow statements	20

THE EXAM PAPER

Format of the paper

November 2001

		Number of marks
Section A:	25 compulsory objective test questions	50
Section B:	two compulsory questions	30
Section C:	one question from two	20
		100

May 2002 onwards 100% of marks will be objective testing style questions.

Time allowed: 3 hours

Analysis of papers

May 2001

Section A

1 Multiple choice questions – 25 questions worth 2 marks each

Section B

2 Prepare a balance sheet and profit and loss account from a trial balance and make five adjustments for closing stocks, accruals and prepayments, provision for doubtful debts and provision for depreciation (14 marks)

Calculate current ratio, gearing and debtor days (6 marks)

3 Correction of errors involving a suspense account (4 marks)

Discuss financial controls (6 marks)

Section C

4 Discussion of depreciation (6 marks)

Prepare ledger accounts for the acquisition, depreciation and part exchange disposal of fixed assets (14 marks)

5 Discuss shock valuations (10 marks)

Calculate gross profit under LIFO and stock days under FIFO and LIFO. Discuss change in gross profit and stock days due to using LIFO rather than FIFO (10 marks)

Pilot Paper

Section A

1 Multiple choice questions – 25 questions worth 2 marks each

Section B

2 Prepare profit and loss account and balance sheet (20 marks)

3 Sales ledger journal entries, amended sales ledger total, amended sales ledger control account (10 marks)

Section C

4 Cash flow statement, discussing usefulness to users of the cash flow statement compared to the profit and loss account (20 marks)

5 Discussion of four methods of valuing fixed assets, the advantages of each method, calculating the NBV of fixed assets and the capital reserve (20 marks)

WHAT THE EXAMINER MEANS

The table below has been prepared by CIMA to help you interpret exam questions.

Learning objective	Verbs used	Definition
1 Knowledge What you are expected to know	• List • State • Define	• Make a list of • Express, fully or clearly, the details of/facts of • Give the exact meaning of
2 Comprehension What you are expected to understand	• Describe • Distinguish • Explain • Identify • Illustrate	• Communicate the key features of • Highlight the differences between • Make clear or intelligible/state the meaning of • Recognise, establish or select after consideration • Use an example to describe or explain something
3 Application Can you apply your knowledge?	• Apply • Calculate/ compute • Demonstrate • Prepare • Reconcile • Solve • Tabulate	• To put to practical use • To ascertain or reckon mathematically • To prove with certainty or to exhibit by practical means • To make or get ready for use • To make or prove consistent/compatible • Find an answer to • Arrange in a table
4 Analysis Can you analyse the detail of what you have learned?	• Analyse • Categorise • Compare and contrast • Construct • Discuss • Interpret • Produce	• Examine in detail the structure of • Place into a defined class or division • Show the similarities and/or differences between • To build up or compile • To examine in detail by argument • To translate into intelligible or familiar terms • To create or bring into existence
5 Evaluation Can you use your learning to evaluate, make decisions or recommendations?	• Advise • Evaluate • Recommend	• To counsel, inform or notify • To appraise or assess the value of • To advise on a course of action

TACKLING OBJECTIVE TEST QUESTIONS

What are objective test (OTs) questions?

Objective test questions (OTs) are designed to ensure that there is **no need for the marker to interpret or grade** the answer as they measure distinct results. Because they **avoid subjectivity,** they can be **marked by a computer**. OTs come in **many formats,** one of which is the multiple choice question (MCQ).

So what are multiple choice questions?

MCQs are a type of objective test question to which you have to **identify the single correct answer from a number of options**.

The Paper 1 exam and objective test questions

OTs in the November 2001 Paper 1 exam

Of the total marks available for the paper, multiple choice questions will comprise:

A 20%
B 50%
C 30%
D 25%

The correct answer is B.

To help you practice MCQs, we have included **lots of them throughout the text**: within each **chapter,** in the **Quick quizzes** at the end of each chapter and in the **Question bank** at the end of the text. And don't forget that we publish a **bank of 150 multiple choice question cards** which you can order using the form at the end of the text.

The MCQs in your exam contain four possible answers. You have to **choose the option that best answers the question**. The three incorrect options are called distracters. There is a skill in answering MCQs quickly and correctly. By practising MCQs you can develop this skill, giving you a better chance of passing the exam.

You may wish to follow the approach outlined below, or you may prefer to adapt it.

Step 1. **Skim read** all the MCQs and **identify** what appear to be the **easier** questions.

Step 2. Attempt each question - **starting with the easier questions** identified in Step 1. Read the question thoroughly. You may prefer to work out the answer before looking at the options, or you may prefer to look at the options at the beginning. Adopt the method that works best for you.

Step 3. Read the four options and see if one matches your own answer. **Be careful with numerical questions,** as the distracters are designed to match answers that incorporate common errors. Check that your calculation is correct. Have you followed the requirement exactly? Have you included every stage of the calculation?

Step 4. You may **find that none of the options matches your answer.**

- Re-read the question to ensure that you understand it and are answering the requirement
- Eliminate any obviously wrong answers
- Consider which of the remaining answers is the most likely to be correct and select the option

Step 5. If you are still **unsure** make a note **and continue to the next question.**

Step 6. **Revisit unanswered** questions. When you come back to a question after a break you often find you are able to answer it correctly straight away. If you are still unsure have a guess. You are not penalised for incorrect answers, so **never leave a question unanswered!**

Exam focus. After extensive practice and revision of MCQs, you may find that you recognise a question when you sit the exam. Be aware that the detail and/or requirement may be different. If the question seems familiar read the requirement and options carefully - do not assume that it is identical.

Computer-based assessment and OTs

Your exam will comprise entirely of a number of different types of **objective test question**. Here are some possible examples.

- **MCQs.** Read through the information above about MCQs and how to tackle them.
- **Data entry.** This type of OT requires you to provide figures such as the correct figure for creditors in a balance sheet.
- **Hot spots.** This question format might ask you to identify which cell on a spreadsheet contains a particular formula or where on a graph marginal revenue equals marginal cost.
- **Multiple response.** These questions provide you with a number of options and you have to identify those which fulfil certain criteria.
- **Matching.** This OT question format could ask you to classify particular costs into one of a range of cost classifications provided, to match descriptions of variances with one of a number of variances listed, and so on.

This text provides you with **plenty of opportunities to practise** these various question types. You will find OTs **within each chapter** in the text, the **Quick quizzes** at the end of each chapter are full of them and there are two OTs linked to each chapter in the **Question bank** at the end of the text.

The **Practice and Revision Kit** for this paper to be published in **January 2002** will be **full of OTs,** providing you with vital revision opportunities at the fundamental techniques and skills you will require in the exam.

Part A
Conceptual and regulatory framework

Chapter 1

THE NATURE AND OBJECTIVES OF ACCOUNTING

Topic List		Syllabus reference	Ability required
1	**What is accounting?**	**(i)**	**Comprehension**
2	**Users of accounting information**	**(i)**	**Comprehension**
3	**Management accounting and financial accounting**	**(i)**	**Comprehension**
4	**The scope of accounting information**	**(i)**	**Comprehension**
5	**The main financial statements**	**(i)**	**Comprehension**

Introduction

The syllabus for the *Financial Accounting Fundamentals* paper begins with the section 'conceptual and regulatory framework'. Before you learn how to prepare financial statements, it is important that you understand **why** accounting information is necessary and the assumptions on which it is based.

In Sections 1 to 2 of this chapter, you will discover the purposes and uses of accounting information.

As you have chosen to train for the CIMA qualification, you may be aware that there is a difference between a **management** accountant and a **financial** accountant. This topic is covered in Section 3.

Accounting is not an exact science. You should be aware that there are limitations on the scope and use of accounting information. This point is explored in Section 4.

Section 5 introduces you to the main financial statements - the profit and loss account and the balance sheet.

Learning outcomes covered in this chapter

- Identify the various user groups who need accounting information and the characteristics of such information necessary to meet their objectives
- Explain the function of and differences between financial and management accounting systems

Syllabus content covered in this chapter

- Users of accounts and the objectives of financial statements
- Functions of financial and management accounts
- Purpose of accounting statements

1 WHAT IS ACCOUNTING?

1.1 To set you thinking, try the first question to see what you already know about accounting.

Question 1

(a) You will often meet with the terms 'an accounting statement' or 'a set of accounts'. Do you know what is meant by these terms?

(b) Who do you think has the task of preparing accounting statements? In an organisation of a reasonable size, would it be one person? One department? Several different departments?

(c) Who are the users of accounting information?

(d) What is the purpose of accounting?

Answer

(a) An accounting statement is, for example, a profit and loss account or a balance sheet. A set of accounts is a number of accounting statements presented together with the intention of showing an overall view of an organisation's income, expenditure, assets and liabilities.

(b) Most organisations of reasonable size will have at least one accounts department, staffed by people with detailed knowledge of accounting systems and theory. In large organisations there may be several departments, or groups, responsible for preparing accounting information to meet the different needs of accounts users.

(c) The users of accounts include a variety of people and organisations, both internal and external, as explained in Section 2 of this chapter, such as current and potential workers, investors, customers and suppliers. Government bodies and the general public may also be interested. The extent of their information needs varies widely.

(d) There are many purposes of accounting. You may have considered the following.

- Control over the use of resources
- Knowledge of what the business owes and owns
- Calculation of profits and losses
- Cash budgeting
- Effective financial planning

Why keep accounts?

KEY TERMS

Accounting is collecting, recording, summarising and communicating financial information.

Accounts are the records in which this information is recorded. Keeping the most basic records is described as **bookkeeping**. The profession responsible for summarising and communicating financial information is the **accountancy** profession.

1.2 Accounts show where money came from and how it has been spent, this

- **aids** the efficient running of a business
- **indicates** how successfully managers are performing
- **provides information** about the resources and activities of a business

1.3 Accounting information **aids** the efficient running of a business in many ways.

(a) A business needs to pay bills for the goods and services it purchases, and collect money from its customers. It must, therefore, keep a record of such bills and invoices so that the correct amounts can be paid or collected at the correct times.

(b) Keeping records of a business's assets (eg its motor vehicles or computers) helps to keep them secure.

1.4 Accounts **indicate how successfully** the managers are performing.

1.5 Modern businesses are often complicated, they seldom have a single owner (some very large enterprises, such as British Telecom, may be owned by millions of shareholders). Frequently the owners are not involved in the day-to-day running of the business but appoint managers to act on their behalf. In addition, there are too many activities and assets for the managers to keep track of simply from personal knowledge and an occasional glance at the bank statement, so accounts which summarise transactions are very useful.

1.6 A business should **provide information** about its resources and activities because there are many groups of people who want or need that information. We will look more closely at the classes of people who might need information about a business in Section 2.

2 USERS OF ACCOUNTING INFORMATION — Pilot Paper

2.1 The following people might be interested in financial information about a large public company.

User group		Comment
(a)	**Managers of the company**	People appointed by the company's owners to supervise the daily activities of the company need information about the company's current and expected future financial situation, to make **planning decisions**.
(b)	**Shareholders of the company**, ie the company's owners	Want to assess how effectively management is performing and how much profit they can withdraw from the business for their own use.
(c)	**Trade contacts**, ie suppliers of goods to the company on credit and customers	Suppliers want to know about the company's **ability** to **pay its debts**; customers need to know that the company is a secure source of supply and is in no danger of closing down.
(d)	**Providers of finance to the company,** ie lenders both short and long term	Lenders will want to ensure that the company is able to meet **interest payments**, and eventually to repay the amounts advanced.
(e)	**The Inland Revenue**	Wants to know about business profits in order to **assess** the tax payable by the company.
(f)	**Employees**	Need to know about the company's financial situation, because their **future** careers and the level of their wages and salaries depend on it.

User group		Comment
(g)	**Financial analysts and advisers**	Need information for their clients. For example, stockbrokers need information to **advise investors,** credit agencies want information to advise potential suppliers of goods to the company, journalists need information for their reading public.
(h)	**Government and their agencies**	Interested in the allocation of resources and in the activities of enterprises. Also require information in order to provide a basis for **national statistics**.
(i)	**The public**	Want information because enterprises affect them in many ways, eg by providing jobs and using local suppliers, or by affecting the environment (eg pollution).

Exam focus point

In the Pilot Paper, you were asked to compare the usefulness of different statements for different users. This subquestion attracted 10 marks.

Question 2

It is easy to see how 'internal' people get hold of accounting information. A manager, for example, can ask the accounts department to prepare whatever accounting statements he needs. But external users of accounts cannot do this. How, in practice, can a business contact or a financial analyst access accounting information about a company?

Answer

Limited companies (though not other forms of business such as partnerships) are required to make certain accounting information public. They send copies of the required information to the Registrar of Companies at Companies House. The information filed at Companies House is available, at a fee, to any member of the public who asks for it. Other sources include financial comment in the press and company brochures.

Question 3

Mark the following statements as true or false.

(a) Shareholders receive annual accounts, prepared in accordance with legal and professional requirements.

(b) The accounts of limited companies are sometimes filed with the Registrar of Companies.

(c) Employees always receive the company's accounts and an employee report.

(d) The Inland Revenue will receive the published accounts and as much supplementary detail as the Inspector of Taxes needs to assess the corporation tax payable on profits.

(e) Banks frequently require more information than is supplied in the published accounts when considering applications for loans and overdraft facilities.

Answer

True

(a) Yes, and, in addition, companies listed on the Stock Exchange have to comply with the regulations in the Stock Exchange's Listing Rules (Yellow Book).

(d)

(e) Yes, banks may require cash flow and profit forecasts and budgets prepared to show management's estimates of future activity in the business.

False

(b) The accounts of limited companies **must always** be filed with the Registrar of Companies and be available for public inspection. In addition, the company itself will often distribute these accounts on request to potential shareholders, the bank and financial analysts. These accounts are all that is usually available to suppliers and customers.

(c) Employees will not necessarily receive company accounts (unless they are shareholders for example), but many companies do distribute the accounts to employees as a matter of policy. Some companies produce employee reports which summarise and expand on matters which are covered in the annual accounts and are of particular interest to them.

REMEMBER!

Many different people use financial statements to acquire information about a business.

3 MANAGEMENT ACCOUNTING AND FINANCIAL ACCOUNTING May 2001

KEY TERMS

Financial accounting is the preparation of accounting reports for external use.

Management accounting is the preparation of accounting reports for internal use.

Exam focus point

The different roles of financial and management accountants was examined in Section A of the May 2001 exam.

3.1 **Management** accounting systems produce detailed information often split between different departments within an organisation (sales, production, finance etc). Although much of the information deals with past events and decisions, management accountants produce information which is forward looking and used to prepare budgets, and make decisions about the **future activities** of a business. They also compare actual performance with budget and try to take corrective action where necessary.

3.2 **Financial** accountants, however, are usually solely concerned with summarising historical data, often from the same basic records as management accountants but in a different way. This difference arises partly because external users have different interests from management and do not need very detailed information. In addition, financial statements are prepared under constraints (such as Financial Reporting Standards) which do not apply to management accounts.

Question 4

Which of the following is a function of the financial accountant in a business which employs several accounting staff?

A Preparing budgets
B Costing products
C Setting selling prices
D Summarising historical accounting data

Answer

D Correct; this is a function of financial accounting.
A This is usually a job for the management accountant.
B This is usually a job for the management accountant.
C This is usually a job for the management accountant.

REMEMBER!

Management accounts are for **internal** use and the financial accounts for **external** use. Management accounts provide information for decision affecting the future, financial accounts provide information about what has happened in the past.

4 THE SCOPE OF ACCOUNTING INFORMATION

4.1 Accounting statements are presented in monetary terms. Therefore they will only include items on which a monetary value can be placed. For example, monetary values can be placed on machinery (eg the original cost, or the amount it would cost to replace it). However the flair of a good manager, or the loyalty and commitment of a dedicated workforce, cannot be valued in monetary terms and so do not appear in the accounts.

4.2 Similarly, there are important factors in the successful running of a business which are non-financial by nature. A manager in a manufacturing business will need a detailed knowledge of his machinery's capabilities, the skills of his production staff and the characteristics of his raw materials. All of these things are important in planning production, but none of them would appear in a set of accounts.

4.3 Subject to these limitations, the range of accounting information is very wide.

- **Profit** earned in a period
- **Assets and liabilities** at a particular date
- **Cost of producing** and/or selling a product or range of products
- **Cost of running** a department or division
- **Quantity of a product** which must be sold in order for it to pay its way (break even)
- Amount of **cash** coming into and leaving a business over a period
- Expected **overdraft** required in the future

Question 5

The above list is far from exhaustive. However to ensure you understand the difference between financial and management accountancy, mark each of the above as most likely to apply financial or management accounting.

Answer

(a) You could have classified this as both financial and management information. Generally the profit earned by the whole business, included in a historical statement (for example for the past 12 months) will be financial accounting. Forecast information or information relating to departments or divisions is management accounting.

(b) This usually falls within the scope of financial accounting, although it may be used as an input to management accounting, for example as a basis for a forecast.

(c) Management accounting.

(d) Management accounting.

(e) Management accounting.

(f) Cash flow accounting is financial information when it is a historical statement and usually management accounting when it is a forecast or budget.

(g) Management accounting.

5 THE MAIN FINANCIAL STATEMENTS

5.1 We end this chapter by looking briefly at the two main financial statements drawn up by financial accountants: the balance sheet and the profit and loss account.

KEY TERM

The **balance sheet** is a list of all the assets owned by a business and all the liabilities owed by a business as at a particular date. It is a snapshot of the financial position of the business at a particular moment.

5.2 Assets are the business's resources eg buildings to operate from, plant and machinery, stock to sell and cars for its employees. These are all resources which it uses in its operations. Also, it may have bank balances, cash and amounts of money owed to it. These provide the funds it needs to carry out its operations and are also assets. It may owe money to the bank or to suppliers, these are liabilities.

KEY TERM

A **profit and loss account** is a record of income generated and expenditure incurred over a given period. The period chosen will depend on the purpose for which the statement is produced. The profit and loss account which forms part of the financial accounts of a limited company will be made up for the period of a year, commencing from the date of the previous year's accounts.

5.3 Management accountants might need quarterly or monthly profit and loss accounts. The profit and loss account shows whether the business has more income than expenditure (a profit) or vice versa (a loss) during a period.

5.4 Organisations which are not run for profit (charities etc) produce a similar statement called an **income and expenditure account** which shows the surplus of income over expenditure (or a deficit where expenditure exceeds income).

Accruals concept — May 2001

THE MAIN POINT!

The **accruals concept** means that income and expenses are included in the profit and loss account of the period in which they are earned or incurred, not received or paid.

Exam focus point

Application of the accruals concept was examined in Section A of the May 2001 exam.

5.5 It is very important to grasp that in nearly all businesses, accounts are not prepared on a cash basis but on an accruals basis, because cash accounting does not present a true picture of the business's activities in any given period.

5.6 EXAMPLE: ACCRUALS CONCEPT

Emma has a business printing and selling T-shirts. In May 20X7 she makes the following purchases and sales.

Invoice date	*Numbers bought/sold*	*Amount*	*Date paid*
Purchases		£	
7.5.X7	20	100	1.6.X7
Sales			
8.5.X7	4	40	1.6.X7
12.5.X7	6	60	1.6.X7
23.5.X7	10	100	1.7.X7

What is Emma's profit for May?

5.7 SOLUTION

	£
Cash basis	
Sales	0
Purchases	0
Profit/loss	0
Accruals basis	
Sales (£40 + £60 + £100)	200
Purchases	(100)
Profit	100

5.8 The accruals basis gives a truer picture than the cash basis. Emma has no cash to show for her efforts until June, but her customers are legally bound to pay her and she is legally bound to pay for her purchases.

5.9 Her balance sheet as at 31 May 20X7 would therefore show her assets and liabilities as follows.

	£
Assets	
Debtors (£40 + £60 + £100)	200
Liabilities	
Creditors	100
Net assets	100
Proprietor's capital	100

KEY TERM

Capital is a special form of liability, representing the amount owed by the business to its proprietor(s).

5.10 In Emma's case it represents the profit earned in May, which she, as owner of the business, is entitled to in full. Capital will also include the proprietor's initial capital, introduced as cash and perhaps equipment or other assets.

5.11 For example, if Emma had begun her business on 30 April 20X7 by opening a business bank account and paying in £100, her balance sheet immediately after this transaction would look like this.

	£
Assets	
Bank	100
Proprietor's capital	100

On 31 May 20X7 the balance sheet would look like this.

	£
Assets	
Debtors (customers who owe Emma money)	200
Bank	100
	300
Liabilities	
Creditors (suppliers to whom Emma owes money)	100
Net assets	200
Proprietor's capital	
Brought forward	100
Profit for the period	100
Carried forward	200

REMEMBER!

This example shows that both the balance sheet and the profit and loss account are summaries of many transactions.

Question 6

By looking at the example of Emma, you may be able to see that there is a simple arithmetical relationship linking capital at the beginning of a period, capital at the end of the period, and profit earned during the period. Can you formulate the relationship?

Answer

The relationship is: opening capital + profit = closing capital. In more complicated examples it would be necessary to make adjustments for new capital introduced during the period, and for any capital withdrawn during the period.

Chapter roundup

- You should have a basic understanding of accounting and its main uses.
- Accounting is the process of collecting, recording, summarising and communicating financial information.
- Accounting information is essential to the efficient running of a business. It helps managers to control the use of resources, keep track of the assets and liabilities of the business and plan effectively for the future.
- Accounting information is required by a wide range of users both within and outside of the business.
- The scope of accounting information is very wide, but it does not embrace every aspect of an organisation's affairs. It is limited to items which have a monetary value.
- The two most important financial statements are the profit and loss account and the balance sheet. Both are prepared on an accruals basis, not a cash basis.
- In Chapter 2 we will develop your understanding of accountancy by considering the concepts, conventions and regulations used in preparing accounts.

Quick quiz

1 How has the increasing complexity of modern business contributed to the development of accounting?

2 Five categories of people who might use accounting information about a business are:

(1) Managers

(2) Public

(3) Inland Revenue

(4) Employees

(5) Shareholders

3 Fill in the blanks.

The main distinction between financial accounting and management accounting is that financial accounting provides historical information to people outside the organisation, whereas management accounting provides Future information to internal management on which they can base planning decisions.

4 Accounting information is limited to items having a monetary value. True or false? True

5 Explain briefly:

(a) What is a balance sheet?
(b) What is a profit and loss account?

6 Fill in the blanks.

The accruals concept means that ________ and ________ are included in the profit and loss account of the period in which they are ________ or ________ not ________ or ________.

Answers to quick quiz

1 There are too many activities for a manager to keep track of by himself and so he needs accounts which summarise transactions to monitor the business' performance.

2 Any five from the following list:

- Managers
- Owners (shareholders)
- Trade contacts
- Providers of finance
- Inland Revenue
- Employees
- Financial analysts and advisers
- Government and its agencies
- The public

3 The main distinction between financial accounting and management accounting is that financial accounting provides **historical** information to people **outside** the organisation, whereas management accounting provides **forward looking** information to **management** on which they can base **decisions**.

4 True. Accounting information is limited to items having a monetary value.

5 (a) A balance sheet shows all the assets and liabilities of a business at a certain date.
(b) A profit and loss account shows the income and expenditure for a period.

6 The accruals concept means that **income** and **expenditure** are included in the profit and loss account of the period in which they are **earned** or **incurred** not **received** or **paid**.

Now try the questions below from the Question Bank

Number	Level	Marks	Time
1	Introductory	15	27 mins
2	Exam	2	3 mins
3	Introductory	5	9 mins

1. The increased complexity of business has increased the complexity of accounts within companies. Therefore it is no longer possible for managers to keep control of there accounts alone. Management accountant are therefore required. Reporting outside the business is also required by law in some cases. This has meant financial accountants are required ✓

5. a) A balance sheet is a snapshot in time of assets and liabilities of a company ✓
b) A profit and loss account is a record of information over a period of time showing expenditure against income to calculate a profit or loss for the company. ✓

Chapter 2

PREPARING ACCOUNTS: CONCEPTS, CONVENTIONS AND REGULATIONS

	Topic List	Syllabus reference	Ability required
1	**Accounting concepts and principles**	(i)	**Comprehension**
2	**Costs and values**	(i)	**Comprehension**
3	**The regulatory framework of accounts**	(i)	**Comprehension**

Introduction

Accounting practice has developed gradually over a period of centuries.

In this chapter we will consider the more important concepts used when preparing accounts. A Financial Reporting Standard FRS 18 describes four concepts as fundamental accounting concepts. Section 1 covers accounting concepts.

Section 2 covers how values are determined.

Section 3 looks at the regulatory framework within which accounts, particularly those of limited companies, are prepared. The purpose of this section is to impress upon you the **importance** of this framework, which is to be studied in much more detail in the later stages of your qualification.

Learning outcomes covered in this chapter

- Identify and explain the fundamental accounting concepts, bases and policies
- Explain the historical cost convention
- Identify the basic methods of valuing assets on current cost, market value and economic value bases and demonstrate their impact on profit measures and balance sheet values
- Explain the influence of legislation and accounting standards on the production of published accounting information for organisations

Syllabus content covered in this chapter

- Fundamental accounting concepts, bases and policies
- Historical cost convention
- Methods of asset valuation and their implications for profit measurement and the balance sheet
- The regulatory influence of company law and accounting standards

1 ACCOUNTING CONCEPTS AND PRINCIPLES

Exam focus point

The accounting concepts and principles are the basis on which all accounts are prepared, they are almost certain to be examined at every sitting.

Eight accounting concepts and principles

1 Entity
2 Money measurement
3 Going concern
4 Prudence
5 Accruals
6 Consistency
7 Separate valuation
8 Materiality

The entity concept

KEY TERM

Entity concept: accountants regard a business as a separate entity, distinct from its owners or managers.

1.1 This concept applies whether the business is a limited company (and so recognised in law as a separate entity) or a sole trader or partnership (in which case the business is not legally separate). So, in the example of Emma in the previous chapter, the money she transferred to her business bank account becomes, in accounting terms, a **business** asset (but legally remains a **personal** asset).

1.2 Acceptance of this concept has important practical consequences. In the case of a small business run by a single individual, the owner's personal affairs and business affairs may appear to be inextricably linked eg Emma may conduct her business from home. In preparing the business accounts, it is essential to separate out her private transactions.

Question 1

Suppose that Emma withdraws a number of T-shirts from her stock to give to friends, how would this be reflected in her accounts?

Answer

The correct accounting treatment is to regard her as having purchased the goods from the business, which is a completely separate entity. The subsequent gift to her friends is then a private transaction and is not recorded in the books of the business. Emma should pay for the T-shirts by taking money from her own purse and putting it into the till, or she should regard the withdrawal as a repayment of capital. Otherwise, the business accounts will give a misleading picture.

The money measurement concept

KEY TERM

Money measurement concept: accounts deal only with items to which a monetary value can be attributed.

1.3 In Chapter 1, we distinguished between an asset such as a machine (which might be valued at its original purchase cost, its replacement cost etc) and an asset such as the flair of a manager or the dedication of the workforce. The machine is valued and included in the balance sheet, flair and dedication are not included, yet they can be of enormous importance to the success of a business. Recognising this, accountants in recent years have tried to suggest ways of 'bringing them on to the balance sheet' by attributing values to them. 'Human resource accounting' is beyond the scope of this book, but you should be aware of the problems it attempts to address.

Question 2

Perhaps it is too glib to say that monetary values can never be attributed to the skill of the workforce. There is at least one high-profile industry where such valuations are commonplace. Can you think of it? And do you know what the accounting consequences are in that industry?

Answer

The industry referred to is of course the world of sport, particularly football, where transfer fees appear to provide an objective valuation of a player's worth. Many football clubs are run as substantial businesses, some of them with shares quoted on the Stock Exchange. As such, their accounting practices are widely publicised and discussed. In almost all cases, however, they make no attempt to include the value of players on their balance sheet, presumably because such values fluctuate wildly with the form and fitness of the players concerned. Almost invariably transfer fees are therefore shown simply as a cost in the profit and loss account.

The going concern concept

KEY TERM

Going concern implies that the business will continue in operation for the foreseeable future, and that there is no intention to put the company into liquidation or to make drastic cutbacks to the scale of operations.

1.4 The main significance of the going concern concept is that the assets of the business should not be valued at their 'break-up' value, which is the amount that they would fetch if they were sold piecemeal and the business were thus broken up. Rather, they are included in the balance sheet at a value which reflects their value to the business.

The prudence concept

Pilot Paper

> **KEY TERM**
>
> **Prudence** is the concept that where alternative procedures (or alternative valuations) are possible, the one selected should be the one which gives the most **cautious** presentation of the business's financial position or results.

1.5 For example, stock should be stated in the balance sheet at cost rather than their selling price so that we do not **anticipate** a profit.

1.6 Also where a loss is foreseen, it should be taken into account immediately. If a business purchases stock for £1,200 but because of a sudden slump only £900 is likely to be realised on sales. The prudence concept values the stock at £900. It is not enough to wait until the stock is sold and then recognise the £300 loss, it must be recognised as soon as it is foreseen.

Question 3

A retailer commences business on 1 January and buys a stock of 20 washing machines, each costing £100. During the year he sells 17 machines at £150 each. How should the remaining machines be valued at 31 December if:

(a) He is forced to close down his business at the end of the year and the remaining machines will realise only £60 each in a forced sale?

(b) He intends to continue his business into the next year?

Answer

(a) If the business is to be closed down, the remaining three machines must be valued at the amount they will realise in a forced sale, ie 3 × £60 = £180.

(b) If the business is regarded as a going concern, the stock unsold at 31 December will be carried forward into the following year. The three machines will therefore appear in the balance sheet at 31 December at cost, 3 × £100 = £300. The prudence concept dictates that they be valued at cost not expected sales value.

Question 4

Samson Feeble trades as a carpenter. He has undertaken to make a range of kitchen furniture for a customer at an agreed price of £1,000. At the end of Samson's accounting year the job is unfinished (being two thirds complete) and the following data has been assembled.

	£
Costs incurred in making the furniture to date	800
Further estimated cost to completion of the job	400
Total cost	1,200

The incomplete job represents **work in progress** at the end of the year which is an asset, like stock. Its cost to date is £800, but by the time the job is completed Samson will have made a loss of £200. What is the effect of this on Samson's balance sheet and profit and loss account?

Answer

The full £200 loss should be charged against profits of the current year. The value of work in progress at the year end should be its **net realisable value**, which is lower than its cost. The net realisable value is costs incurred to date £800, less loss foreseen £200 (£600).

1.7 Sales revenue will be 'realised' and so 'recognised' in the profit and loss account in the following cases.

(a) The sale transaction is for a specific quantity of goods at a known price, so that the sales value of the transaction is known for certain.

(b) The sale transaction has been completed, or else it is certain that it will be completed (eg in the case of long-term contract work, when the job is well under way but not yet completed by the end of an accounting period).

(c) The **critical event** in the sale transaction has occurred ie when it becomes virtually certain that cash will eventually be received from the customer or cash is actually received.

1.8 Usually, revenue is 'recognised' either when a cash sale is made, or when the customer promises to pay on or before a specified future date, and the debt is legally enforceable.

1.9 The prudence concept is applied here in the sense that revenue should not be anticipated, before it is reasonably certain to 'happen'.

Question 5

A realised profit arises when?

A A customer's order is received
B A debtor pays an invoice
C A property is revalued upwards
D Goods are sent to a customer, who will purchase on credit, the invoice will be sent later

Answer

B Correct.

A The sale has not yet occurred, it is far too early to recognise profit.

C This is an unrealised surplus, it will only become realised if the property is sold.

D This is too early in the sales cycle to recognise a profit. The sale is not for cash and the customer has not yet accepted the goods.

The accruals concept or matching concept

KEY TERM

The **accruals concept** states that, in computing profit, revenue earned must be matched against the expenditure incurred in earning it, and that amounts are included in the accounts when they are earned or incurred, not received or paid.

1.10 This is illustrated in the example of Emma (5.6 in Chapter 1). Profit of £100 was computed by matching the revenue (£200) earned from the sale of 20 T-shirts against the cost (£100) of acquiring them.

1.11 However, if Emma sold 18 T-shirts, it is be incorrect to charge her profit and loss account with the cost of 20 T-shirts, as she still has two T-shirts in stock. Therefore, only the purchase cost of 18 T-shirts (£90) is matched with her sales revenue (£180), leaving her with a profit of £90.

1.12 Her balance sheet will therefore look like this.

	£
Assets	
Stock (at cost, ie 2 × £5)	10
Debtors (18 × £10)	180
	190
Liabilities	
Creditors	100
Net assets	90
Proprietor's capital (profit for the period)	90

1.13 In this example, the concepts of going concern and matching are linked. As the business is assumed to be a going concern, it is possible to carry forward the cost of the unsold T-shirts as a charge against profits of the next period.

Exam focus point

Application of the accruals concept to stock calculations was examined in Section A of the May 2001 exam.

Question 6

If Emma decided to give up selling T-shirts, how would the two T-shirts in the balance sheet be valued?

Answer

The going concern concept no longer applies and the value of the two T-shirts in the balance sheet will be a break-up valuation rather than cost. Similarly, if the two unsold T-shirts are unlikely to be sold at more than their cost of £5 each (say, because of damage or a fall in demand) then they will be shown on the balance sheet at their net realisable value (ie the likely eventual sales price less any expenses to make them saleable, eg repairs) rather than cost. This shows the application of the prudence concept. The prudence concept will always override the accruals concept, where the two conflict.

1.14 Company legislation gives legal recognition to the accruals concept, stating that: 'all income and charges relating to the financial year to which the accounts relate shall be taken into account, without regard to the date of receipt or payment.' This requires businesses to take account of sales and purchases when made (rather than when paid for) and to carry unsold stock forward in the balance sheet rather than to deduct its cost from profit for the period.

The consistency concept

1.15 Accounting is not an exact science. There are many areas where judgement must be used in determining money values for items appearing in accounts. Certain procedures and principles are recognised as good accounting practice, but there are often various acceptable methods of accounting for similar items.

KEY TERM

The **consistency concept** states that in preparing accounts consistency should be observed in two respects.

(a) **Similar** items within a single set of accounts should be given **similar** accounting treatment.

(b) The **same** treatment should be applied from one period to **another** in accounting for similar items. This enables valid comparisons to be made from one period to the next.

Question 7

Mark the following statements as true or false.

(a) The entity concept is that accountants regard a business as a separate legal entity, distinct from its owners or managers.

(b) Accounts deal only with items to which a monetary value can be attributed.

(c) Where the prudence and accruals concepts conflict, preparers of accounts may follow either.

(d) The accruals, prudence, going concern and consistency concepts are contained in SSAP 2.

Answer

True

(b)

(d) Yes. Company law adds a fifth, the separate valuation principle.

False

(a) No. The entity concept is that accountants regard a business as a separate entity, but it is not always a legal difference. For example, legally a sole trader is not separate from his business.

(c) Where the prudence and accruals concepts conflict, prudence overrides accruals.

The separate valuation principle

1.16 Company law recognises the same four fundamental accounting concepts of going concern, prudence, accruals and consistency, although it describes them not as concepts but as **accounting principles**. The Act also mentions a fifth principle, the separate valuation principle.

KEY TERM

The **separate valuation principle** states that, in determining the amount to be attributed to an asset or liability in the balance sheet, each component item of the asset or liability must be valued separately.

1.17 These separate valuations are then totalled to arrive at the balance sheet figure. For example, if a company's stock comprises 50 separate items, each item must (in theory) be valued separately. The 50 values are then totalled and this is the stock figure in the accounts.

The materiality concept

1.18 Apart from error, there will be many areas where two different accountants will come up with different figures for the same item. The materiality concept is relevant in this context.

KEY TERM

A matter is **material** if its omission or misstatement would reasonably influence the decisions of a user of the accounts.

1.19 In preparing accounts it is important to decide what is material and what is not, so that time and money are not wasted in the pursuit of excessive detail.

1.20 Determining whether an item is material is very subjective. There is no absolute measure of materiality. It is common to apply a convenient rule of thumb (for example to define material items as those with a value greater than 5% of the net profit in the accounts). However, it is not only the value of the item which needs to be considered, the context is also important.

(a) A balance sheet shows fixed assets of £2m and stocks of £30,000. An error of £20,000 in the fixed asset valuation may be immaterial, but an error of £20,000 in the stock valuation is material. Therefore, the total of which the error forms a part must be considered.

(b) A business has a bank loan of £50,000 and a £55,000 balance on bank deposit account. It would be a material misstatement if these two amounts were shown on the balance sheet as 'cash at bank £5,000'. In other words, incorrect presentation can be material misstatement even if there is no monetary error.

1.21 The assessment of an item as material or immaterial may affect its treatment in the accounts. The profit and loss account shows the expenses incurred by the business grouped under suitable headings (heating and lighting, rent and rates, etc). However, very small expenses can be lumped together under a heading such as 'sundry expenses', because a more detailed breakdown is inappropriate for such immaterial amounts.

Question 8

(a) You depreciate your office equipment by 20% each year because it has a useful life, on average, of five years. This year your profitability is down and you think you can squeeze an extra year's life out of your equipment. Is it acceptable not to charge any depreciation this year?

(b) You have recently paid £4.95 for a waste paper bin which should have a useful life of about five years. Should you treat it as a fixed asset?

Answer

(a) No, because of the consistency concept. Once the depreciation policy has been established, it should not be changed without good cause.

(b) No, because of the materiality concept. The cost of the bin is very small. Treat the £4.95 as an expense in this year's profit and loss account.

Clashes between accounting concepts

1.22 Sometimes inconsistencies arise between the different accounting concepts. Consider the following two examples.

(a) **Accruals and prudence**. The accruals concept requires future income to be accrued. The prudence concept says that caution should be exercised, so that if there is doubt about the subsequent receipt, no accrual should be made.

(b) **Consistency and prudence.** If circumstances change, prudence may conflict with the consistency concept, which requires the same treatment year after year.

1.23 In all situations where prudence conflicts with another accounting concept, prudence must prevail and the other concept must be over-ridden.

Exam focus point

These accounting concepts are likely to be tested in every exam.

Make sure that you can define each of these fundamental accounting concepts and also explain their relevance. If you understand them they will earn you some easy marks in the exam.

2 COSTS AND VALUES

KEY TERM

A basic principle of accounting (some writers include it in the list of fundamental accounting concepts) is that resources are normally stated in accounts at **historical cost,** ie at the amount which the business paid to acquire them.

2.1 An important advantage of doing this is the objectivity of accounts is maximised: there is usually documentary evidence to prove the amount paid to buy an asset or pay an expense. In general, accountants prefer to deal with costs, rather than 'values'. Valuations tend to be subjective and to vary according to what the valuation is for.

2.2 A company acquires a machine to manufacture its products, with an expected useful life of four years. At the end of two years the company is preparing a balance sheet and has to value the asset.

2.3 **Possible costs and values**

- **Original cost** (historical cost)
- **Half** of the historical cost (half of its useful life has expired)
- **Secondhand value**
- **Replacement cost** of an **identical** machine
- **Replacement cost** of a **more modern** (technologically advanced) machine
- **Economic value** (ie the amount of the profits it is expected to generate during its remaining life)

2.4 All of these valuations have something to commend them, but the great advantage of the first two is that they are based on the machine's historical cost, which is verifiable. The subjective judgement involved in the other valuations, particularly the last, is so great as to lessen the reliability of any accounts based on them. The second method, or a variation of it, is the one which will normally be used (see Chapter 11).

2.5 EXAMPLE: COSTS AND VALUES

Brian sets up in business on 1 January 20X6 selling accountancy textbooks. He buys 100 books for £5 each and by 31 December 20X6 he manages to sell his entire stock, all for cash, at a price of £8 each. On 1 January 20X7 he replaces his stock by purchasing another 100 books. This time the cost of the books has risen to £6 each. Calculate the profit for 20X6.

2.6 SOLUTION

In conventional historical cost accounting, Brian's profit would be computed as follows.

	£
Sale of 100 books (@ £8 each)	800
Cost of 100 books (@ £5 each)	500
Profit for the year	300

2.7 The purchase of the books is stated at their historical cost. Although this is accepted accounting practice, and is the method we will be using, it involves an anomaly which can be seen if we look at how well off the business is.

2.8 On 1 January 20X6 the assets of the business consist of the 100 books which Brian has purchased as stock. On 1 January 20X7 the business has an identical stock of 100 books, and also has cash of £200 (ie £800 received from customers, less the £600 cost of replacing stock). So despite making a profit of £300, measured in the conventional way, the business appears to be only £200 better off.

2.9 This anomaly can be removed if an alternative accounting convention is used. Suppose that profit is the difference between the selling price of goods and the cost of replacing the goods sold. Brian's profit is as follows.

	£
Sale of 100 books	800
Cost of replacing 100 books sold @ £6 each	600
Profit for the year	200

2.10 Now the profit for the year is exactly matched by the increase in the company's assets over the year.

Capital maintenance — Pilot Paper

KEY TERM

The **capital** of a business (also called its net worth) is the excess of its **assets** over its **liabilities**, and represents the proprietor's interest in the business.

2.11 One way of calculating profit measures how well off a business is at the beginning of a period compared to the end of the period. The difference (after allowing for drawings and injections of new capital) is the profit or loss for the period. On this basis, profit depends on the valuation of the assets and liabilities

2.12 Returning the example of Brian and using historical cost, the value of his business at 1 January 20X6 and 1 January 20X7 is as follows.

	20X6	*20X7*
	£	£
Stocks (at historical cost)	500	600
Cash	0	200
	500	800

2.13 The value of the business has risen by £300 over the year and this is the amount of profit we calculated on the historical cost basis. We can say that the original capital of the business, £500, has been maintained and an additional £300 created.

2.14 Instead of using historical costs, it is theoretically possible to measure capital in physical terms. Brian's physical capital was originally 100 books; on 1 January 20X7, it consists of an identical 100 books plus £200 cash. We can say that Brian's original physical capital has been maintained and an addition to capital of £200 has been created. This is equivalent to the profit we computed on a replacement cost basis.

2.15 A system of accounting based principally on replacement costs, and measuring profit as the increase in physical capital, was used in the UK for some years (called **current cost accounting**).

2.16 The main accounting system has always been, and will continue to be, historical cost accounting. However current cost accounting was developed as a possible solution to certain problems which arise in periods of rising prices. Theoretical and practical problems in the current cost accounting system led to its withdrawal in the UK.

Accounting in periods of rising prices — Pilot Paper

2.17 In periods of **inflation**, businessmen and accountants face a number of problems.

Problem		Comment
(a)	For businessmen the major difficulty is in **decision making**.	Successful decisions depend on correct estimates of future events. This is complicated when future costs and prices are affected by inflation. The difficulty is more acute when the effects of the decision extend over a long period of time, but even short-term decisions such as price increases are affected.
(b)	Businessmen rely on accounts to show the **profit** earned by a business, partly so that the owners can decide how much profit can safely be withdrawn from the business.	When prices are rising, at least some of the profit shown by historical cost accounts must be ploughed back into the business just to maintain its previous capacity.
(c)	The accountant must prepare accounts expressed in terms of a **monetary unit** (eg the £ in the UK).	In times of rising prices the value of the unit is not constant and comparisons between the accounts of the current year with those of previous years may be misleading.
(d)	The accountant must cope with difficulties in **measuring** asset values and profit.	Asset values can become out of date, particularly fixed assets eg a freehold factory purchased 20 years ago is shown at its original cost, even though its value is likely to have increased greatly over the period of ownership. Profit figures can be distorted by increases in the cost of goods purchased during the accounting period, because the cost of goods sold is computed on the basis of their historical cost.

2.18 Attempts to solve the problems of inflation have a long history in the UK and abroad. One step common in practice is to prepare **modified** historical cost accounts. This means that up-to-date valuations are included in the historical cost balance sheet for some or all of a company's fixed assets, without any other adjustments being made. No attempt is made to tackle the difficulties of profit measurement.

2.19 The two alternative systems which have found favour, at different times, in the UK are **current cost accounting** (CCA) and **current purchasing power accounting** (CPP). CCA has already been briefly described. CPP tackles the problems of inflation by attempting to express accounting values in terms of a stable monetary unit.

2.20 For the foreseeable future, historical cost accounting is likely to be the most important system in the UK, despite its inability to reflect the effects of inflation.

There are a number of reasons why this is so.

(a) It is **easy and cheap**. Other methods tend to be far more complicated and onerous to use, particularly for small businesses. Also, there is no agreement on an alternative.

(b) The fact that **fixed asset revaluation** is permitted or encouraged means that there is less likelihood of a serious understatement of actual value distorting the balance sheet valuation of the business.

(c) It is easy to understand and users are **aware of its limitations**, so make appropriate allowances. Alternative methods generally involve much more complex concepts.

(d) The figures are easy to obtain and are **objective** and **readily verifiable**, being tied to actual transactions. Other methods depend more on subjective valuations.

2.21 It is important to note that, legally, a business does not have to account for inflation.

Question 9

In a period when prices are rising, the profit shown under the historical cost convention will differ from that shown under the current cost convention. In the case of a retail trading company, which of the two profit figures will be higher?

Answer

The profit shown under the historical cost convention will be higher. This is because the value of the resources used is their cost at the time they were purchased. Under the current cost convention, the value of these resources is their cost at the (later) time when they were replaced. Given that prices are rising, this cost will be higher and so reported profits will be less.

Exam focus point

Both the pilot paper and the May 2001 exam contained a question in Section A comparing the historical cost convention with the current cost convention.

3 THE REGULATORY FRAMEWORK OF ACCOUNTS

3.1 There is a wide range of accounting concepts in use. There are also different conventions under which accounts can be prepared. It may seem as though almost anything goes. What rules are there?

3.2 For an **unincorporated** business, any form of accounting information is adequate if it gives the owner(s) of the business a basis for planning and control, and satisfies the requirements of external users such as the Inland Revenue.

3.3 The activities of **limited companies**, including the way they prepare their accounts, are closely regulated.

THE MAIN POINTS

The regulations on accounts come from four main sources.

- Company law enacted by the UK Parliament
- Statements of standard accounting practice and financial reporting standards issued by the professional accountancy bodies in the UK and Ireland
- International accounting standards
- For quoted companies, the requirements of the Stock Exchange

Company law

3.4 Limited companies are required by law to prepare accounts annually for distribution to their shareholders. A copy of these accounts must be lodged with the Registrar of Companies and is available for inspection by any member of the public. For this reason a company's statutory annual accounts are often referred to as its published accounts.

3.5 In 1985, all existing companies legislation was brought together in a number of consolidating Acts, of which by far the most important being the Companies Act 1985 (CA 1985). This was substantially amended on the enactment of the Companies Act 1989 (CA 1989).

3.6 This book reflects the 1985 Act **as amended by the** 1989 Act. Unless otherwise stated, all statutory references are to the amended CA 1985. Occasionally, where there is no parallel provision, a section number is followed by 'CA 1989' to indicate a section of the new Act itself.

3.7 There are many differences between accounting systems found in the various European Union (EU) member states. For example, in the UK a 'true and fair view' is sought, whereas in West Germany a 'legal and correct view' is observed. Taxation and accounting principles differ and consolidation practices vary.

3.8 Since the United Kingdom became a member of the EU it has been obliged to comply with legal requirements decided on by the EU. It does this by enacting UK laws to implement EU directives. For example, the CA 1989 was enacted in part to implement the provisions of the seventh and eighth EU directives, which deal with consolidated accounts and auditors.

3.9 As far as the preparation of accounts is concerned, the overriding requirement of companies legislation is that accounts should show a 'true and fair view'. This phrase is not defined in the Companies Acts. What it certainly does **not** mean is that company accounts are to be exact to the penny. For one thing, many of the figures appearing in a set of accounts are arrived at least partly by the exercise of judgement. For another, the amount of time and effort that such a requirement would cost would be out of all proportion to the advantages derived from it (see the discussion earlier in this chapter of the materiality concept).

3.10 The legislation also requires that the accounts of a limited company (except certain small companies) must be **audited**. An audit, for this purpose, may be defined as an 'independent examination of, and expression of opinion on, the financial statements of an enterprise'.

3.11 This means that a limited company must engage a firm of chartered or certified accountants to conduct an examination of its accounting records and its financial statements in order to form an opinion as to whether the accounts present a 'true and fair view'. At the conclusion of their audit, the auditors issue a report (addressed to the owners of the company, ie its **members** or **shareholders**) which is published as part of the accounts.

3.12 Audit is discussed in more detail in Chapter 21 of this Study Text.

Non-statutory regulation

3.13 Apart from company law, the main regulations affecting accounts in the UK derive from pronouncements issued by the professional accounting. Six accountancy bodies in the UK are represented on the Consultative Committee of Accountancy Bodies (CCAB). They are as follows.

- The Chartered Institute of Management Accountants (CIMA)
- The Institute of Chartered Accountants in England and Wales (ICAEW)
- The Institute of Chartered Accountants of Scotland (ICAS)
- The Institute of Chartered Accountants in Ireland (ICAI)
- The Association of Chartered Certified Accountants (ACCA)
- The Chartered Institute of Public Finance and Accountancy (CIPFA)

3.14 The CCAB is a major influence on the way in which accounts are prepared. Our main interest will be in the accounting standards published to lay down accounting treatments in areas where a variety of approaches might be taken. The value of accounts would be reduced if users were not able to count on a measure of comparability between them. The aim of accounting standards is to ensure that such comparability exists.

The Accounting Standards Committee (ASC) and the Accounting Standards Board (ASB)

3.15 The ASC was set up in January 1970 with the aim of publishing accounting standards in order to crack down on manipulation of published accounts. This was the beginning of a long line of attempts to protect investors in the wake of accounting scandals.

Question 10

You will be aware from your reading that such attempts have not yet been entirely successful. For fun, list a few of the more recent accounting scandals you can think of.

Answer

The list is almost endless, but among the most recent are the Maxwell empire and Barings Bank.

3.16 The procedure of the ASC was to publish an **exposure draft** (ED), outlining its proposed accounting treatment for the area under consideration. Comments were invited from interested parties, and in the light of such comments a final document was issued in the form of a **Statement of Standard Accounting Practice** (SSAP). Under the CA 1989, large companies are required to state that their accounts have been prepared in accordance with applicable accounting standards. The ASC issued 25 SSAPs before it was replaced by a successor body on 1 August 1990.

3.17 In response to criticisms of the ASC's ineffectiveness, CCAB appointed a committee under the chairmanship of Sir Ron Dearing to review and make recommendations on the process by which accounting standards are issued. The Committee reported in 1988 and as a result of its recommendations a new standard-setting process was introduced. Under this system, there are four bodies you need to know about.

- The Financial Reporting Council (FRC)
- The Accounting Standards Board (ASB)
- The Financial Reporting Review Panel (FRRP)
- The Urgent Issues Task Force (UITF)

3.18 The **Financial Reporting Council**. The FRC draws its membership from a wide spectrum of accounts preparers and users. Its chairman is appointed by the Government. The FRC operates through two arms: the FRRP and the ASB.

3.19 The **Accounting Standards Board**. The ASB is, in effect, the successor body to the ASC and is responsible for the issue of accounting standards. Accounting standards issued by the ASB are called **Financial Reporting Standard** (FRSs), of which sixteen have so far been published.

3.20 Prior to publication, the ASB circulates its proposals in the form of a financial reporting exposure draft (inevitably referred to as a FRED) and invites comments. To avoid chaos, the ASB has 'adopted' those SSAPs still extant and they therefore remain in force.

3.21 The **Financial Reporting Review Panel**. The FRRP is the second operating arm of the FRC. Its task is to examine accounts published by companies if it appears that Companies Act requirements have been breached - in particular, the requirement that accounts should show a true and fair view. The panel has legal backing: if a public company departs from an accounting standard, the panel may apply to the courts, which may in turn instruct the company to prepare revised accounts.

3.22 The **Urgent Issues Task Force**. The UITF is an offshoot of the ASB. Its role is to assist the ASB in areas where an accounting standard or Companies Act provision already exists, but where unsatisfactory or conflicting interpretations have developed. As its name suggests, the UITF is designed to act quickly (more quickly than the full standard-setting process is capable of) when an authoritative ruling is urgently needed.

International accounting standards

3.23 The International Accounting Standards Committee (IASC) was set up in June 1973 in an attempt to co-ordinate the development of international accounting standards. It includes representatives from many countries throughout the world, including the USA and the UK.

NOTE

From 1 April 2001, the International Accounting Standards Board (IASB) has replaced the IASC.

3.24 International standards are not intended to override local regulations. In the UK, however, the ASC and ASB expressed their support for international standards by incorporating them within the UK standards. However, not all IAS have been incorporated in this way.

The Stock Exchange regulations

3.25 The Stock Exchange is a market for stocks and shares, and a company whose securities are traded in this market is known as a 'quoted' or 'listed' company.

3.26 When a share is granted a quotation on The Stock Exchange, it appears on the 'Official List' which is published in London each business day. The Official List shows the 'official quotation' or price for the share for that day. It is drawn up by the Quotations Department of The Stock Exchange, which derives its prices from those actually ruling in the market.

3.27 In order to receive a quotation for its securities, a company must conform with Stock Exchange Listing Rules issued by the Council of The Stock Exchange. The company commits itself to certain procedures and standards, including matters concerning the disclosure of accounting information, which are more extensive than the disclosure requirements of the Companies Acts. These include issuing the annual report within six months of the year end and publishing an interim report giving profit and loss information.

Question 11

To ensure you understand which regulations apply to which type of business, fill in the table below with a 'yes' where compliance is required and 'no' where it is not.

Type Of Business	Companies Act	FRSs/SSAPs	IASs	Stock Exchange Listing Rules
Public Listed Company				
Private Limited Company				
Sole Tradership				

Answer

Type Of Business	Companies Act	FRSs/SSAPs	IASs	Stock Exchange Listing Rules
Public Listed Company	YES	YES	NO	YES
Private Limited Company	YES	YES	NO	NO
Sole Tradership	NO	NO	NO	NO

Chapter roundup

- A large number of accounting concepts are used in the preparation of a set of accounts.
- Different accounting conventions can lead to different reported results. Of the various possible conventions that could be adopted, the historical cost convention is the only one enjoying wide currency at present. However, you should also be aware of the current cost and current purchasing power conventions.
- Order is provided by a comprehensive regulatory framework, based on UK company legislation, accounting standards (UK and international) and Stock Exchange requirements.

Quick quiz

1 The 8 accounting concepts or principles are:

(1) entity

(2) monetary measurement

(3) going concern

(4) prudence

(5) accural

(6) separate valuation

(7) materiality

(8) consistency

2 Fill in the blanks.

(a) The entity concept means that a business is treated as a separate entity, distinct from its owners or shareholders.

(b) The money measurement concept means that accounts deal only with items of monetry value.

(c) The going concern concept implies that a business values it's assets at the value to the business as the current time.

(d) The prudence concept means that accounts give the least optimistic presentation of a business's financial position or results.

(e) The accruals concept means that revenue earned must be ______.

(f) The consistency concept means that similar items in a set of accounts must be treated by the same means and that the same treatment should be applied from period to period.

(g) The separate valuation principle means that each component of an asset or liability must be treated as a seperate entity.

(h) The materiality concept states that a matter is material if its going to affect the way in which the accounts are interpreted.

3 At what stage is it normal to recognise the revenue arising from a credit sale?

4 Are these statements true or false?

(a) If the accruals concept and the prudence concept conflict, prudence prevails.
(b) If the consistency concept and the prudence concept conflict, prudence prevails.

5 Six possible values that might be attributed to a piece of machinery in a balance sheet are:

(1) at buying price

(2) at buying price - shelf life %.

(3) to buy new . replace

(4) to buy second hand

(5) to buy and upgraded version

(6) cost of machine + sales revenue lost.

6 Financial capital maintenance means?

A The business has the same quantity of assets at the end of the year as it had at the start

B The business has made a profit in the year

C The business proprietor has withdrawn only sufficient profits so that the business is able to replace its stock

D The original financial capital of the business is the same at the end of the year as it was at the start allowing for profit and drawings ✓

7 Which of the following is an advantage of historic cost accounting (HCA)?

A Assets are measured using objective historic costs ✓
B Profits will be overstated in times of rising prices
C Depreciation charges will be understated in times of rising prices
D Distributions to owners may be high

8 Fill in the blanks.

The main statute governing the content of limited company accounts in the UK is company law.

9 Fill in the blanks on this diagram showing the relationship of the four bodies responsible for the issue and enforcement of accounting regulations in the UK.

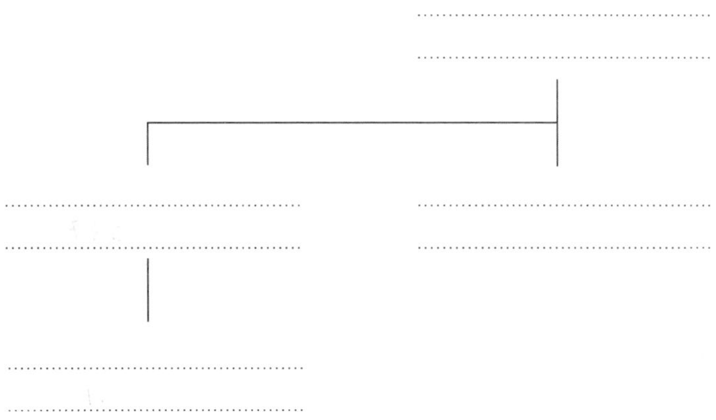

3. When it is certain that the sale is going to be paid.

Answers to quick quiz

1 (1) Entity
(2) Money measurement
(3) Going concern
(4) Prudence
(5) Accruals
(6) Consistency
(7) Separate valuation
(8) Materiality

2 (a) The entity concept means that a business is treated as a **separate entity**, distinct from its **owners** or **managers** .

(b) The money measurement concept means that accounts deal only with items **to which a monetary value can be attributed**.

(c) The going concern concept implies that a business **will continue in operation for the foreseeable future**

(d) The prudence concept means that accounts give **the most cautious** presentation of a business's financial position or results.

(e) The accruals concept means that revenue earned must be **matched against the expenditure incurred in earning it**.

(f) The consistency concept means that similar items in a set of accounts **should be given similar accounting treatment** and that the same treatment should be applied **from one period to another in accounting for similar items**.

(g) The separate valuation principle means that each component of an asset or liability must be **valued separately**.

(h) The materiality concept states that a matter is material if its **omission or mistatement would reasonably influence the decision of a user of accounts**.

3 When the sale has been completed and the customer has accepted the goods. At this point the debt is legally enforceable.

4 Both (a) and (b) are true.

5 (1) Original cost
(2) Original cost, written down across its useful life
(3) Secondhand value
(4) Replacement cost of an identical machine
(5) Replacement cost of a more modern machine
(6) Economic value

6 D Correct. This is the characteristic of a financial capital system.

A This describes one of the key elements of a system of current cost accounting.

B Under historic accounting, net profit equals the increase in net assets for the period. If no drawings are made, financial capital will increase.

C This reflects a system of capital maintenance in real terms.

7 A Correct. Asset values can be verified against historic purchase costs, thus avoiding subjective valuation judgements.

B Profits will be overstated because of holding gains, this is seen as a disadvantage of HCA.

C Depreciation will be based upon historic costs and may therefore be too low, leading to excessive profits being recorded.

D If profits are overstated, distributions may be excessive leading to erosion of the company capital base.

8 The main statute governing the content of limited company accounts in the UK is **CA 1985, as modified by CA 1989**.

9

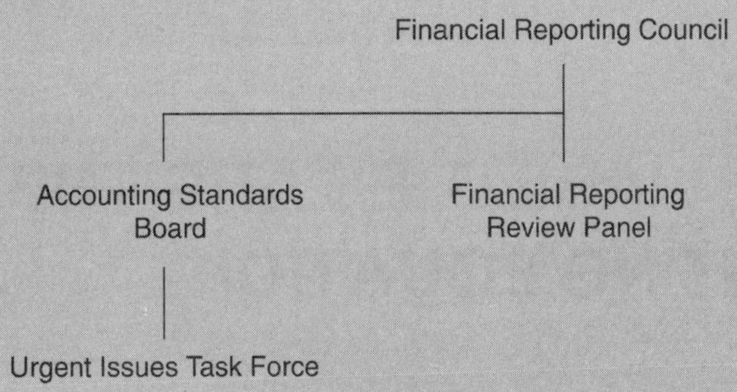

Now try the questions below from the Exam Question Bank

Number	Level	Marks	Time
4	Introductory	15	27 mins
5	Exam	2	3 mins
6	Exam	2	3 mins

Chapter 3

ASSETS, LIABILITIES AND THE ACCOUNTING EQUATION

Topic List		Syllabus reference	Ability required
1	**The nature of a business: assets and liabilities**	(i)	**Comprehension**
2	**The balance sheet**	(i)	**Comprehension**
3	**The accounting equation**	(i)	**Comprehension**
4	**The business equation**	(i)	**Comprehension**

Introduction

We have used the terms 'business', 'assets' and 'liabilities' without looking too closely at their meaning. It is important to have a thorough understanding of how these terms are used in an accounting context.

Sections 3 and 4 of the chapter introduce two concepts which it is important for you to grasp: the **accounting equation** and the **business equation**. You may already realise that a balance sheet has to balance. You are about to learn why!

Learning outcomes covered in this chapter

- Explain the concept of capital and revenue, cash and profit, income and expenditure and assets and liabilities

Syllabus content covered in this chapter

- The accounting equation
- Cash and profit
- Income, expenditure, assets and liabilities

Exam focus point

Do not rush this chapter. This is the foundation on which you will master more complex topics later in your studies. The examiner has stated that he is keen to ensure students have grasped the basics!

1 THE NATURE OF A BUSINESS: ASSETS AND LIABILITIES

Question 1

You may already be familiar with certain terms. Can you distinguish, for example, between the terms 'an enterprise', 'a business', 'a company' and 'a firm'?

Answer

An 'enterprise' is the most general term, referring to just about any organisation in which people join together to achieve a common end. In the context of accounting it can refer to a multinational conglomerate, a small club, a local authority and so on *ad infinitum.*

A 'business' is also a very general term, but it does not extend as widely as the term 'enterprise' as it would not include a charity or a local authority. Any organisation existing to trade and make a **profit** could be called a business.

A 'company' is an enterprise constituted in a particular legal form, usually involving limited liability for its members. Companies need not be businesses eg many charities are constituted as companies.

A 'firm' is a much vaguer term. It is sometimes used loosely in the sense of a business or a company. Some writers, more usefully, try to restrict its meaning to that of an unincorporated business (ie a business **not** constituted as a company eg a partnership).

KEY TERM

A **business** is an organisation which sells something or provides a service with the objective of profit.

1.1 Business's range from very small businesses (the local shopkeeper or plumber) to very large ones (ICI), but the objective of earning profit is common to all of them.

KEY TERM

Profit is the excess of income over expenditure. When expenditure exceeds income, the business is running at a **loss.**

1.2 One of the jobs of an accountant is to measure income, expenditure and profit. It is not a straightforward exercise and in later chapters we will look at some of the theoretical and practical problems.

1.3 **Non profit making enterprises**

Organisations	Comment
(a) **Charities** - exist to provide help to the needy.	Must keep expenditure within the level of income or cannot continue in operation.
(b) **Public sector organisations** - exist to serve the community rather than to make profits.	Include government departments and services (eg the fire service, police force, national health service etc). Can only spend the money allowed to them by the government. Must be cost- conscious.
(c) Certain **clubs and associations** - exist to provide services to their members.	To maintain and improve the services they offer, must ensure that income is at least as great as expenditure.

THE MAIN POINT!

All enterprises, profit making or not, will produce financial statements to provide information to interested parties. For a business, the most important statements are the **balance sheet** and the **profit and loss account**.

Both statements are based on the separate entity convention.

The business as a separate entity

KEY TERM

Limited liability: the liability of shareholders to the company is **limited** to the amount the company asks for their shares on issue.

1.4 It is crucial that you understand the convention adopted in preparing accounts (the *entity concept*) is **always** to treat a business as a separate entity from its owner(s). This applies whether or not the business is recognised in law as a separate entity.

1.5 Suppose that Fiona Middleton sets up a business as a hairdresser as 'Fiona's Salon'. The law sees no distinction between Fiona Middleton, the individual, and the business known as 'Fiona's Salon'. Any debts of the business which cannot be met from business assets must be met from Fiona's private resources.

1.6 But the law recognises a company as a legal entity, quite separate from its owners (the shareholders). A company may acquire assets, incur debts and enter into contracts. If a company's assets become insufficient to meet its liabilities, the company might become 'bankrupt'. But the shareholders are not usually required to pay the deficit from their own private resources. The debts belong to the company alone, and the shareholders have limited liability.

IMPORTANT POINT

Financial statements always treat the business as a separate entity.

Question 2

Fill in the missing words to make sure you understand the entity concept and how the law differs from accounting practice.

The entity concept regards a business as a ___ entity, distinct from its____ . The concept applies to _ businesses. However, the law only recognises a ______ as a legal entity separate from its _________. The liability of shareholders to the company is _ to the amount the company asks them to pay for their shares.

Answer

The missing words are:

separate; owners; all; company; owners; limited.

REMEMBER

The balance sheet is a list of all the assets owned by a business and all the liabilities owed by it at a particular date.

The profit and loss account is a record of income generated and expenditure incurred over a given period.

2 THE BALANCE SHEET

KEY TERM

An **asset** is something valuable which a business owns.

2.1 Fixed assets are held and used in operations to generate profit, such as an office building, or a machine. Current assets are held for only a short time with the intention of turning them into cash in the ordinary course of business.

2.2 **Examples of assets**

Long-term (fixed) assets

- Factories
- Office building
- Warehouse
- Delivery vans
- Lorries
- Plant and machinery
- Computer equipment
- Office furniture

Short-term (current) assets

- Cash
- Raw materials
- Finished goods held for sale to customers
- Money owned by customers
- Cash and bank accounts

KEY TERM

A **liability** is something which is owed to somebody else. 'Liabilities' is the accounting term for the amounts a business owes (the debts of the business).

2.3 **Examples of liabilities**

- A bank loan or bank overdraft
- Amounts owed to suppliers for goods purchased but not yet paid for
- Taxation owed to the government

Question 3

Classify the following items as fixed assets, current assets or liabilities.

(a) A personal computer used in the accounts department of a retail store
(b) A personal computer on sale in an office equipment shop
(c) Wages due to be paid to staff at the end of the week
(d) A van for sale in a motor dealer's showroom
(e) A delivery van used in a grocer's business
(f) An amount owing to a leasing company for the acquisition of a van

Answer

(a) Fixed asset
(b) Current asset
(c) Liability
(d) Current asset
(e) Fixed asset
(f) Liability

FORMULA TO LEARN

Net assets = Assets – Liabilities

KEY TERM

Capital is the amount owed to the owner of the business by the business.

2.4 Owners put in money to start a business, and are owed any profits which are generated by the business.

3 THE ACCOUNTING EQUATION

FORMULA TO LEARN

The accounting equation is that in a balance sheet:

Assets = Capital + Liabilities

3.1 EXAMPLE: THE ACCOUNTING EQUATION

On 1 July 20X6, Courtney Spice opened a stall in the market, to sell herbs and spices. She had £2,500 to put into her business.

When the business is set up, it owns the cash that Courtney has put into it, £2,500. But does it owe anything?

The answer is yes. The business is a separate entity in accounting terms. It has obtained its assets (in this example cash) from its owner, Courtney Spice. It therefore owes this amount of money to its owner. If Courtney changed her mind and decided not to go into business after all, the business would have to repay the cash to Courtney.

The money put into a business by its owners is **capital**. A business proprietor invests capital with the intention of earning profit.

When Courtney Spice sets up her business:

Capital invested	=	£2,500
Cash	=	£2,500

Capital is a form of liability, because it is an amount owed by the business to its owner(s). As liabilities and assets are always equal amounts, we can state the accounting equation as follows.

Assets	=	*Capital*	+	*Liabilities*

For Courtney Spice, as at 1 July 20X6:

£2,500 (cash)	=	£2,500	+	£0

3.2 EXAMPLE CONTINUED

Courtney Spice uses some of the money invested to buy a market stall for £1,800. She also purchases some herbs and spices at a cost of £650.

This leaves £50 in cash (£2,500 – £1,800 – £650). Courtney puts £30 in the bank and keeps £20 in small change. She is now ready for her first day of market trading on 3 July 20X6.

The assets and liabilities of the business have altered. At 3 July, before trading begins, the state of her business is as follows.

Assets		=	*Capital*	+	*Liabilities*
	£				
Stall	1,800	=	£2,500	+	£0
Herbs and spices	650				
Cash at bank	30				
Cash in hand	20				
	2,500				

3.3 EXAMPLE CONTINUED: PROFIT INTRODUCED INTO THE ACCOUNTING EQUATION

On 3 July Courtney has a very successful day. She is able to sell all of her herbs and spices for £900 cash. Courtney has sold goods costing £650 to earn revenue of £900, we can say that she has earned a profit of £250 on the day's trading.

Profits belong to the owners of a business. So the £250 belongs to Courtney and are treated as an addition to the proprietor's capital.

Assets		=	*Capital*		+	*Liabilities*
	£			£		
Stall	1,800		Original investment	2,500		
Herbs and spices	0					
Cash at bank	30					
Cash in hand (20 + 900)	920		Retained profit	250		
	2,750			2,750	+	£0

We can re-arrange the accounting equation to help us to calculate the capital balance.

Assets – liabilities	=	Capital, or
Net assets	=	Capital

At the beginning and end of 3 July 20X6, Courtney's financial position is shown below.

	Net Assets	Capital
(a) At the beginning of the day:	£(2,500 – 0) = £2,500	= £2,500
(b) At the end of the day:	£(2,750 – 0) = £2,750	= £2,750

There has been an increase of £250 in net assets, which is the amount of profits earned during the day.

Drawings

KEY TERM

Drawings are amounts taken out of a business by its owner.

3.4 Courtney Spice has made a profit of £250 from her first day's work, she may decide to draw some of the profits out of the business for living expenses. Courtney decides to pay herself £180. This £180 is not an expense to be deducted in arriving at net profit. In other words, it would be incorrect to calculate the net profit earned by the business as follows.

	£
Profit on sale of herbs and spices	250
Less 'wages' paid to Courtney	180
Net profit earned by business (incorrect)	70

3.5 Any amounts paid by a business to its proprietor are treated by accountants as withdrawals of profit (drawings) and not as expenses incurred by the business.

In Courtney's case, the true position is that the net profit earned is the £250 surplus on sale of herbs and spices.

	£
Net profit earned by business	250
Less profit withdrawn by Courtney	180
Net profit retained in the business	70

3.6 The drawings are taken in cash, reducing the cash assets by £180. After the withdrawals, the accounting equation would be restated.

(a) *Assets*		=	*Capital*		+	*Liabilities*
	£			£		
Stall	1,800		Original investment	2,500		
Herbs and spices	0		Retained profit			
Cash at bank	30		(250 – 180)	70		
Cash in hand (920-180)	740					
	2,570			2,570	+	£0

(b) Alternatively	*Net assets*		*Capital*
	£(2,570 – 0)	=	£2,570

The increase in net assets is now only £(2,570 – 2,500) = £70, which is the amount of the retained profits.

IMPORTANT POINTS

A balance sheet balances, ie Assets = Capital + liabilities.

Liabilities are what the business owes to third parties.

Capital is what the business owes to its owner.

Capital = Original investment *plus* profit *less* drawings

Profit = Income – expenditure

Drawings = Amounts taken out of a business by its owner.

4 THE BUSINESS EQUATION **May 2001**

4.1 The business equation gives a definition of profits earned. The previous section has shown that the amount of profit earned is related to the increase in the net assets of the business and the drawings of profits by the proprietor.

FORMULA TO LEARN

The business equation is:

$$P = I + D - C_i$$

where

P	represents profit
I	represents the increase in net assets, after drawings have been taken out by the proprietor
D	represents drawings
C_i	represents the amount of extra capital introduced into the business during the period.

4.2 In our example of Courtney Spice's business on 3 July 20X6, after drawings.

Profit = £70 + £180 – £0
= £250

Exam focus point

The **business equation** was examined in Section A of the May 2001 exam.

4.3 EXAMPLE CONTINUED

The next market is on 10 July and Courtney purchases more herbs and spices for £740 cash. She is not feeling well, however, and so she accepts help for the day from her cousin Bianca, for a wage of £40. On 10 July, they sell all the goods for £1,100 cash. Courtney pays Bianca her wage of £40 and draws out £200 for herself.

Required

(a) State the accounting equation before trading began on 10 July.

(b) State the accounting equation at the end of 10 July, after paying Bianca

(i) but before drawings are taken out.
(ii) after drawings have been made.

(c) State the business equation to compute profits earned on 10 July.

The accounting equation for the business at the end of transactions for 3 July is given in 3.6(a).

4.4 SOLUTION

(a) After the purchase of the goods for £740.

Assets		=	*Capital*	+	*Liabilities*
	£				
Stall	1,800				
Goods	740				
Cash at bank	30				
Cash in hand (740 – 740)	0				
	2,570	=	£ 2,570	+	£0

(b) (i) On 10 July after Bianca is paid £40.

	£	£
Sales		1,100
Less cost of goods sold	740	
Bianca's wage	40	
		780
Profit		320

Assets		=	*Capital*		+	*Liabilities*
	£			£		
Stall	1,800		At beginning of 10 July	2,570		
Goods	0		Profits earned	320		
Cash at bank	30					
Cash in hand (0 + 1,100 – 40)	1,060					
	2,890			2,890	+	£0

(ii) After Courtney has taken drawings of £200.

Assets		=	*Capital*		+	*Liabilities*
	£			£		
Stall	1,800		At beginning of 10 July	2,570		
Goods	0		Retained profits (320 – 200)	120		
Cash at bank	30					
Cash in hand (1,060 – 200)	860					
	2,690			2,690	+	£0

(c)

	£
Net assets at end of 10 July	2,690
Net assets at beginning of 10 July	2,570
Increase in net assets	120

The business equation is:

$$P = I + D - C_i$$
$$= £120 + £200 - £0$$
$$= £320$$

This confirms the calculation of profit made in b(i).

Tutorial note. It is very important you should understand the principles described so far. Do not read on until you are confident that you understand the solution to this example.

Creditors and debtors

KEY TERM

A **creditor** is a person to whom a business owes money and is therefore a liability of a business.

A **debtor** is a person who owes money to the business and is therefore an asset of the business.

4.5 It is common business practice to make purchases on credit, with a promise to pay within 30 days or two months or three months from the date of the bill (or 'invoice') for the goods. For example, A buys goods costing £2,000 on credit from B. B sends A an invoice for £2,000, dated 1 March, with credit terms that payment must be made within 30 days. If A pays on 31 March, B will be a creditor of A between 1 and 31 March for £2,000.

4.6 Just as a business might buy goods on credit, so might it sell goods to customers on credit. A customer who buys goods on credit is a **debtor**. Taking the example in 3.5, **A is a debtor of B** for £2,000 between 1 and 31 March.

4.7 EXAMPLE CONTINUED

Courtney Spice's market stall continues to trade during the following week to 17 July 20X6. (See Paragraph 4.4 (b)(ii) for the situation as at the end of 10 July.)

(a) Courtney needs more money in the business and so she makes the following arrangements.

  (i) She invests a further £250 of her own savings.

  (ii) She persuades her Uncle Phil to lend her £500 immediately. Uncle Phil tells her that she can repay the loan whenever she likes but, in the meantime, she must pay him interest of £5 each week at the end of the market day. They agree that it will probably be quite a long time before the loan is eventually repaid.

(b) She decides that she can afford to buy a second hand van to pick up herbs and spices from her supplier and bring them to her stall in the market. She buys a van on credit for £700. Courtney agrees to pay for the van after 30 days' trial use.

(c) During the week before the next market day (17 July), Courtney's Uncle Grant asks her if she could sell him some spice racks and herb chopping boards as presents for his friends. Courtney agrees and she buys what Uncle Grant wants, paying £300 in cash. Uncle Grant accepts delivery of the goods and agrees to pay £350 to Courtney for them, but he asks if she can wait until the end of the month for payment. Courtney agrees.

(d) Courtney buys herbs and spices costing £800. Of these purchases £750 are paid for in cash, with the remaining £50 on seven days' credit. Courtney decides to use Bianca's services again as an assistant on market day, at an agreed wage of £40.

(e) On 17 July, Courtney once again sells all her goods, earning revenue of £1,250 cash. She takes out drawings of £240 for her week's work and pays Bianca £40 in cash. She will make the interest payment to her Uncle Phil the next time she sees him.

(f) Ignore any van expenses for the week, for the sake of relative simplicity.

Required

(a) State the accounting equation

  (i) After Courtney and Uncle Phil have put more money into the business and after the purchase of the van.

  (ii) After the sale of goods to Uncle Grant.

  (iii) After the purchase of goods for the weekly market.

  (iv) At the end of the day's trading on 17 July, after drawings have been 'appropriated' out of profit.

(b) State the business equation showing profit earned during the week ended 17 July.

4.8 SOLUTION

This solution deals with each transaction one at a time in chronological order.

(a) (i) *The addition of Courtney's extra capital and Uncle Phil's loan*

To the business, Uncle Phil is a long-term creditor and, therefore, his investment is a liability of the business and not business capital.

Assets		=	*Capital*		+	*Liabilities*	
	£			£			£
Stall	1,800		As at end of 10 July	2,690		Loan	500
Goods	0		Additional capital put in	250			
Cash (30+860+ 250+500)	1,640						
	3,440	=		2,940	+		500

The purchase of the van (cost £700) is on credit.

Assets		=	*Capital*		+	*Liabilities*	
	£			£			£
Stall	1,800		As at end of 10 July	2,690		Loan	500
Van	700		Additional capital	250		Creditor	700
Cash	1,640						
	4,140	=		2,940	+		1,200

(ii) *The sale of goods to Uncle Grant on credit (£350) at a cost of £300 (cash)*

Assets		=	*Capital*		+	*Liabilities*	
	£			£			
Stall	1,800		As at end of 10 July	2,690		Loan	500
Van	700		Additional capital	250		Creditor	700
Debtors	350		Profit on sale to				
Cash(1,640 – 300)	1,340		Uncle Grant (350 – 300)	50			
	4,190	=		2,990	+		1,200

(iii) *After the purchase of goods (£750 paid in cash and £50 on credit)*

Assets		= *Capital*		+ *Liabilities*	
	£		£		£
Stall	1,800	As at end of 10 July	2,690	Loan	500
Van	700			Creditor for van	700
Goods	800	Additional capital	250	Creditor for goods	50
Debtors	350	Profit on sale to			
Cash(1,340 – 750)	590	Uncle Grant	50		
	4,240 =		2,990 +		1,250

(iv) *After market trading on 17 July*

	£	£
Sales		1,250
Cost of goods sold	800	
Wages	40	
Interest payable	5	
		845
Profit earned on 17 July		405
Profit on sale of goods to Uncle Grant		50
Profit for the week		455
Drawings appropriated out of profits		240
Retained profit		215

Assets		= *Capital*		+ *Liabilities*	
	£		£		£
Stall	1,800	As at end of 10 July	2,690	Loan	500
Van	700	Additional capital	250	Creditor for van	700
Goods	0			Creditor for goods	50
Debtors	350				
Cash (590+ 1,250 – 40 – 240)	1,560	Profits retained	215	Creditor for interest payment	5
	4,410		3,155		1,255

(b)

	£
Net assets as at the end of 17 July £(4,410 – 1,255)	3,155
Net assets as at the end of 10 July (Paragraph 4.4(b)(ii))	2,690
Increase in net assets	465

(Remember that extra capital of £250 was invested by Courtney.)

$$P = I + D - C_i$$
$$= £465 + £240 - £250$$
$$= £455$$

This confirms the calculation of profit for the week in (a)(iv) above.

Question 4

Calculate the profit for the year ended 31 December 20X1 from the following information.

	1 January 20X1		*31 December 20X1*	
	£	£	£	£
Assets				
Property	20,000		20,000	
Machinery	6,000		9,000	
Debtors	4,000		8,000	
Cash	1,000		1,500	
		31,000		38,500
Liabilities				
Overdraft	6,000		9,000	
Creditors	5,000		3,000	
		(11,000)		(12,000)
Net assets		20,000		26,500
Drawings during the year				£4,500
Additional capital introduced by the proprietor during the year				£5,000

Answer

The increase in net assets during the year was £(26,500 - 20,000) = £6,500.

$P = I + D - C_i$
= £6,500 + £4,500 - £5,000
= £6,000

Chapter roundup

- A **business** owns assets and owes liabilities. It is important to keep business assets and liabilities separate from the personal assets and liabilities of the proprietor(s).
- **Assets** are items belonging to a business and used in the running of the business. They may be fixed (such as machinery or office premises) or current (such as goods, debtors and cash).
- **Liabilities** are amounts owed by a business to outsiders (eg a bank or a trade creditor).
- The assets of a business are always equal to its liabilities (including capital).
- The accounting equation and the business equation are useful concepts in accounting because:
  - The accounting equation emphasises the equality between assets and liabilities (including capital as a liability).
  - The business equation emphasises the inter-relationship between profits, net assets, appropriations of profit (drawings) and new capital investment.
- You should now be able to account for simple business transactions.
  - Restate the assets and liabilities of the business after the transactions have taken place.
  - State the profit or loss, if any, arising as a result of the transactions.
- The assets and liabilities of a business at any moment in time are shown in a balance sheet. This is very similar to the accounting equation.
- The profit (or loss) earned by a business during a given period of time is shown in a trading, profit and loss account.

  These will be described in more detail in the following chapter.

Quick quiz

1 Fill in the blanks.

If income exceeds expenditure, the business makes a ___profit___.

If expenditure exceeds income, the business makes a ___loss___.

2 Limited liability means that?

A Members of a company need only pay part of the debts if the company becomes insolvent

B Shareholders will receive only partial return of their investment if the company becomes insolvent

C Upon liquidation, the maximum amount which a member can be called upon to pay is any outstanding monies on shares purchased

D Losses of an insolvent company are shared between creditors and members

3 State whether the following are fixed assets, current assets, liabilities, capital or drawings.

(a) A delivery van fixed
(b) Money owed to a supplier liability
(c) A mortgage owed to a bank liability
(d) Money put into the business bank by the owner of the business capital
(e) Profit made by a business capital
(f) Money owed by a customer current asset
(g) Raw materials not yet used in production current asset
(h) Money taken from the business bank account by the owner of a business. drawing

4 Which of the following is a correct version of the 'fundamental accounting equation'?

A Assets = liabilities
B Assets = capital less liabilities
C Assets plus liabilities = capital
D Assets = capital + liabilities

5 Capital is?

A The amount borrowed to set up a business
B The amount owed by a business to its proprietor(s)
C The value of the assets in a business
D The total amount invested in a business by all the providers of capital

6 Complete the business equation

P = I + D - Ci

7 What do P, I, D and C_i stand for in the business equation? Profit Net loss drawing Capital investment

8 Profit for a period was £400, and the increase in net assets (after drawings of £200 have been taken into account) was £1,000. How much additional capital has the proprietor introduced in the period?

A nil
B £400
C £800
D 1,200

Answers to quick quiz

1 If income exceeds expenditure, the business makes a **profit**.

If expenditure exceeds income, the business makes a **loss**.

2 C This is correct, obviously the members lose their investments.

A Incorrect; members cannot be called upon to meet any of the debts unless they have personally guaranteed them.

B Ordinary shareholders and preference shareholders will only receive a return of investment if funds exist to pay them in a liquidation (which is usually unlikely).

D Company law is designed to protect creditors.

3 (a) Fixed asset
(b) Liability
(c) Liability
(d) Capital
(e) Capital
(f) Current asset
(g) Current asset
(h) Drawings

4 D Correct.
A This is correct, but it is usual to subdivide liabilities between 'capital' and other liabilities.
B Incorrect.
C Incorrect, assets less liabilities = net assets = capital.

5 B Correct.
A Borrowings are liabilities of a business, not capital.
C Capital will equal net assets employed at a point in time.
D Loan capital could be provided – so this definition is not precise.

6 $P = I + D - C_i$

7 P = Profit
I = Increase in net assets (after allowing for drawings)
D = Drawings
C_i = Capital introduced

8 C

Now try the questions below from the Exam Question Bank

Number	Level	Marks	Time
7	Introductory	15	27 mins
8	Exam	2	3 mins
9	Introductory	5	9 mins

Chapter 4

AN INTRODUCTION TO FINAL ACCOUNTS

Introduction

In Chapter 3 you met the accounting equation and the balance sheet. You also have some idea of what is meant by the profit and loss account.

A **balance sheet** shows the liabilities, capital and assets of a business at a given moment in time. It is like a 'snapshot', since it captures a still image of something which is continually changing. Typically, a balance sheet is prepared to show the position at the end of the accounting period.

Only the basic details of a balance sheet are described in this chapter. We will add more detail in later chapters, as we look at other ideas and accounting methods.

The **profit and loss account** matches the revenue earned in a period with the costs incurred in earning it. It is usual to distinguish between a **gross profit** (sales revenue less the cost of goods sold) and a **net profit** (the gross profit less the expenses of selling, distribution, administration etc).

There is a fair amount to learn before you will be able to prepare these statements yourself. It is important to introduce the financial statements now so you can see the final result. Keep them in mind as you tackle the basics of ledger accounting in the next few chapters.

If you buy an asset which you can use in the business over the next twenty years, it would be misleading to charge all the expenses in the first year. This is the principle behind the important distinction between **capital and revenue expenditure** which is explored in Section 3 of the chapter.

Learning outcomes covered in this chapter

- Explain the concepts of capital and revenue, cash and profit, income and expenditure and assets and liabilities

Syllabus content covered in this chapter

- Items in formats for published accounts
- Capital and revenue

1 THE BALANCE SHEET **Pilot Paper**

> **REMEMBER**
>
> A balance sheet is a statement of the assets and liabilities of a business at a point in time.

1.1 A balance sheet can be presented in two ways.

- Assets in one half and capital and liabilities in the other
- Net assets in one half and capital in the other

1.2 **An illustrated balance sheet**

(a) NAME OF BUSINESS
BALANCE SHEET AS AT (DATE)

	£
Assets (item by item)	X
	X
	X

	£
Capital	X
Liabilities (item by item)	X
	X

(b) NAME OF BUSINESS
BALANCE SHEET AS AT (DATE)

	£
Assets	X
Less liabilities	X
Net assets	X
Capital	X

Method (a) is the format preferred under International Standards, while method (b) is the usual format under UK Standards. This Study Text generally uses method (b).

1.3 In either format, the total value in one half of the balance sheet will equal the total value in the other half. You should understand this from the accounting equation.

1.4 Capital, liabilities and assets are usually shown in more detail in a balance sheet. The following paragraphs give examples of this.

Capital (sole trader)

> **REMEMBER**
>
> Capital is what the business owes to the owner.

1.5 The proprietor's capital can be analysed into difference sources.

	£	£
Capital as at the beginning of the accounting period (ie capital 'brought forward')		X
Add additional capital introduced during the period		X
		X
Add profit earned during the period	X	
Less drawings	(X)	
Retained profit for the period		X
Capital as at the end of the accounting period (ie capital 'carried forward')		X

1.6 '**Brought forward**' means 'brought forward from the previous period', and '**carried forward**' means 'carried forward to the next period'. The carried forward amount at the end of one period is also the brought forward amount of the next period. The word 'down' is sometimes used instead of 'forward'.

Liabilities

REMEMBER

Liabilities are what the business owes to third parties.

1.7 The various liabilities are detailed separately. A distinction is made between current liabilities and long-term liabilities.

Current liabilities (amounts falling due within one year)

KEY TERM

Current liabilities are debts of the business that must be paid within a fairly short period of time. By convention, a 'fairly short period of time' is taken as one year.

1.8 In the accounts of limited companies, the CA 1985 requires the use of the term 'creditors: amounts falling due within one year' rather than 'current liabilities'.

Examples of current liabilities

- **Loans** repayable within one year
- **Bank overdraft** (repayable on demand, in theory)
- **Trade creditors** (suppliers to whom the business owes money)
- **Taxation** payable
- **Accrued expenses** (eg gas used between the date of the last bill and the end of the accounting period for which a bill has not yet been received)

Accrued expenses will be described more fully in a later chapter.

Long-term liabilities (amounts falling due after more than one year)

KEY TERM

A **long-term liability** is a debt which is not payable within the 'short term' and so any liability which is not current must be long-term.

1.9 By convention 'long-term' means more than one year. In limited company accounts, the CA 1985 requires use of the term: 'Creditors: amounts falling due after more than one year'.

1.10 **Examples of long-term liabilities**

(a) **Loans** which are not repayable for more than one year, such as a bank loan or a loan from an individual.

(b) A **mortgage loan**, which is secured against a property. The lender then has 'first claim' on the property and can force its sale if the business fails to repay the loan.

(c) **Debentures** or debenture loans, which are securities issued by a limited company at a fixed rate of interest. They are repayable on agreed terms by a specified date in the future. The holders' interests, including security for the loan, are protected by the terms of a trust deed.

Assets

REMEMBER

Assets are what the business owns.

1.11 Assets in the balance sheet are divided into two groups.

(a) Fixed assets

- Tangible fixed assets
- Intangible fixed assets
- Investments (long term)

(b) Current assets

Fixed assets

KEY TERM

A **fixed asset** is an asset acquired for continuing use within the business, with a view to earning income or making profits from its use, either directly or indirectly.

1.12 A fixed asset is not acquired for sale to a customer.

(a) In manufacturing, a production machine is a fixed asset as it makes goods for sale.

(b) In a service industry, equipment used by employees giving service to customers is a fixed asset (eg the equipment used in a garage, furniture in a hotel).

(c) Factory premises, office furniture, computer equipment, company cars, delivery vans or pallets in a warehouse are all fixed assets.

In addition the asset must have a 'life' in use of more than one year (strictly, more than one 'accounting period' which might be less than one year).

KEY TERM

A **tangible fixed asset** is a physical asset, ie one that can be touched. It has a real, 'solid' existence.

1.13 All the examples mentioned above are tangible fixed assets.

KEY TERM

An **intangible fixed asset** is an asset which does not have a physical existence. It cannot be 'touched'.

1.14 An example of an 'intangible fixed asset' is the 'goodwill' from customers that a business builds up over the years. Detailed knowledge of this point is outside the scope of your syllabus.

1.15 An **investment** can be a fixed asset. Investments are commonly found in the published accounts of large limited companies. Company A might invest in another company B, by purchasing some of its shares. These shares would earn income for A in the form of dividends paid out by B. If the investments are purchased by A with a view of holding them for more than one year, they would be fixed assets of A.

Fixed assets and depreciation

1.16 Fixed assets can be held and used by a business for a number of years, but they wear out or lose their usefulness over time. Every tangible fixed asset has a limited life. (The only exception is land held freehold or on a very long leasehold.)

1.17 The accounts of a business try to recognise that the cost of a fixed asset is gradually used up with time. This is done by writing off the asset's cost in the profit and loss account over several accounting periods. For example, a machine costs £1,000 and is expected to wear out after ten years. Therefore, we can write off the cost by £100 each year. This process is known as **depreciation**.

1.18 If a balance sheet is drawn up four years after the asset was purchased, the amount of depreciation accumulated is 4 × £100 = £400. The machine then appears in the balance sheet in the following way.

	£
Machine at original cost	1,000
Less accumulated depreciation	400
Net book value*	600

* ie the value of the asset in the books of account, net of depreciation.

After ten years the asset would be fully depreciated and would appear in the balance sheet with a net book value of zero.

Current assets

KEY TERM

Current assets are either:

(a) items owned by the business with the intention of turning them into cash within one year; or

(b) cash, including money in the bank, owned by the business.

1.19 These assets are 'current' because they are continually flowing through the business. For example, a trader, David Wickes, runs a business selling motor cars and purchases a showroom, which he stocks with cars for sale.

(a) If he sells a car in a cash sale, the goods are immediately converted into cash.

(b) If he sells a car in a credit sale, the car will be given to the customer who becomes a debtor of the business. Eventually, the debtor will pay what he owes in cash.

1.20 The following current assets can be identified from this example.

(a) The cars (goods) held in stock for re-sale are current assets, because David Wickes intends to sell them within one year.

(b) Debtors are current assets, if they are expected to pay all they owe within one year.

(c) Cash is a current asset.

1.21 The transactions described above could be shown as a cash cycle.

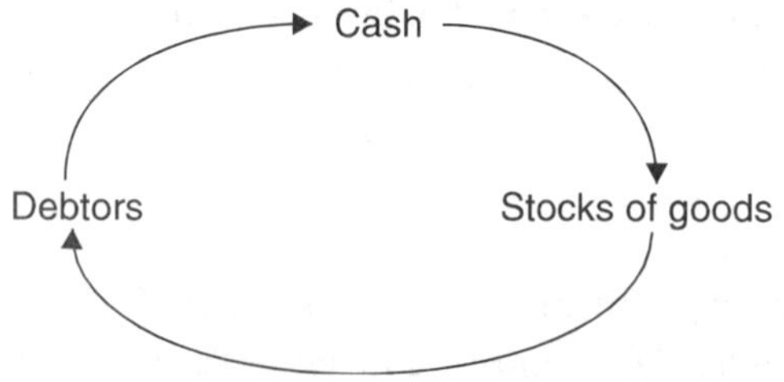

1.22 Cash is used to buy goods which are sold. Sales on credit create debtors, but eventually cash is received. Some, perhaps most, of the cash is then used to replenish stocks.

1.23 **Main items of current assets**

- Stocks
- Debtors
- Cash

1.24 It is important to realise that cars are current assets of David Wickes because he is a car trader. If he also has a car which he keeps and uses on business, this car would be a fixed asset. The difference between a fixed and a current asset is the purpose for which it is used in the business.

1.25 **Some other categories of current assets**

(a) **Short-term investments**. These are stocks and shares of other businesses held with the intention of selling them in the near future, eg shares in Marks and Spencer, ICI or GEC. The shares will be sold when the business needs the cash again. If share prices rise in the meantime, the business will make a profit.

(b) **Prepayments.** These are amounts already paid by the business for benefits which will be enjoyed within the next accounting period. A business pays an annual insurance premium of £240 to insure its premises against fire and theft. The premium is payable annually in advance on 1 December. If the business has an accounting year end of 31 December, it will only enjoy one month's insurance cover by the end of the year. The remaining 11 months' cover (£220) will be enjoyed in the next year. The prepayment of £220 is shown in the balance sheet at 31 December as a current asset.

A prepayment can be thought of as a form of debtor. At 31 December, the insurance company still owes the business 11 months' worth of insurance cover.

Trade debtors and other debtors

1.26 Although it is convenient to think of debtors as customers who buy goods on credit, it is more accurate to say that a debtor is anyone who owes the business money.

1.27 A distinction can be made between two groups of debtors.

(a) Trade debtors, ie customers who still owe money for goods or services bought on credit in the course of the trading activities of the business.

(b) Other debtors, ie anyone else owing money to the business (including prepayments).

Question 1

Are the following, tangible fixed assets, intangible fixed assets, investments, current assets, current liabilities or long term liabilities.

(a) Shares in BP, intended to be held long term invest.
(b) Machinery used in production fa
(c) Raw materials intended for use in production ca
(d) An overdraft cl
(e) A mortgage ltl
(f) Trade creditors cl
(g) Trade debtors ca
(h) Goodwill ifa
(i) Prepayments ca
(j) Accrued expenses cl

Answer

(a) Investments
(b) Tangible fixed assets
(c) Current assets
(d) Current liabilities
(e) Long term liabilities
(f) Current liabilities
(g) Current assets
(h) Intangible fixed assets
(i) Current assets
(j) Current liabilities

1.28 EXAMPLE: BALANCE SHEET PREPARATION

You might like to attempt to prepare a balance sheet yourself before reading the solution.

Prepare a balance sheet for the Ted Hills Hardware Store as at 31 December 20X6, given the information below.

	£
Capital as at 1 January 20X6	47,600
Profit for the year to 31 December 20X6	8,000
Freehold premises, net book value at 31 December 20X6	50,000
Motor vehicles, net book value at 31 December 20X6	9,000
Fixtures and fittings, net book value at 31 December 20X6	8,000
Long-term loan (mortgage)	25,000
Bank overdraft*	2,000
Goods held in stock for resale	16,000
Debtors	500
Cash in hand*	100
Creditors	1,200
Taxation payable	3,500
Drawings	4,000
Accrued costs of rent	600
Prepayment of insurance	300

* A shop might have cash in its cash registers, but an overdraft at the bank.

1.29 SOLUTION

TED HILLS BALANCE SHEET
AS AT 31 DECEMBER 20X6

	£	£
Fixed assets at net book value		
Freehold premises		50,000
Fixtures and fittings		8,000
Motor vehicles		9,000
		67,000
Current assets		
Stocks	16,000	
Debtors	500	
Prepayment	300	
Cash	100	
	16,900	
Current liabilities		
Bank overdraft	2,000	
Creditors	1,200	
Taxation payable	3,500	
Accrued costs	600	
	7,300	
Net current assets		9,600
		76,600
Long-term liabilities		
Loan		(25,000)
Net Assets		51,600
Capital		
Capital as at 1 January 20X6		47,600
Profit for the year		8,000
		55,600
Less drawings		(4,000)
Capital as at 31 December 20X6		51,600

Question 2

Prepare the balance sheet for Abbax as at 31 December 20X4 from the information below.

	£
Freehold premises	80,000
Stocks	2,500
Creditors	4,000
Profit for the year to 31.12.X4	6,600
Capital introduced in the year to 31.12.X4	5,000
Debtors	3,000
Furniture	27,000
Accruals	500
Drawings in the year to 31.12.X4	3,000
Prepayments	1,000
Delivery vans	15,000
Cash at bank	4,600
Mortgage	70,000
Capital brought forward at 1.1.X4	50,000

Answer

	£	£	£
Fixed assets at net book value			
Freehold premises			80,000
Furniture			27,000
Delivery vans			15,000
			122,000
Current assets			
Stocks		2,500	
Debtors		3,000	
Prepayments		1,000	
Cash		4,600	
		11,100	
Current liabilities			
Creditors	4,000		
Accruals	500		
		(4,500)	
Net current assets			6,600
Long term liabilities			
Mortgage			(70,000)
Net assets			58,600
Capital			
Capital brought forward at 1.1.X4			50,000
Capital introduced in the year			5,000
			55,000
Profit for the year			6,600
			61,600
Less: drawings			3,000
Capital carried forward at 31.12.X4			58,600

The order of items in the balance sheet

1.30 The balance sheet format most commonly used is the vertical format. The following versions exist.

(a) Net assets above and capital below (as in the example above)

(b) Fixed assets and net current assets above, with capital and long-term liabilities below

(c) Assets above with capital and liabilities below

(d) Capital and liabilities above, with assets below

There is no general rule about which version of a vertical balance sheet should be used. However CA 1985 requires (a) to be used for the published accounts of most limited companies. This format is therefore the one you should try to familiarise yourself with and use as a matter of habit. (If you are studying the International syllabus, then format (c) is the one to be used).

Order of items within categories

1.31 By convention, a balance sheet lists assets and liabilities in a particular order.

(a) **Fixed assets** are listed in a descending order of 'length of useful life'. Property has a longer life than fixtures and fittings, which usually have a longer life than motor vehicles. This is why the fixed assets in the example above are listed in that order.

(b) **Current assets** are listed in descending order of the length of time it might be before the asset will be converted into cash. Broadly speaking, stocks will convert into debtors, and debtors will convert into cash. So stock, debtors and cash will be listed in that order. Prepayments, because they are similar to debtors, should be listed after debtors and before cash.

(c) **Current liabilities** are listed in the descending order in which payment is due. Since bank overdrafts are strictly repayable on demand, they are listed first. Then come creditors and accruals. In the above example 'Taxation payable' is separately listed after creditors, as it is a specific type of creditor.

Working capital, or net current assets

KEY TERM

The **working capital** of a business is the difference between its current assets and current liabilities, ie net current assets.

1.32 In the balance sheet above, the Ted Hills Hardware Store has net current assets of £(16,900 – 7,300) = £9,600.

Exam focus point

Unless examination questions specify otherwise, method (a) is now the format of balance sheet we would recommend that you try to use.

2 THE TRADING, PROFIT AND LOSS ACCOUNT — Pilot Paper

KEY TERM

The **trading, profit and loss account** is a statement showing in detail how the profit (or loss) of a period has been made.

2.1 The owners and managers of a business want to know how much profit or loss has been made, but there is only limited information value in the figure for profit shown in a balance sheet.

2.2 In order to exercise financial control effectively, managers need to know how much income has been earned, what costs have been incurred and whether the performance of sales or the control of costs appears to be satisfactory. This is the basic reason for preparing the trading, profit and loss account.

2.3 There are two parts to the statement, a trading account and a profit and loss account.

(a) **The trading account**. This shows the **gross profit** for the accounting period.

> **KEY TERM**
>
> **Gross profit** is the difference between the value of sales (excluding value added tax) and the cost of the goods sold

In a retail business, the cost of the goods sold is their purchase cost from the suppliers. In a manufacturing business, the cost of goods sold is the cost of raw materials plus the cost of the labour required to make the goods, and often plus an amount of production 'overhead' costs.

(b) **The profit and loss account**. This shows the **net profit** of the business.

> **KEY TERM**
>
> **Net profit** can be illustrated by the formula below.
>
> Net profit = Gross profit + Income from other sources − Other business expenses

Detail in the profit and loss account

2.4 **Examples of income from other sources**

- Dividends or interest received from investments
- Profits on the sale of fixed assets
- Rental income
- Discounts received from suppliers

2.5 **Examples of other business expenses**

(a) **Selling and distribution expenses**. These are expenses associated with the process of selling and delivering goods to customers.

- Salaries of the sales director and sales management
- Salaries and commissions of salesmen
- Travelling and entertainment expenses of salesmen
- Marketing costs (eg advertising and sales promotion expenses)
- Costs of running and maintaining delivery vans
- Discounts allowed to customers (eg 5% discount for cash)
- Bad debts written off (ie when a customer does not pay all they owe)

Discounts and bad debts are described in more detail in a later chapter.

(b) **Administration expenses**. These are the expenses of providing management and administration for the business.

- Salaries of directors, management and office staff

- Rent and rates
- Insurance
- Telephone and postage
- Printing and stationery
- Heating and lighting

(c) **Finance expenses.**

- Interest on a loan
- Bank overdraft interest

You should try to group items of expenses (as shown above), but this will be dealt with in more detail in later chapters.

2.6 EXAMPLE: TRADING, PROFIT AND LOSS ACCOUNT

On 1 June 20X5, Beppe de Marco commenced trading as an ice cream salesman.

(a) He rented a van at a cost of £1,000 for three months. Running expenses for the van averaged £300 per month.

(b) He hired a part time helper at a cost of £100 per month.

(c) He borrowed £2,000 from his bank and the interest cost of the loan was £25 per month.

(d) His main business was selling ice cream from the van, but he also did some special catering supplying ice creams for office parties. Sales to these customers were usually on credit.

(e) For the three months to 31 August 20X5, his total sales were £10,000 (cash £8,900, credit £1,100).

(f) He purchased his ice cream from a local manufacturer, Palmer Ltd. The cost of purchases in the three months to 31 August 20X5 was £6,200 and at 31 August he had sold every item of stock. He still owed £700 to Palmer Ltd for purchases on credit.

(g) One of his credit sale customers has gone bankrupt, owing Beppe £250. Beppe has decided to write off the debt in full.

(h) He used his own home for his office work. Telephone and postage expenses for the three months to 31 August were £150.

(i) During the period he paid himself £300 per month.

Required

Prepare a trading, profit and loss account for the three months 1 June to 31 August 20X5.

2.7 SOLUTION

BEPPE DE MARCO
TRADING, PROFIT AND LOSS ACCOUNT
FOR THE THREE MONTHS ENDED 31 AUGUST 20X5

	£	£
Sales		10,000
Less cost of sales		6,200
Gross profit		3,800
Wages (3 × £100)	300	
Van rental	1,000	
Van expenses (3 × £300)	900	
Bad debt written off	250	
Telephone and postage	150	
Interest charges (3 × £25)	75	
		2,675
Net profit (transferred to the balance sheet)		1,125

Note: The cost of sales is £6,200 even though £700 of the costs have not yet been paid. This will be reflected in the balance sheet as a creditor. The amount of £300 per month that Beppe paid to himself are drawings and so will be taken to the capital section of the balance sheet.

Question 3

On 1 January 20X2, Fred started a dress shop.

(a) He rented a shop at £200 per month and spent £10,000 on fixtures and fittings.

(b) He employed a shop assistant at £1,000 a month.

(c) He bought stock of dresses on credit for £38,000.

(d) He sold three quarters of his stock for £50,000.

(e) He estimates he has used £2,000 worth of electricity (he has so far received bills for January–September for £1,400)

(f) Fred estimates that his fixtures and fittings will last 10 years.

Required

Prepare a trading, profit and loss account for the year to 31 December 20X2.

Answer

FRED's BUSINESS
TRADING, PROFIT AND LOSS ACCOUNT
AS AT 31 DECEMBER 20X2

	£	£
Sales		50,000
Less cost of sales (¾ × £38,000)		(28,500)
Gross profit		21,500
Rent (£200 × 12)	2,400	
Depreciation (£10,000 ÷ 10)	1,000	
Wages	12,000	
Electricity	2,000	
		17,400
Net profit		4,100

3 CAPITAL AND REVENUE EXPENDITURE

KEY TERMS

Capital expenditure is expenditure which results in the acquisition of fixed assets, or an improvement in their earning capacity.

Revenue expenditure is expenditure which is incurred for either of the following reasons.

(a) For the purpose of the **trade** of the business. This includes expenditure classified as selling and distribution expenses, administration expenses and finance charges.

(b) To **maintain** the existing earning capacity of fixed assets.

3.1 Revenue expenditure is charged to the profit and loss account. For example, a business buys ten widgets for £200 (£20 each) and sells eight of them during an accounting period. It will have two widgets left in stock at the end of the period. The full £200 is revenue expenditure, but only £160 is a cost of goods sold during the period. The remaining £40 will be included in the balance sheet in the stock of goods held - ie as a **current asset** valued at £40.

3.2 A business purchases a building for £30,000. It then adds an extension to the building at a cost of £10,000. The building needs to have a few broken windows mended, its floors polished and some missing roof tiles replaced. These cleaning and maintenance jobs cost £900.

3.3 The original purchase (£30,000) and the cost of the extension (£10,000) are capital expenditures, because they are incurred to acquire and then improve a fixed asset. The other costs of £900 are revenue expenditure, because these merely maintain the building and so its 'earning capacity'. The £40,000 will appear as fixed assets in the balance sheet, while the £900 will be shown as an expense in the profit and loss account.

Capital income and revenue income

3.4 Capital income is the proceeds from the sale of fixed assets, including fixed asset investments. The profits (or losses) from the sale of fixed assets are included in the profit and loss account for the accounting period in which the sale takes place.

3.5 Revenue income comes from the following sources.

- Sale of trading assets
- Interest and dividends received from investments held by the business

Capital transactions

3.6 The above items do not include raising additional capital from the owner(s) of the business, or raising and repaying loans. These transactions add to the cash assets of the business, thereby creating a corresponding increase in capital or loan. When a loan is repaid, it reduces the liabilities (loan) and the assets (cash) of the business.

None of these transactions would be reported through the profit and loss account.

Why is the distinction between capital and revenue items important?

3.7 Since revenue items and capital items are accounted for in different ways, the correct calculation of profit for any accounting period depends on the correct classification of items as revenue or capital.

Exam focus point

The distinction between capital and revenue expenditure was examined in Section A of the May 2001 exam.

Question 4

Classify each of the following items as 'capital' or 'revenue' expenditure or income.

(a) The purchase of leasehold premises. capital

(b) The annual depreciation of leasehold premises. revenue

(c) Solicitors' fees in connection with the purchase of leasehold premises. capital

(d) The costs of adding extra storage capacity to a mainframe computer used by the business. capital

(e) Computer repairs and maintenance costs. revenue

(f) Profit on the sale of an office building. capital

(g) Revenue from sales by credit card. revenue

(h) The cost of new machinery. capital

(i) Customs duty charged on the machinery when imported into the country. capital

(j) The 'carriage' costs of transporting the new machinery from the supplier's factory to the premises of the business purchasing the machinery. capital

(k) The cost of installing the new machinery in the premises of the business. capital

(l) The wages of the machine operators revenue

Answer

(a) Capital expenditure.

(b) Depreciation of a fixed asset is a revenue expenditure.

(c) The legal fees associated with the purchase of a property may be added to the purchase price and classified as capital expenditure.

(d) Capital expenditure (enhancing an existing fixed asset).

(e) Revenue expenditure.

(f) Capital income.

(g) Revenue income (trading income).

(h) Capital expenditure.

(i) If customs duties are borne by the purchaser of the fixed asset, they may be added to the cost of the machinery and classified as capital expenditure.

(j) Similarly, if carriage costs are paid for by the purchaser of the fixed asset, they may be included in the cost of the fixed asset and classified as capital expenditure.

(k) Installation costs of a fixed asset are also added to the fixed asset's cost and classified as capital expenditure.

(l) Revenue expenditure.

Chapter roundup

- This chapter has added detail to the balance sheet and the trading, profit and loss account.
- A balance sheet shows the financial position of a business at a given moment in time.
- A trading, profit and loss account shows in detail how the profit or loss of a period arises.
- A distinction is made in the balance sheet between long-term liabilities and current liabilities, and between fixed assets and current assets.
- 'Current' means 'within one year'. Current assets are expected to be converted into cash within one year. Current liabilities are debts which are payable within one year.
- Fixed assets are those acquired for long-term use within the business. They are normally valued at cost less depreciation.
- Capital expenditure is expenditure which results in the acquisition of fixed assets or an improvement in their earning capacity.
- Revenue expenditure is incurred for the purpose of trade of the business or to **maintain the existing** earning capacity of fixed assets.

Quick quiz

1 What is a balance sheet? (Assume historic accounting is being used.)

A A list of all the assets and liabilities of a business.
B A statement of the net worth of a business.
C A statement which shows how the net assets of a business have changed over time.
D A statement of the assets and liabilities of a business at a point in time in financial terms. ✓

2 Fill in the blanks.

Morgage_______ and _______________ are examples of long term liabilities.

3 Which of the following is *not* a current asset?

A Machinery ✓
B Stock
C Prepayments
D Debtors

4 Working capital is another term for net assets. True or false? True.

5 Gross profit is best described as?

A Sales less expenses ✓
B Invoiced sales less purchases of stock
C Net profit less business overheads
D Sales less cost of goods sold

6 Three sources of income other than the sale of goods which could appear in a profit and loss account are:

(i) _______________
(ii) _______________
(iii) _______________

7 Four items which might be included in selling and distribution expenses are:

(i) _______________
(ii) _______________
(iii) _______________
(iv) _______________

8 Which two statements explain the distinction between capital and revenue expenditure?

(i) Revenue expenditure is an expense in the profit and loss account, capital expenditure is an asset in the balance sheet.

(ii) Revenue expenditure is an expense in the profit and loss account, capital expenditure is a liability in the balance sheet.

(iii) Capital expenditure results in the acquisition or improvement of fixed assets, revenue expenditure is incurred for the purpose of trade or to maintain the earning capacity of fixed assets.

(iv) Revenue expenditure results in the acquisition or improvement of fixed assets, capital expenditure is incurred for the purpose of trade or to maintain the earning capacity of fixed assets.

Answers to quick quiz

1 D Correct, the balance sheet is only correct at a point in time.

A Incorrect; businesses have assets (and liabilities) which do not appear on the balance sheet (eg the skills of the employees).

B Incorrect because the balance sheet is not intended to represent the true values of the net assets.

C Incorrect, the profit and loss account will reveal the extent to which profits (or losses) have increased (or decreased) net assets in the period.

2 Chose from: loans, mortgage, debenture.

3 A Correct. Machinery is an asset which will be consumed over its useful life in excess of one year.

B, C and D are all current assets.

4 False. Working capital is another term for net current assets.

5 D Correct; cost of goods sold will include certain overheads such as carriage costs of purchases.

6 Choose from:

(i) Profit on sale of fixed assets
(ii) Interest or dividends from investments
(iii) Discounts received
(iv) Rental income

7 Choose from:

(i) Salaries, commission or expenses paid to sales personnel
(ii) Marketing costs
(iii) Delivery van costs
(iv) Discounts allowed to customers
(v) Bad debts written off.

8 Capital expenditure buys or improves a fixed asset. Revenue expenditure maintains fixed assets or is incurred for the purpose of the trade.

Now try the questions below from the Question Bank

Number	Level	Marks	Time
10	Introductory	10	18 mins
11	Exam	2	3 mins
12	Exam	2	3 mins

Part B

Accounting systems and accounts preparation

Chapter 5

SOURCES, RECORDS AND THE BOOKS OF PRIME ENTRY

Topic List		Syllabus reference	Ability required
1	The role of source documents	(ii)	Comprehension
2	Books of prime entry	(ii)	Comprehension
3	Sales and purchase day books	(ii)	Application
4	Sales and purchase returns day books	(ii)	Application
5	Cash books	(ii)	Application
6	Coding systems	(ii)	Application

Introduction

From your studies of Part A you have grasped important points about the nature and purpose of accounting. You will realise that most organisations exist to make a profit for their owners, which they do by receiving money for goods and services provided. The role of the accounting system is to record these transactions and create information about them. You also understand the basic principles underlying the balance sheet and profit and loss account and have an idea of what they look like.

We now turn our attention to how a business transaction works its way through to the financial statements.

It is usual to record a business transaction on a **document**. Such documents include invoices, orders, credit notes and goods received notes, all of which will be discussed in Section 1 of this chapter. In terms of the accounting system these are known as **source documents**. The information on them is processed by the system by, for example, aggregating (adding together) or classifying.

Records of source documents are kept in '**books of prime entry**', which, as the name suggests, are the first stage at which a business transaction enters into the accounting system. The various types of books of prime entry are discussed in Sections 2 to 5.

In the next chapter we consider what happens to transactions after the books of prime entry stage.

Learning outcomes covered in this chapter

- Explain the purpose of accounting records and their role in the accounting system
- Prepare accounts for sales and purchases
- Prepare cash and bank accounts
- Prepare petty cash statements under an imprest system
- Identify the necessity for financial accounting codes and construct a simple coding system

Syllabus content covered in this chapter

- The accounting system and accounting records
- Accounting for sales and purchases
- Preparation of accounts for cash and bank
- Financial accounting codes and their uses

1 THE ROLE OF SOURCE DOCUMENTS

KEY TERMS

Source documents record business transactions. Examples are invoices, sales and purchase orders, wage slips, credit notes, goods received notes, till rolls etc. They are the source of all information for the financial statements

Business transactions are sales or purchases, the paying or receiving of money or recognising that money is owed or owing.

Sales and purchase orders

1.1 Sales orders record customer's requests for goods or services. Purchase orders record a business requests to its suppliers for goods or services.

Invoices

1.2 An **invoice** relates to a sales order or a purchase order.

(a) When a business sells goods or services on credit to a customer, it sends out an invoice. The details on the invoice should match up with the details on the sales order. The invoice is a request for the customer to pay what he owes.

(b) When a business buys goods or services on credit it receives an invoice from the supplier. The details on the invoice should match up with those on the purchase order.

1.3 The invoice is primarily a demand for payment, but it is used for other purposes as well. Since it has several uses, an invoice is often produced on multi-part stationery, or photocopied, or carbon-copied. The top copy will go to the customer and other copies will be used by various people within the business. The following information is usually shown on an invoice.

- Invoice number
- Name and address of the seller and the purchaser
- Date of the sale
- Reference number of the sales order (if applicable)
- Description of what is being sold
- Quantity and unit price of what has been sold (eg 20 pairs of shoes at £25 a pair)
- Details of trade discount, if any (eg 10% reduction in cost if buying over 100 items)
- Total amount of the invoice including (in the UK) any details of VAT
- Sometimes, the date by which payment is due and other terms of sale

Credit notes

1.4 A credit note reduces or cancels an invoice because the goods or services were not received or were rejected as substandard, or there was an error on the invoice. A credit note is sometimes printed in red to distinguish it from an invoice. Otherwise, it will be made out in much the same way as an invoice.

1.5 A **debit note** is issued to a supplier to formally request a credit note.

1.6 **Goods received notes** (GRNs) record a receipt of goods, most commonly in a warehouse. Often the accounts department will want to see the relevant GRN before paying a supplier's invoice. Even where GRNs are not routinely used, the details of a consignment from a supplier which arrives without an advice note must always be recorded.

2 BOOKS OF PRIME ENTRY

KEY TERM

Books of prime entry are used to list and summarise the information on source documents.

2.1 The following are the main books of prime entry.

- Sales day book
- Purchase day book
- Sales returns day book
- Purchases returns day book
- Cash book
- Petty cash book
- Journal (described in the next chapter)

2.2 For convenience, this chapter describes books of prime entry as if they are actual books. Books of prime entry are often not books at all, but rather files in the memory of a computer. However, the principles remain the same whether they are manual or computerised.

3 SALES AND PURCHASE DAY BOOKS

The sales day book

KEY TERM

The **sales day book** lists all invoices sent out to customers.

3.1 An extract from a sales day book might look like this.

SALES DAY BOOK

Date	*Invoice*	*Customer*	*Sales ledger folio*	*Total amount invoiced*
20X0				£
Jan 10	247	Jones & Co	SL14	105.00
	248	Smith Ltd	SL 8	86.40
	249	Alex & Co	SL 6	31.80
	250	Enor College	SL 9	1,264.60
				1,487.80

3.2 The column called 'sales ledger folio' is a reference to the sales ledger which is a record of what each customer owes the business. It means, for example, that the sale to Jones & Co for £105 is also recorded on folio (page) 14 of the sales ledger.

3.3 Most businesses 'analyse' their sales as it gives the managers of the business useful information which helps them to decide how best to run the business. For example, a business sells boots and shoes. The sale to Smith was entirely boots, the sale to Alex was entirely shoes and the other two sales were a mixture of both. Then the sales day book might look like this.

SALES DAY BOOK

Date	*Invoice*	*Customer*	*Sales ledger folio*	*Total amount invoiced*	*Boot sales*	*Shoe sales*
20X0				£	£	£
Jan 10	247	Jones & Co	SL 14	105.00	60.00	45.00
	248	Smith Ltd	SL 8	86.40	86.40	
	249	Alex & Co	SL 6	31.80		31.80
	250	Enor College	SL 9	1,264.60	800.30	464.30
				1,487.80	946.70	541.10

The purchase day book

> **KEY TERM**
>
> The **purchases day book** lists all invoices received from suppliers.

3.4 An extract from a purchase day book might look like this.

PURCHASE DAY BOOK

Date	*Supplier*	*Purchase ledger folio*	*Total amount invoiced*	*Purchases*	*Electricity etc*
20X8			£	£	£
Mar 15	Cook & Co	PL 31	315.00	315.00	
	W Butler	PL 46	29.40	29.40	
	EEB	PL 42	116.80		116.80
	Show Fair Ltd	PL 12	100.00	100.00	
			561.20	444.40	116.80

3.5 The 'purchase ledger folio' is a reference to the purchase ledger which is a record of what each supplier is owed.

3.6 There is no 'invoice number' column, because the purchase day book records other people's invoices, which have all sorts of different numbers.

3.7 The purchase day book analyses the invoices which have been received. In this example, three of the invoices related to goods which the business intends to re-sell (called simply 'purchases') and the fourth invoice was an electricity bill.

4 SALES AND PURCHASE RETURNS DAY BOOK

The sales returns day book

> **KEY TERM**
>
> The **sales returns day book** lists goods (or services) returned (or rejected) by customers for which credit notes are issued.

4.1 An extract from the sales returns day book might look like this.

SALES RETURNS DAY BOOK

Date	*Customer and goods*	*Sales ledger folio*	*Amount*
20X8			£
30 April	Owen Plenty		
	3 pairs 'Texas' boots	SL 82	135.00

4.2 Some sales returns day books analyse what goods were returned, it makes sense to keep as complete a record as possible.

The purchase returns day book

KEY TERM

The **purchase returns day book** lists goods (or services) returned to suppliers (or rejected) for which credit notes have been received or are expected.

4.3 An extract from the purchase returns day book might look like this.

PURCHASE RETURNS DAY BOOK

Date	*Supplier and goods*	*Purchase ledger folio*	*Amount*
20X8			£
29 April	Boxes Ltd		
	300 cardboard boxes	PL 123	46.60

Question 1

An invoice received from supplier is recorded in:

A The sales book
B The purchase book
C The sales returns book
D The purchases returns book

Answer

B is correct.

Question 2

An invoice sent to a customer is recorded in:

A The sales book
B The purchases book
C The sales returns book
D The purchases returns book

Answer

A is correct.

5 CASH BOOKS

The cash book

KEY TERM

The **cash book** lists all money received into and paid out of the business bank account.

5.1 Some cash, in notes and coins, is usually kept on the premises in order to make occasional payments for small items of expense. This cash is accounted for separately in a **petty cash book** (which we will look at shortly).

5.2 EXAMPLE: CASH BOOK

At the beginning of 1 September, Robin Plenty had £900 in the bank.

During 1 September 20X7, Robin Plenty had the following receipts and payments.

(a) Cash sale - receipt of £80
(b) Payment from credit customer Hay £400 less discount allowed £20
(c) Payment from credit customer Been £720
(d) Payment from credit customer Seed £150 less discount allowed £10
(e) Cheque received for cash to provide a short-term loan from Len Dinger £1,800
(f) Second cash sale - receipts of £150
(g) Cash received for sale of machine £200
(h) Payment to supplier Kew £120
(i) Payment to supplier Hare £310
(j) Payment of telephone bill £400
(k) Payment of gas bill £280
(l) £100 in cash withdrawn from bank for petty cash
(m) Payment of £1,500 to Hess for new plant and machinery

5.3 SOLUTION

The receipts part of the cash book for 1 September would look like this.

CASH BOOK (RECEIPTS)

Date	*Narrative*	*Folio*	*Total*
20X7			£
1 Sept	Balance b/d*		900
	Cash sale		80
	Debtor: Hay		380
	Debtor: Been		720
	Debtor: Seed		140
	Loan: Len Dinger		1,800
	Cash sale		150
	Sale of fixed asset		200
			4,370
2 Sept	Balance b/d*		1,660

* 'b/d' = brought down (ie brought forward)

The cash received in the day amounted to £3,470. Added to the £900 at the start of the day, this comes to £4,370. However this is not the amount to be carried forward to the next day. First we have to subtract all the payments made during 1 September.

The payments part of the cash book for 1 September would look like this.

CASH BOOK (PAYMENTS)

Date	*Narrative*	*Folio*	*Total*
20X7			£
1 Sept	Creditor: Kew		120
	Creditor: Hare		310
	Telephone		400
	Gas bill		280
	Petty cash		100
	Machinery purchase		1,500
	Balance c/d		1,660
			4,370

Payments during 1 September totalled £2,710. We know that the total of receipts was £4,370. That means that there is a balance of £4,370 – £2,710 = £1,660 to be 'carried down' to the start of the next day. As you can see this 'balance carried down' is noted at the end of the payments column, so that the receipts and payments totals show the same figure of £4,370 at the end of 1 September. And if you look to the receipts part of this example, you can see that £1,660 has been brought down ready for the next day.

5.4 It is usual to analyse the receipts and payments. With analysis columns completed, the cash book given in the examples above might look as follows.

CASH BOOK (RECEIPTS)

Date	*Narrative*	*Folio*	*Total*	*Debtors*	*Cash sales*	*Other*
			£	£	£	£
20X7						
1 Sept	Balance b/d		900			
	Cash sale		80		80	
	Debtor - Hay		380	380		
	Debtor - Been		720	720		
	Debtor - Seed		140	140		
	Loan - Len Dinger		1,800			1,800
	Cash sale		150		150	
	Sale of fixed asset		200			200
			4,370	1,240	230	2,000

CASH BOOK (PAYMENTS)

Date	*Narrative*	*Folio*	*Total*	*Creditors*	*Petty cash*	*Wages*	*Other*
			£	£	£	£	£
20X7							
1 Sept	Creditor - Kew		120	120			
	Creditor - Hare		310	310			
	Telephone		400				400
	Gas bill		280				280
	Petty cash		100		100		
	Machinery purchase		1,500				1,500
	Balance c/d		1,660				
			4,370	430	100	-	2,180

Bank statements

5.5 Weekly or monthly, a business will receive a **bank statement**. Bank statements are used to check that the balance shown in the cash book agrees with the amount on the bank statement. This agreement or '**reconciliation**' is the subject of a later chapter.

Petty cash book **May 2001**

KEY TERM

The **petty cash book** lists all cash payments for small items, and occasional small receipts.

5.6 Most businesses keep a small amount of cash on the premises to make occasional small payments in cash - eg to pay the milkman, to buy a few postage stamps etc. This is often called the cash float or petty cash account. Petty cash can also be used for occasional small receipts, such as cash paid by a visitor to make a phone call or to take some photocopies.

5.7 There are usually more payments than receipts and petty cash must be 'topped up' with cash from the business bank account.

5.8 Under what is called the **imprest system,** the amount of money in petty cash is kept at an agreed sum or 'float' (say £100). Expense items are recorded on vouchers as they occur.

	£
Cash still held in petty cash	X
Plus voucher payments	X
Must equal the agreed sum or float	X

The total float is made up regularly (to £100, or whatever the agreed sum is) by means of a cash payment from the bank account into petty cash. The amount paid into petty cash will be the total of the voucher payments since the previous top-up.

Exam focus point

Writing up the petty cash book with an imprest system was examined in Section A of the May 2001 exam.

5.9 The format of a petty cash book is the same as for the cash book, with analysis columns for items of expenditure.

THE MAIN POINT

Business transactions are recorded on source documents which are listed and summarised in books of prime entry.

Question 3

State in which books of prime entry the following transactions would be entered.

(a) Your business pays A Brown (a supplier) £450.00.
(b) You send D Smith (a customer) an invoice for £650.
(c) Your accounts manager asks you for £12 urgently in order to buy some envelopes.
(d) You receive an invoice from A Brown for £300.
(e) You pay D Smith £500.
(f) F Jones (a customer) returns goods to the value of £250.
(g) You return goods to J Green to the value of £504.
(h) F Jones pays you £500.

Answer

(a) Cash book
(b) Sales day book
(c) Petty cash book
(d) Purchases day book
(e) Cash book
(f) Sales returns day book
(g) Purchase returns day book
(h) Cash book

6 CODING SYSTEMS

6.1 Each account in an accounting system has a **unique code** used to identify the correct account for a posting (to be keyed into the computer if the system is computerised). If there are two suppliers called Jim Jones, you can only tell their accounts apart by a different code.

6.2 Coding also saves time in copying out data because **codes are shorter** than 'longhand' descriptions. For the same reason, and also to save storage space, computer systems make use of coded data.

6.3 In purchase accounting systems, the most obvious examples of codes are as follows.

- Supplier account numbers
- General ledger account numbers
- Stock item codes

These are all codes a business sets up and applies internally. External codes which affect the business include **bank account numbers** and **bank sort codes**.

6.4 Various coding systems (or combinations of them) may be used when designing codes. The systems are described below.

Sequence codes

6.5 **Sequence codes** make no attempt to classify the item to be coded. It is simply given the next available number in a rising sequence. New items can only be inserted at the end of the list and therefore the codes for similar items may be very different. For example:

1 = saucepans
2 = kettles
3 = pianos
4 = dusters

6.6 Sequence codes are rarely used when a large number of items are involved, except for document numbering (eg invoice numbers).

Block codes

6.7 **Block codes** provide a different sequence for each different group of items. For example , suppliers may be divided up according to area.

North East	code numbers 10,000-19,999
North West	code numbers 20,000-29,999
Scotland	code numbers 30,000-39,999

The coding of supplier accounts is then sequential within each block.

Significant digit codes

6.8 **Significant digit codes** use some digits which are part of the description of the item being coded. An example is:

5000	Electric light bulbs
5025	25 watt
5040	40 watt
5060	60 watt
5100	100 watt
etc	

Hierarchical codes

6.9 **Hierarchical codes** are allocated on the basis of a tree structure, where the relationship between items is of utmost importance. A well known example is the Universal Decimal Code used by most libraries. For example:

5	Business
5 2	Finance
5 2 1	Cost accounting
5 2 1.4	Standard costing
5 2 1.4 7	Variance analysis
5 2 1.4 7 3	Fixed overhead variances

Faceted codes

6.10 **Faceted codes** consist of a number of sections, each section of the code representing a different feature of the item. For example in a clothing store there might be a code based on the following facets.

Garment type	*Customer type*	*Colour*	*Size*	*Style*

If SU stood for suit, M for man and B for blue, a garment could be given the code SU M B 40 17. Similarly ND F W 14 23 could stand for a woman's white nightdress size 14, style 23. One of the great advantages of this system is that the type of item can be recognised from the code.

Faceted codes may be entirely numeric. For example, a large international company allocates code numbers for each suppliers' representative.

Digit 1	Continent (eg America - 1, Europe - 2)
Digits 2/3	Country (eg England - 06)
Digit 4	Area (eg North - 3)
Digits 5/6	Representative's name (eg Mr J Walker - 14)

The code number is then expressed as 2/06/3/14.

Coding in the general ledger

6.11 A general ledger will consist of a **large number of coded accounts**. For example, part of a general ledger might be as follows.

Account code	Account name
100200	Plant and machinery (cost)
100300	Motor vehicles (cost)
300000	Total debtors
400000	Total creditors
500130	Wages and salaries
500140	Rent and rates
500150	Advertising expenses
500160	Bank charges
500170	Motor expenses
500180	Telephone expenses
600000	Sales
700000	Cash

6.12 A business will, of course, choose its own codes for its general ledger accounts. The codes given in the above table are purely imaginary.

Question 4

State what type of code is being used in paragraph 6.11 above. Explain your answer.

Answer

This is a significant digit code. The digits are part of the description of the item being coded. So 100000 represents fixed assets and the '200' in 100200 represents plant and machinery.

Chapter roundup

- Business transactions are recorded on source documents. These include the following.
    - Sales orders
    - Purchase orders
    - Invoices
    - Credit notes
- These transactions are recorded in books of prime entry of which there are seven.
    - Sales day book
    - Sales returns day book
    - Purchase day book
    - Purchase returns day book
    - Cash book
    - Petty cash book
    - Journal
- Most businesses keep petty cash on the premises which is topped up from the main bank account. Under the imprest system the petty cash is kept at an agreed sum.
- You must be aware of which transactions go in each book of prime entry.
- Be aware of the different coding systems available.

Quick quiz

1 Five pieces of information normally shown on an invoice are:

(1) invoice number

(2) customer

(3) goods

(4) price

(5) quantity

2 A business issues a credit note. Where is this first recorded?

A In the sales ledger
B In the sales returns day book
C In the sales day book
D In the journal

3 The sales day book is:

A A record of cash received from customers
B A record of the balances on customers accounts
C A record of invoices received
D A record of credit sales made

4 The purchases day book is:

A A record of cash paid to suppliers
B A record of the balances on suppliers accounts
C A record of invoices received from suppliers
D A record of invoices sent to customers

5 Fill in the blanks.

The cash book records transations going in and out of the businesses bank account.

The petty cash book records transactions of small amounts of cash going in and out (although out mostly) of petty cash on site.

6 On June there was £90 in the petty cash tin. By the end of June there were vouchers for £35 of expenses and £5 had been paid in (by a member of staff for some private phone calls). A cheque for £30 was cashed to 'top up' the petty cash. What is the imprest total?

A £30
B £40
C £60
D £90

Answers to quick quiz

1 Choose five from:

(1) Name and address of supplier and customer
(2) Details of goods purchased
(3) Details of any discount
(4) Date of the sale
(5) Total amount due
(6) Invoice number
(7) Reference number of sales order
(8) VAT details
(9) Sometimes, the payment terms

2 B Correct

A Incorrect, the ledgers are posted from day books

C Incorrect, an invoice would be recorded in the sales day book.

D Incorrect, the journal is used to make transfers or correct errors or to record transactions which do not go through another prime entry record

3 D Correct
A This would be recorded in the cash book
B This would be referred to as the sales ledger
C This would be the purchase day book

4 C Correct
A This would be recorded in the cash book
B This would be referred to as the purchase ledger
D This would be the sales day book

5 The cash book records money received into and paid out of the business bank account.

The petty cash book records minor items of expenditure (eg postage stamps) paid or received in cash.

6 D is correct (90 – 35 + 5 + 30 = 90). The imprest total is the balance to which the petty cash is restored at the end of each month.

Now try the questions below from the Question Bank

Number	Level	Marks	Time
13	Introductory	10	18 mins
14	Introductory	15	27 mins
15	Exam	2	3 mins

Chapter 6

LEDGER ACCOUNTING AND DOUBLE ENTRY

Topic List		Syllabus reference	Ability required
1	The nominal ledger	(ii)	Application
2	Double entry bookkeeping	(ii)	Application
3	The journal	(ii)	Application
4	Posting from day books to nominal ledger accounts	(ii)	Application
5	The imprest system	(ii)	Application
6	The sales and purchase ledgers	(ii)	Application

Introduction

We have studied the theory of preparing accounts for a business. We have seen, by means of the accounting and the business equations, that it is possible to prepare a profit and loss account and a balance sheet on any date, relating to any period of time. A business is continually making transactions and we do not want to prepare accounts after every transaction. To do so is too time-consuming.

A business should keep a record of its transactions and, when the time comes to prepare the accounts, the relevant information can be taken from those records. The records of transactions, assets and liabilities should be in chronological order and dated so that transactions can be related to a particular period of time (eg daily, weekly, monthly, yearly).

We have already seen the first step in this process, which is to list all the transactions in various books of prime entry. Now we study the method used to summarise these records.

This chapter introduces **double entry bookkeeping**, the cornerstone of accounts preparation.

Learning outcomes covered in this chapter

- Explain the purpose of accounting records and their role in the accounting system
- Prepare cash and bank accounts
- Prepare petty cash statement under an imprest system
- Prepare accounts for sales and purchases including personal accounts
- Prepare nominal ledger accounts
- Prepare journal entries

Syllabus content covered in this chapter

- Ledger accounts
- Double-entry bookkeeping
- Preparation of accounts for cash and bank
- Imprest system for petty cash
- Accounting for sales and purchases including personal accounts
- Nominal ledger accounting
- Journal entries

1 THE NOMINAL LEDGER

KEY TERM

The **nominal ledger** is an accounting record which summarises the financial affairs of a business. It contains accounts for each asset, liability and capital, income and expenditure and profit and loss.

1.1 The nominal ledger is sometimes called the '**general ledger**'. It consists of a large number of different accounts, each account having its own purpose or 'name' and an identity or code.

1.2 **Examples of accounts included in the nominal ledger**

- Plant and machinery at cost (fixed asset)
- Motor vehicles at cost (fixed asset)
- Plant and machinery, provision for depreciation (liability)
- Motor vehicles, provision for depreciation (liability)
- Proprietor's capital (liability)
- Stocks - raw materials (current asset)
- Stocks - finished goods (current asset)
- Total debtors (current asset) often called sales ledger control account
- Total creditors (current liability) often called purchase ledger control account
- Wages and salaries (expense item)
- Rent and rates (expense item)
- Advertising expenses (expense item)
- Bank charges (expense item)
- Motor expenses (expense item)
- Telephone expenses (expense item)
- Sales (income)
- Total cash or bank overdraft (current asset or liability) often called cash control account
- Petty cash

THE MAIN POINT

The nominal ledger contains a separate account for each item which appears in a balance sheet or profit and loss account.

The format of a ledger account

1.3 If a ledger account is kept in an actual book, its format is as follows.

ADVERTISING EXPENSES

Date	*Narrative*	*Folio*	£	*Date*	*Narrative*	*Folio*	£
20X6							
15 April	JFK Agency for quarter to 31 March	PL 348	2,500				

Only one entry is shown here, as an example simply to illustrate the general format.

1.4 There are two sides to the account and a heading on top, so it is usually called a '**T**' **account.**

NAME OF ACCOUNT

DEBIT SIDE	£	CREDIT SIDE	£

2 DOUBLE ENTRY BOOKKEEPING **Pilot Paper**

2.1 Remember the accounting equation said that the total of liabilities plus capital is always equal to total assets so any transaction which changes the amount of total assets must also change the total liabilities plus capital, and vice versa. Alternatively, a transaction uses up assets of a certain value to obtain other assets of the same value. For example, a business pays £50 for some goods. Its total assets will be unchanged, but the amount of cash falls by £50 and the value of goods in stock rises by £50.

2.2 Ledger accounts, with their **debit** and **credit** sides, allow the two-sided nature of business transactions to be recorded. This system of accounting was first used in Venice in 1494 AD.

KEY TERM

The **double entry system of bookkeeping** means that for every debit there is an equal credit. This is sometimes referred to as the concept of **duality.**

THE MAIN POINT!

The rules of double entry bookkeeping

The basic rule is that **every** financial transaction gives rise to two accounting entries, one a debit and a credit. The total value of debit entries in the nominal ledger is therefore always equal to the total value of credit entries.

Debit	Credit
• Increase in an expense (eg purchase of stationery)	• Increase in income (eg a sale)
• Increase in an asset (eg a purchase of office furniture)	• Increase in a liability (eg obtaining a bank loan)
• Decrease in a liability (eg paying a creditor)	• Decrease in an asset (eg making a cash payment)

2.3 A good starting point is the cash account where receipts and payments of cash are recorded. The rule to remember about the cash account is as follows.

(a) A cash **payment** is a **credit** entry, because the cash asset is decreasing. Cash may be used to pay an expense (eg rates) or to purchase an asset (eg a machine). The matching debit entry is made in the appropriate expense or asset account.

(b) A cash **receipt** is a **debit** entry, because the cash asset is increasing. Cash is received by a retailer who makes a cash sale. The credit entry is then made in the sales account.

2.4 EXAMPLE: DOUBLE ENTRY FOR CASH TRANSACTIONS

A business has the following transactions.

(a) A cash sale (ie a receipt) of £2
(b) Payment of a rent bill totalling £150
(c) Buying some goods for cash at £100
(d) Buying some shelves for cash at £200

How would these four transactions be posted to the ledger accounts?

2.5 SOLUTION

(a) The two sides of the transaction are cash is received (debit entry in the cash account) because the asset cash is increasing) and sales increase by £2 (credit entry in the sales account because sales income is increasing).

CASH ACCOUNT

	£		£
Sales a/c	2		

SALES ACCOUNT

	£		£
		Cash a/c	2

(Note how the entry in the cash account is cross-referenced to the sales account and vice-versa. This enables a person looking at one of the accounts to trace where the other half of the double entry can be found.)

(b) The two sides of the transaction are cash is paid (credit entry in the cash account because the asset cash is reduced) and rent expense increases by £150 (debit entry in the rent account because the expense is increasing).

CASH ACCOUNT

	£		£
		Rent a/c	150

RENT ACCOUNT

	£		£
Cash a/c	150		

(c) The two sides of the transaction are cash is paid (credit entry in the cash account because the asset cash is reduced) and purchases increase by £100 (debit entry in the purchases account because purchase expense is increasing).

CASH ACCOUNT

	£		£
		Purchases a/c	100

PURCHASES ACCOUNT

	£		£
Cash a/c	100		

(d) The two sides of the transaction are cash is paid (credit entry in the cash account because the asset cash is reduced) and assets increase by £200 (debit entry in shelves account because the fixed asset is increasing).

CASH ACCOUNT

	£		£
		Shelves a/c	200

SHELVES (ASSET) ACCOUNT

	£		£
Cash a/c	200		

The cash account of the business would end up looking as follows.

CASH ACCOUNT

	£		£
Sales a/c	2	Rent a/c	150
		Purchases a/c	100
		Shelves a/c	200

Question 1

Show how these transactions would be recorded in the accounts in the nominal ledger.

The bank has a balance of £1,000.

(a) Buy goods for resale costing £100
(b) Sell goods for £150
(c) Pay electricity bill for £120
(d) Buy a delivery van for £600
(e) Buy petrol costing £10

Answer

CASH ACCOUNT

	£		£
Balance b/d	1,000	Purchases a/c	100
Sales a/c	150	Electricity expense a/c	120
		Fixed asset van a/c	600
		Motor expense a/c	10

PURCHASES ACCOUNT

	£		£
Cash a/c	100		

SALES ACCOUNT

	£		£
		Cash a/c	150

ELECTRICY EXPENSE ACCOUNT

	£		£
Cash a/c	120		

FIXED ASSET VAN ACCOUNT

	£		£
Cash a/c	600		

MOTOR EXPENSES ACCOUNT

	£		£
Cash a/c	10		

Credit transactions

2.6 Not all transactions are settled immediately in cash. A business can purchase goods or fixed assets from its suppliers on credit terms. Equally, the business can grant credit terms to its customers. Clearly no entries can be made in the cash book when a credit transaction occurs, because no cash has been received or paid. The solution is to use debtors and creditors accounts instead. A debtor is someone who owes money to the business. A creditor is someone to whom the business owes money.

2.7 EXAMPLE: CREDIT TRANSACTIONS

Recorded in the sales day book and the purchase day book are the following transactions.

(a) The business sells goods on credit to a customer Mr A for £2,000.
(b) The business buys goods on credit from a supplier B Ltd for £100.

How and where are these transactions posted in the ledger accounts?

2.8 SOLUTION

(a)

DEBTORS ACCOUNT

	£		£
Sales a/c	2,000		

SALES ACCOUNT

	£		£
		Debtors account	2,000

(b)

CREDITORS ACCOUNT

	£		£
		Purchases a/c	100

PURCHASES ACCOUNT

	£		£
Creditors a/c	100		

When cash is paid to creditors or by debtors

2.9 What happens when a credit transaction is eventually settled in cash?

2.10 EXAMPLE CONTINUED

Suppose that, in the example above, the business paid £100 to B Ltd one month after the goods were acquired. The two sides of this new transaction are cash is paid (credit entry in the cash account) and the amount owing to creditors is reduced (debit entry in the creditors account).

CASH ACCOUNT

	£		£
		Creditors a/c (B Ltd)	100

CREDITORS ACCOUNT

	£		£
Cash a/c	100		

Bringing together the two parts of this example.

CASH ACCOUNT

	£		£
		Creditors a/c	100

PURCHASES ACCOUNT

	£		£
Creditors a/c	100		

CREDITORS ACCOUNT

	£		£
Cash a/c	100	Purchases a/c	100

2.11 The two entries in the creditors account cancel each other out, indicating that no money is owing to creditors any more. We are left with a credit entry of £100 in the cash account and a debit entry of £100 in the purchases account. These are exactly the entries which would have been made to record a **cash** purchase of £100 (compare example above). After the business has paid off its creditors, it is in exactly the same position as if it had made cash purchases of £100.

2.12 Similar reasoning applies when a customer settles his debt. In the example above when Mr A pays his debt of £2,000 the two sides of the transaction are cash is received (debit entry in the cash account) and the amount owed by debtors is reduced (credit entry in the debtors account).

CASH ACCOUNT

	£		£
Debtors a/c	2,000		

DEBTORS ACCOUNT

	£		£
		Cash a/c	2,000

2.13 The accounts recording this sale to, and payment by, Mr A now appear as follows.

CASH ACCOUNT

	£		£
Debtors a/c	2,000		

SALES ACCOUNT

	£		£
		Debtors a/c	2,000

DEBTORS ACCOUNT

	£		£
Sales a/c	2,000	Cash a/c	2,000

2.14 The two entries in the debtors account cancel each other out; while the entries in the cash account and sales account reflect the same position as if the sale had been made for cash.

Question 2

Identify the debit and credit entries for the following transactions.

(a) Bought a machine on credit from A, cost £8,000.
(b) Bought goods on credit from B, cost £500.
(c) Sold goods on credit to C, value £1,200.
(d) Paid D (a creditor) £300.
(e) Collected £180 from E, a debtor.
(f) Paid wages £4,000.
(g) Received rent bill of £700 from landlord G.
(h) Paid rent of £700 to landlord G.
(i) Paid insurance premium £90.

Answer

			£	£
(a)	DEBIT	Machine account (fixed asset)	8,000	
	CREDIT	Creditors (A)		8,000
(b)	DEBIT	Purchases account	500	
	CREDIT	Creditors (B)		500
(c)	DEBIT	Debtors (C)	1,200	
	CREDIT	Sales		1,200
(d)	DEBIT	Creditors (D)	300	
	CREDIT	Cash		300
(e)	DEBIT	Cash	180	
	CREDIT	Debtors (E)		180
(f)	DEBIT	Wages account	4,000	
	CREDIT	Cash		4,000

			£	£
(g)	DEBIT	Rent account	700	
	CREDIT	Creditors (G)		700
(h)	DEBIT	Creditors (G)	700	
	CREDIT	Cash		700
(i)	DEBIT	Insurance costs	90	
	CREDIT	Cash		90

Question 3

Record the ledger entries for the following transactions? Ron Knuckle set up a business selling keep fit equipment. He put £7,000 of his own money into a business bank account (transaction A) and in his first period of trading, the following transactions occurred.

Transaction		£
B	Paid rent of shop for the period	3,500
C	Purchased equipment (stocks) on credit	5,000
D	Raised loan from bank	1,000
E	Purchase of shop fittings (for cash)	2,000
F	Sales of equipment: cash	10,000
G	Sales of equipment: on credit	2,500
H	Payments to trade creditors	5,000
I	Payments from debtors	2,500
J	Interest on loan (paid)	100
K	Administration expenses (all paid in cash)	1,900
L	Drawings	1,500

All stocks purchased during the period were sold and so there were no closing stocks of equipment.

Try to do as much of this exercise as possible yourself before reading the solution.

Answer

CASH ACCOUNT

	£		£
Capital – Ron Knuckle (A)	7,000	Rent (B)	3,500
Bank loan (D)	1,000	Shop fittings (E)	2,000
Sales (F)	10,000	Trade creditors (H)	5,000
Debtors (I)	2,500	Bank loan interest (J)	100
		Other expenses (K)	1,900
		Drawings (L)	1,500
			14,000
		Balancing figure – the amount of cash left over after payments have been made	6,500
	20,500		20,500

CAPITAL (RON KNUCKLE) ACCOUNT

	£		£
		Cash (A)	7,000

BANK LOAN ACCOUNT

	£		£
		Cash (D)	1,000

PURCHASES ACCOUNT

	£		£
Trade creditors (C)	5,000		

CREDITORS ACCOUNT

	£		£
Cash (H)	5,000	Purchases (C)	5,000

RENT EXPENSE ACCOUNT

	£		£
Cash (B)	3,500		

FIXED ASSETS (SHOP FITTINGS) ACCOUNT

	£		£
Cash (E)	2,000		

SALES ACCOUNT

	£		£
		Cash (F)	10,000
		Debtors (G)	2,500
			12,500

DEBTORS ACCOUNT

	£		£
Sales (G)	2,500	Cash (I)	2,500

BANK LOAN INTEREST ACCOUNT

	£		£
Cash (J)	100		

OTHER EXPENSES ACCOUNT

	£		£
Cash (K)	1,900		

DRAWINGS ACCOUNT

	£		£
Cash (L)	1,500		

If you want to make sure that this solution is complete, you should go through all the transactions ticking each off in the ledger accounts, once as a debit and once as a credit. When you have finished, all transactions in the 'T' account should be ticked, with only totals left over.

There is an easier way to check that the solution does 'balance' properly, which we will meet in the next chapter. It is called a trial balance.

3 THE JOURNAL — Pilot Paper

3.1 As mentioned in the last chapter, one of the books of prime entry is the journal.

KEY TERM

The **journal** is a record of unusual transactions. It is used to record any double entries made which do not arise from the other books of prime entry.

3.2 Whatever type of transaction is being recorded, the format of a journal entry is as follows.

Date	*Folio*	*Debit*	*Credit*
		£	£
Account to be debited		X	
Account to be credited			X
(Narrative to explain the transaction)			

3.3 A narrative explanation must accompany each journal entry. It is required for audit and control, to indicate the purpose and authority of every transaction which is not first recorded in a book of prime entry.

Exam focus point

In the Pilot Paper, a subquestion of 3 marks required the preparation of journal entries (**without** a narrative). However the remaining 7 marks of the question, then relied on these journal entries being correct. Section A of the May 2001 exam had a question on recording transactions in journals, and Section B had a 10 mark question on the correction of errors by journal entries.

3.4 EXAMPLE: JOURNAL ENTRIES

The following is a summary of the transactions of 'Hair by Fiona Middleton'.

1 January	Put in cash of £2,000 as capital Purchased brushes and combs for cash £50 Purchased hair driers from Gilroy Ltd on credit £150
30 January	Paid three months rent to 31 March £300 Collected and paid in takings £600
31 January	Gave Mrs Sullivan a perm, highlights etc on credit £80

Although these entries would normally go through the other books of prime entry (eg the cash book), it is good practice for you to show these transactions as journal entries.

3.5 SOLUTION

JOURNAL

			£	£
1 January	DEBIT	Cash account	2,000	
	CREDIT	Fiona Middleton – capital account		2,000
	Initial capital introduced			
1 January	DEBIT	Brushes and combs (asset) account	50	
	CREDIT	Cash account		50
	The purchase for cash of brushes and combs as fixed assets			
1 January	DEBIT	Hair dryer asset account	150	
	CREDIT	Sundry creditors account *		150
	The purchase on credit of hair driers as fixed assets			

			£	£
30 January	DEBIT	Rent expense account	300	
	CREDIT	Cash account		300
	The payment of rent to 31 March			
30 January	DEBIT	Cash account	600	
	CREDIT	Sales account		600
	Cash takings			
31 January	DEBIT	Debtors account	80	
	CREDIT	Sales account		80
	The provision of a hair-do on credit			

* *Note*. Creditors who have supplied **fixed assets** are included amongst sundry creditors. Creditors who have supplied raw materials or goods for resale are **trade creditors**. It is quite common to have separate creditors accounts for trade and sundry creditors.

The correction of errors

3.6 The journal is commonly used to record **corrections** of **errors** that have been made in writing up the nominal ledger accounts.

3.7 There are several types of error which can occur. They are looked at in detail in a later chapter along with the way of using journal entries to correct them.

4 POSTING FROM DAY BOOKS TO NOMINAL LEDGER ACCOUNTS

4.1 So far, in this session, we have made entries in nominal ledger accounts for each individual transaction, ie each source document has been recorded by a separate debit and credit. This means that every accounts department would need a lot of people who understand the double entry system, and that nominal ledger accounts would contain a huge number of entries. These two problems are avoided by using the books of prime entry or day books (remember these are lists of similar transactions). In practice, source documents are recorded in books of prime entry, and totals are posted from them to the nominal ledger accounts.

THE MAIN POINTS!

Individual transactions are recorded in day books. Day book totals are recorded in double entry in the nominal ledger.

4.2 In the previous chapter, we used the following example of four transactions entered into the sales day book.

SALES DAY BOOK

Date	*Invoice*	*Customer*	*Sales ledger folios*	*Total amount invoiced*	*Boot sales*	*Shoe sales*
20X0			£	£	£	£
Jan 10	247	Jones & Co	SL 14	105.00	60.00	45.00
	248	Smith Ltd	SL 8	86.40	86.40	
	249	Alex & Co	SL 6	31.80		31.80
	250	Enor College	SL 9	1,264.60	800.30	464.30
				1,487.80	946.70	541.10

This day book could be posted to the ledger accounts as follows.

DEBIT	Debtors account	£1,487.80	
CREDIT	Total sales account		£1,487.80

4.3 However a total sales account is not very informative. In our example, it is better to have a 'sale of shoes' account and a 'sale of boots' account.

		£	£
DEBIT	Debtors account	1,487.80	
CREDIT	Sale of shoes account		541.10
	Sale of boots account		946.70

4.4 This is why the sales are analysed in the day book. Exactly the same reasoning lies behind the analyses kept in other books of prime entry, so that we can record it in the nominal ledger.

Question 4

The correct posting for the total column of the purchase day book is:

A Debit creditors account
Credit purchases account

B Debit purchases account
Credit creditors account

C Debit debtors account
Credit sales account

D Debit sales account
Credit debtors account

Answer

B is correct.

---

5 THE IMPREST SYSTEM

5.1 In the last chapter, we saw how the petty cash book was used to operate the **imprest** system for petty cash. It is now time to see how the double entry works in the imprest system.

5.2 EXAMPLE

A business starts off a cash float on 1.3.20X7 with £250. This will be a payment from cash at bank to petty cash.

DEBIT	Petty cash	£250	
CREDIT	Cash at bank		£250

Five payments were made out of petty cash during March 20X7.

				Payments	
Receipts	*Date*	*Narrative*	*Total*	*Postage*	*Travel*
£			£	£	£
250.00	1.3.X7	Cash			
	2.3.X7	Stamps	12.00	12.00	
	8.3.X7	Stamps	10.00	10.00	
	19.3.X7	Travel	16.00		16.00
	23.3.X7	Travel	5.00		5.00
	28.3.X7	Stamps	11.50	11.50	
250.00			54.50	33.50	21.00

At the end of each month (or at any other suitable interval) the total credits in the petty cash book are posted to ledger accounts. For March 20X7, £33.50 would be debited to postage account and £21.00 to travel account. The cash float would need to be topped up by a payment of £54.50 from the main cash book.

		£	£
DEBIT	Petty cash	54.50	
CREDIT	Cash		54.50

The petty cash book for the month of March 20X7 will look like this.

Receipts	*Date*	*Narrative*	*Total*	*Payments* *Postage*	*Travel*
£			£	£	£
250.00	1.3.X7	Cash			
	2.3.X7	Stamps	12.00	12.00	
	8.3.X7	Stamps	10.00	10.00	
	19.3.X7	Travel	16.00		16.00
	23.3.X7	Travel	5.00		5.00
	28.3.X7	Stamps	11.50	11.50	
	31.3.X7	Balance c/d	195.50		
250.00			250.00	33.50	21.00
195.50	1.4.X7	Balance b/d			
54.50	1.4.X7	Cash			

The cash float is back up to £250 on 1.4.X7, ready for more payments to be made.

6 THE SALES AND PURCHASE LEDGERS

Impersonal accounts and personal accounts

6.1 The accounts in the nominal ledger (ledger accounts) give figures for the balance sheet and profit and loss account. They are called **impersonal** accounts. However, there is also a need for **personal** accounts (most commonly for debtors and creditors) and these are contained in the sales ledger and purchase ledger.

> **KEY TERM**
>
> **Personal accounts** are not part of the double entry system. They record how much is owed by a customer or to a supplier. They are **memorandum** accounts only.

The sales ledger

> **KEY TERM**
>
> The **sales ledger** contains separate accounts for each credit customer, so that, at any time, a business knows how much it is owed by each customer.

6.2 The **sales day book** provides a chronological record of invoices sent out by a business to credit customers. For many businesses, this can involve very large numbers of invoices per day or per week. The same customer can appear in several different places in the sales day book. So at any point in time, a customer may owe money on several unpaid invoices.

6.3 A business needs to keep a record of how much money each individual credit customer owes because:

(a) A customer might telephone, and ask how much he currently owes.

(b) It provides the information needed for statements sent to credit customers at the end of each month.

(c) It assists the business in keeping a check on the credit position of each customer to ensure that he is not exceeding his credit limit.

(d) Most important is the need to match payments received against invoices. If a customer makes a payment, the business must set it off against the correct invoice.

6.4 Sales ledger accounts are written up in the following way.

(a) When entries are made in the sales day book (invoices sent out), they are recorded on the **debit side** of the relevant customer account in the sales ledger.

(b) Similarly, when entries are made in the cash book (payments received) or in the sales returns day book, they recorded on **credit side** of the customer account.

6.5 Each customer account is given a reference or code number, the 'sales ledger folio' in the **sales day book**.

6.6 EXAMPLE: A SALES LEDGER ACCOUNT

ENOR COLLEGE

A/c no: SL 9

		£		£
	Balance b/f	250.00		
10.1.X0	Sales - SDB 48 (invoice no 250)	1,264.60	Balance c/d	1,514.60
		1,514.60		1,514.60
11.1.X0	Balance b/d	1,514.60		

6.7 The debit side of this personal account shows amounts owed by Enor College. When Enor pays some of the money it owes it will be entered into the cash book (receipts) and subsequently entered in the credit side of the personal account. For example, if the college paid £250 on 10.1.20X0.

ENOR COLLEGE

A/c no: SL 9

		£		£
	Balance b/f	250.00	10.1.X0 Cash	250.00
10.1.X0	Sales - SDB 48 (invoice no 250)	1,264.60	Balance c/d	1,264.60
		1,514.60		1,514.60
11.1.X0	Balance b/d	1,264.60		

The purchase ledger (bought ledger)

KEY TERM

The **purchase ledger** contains separate accounts for each credit supplier, so that, at any time a business knows how much it owes to each supplier.

6.8 The purchase ledger, like the sales ledger, consists of a number of personal accounts. These are separate accounts for each individual supplier and they enable a business to keep a check on how much it owes each supplier.

6.9 **The purchase invoice is recorded in the purchases day book**. Then the purchases day book is used to update accounts in the purchase ledger.

6.10 EXAMPLE: PURCHASE LEDGER ACCOUNT

COOK & CO

A/c no: PL 31

	£		£
Balance c/d	515.00	Balance b/f	200.00
		15 Mar 20X8	
		Invoice received	
		PDB 37	315.00
	515.00		515.00
		16 March 20X8	
		Balance b/d	515.00

The credit side of this personal account shows amounts owing to Cook & Co. If the business paid Cook & Co some money, it would be entered into the cash book (payments) and subsequently be posted to the debit side of the personal account. For example, if the business paid Cook & Co £100 on 15 March 20X8.

COOK & CO

A/c no: PL 31

		£			£
15.3.X8	Cash	100.00	15.3.X8	Balance b/f	200.00
			15.3.X8	Invoice received	
	Balance c/d	415.00		PDB 37	315.00
		515.00			515.00
			16.3.X8	Balance b/d	415.00

6.11 The roles of the sales day book and purchases day book are very similar, with one book dealing with invoices sent out and the other with invoices received. The sales ledger and purchase ledger also serve similar purposes, with one consisting of personal accounts for credit customers and the other consisting of personal accounts for credit suppliers.

Question 5

At 1 May 20X3 amounts owing to Omega by his customers in respect of their April purchases were:

	£
Alpha	210
Beta	1,040
Gamma	1,286
Delta	279
Epsilon	823

The amounts owing by Omega to his suppliers at 1 May were:

	£
Zeta	2,173
Eta	187
Theta	318

Sales made by Omega during May were as follows.

	£
Gamma	432
Epsilon	129
Beta	314
Epsilon	269
Alpha	88
Delta	417
Epsilon	228

Purchases during May

	£
Eta	423
Zeta	268
Eta	741

Returns inwards (ie sales returns)

	£
Epsilon	88

Cash payments

	£
Eta	187
Theta	318
Zeta	1,000

Cash receipts

	£
Beta	1,040
Delta	279
Gamma	826
Epsilon	823

Required

(a) Open accounts for Omega's customers and suppliers and record therein the 1 May balances.
(b) Record the transactions in the appropriate personal account and nominal ledger accounts.
(c) Balance the personal accounts where necessary.
(d) Extract a list of debtors at 31 May.

Answer

(a),(b),(c)

ALPHA

	£		£
Opening balance	210		
May sales	88	Balance c/d	298
	298		298

BETA

	£		£
Opening balance	1,040	Cash	1,040
May sales	314	Balance c/d	314
	1,354		1,354

GAMMA

	£		£
Opening balance	1,286	Cash	826
May sales	432	Balance c/d	892
	1,718		1,718

DELTA

	£		£
Opening balance	279	Cash	279
May sales	417	Balance c/d	417
	696		696

EPSILON

	£		£
Opening balance	823	Cash	823
May sales	129	Returns	88
May sales	269	Balance c/d	538
May sales	228		
	1,449		1,449

ZETA

	£		£
Cash	1,000	Opening balance	2,173
Balance c/d	1,441	May purchases	268
	2,441		2,441

ETA

	£		£
Cash	187	Opening balance	187
Balance c/d	1,164	May purchases	423
		May purchases	741
	1,351		1,351

THETA

	£		£
Cash	318	Opening balance	318

SALES ACCOUNT

	£		£
		May sales	1,877

PURCHASES ACCOUNT

	£		£
May purchases	1,432		

RETURNS ACCOUNT

	£		£
May returns	88		

CASH ACCOUNT

	£		£
May receipts	2,968	May payments	1,505

(d) DEBTORS AS AT 31 MAY

	April	*May*	*Total*
	£	£	£
Alpha	210	88	298
Beta	-	314	314
Gamma	460	432	892
Delta	-	417	417
Epsilon	-	538	538
	670	1,789	2,459

THE MAIN POINTS!

(a) Business transactions are recorded on source documents.

(b) Source documents are recorded in day books.

(c) Totals of day books are recorded by double entry in nominal ledger accounts.

(d) Single transactions are recorded from day books to individual customer and supplier accounts by single entry.

(e) Customer accounts are in the sales ledger

(f) Supplier accounts are in the purchase ledger

(g) The sales and purchase ledger are not part of the double entry system

(h) The nominal ledger contains one account for each item in the balance sheet and profit and loss account.

Question 6

The following is a summary of the petty cash transactions of Jockfield Ltd for May 20X2.

May	1	Received from cashier £300 as petty cash float	
			£
	2	Postage	18
	3	Travelling	12
	4	Cleaning	15
	7	Petrol for delivery van	22
	8	Travelling	25
	9	Stationery	17
	11	Cleaning	18
	14	Postage	5
	15	Travelling	8
	18	Stationery	9
		Cleaning	23
	20	Postage	13
	24	Delivery van 5,000 miles service	43
	26	Petrol	18
	27	Cleaning	21
	29	Postage	5
	30	Petrol	14

Required

(a) Rule up a suitable petty cash book with analysis columns for expenditure on cleaning, motor expenses, postage, stationery, travelling.

(b) Enter the month's transactions.

(c) Enter the receipt of the amount necessary to restore the imprest and carry down the balance for the commencement of the following month.

(d) State how the double entry for the expenditure is completed.

Answer

(a),(b),(c)

PETTY CASH BOOK

Receipts	*Date*	*Narrative*	*Total*	*Postage*	*Travelling*	*Cleaning*	*Stationery*	*Motor*
£			£	£	£	£	£	£
300	May 1	Cash						
	May 2	Postage	18	18				
	May 3	Travelling	12		12			
	May 5	Cleaning	15			15		
	May 7	Petrol	22					22
	May 8	Travelling	25		25			
	May 9	Stationery	17				17	
	May 11	Cleaning	18			18		
	May 14	Postage	5	5				
	May 15	Travelling	8		8			
	May 18	Stationery	9				9	
	May 18	Cleaning	23			23		
	May 20	Postage	13	13				
	May 24	Van service	43					43
	May 26	Petrol	18					18
	May 27	Cleaning	21			21		
	May 29	Postage	5	5				
	May 30	Petrol	14					14
			286	41	45	77	26	97
286	May 31	Cash						
		Balance c/d	300					
586			586					
300	June 1	Balance b/d						

(d) The analysis totals are posted to the relevant ledger accounts by double entry:

		£	£
DEBIT	Postage expense account	41	
DEBIT	Travelling expense account	45	
DEBIT	Cleaning expense account	77	
DEBIT	Stationery expense account	26	
DEBIT	Motor expense account	97	
CREDIT	Petty cash account		286

and

		£	£
DEBIT	Petty cash account	286	
CREDIT	Cash account		286

Chapter roundup

- Double entry bookkeeping is based on the same idea as the accounting equation. Every accounting transaction alters the make-up of a business's assets and liabilities. Since the equality of assets and liabilities is always preserved, it follows that each transaction must have two equal but opposite effects.
- In a system of double entry bookkeeping every accounting event must be entered in ledger accounts both as a debit and as an equal but opposite credit. The principal accounts are contained in a ledger called the nominal ledger.
- Some accounts in the nominal ledger represent the total of very many smaller balances. For example, the debtors accounts represents all the balances owed by individual customers of the business, while the creditors account represents all amounts owed by the business to its suppliers.
- To keep track of individual customer and supplier balances, it is common to maintain subsidiary ledgers (called the sales ledger and the purchase ledger respectively). Each account in these ledgers represents the balance owed by or to an individual customer or supplier. These subsidiary ledgers are kept purely for reference and are therefore known as **memorandum** records. They do **not** normally form part of the double entry system
- The rules of double entry bookkeeping are best learnt by considering the cash book. In the cash book a **credit** entry indicates a payment made by the business; the matching debit entry is then made in an account denoting an expense paid, an asset purchased or a liability settled. A **debit** entry in the cash book indicates cash received by the business; the matching credit entry is then made in an account denoting revenue received, a liability created or an asset sold.

Quick quiz

1 The suppliers personal accounts will appear in which of the following business records?

A The general (or nominal) ledger
B The sales ledger
C The purchase journal
D The purchase ledger ✓

2 The double entry to record a cash sale of £50 is:

DEBIT Cash account. £50

CREDIT sales account £50

3 The double entry to record a purchase of office chairs for £1,000 is:

DEBIT Assets account £1,000

CREDIT Cash account. £1,000

4 The double entry to record a credit sale is:

DEBIT debtors account

CREDIT sales account.

5 Which of these statements are correct?

(i) The purchases book is part of a double entry system.
(ii) The purchases ledger is part of a double entry system.

A (i) only
B (i) and (ii)
C (ii) only
D Both are false ✓

6 Personal accounts contain records of?

A Debtors and creditors ✓
B Assets and liabilities
C Income and expenditure
D Transactions with the proprietor of the business

Answers to quick quiz

1 D This is correct
A These ledgers are used to record impersonal accounts.
B Customers accounts are kept in the sales ledger.
C This is simply a record of purchase invoices received.

2 DEBIT: CASH £50; CREDIT: SALES £50

3 DEBIT: FIXED ASSETS £1,000; CREDIT: CASH £1,000

4 DEBIT: DEBTORS; CREDIT: SALES

5 D is correct. The purchases book is a day book, and the purchases ledger shows balances on suppliers accounts.

6 A Correct, these should be reconciled to control accounts periodically.

B These would be in the nominal ledger.

C These would be in the nominal ledger.

D These would be in either the nominal ledger or a 'private ledger' not accessible by accounting staff.

Now try the questions below from the Exam Question Bank

Number	Level	Marks	Time
16	Exam	15	27 mins
17	Exam	2	3 mins
18	Exam	2	3 mins

Chapter 7

FROM TRIAL BALANCE TO FINANCIAL STATEMENTS

Topic List		Syllabus reference	Ability required
1	The trial balance	(ii)	Application
2	The trading, profit and loss account	(iv)	Application
3	The balance sheet	(iv)	Application
4	Balancing accounts and preparing financial statements	(iv)	Application

Introduction

In the previous chapters you learned the principles of double entry and how to post to the ledger accounts. The next step in our progress towards the financial statements is the trial balance.

Before transferring the relevant balances at the year end to the profit and loss account and putting closing balances carried forward into the balance sheet, it is usual to test the accuracy of the double entry bookkeeping records by preparing a trial balance. This is done by taking all the balances on every account. Due to the nature of double entry, the total of the debit balances will be exactly equal to the total of the credit balances.

In very straightforward circumstances, it is possible to prepare accounts directly from a trial balance. This is covered in Section 4.

Exam questions at all levels in financial accounting involve preparation of final accounts from trial balance. Also, you may end up having to do it in 'real life'!

Learning outcomes covered in this chapter

- Prepare a trial balance
- Prepare trading accounts, profit and loss accounts, appropriation of profit and balance sheets from trial balance

Syllabus content covered in this chapter

- Trial balance
- Trading, profit and loss accounts and balance sheets from trial balance
- Accounting for the appropriation of profit

1 THE TRIAL BALANCE

KEY TERM

A **trial balance** is a list of nominal ledger account balances. It is prepared to check that the total of debit balances is the same as the total of credit balances and offer reassurance that the double entry recording from day books has been done correctly.

1.1 EXAMPLE

Here are the accounts of Ron Knuckle from Question 2 in the last chapter.

CASH

	£		£
Capital - Ron Knuckle	7,000	Rent	3,500
Bank loan	1,000	Shop fittings	2,000
Sales	10,000	Trade creditors	5,000
Debtors	2,500	Bank loan interest	100
		Incidental expenses	1,900
		Drawings	1,500
			14,000
		Balancing figure - the amount of cash left over after payments have been made	6,500
	20,500		20,500

CAPITAL (RON KNUCKLE)

	£		£
		Cash	7,000

BANK LOAN

	£		£
		Cash	1,000

PURCHASES

	£		£
Trade creditors	5,000		

TRADE CREDITORS

	£		£
Cash	5,000	Purchases	5,000

RENT

	£		£
Cash	3,500		

SHOP FITTINGS

	£		£
Cash	2,000		

SALES

	£		£
		Cash	10,000
		Debtors	2,500
			12,500

DEBTORS

	£		£
Sales	2,500	Cash	2,500

BANK LOAN INTEREST

	£		£
Cash	100		

OTHER EXPENSES

	£		£
Cash	1,900		

DRAWINGS ACCOUNT

	£		£
Cash	1,500		

Balancing ledger accounts

1.2 At the end of an accounting period, a balance is struck on each account in turn. This means that all the debits on the account are totalled and so are all the credits. If the total debits exceed the total credits there is said to be a debit balance on the account. If the credits exceed the debits, then the account has a credit balance.

1.3 In our example, there is very little balancing to do. Both the trade creditors account and the debtors account balance off to zero. The cash account has a debit balance of £6,500 and the total on the sales account is £12,500, which is a credit balance. Otherwise, the accounts have only one entry each, so there is no totalling to do to arrive at the balance on each account.

1.4 If the basic principle of double entry has been correctly applied throughout the period, the credit balances equal the debit balances in total.

	Debit	*Credit*
	£	£
Cash	6,500	
Capital		7,000
Bank loan		1,000
Purchases	5,000	
Trade creditors	-	-
Rent	3,500	
Shop fittings	2,000	
Sales		12,500
Debtors	-	-
Bank loan interest	100	
Other expenses	1,900	
Drawings	1,500	
	20,500	20,500

1.5 It does not matter in what order the various accounts are listed, because the trial balance is not a document that a company **has** to prepare. It is just a method used to test the accuracy of the double entry bookkeeping.

What if the trial balance shows unequal debit and credit balances?

1.6 If the two columns of the trial balance are not equal, there must be an error in recording the transaction. However, a trial balance will not disclose the following types of errors.

- Complete **omission** of a transaction, because neither a debit nor a credit is made. This is called an error or omission.
- Posting of a transaction to the correct side of the ledger, but to a wrong **account**. This is called an error of commission.
- **Compensating** errors (eg an error of £100 is exactly cancelled by another £100 error elsewhere)
- Errors of **principle** (eg cash received from debtors being debited to the debtors account and credited to cash instead of the other way round)

Question 1

As at 30.3.20X7, your business has the following balances on its ledger accounts.

Accounts	*Balance*
	£
Bank loan	12,000
Cash	11,700
Capital	13,000
Rates	1,880
Trade creditors	11,200
Purchases	12,400
Sales	14,600
Sundry creditors	1,620
Debtors	12,000
Bank loan interest	1,400
Other expenses	11,020
Vehicles	2,020

On 31.3.X7 the business made the following transactions.

(a) Bought materials for £1,000, half for cash and half on credit.
(b) Made £1,040 sales, £800 of which was for credit.

(c) Paid wages to shop assistants of £260 in cash.

Required

Draw up a trial balance showing the balances as at the end of 31.3.X7.

Answer

First you must put the original balances into a trial balance - ie decide which are debit and which are credit balances.

Account	*Dr*	*Cr*
	£	£
Bank loan		12,000
Cash	11,700	
Capital		13,000
Rates	1,880	
Trade creditors		11,200
Purchases	12,400	
Sales		14,600
Sundry creditors		1,620
Debtors	12,000	
Bank loan interest	1,400	
Other expenses	11,020	
Vehicles	2,020	
	52,420	52,420

Now we must take account of the effects of the three transactions which took place on 31.3.X7.

			£	£
(a)	DEBIT	Purchases	1,000	
	CREDIT	Cash		500
		Trade creditors		500
(b)	DEBIT	Cash	240	
		Debtors	800	
	CREDIT	Sales		1,040
(c)	DEBIT	Other expenses	260	
	CREDIT	Cash		260

When these figures are included in the trial balance, it becomes:

Account	*Dr*	*Cr*
	£	£
Bank loan		12,000
Cash (11,700 – 500 + 240 – 260)	11,180	
Capital		13,000
Rates	1,880	
Trade creditors (11,200 + 500)		11,700
Purchases (12,400 + 1,000)	13,400	
Sales (14,600 + 1,040)		15,640
Sundry creditors		1,620
Debtors (12,000 + 800)	12,800	
Bank loan interest	1,400	
Other expenses (11,020 + 260)	11,280	
Vehicles	2,020	
	53,960	53,960

And it balances!

THE MAIN POINT!

A trial balance is done prior to producing the financial statements. It provides reassurance that the double entry bookkeeping has been done correctly, but it does not reveal all possible errors.

2 THE TRADING, PROFIT AND LOSS ACCOUNT — Pilot Paper

2.1 The first step in preparing the financial statements is to open up another ledger account in the nominal ledger called the trading, profit and loss account. In it a business summarises its results for the period by gathering together all the ledger account balances relating to income and expenses. This account is still part of the double entry system, so the basic rule of double entry still applies: every debit must have an equal and opposite credit entry.

2.2 This trading, profit and loss account is not the financial statement we are aiming for, even though it has the same name. The difference between the two is not very great, because they contain the same information. However, the financial statement lays it out differently and may be much less detailed.

2.3 The first step is to look through the ledger accounts and identify which ones relate to income and expenses. In the case of Ron Knuckle, the income and expense accounts consist of purchases, rent, sales, bank loan interest, and other expenses.

2.4 The balances on these accounts are then transferred to the new trading, profit and loss account. For example:

		£	£
Debit	Trading profit and loss account	5,000	
Credit	Purchases account		5,000

PURCHASES

	£		£
Trade creditors	5,000	Trading, P & L a/c	5,000

RENT

	£		£
Cash	3,500	Trading, P & L a/c	3,500

SALES

	£		£
Trading, P & L a/c	12,500	Cash	10,000
		Debtors	2,500
	12,500		12,500

BANK LOAN INTEREST

	£		£
Cash	100	Trading, P & L a/c	100

OTHER EXPENSES

	£		£
Cash	1,900	Trading, P & L a/c	1,900

TRADING, PROFIT AND LOSS ACCOUNT

	£		£
Purchases	5,000	Sales	12,500
Rent	3,500		
Bank loan interest	100		
Other expenses	1,900		

(Note that the trading, profit and loss account is not yet balanced off.)

2.5 The items we have gathered together in the trading, profit and loss account are the same items needed to draw up the trading, profit and loss account in the form of a financial statement. With a little rearrangement they could be presented as follows.

RON KNUCKLE: TRADING, PROFIT AND LOSS ACCOUNT

	£	£
Sales		12,500
Cost of sales (= purchases in this case)		(5,000)
Gross profit		7,500
Expenses		
Rent	3,500	
Bank loan interest	100	
Other expenses	1,900	
		(5,500)
Net profit		2,000

3 THE BALANCE SHEET **Pilot Paper**

3.1 Look back at the ledger accounts of Ron Knuckle, which ones are left? We still have cash, capital, bank loan, trade creditors, shop fittings, debtors and the drawings account.

3.2 Are these the only ledger accounts left? No: there is still the last one we opened up, the trading, profit and loss account. The balance on this account represents the profit earned by the business it has a credit balance - a profit - of £2,000. (This is the figure shown in the trading profit and loss account financial statement.)

3.3 These remaining accounts must also be balanced off, but since they represent assets and liabilities of the business (not income and expenses) their balances are **carried down** in the books of the business. This means that they become opening balances for the next accounting period.

3.4 The usual method of balancing off a ledger account at the end of an accounting period is illustrated by the bank loan account in Ron Knuckle's books.

BANK LOAN ACCOUNT

	£		£
Balance carried down (c/d)	1,000	Cash	1,000
		Balance brought down (b/d)	1,000

3.5 A credit balance brought down denotes a liability. An asset is represented by a debit balance brought down.

3.6 A proprietor's capital comprises any cash introduced by him, plus any profits less any drawings. These three elements are contained in different ledger accounts: cash introduced of £7,000 appears in the capital account, drawings of £1,500 in the drawings account and the profit is the £2,000 credit balance on the trading profit and loss account. It is convenient to gather together all these amounts into one capital account, in the same way as we earlier gathered together income and expense accounts into one trading and profit and loss account.

DRAWINGS

	£		£
Cash	1,500	Capital a/c	1,500

TRADING, PROFIT AND LOSS ACCOUNT

	£		£
Purchases	5,000	Sales	12,500
Rent	3,500		
Bank loan interest	100		
Other expenses	1,900		
Capital a/c	2,000		
	12,500		12,500

CAPITAL

	£		£
Drawings	1,500	Cash	7,000
Balance c/d	7,500	Trading, P & L a/c	2,000
	9,000		9,000
		Balance b/d	7,500

3.7 A re-arrangement of the outstanding balances completes Ron Knuckle's balance sheet.

RON KNUCKLE
BALANCE SHEET AT END OF FIRST TRADING PERIOD

	£
Fixed assets	
Shop fittings	2,000
Current assets	
Cash	6,500
Total assets	8,500
Liabilities	
Bank loan	(1,000)
Net assets	7,500
Proprietor's capital	7,500

3.8 When a balance sheet is drawn up for an accounting period which is not the first one, then it ought to show the capital at the start of the accounting period and the capital at the end of the accounting period. This will be illustrated in the next example.

Exam focus point

Do not proceed unless you are 100 per cent confident that you understand the basics of preparing a trading, profit and loss account and balance sheet. The rest of your studies will build on these foundations.

THE MAIN POINT!

At the end of an accounting period, in preparation for producing the balance sheet and profit and loss account:

(a) Ledger accounts are balanced

(b) A trial balance is prepared to check that the total of debit balances equals the total of credit balances

(c) A new ledger account called profit and loss account is opened

(d) Using double entry, accounts relating to income and expenses are transferred to the new profit and loss ledger account

(e) Accounts relating to balance sheet items are left as balances in the nominal ledger

4 BALANCING ACCOUNTS AND PREPARING FINANCIAL STATEMENTS

May 2001

4.1 The exercise which follows is the most important so far. It uses all the accounting steps from entering up ledger accounts to preparing the financial statements, and is set out in a style which you might well find in an examination. It is very important that you try the question by yourself: if you do not, you will be missing out a vital part of this text.

Question 2

A business is established with capital of £2,000, and this amount is paid into a business bank account by the proprietor. During the first year's trading, the following transactions (in summary) occurred:

	£
Purchases of goods for resale, on credit	4,300
Payments to trade creditors	3,600
Sales, all on credit	5,800
Payments from debtors	3,200
Fixed assets purchased for cash	1,500
Other expenses, all paid in cash	900

The bank has provided an overdraft facility of up to £3,000.

Prepare the ledger accounts, a trading, profit and loss account for the year and a balance sheet as at the end of the year.

Answer

Open the ledger accounts so that the transactions can be posted. The next step is to work out the double entry bookkeeping for each transaction. Normally you would write them straight into the accounts, but to make this example easier to follow, they are first listed below.

(a)	Establishing business (£2,000)	DR	Cash	CR	Capital
(b)	Purchases (£4,300)	DR	Purchases	CR	Creditors
(c)	Payments to creditors (£3,600)	DR	Creditors	CR	Cash
(d)	Sales (£5,800)	DR	Debtors	CR	Sales
(e)	Payments by debtors (£3,200)	DR	Cash	CR	Debtors
(f)	Fixed assets (£1,500)	DR	Fixed assets	CR	Cash
(g)	Other (cash) expenses (£900)	DR	Other expenses	CR	Cash

CASH

	£		£
Capital	2,000	Creditors	3,600
		Fixed assets	1,500
Debtors	3,200	Other expenses	900

CAPITAL

	£		£
		Cash	2,000

TRADE CREDITORS

	£		£
Cash	3,600	Purchases	4,300

PURCHASES

	£		£
Creditors	4,300		

FIXED ASSETS

	£		£
Cash	1,500		

SALES

	£		£
		Debtors	5,800

DEBTORS

	£		£
Sales	5,800	Cash	3,200

OTHER EXPENSES

	£		£
Cash	900		

The next thing to do is to balance all these accounts. It is at this stage that you could draw up a trial balance to make sure the double entries are accurate. There is not very much point in this simple example, but if you did draw up a trial balance, it would look like this.

	Dr	*Cr*
	£	£
Cash		800
Capital		2,000
Creditors		700
Purchases	4,300	
Fixed assets	1,500	
Sales		5,800
Debtors	2,600	
Other expenses	900	
	9,300	9,300

After balancing the accounts, the trading, profit and loss account is opened and all the balances relating to income and expenses are transferred.

CASH

	£		£
Capital	2,000	Trade creditors	3,600
Debtors	3,200	Fixed assets	1,500
Balance c/d	800	Other expenses	900
	6,000		6,000
		Balance b/d (overdraft)	800

CAPITAL

	£		£
Balance c/d	2,600	Cash	2,000
		P & L a/c	600
	2,600		2,600

TRADE CREDITORS

	£		£
Cash	3,600	Purchases	4,300
Balance c/d	700		
	4,300		4,300
		Balance b/d	700

PURCHASES ACCOUNT

	£		£
Trade creditors	4,300	Trading a/c	4,300

FIXED ASSETS

	£		£
Cash	1,500	Balance c/d	1,500
Balance b/d	1,500		

SALES

	£		£
Trading a/c	5,800	Debtors	5,800

DEBTORS

	£		£
Sales	5,800	Cash	3,200
		Balance c/d	2,600
	5,800		5,800
Balance b/d	2,600		

OTHER EXPENSES

	£		£
Cash	900	P & L a/c	900

TRADING, PROFIT AND LOSS ACCOUNT

	£		£
Purchases account	4,300	Sales	5,800
Gross profit c/d	1,500		
	5,800		5,800
Other expenses	900	Gross profit b/d	1,500
Net profit (transferred to capital account)	600		
	1,500		1,500

So the financial statements will be as follows.

TRADING, PROFIT AND LOSS ACCOUNT
FOR THE ACCOUNTING PERIOD

	£
Sales	5,800
Cost of sales (purchases)	(4,300)
Gross profit	1,500
Expenses	900
Net profit	600

BALANCE SHEET AS AT THE END OF THE PERIOD

	£	£
Fixed assets		1,500
Current assets		
Debtors	2,600	
Current liabilities		
Bank overdraft	800	
Trade creditors	700	
	1,500	
Net current assets		1,100
		2,600
Capital		
At start of period		2,000
Net profit for period		600
At end of period		2,600

Exam focus point

Section B of the May 2001 exam had a 14 mark question on preparing final accounts from a trial balance (with a few adjustments).

Chapter roundup

- At suitable intervals, the entries in each ledger accounts are totalled and a balance is struck. Balances are usually collected in a trial balance which is then used as a basis for preparing a profit and loss account and a balance sheet.
- A trial balance can be used to test the accuracy of the double entry accounting records. It works by listing the balances on ledger accounts, some of which will be debits and some credits, to see if they balance.
- A profit and loss ledger account is opened up to gather all items relating to income and expenses. When rearranged, the items make up the profit and loss account financial statement.
- The balances on all remaining ledger accounts (including the profit and loss account) can be listed and rearranged to form the balance sheet.

Quick quiz

1 Fill in the blanks.

A trial balance is a list of ______________________________

______________________________.

2 Four circumstances in which a trial balance might balance although some of the balances are wrong are:

(1) ____________

(2) ____________

(3) ____________

(4) ____________

3 Which of the following errors would result in a trail balance failing to agree?

A Failing to record an invoice from a supplier in the accounting system

B Recording a fixed asset purchase as an item of revenue expenditure

C Recording an expense payment as:
Dr bank a/c Cr expense a/c

D Recording an expense payment as:
Dr expense a/c Dr bank a/c

4 When preparing a trial balance, the clerk omits the balance of £2,000 on the debtors account. This error means that the total of debit balances will exceed the total of credit balances by £2,000. True or false?

Answers to quick quiz

1 A trial balance is a list of nominal ledger account balances.

2 (1) Omission of a transaction completely
(2) Posting to the wrong ledger account
(3) Compensating errors
(4) Errors of principle

3 D This is an example of a failure of the basic rules of double entry, so the trial balance will not agree.

A This is an error of omission, the financial records will be incomplete but the integrity of the double entry process is not impaired.

B This is an error of principle, confusion between capital and revenue expenditure has occurred.

C This is a reversal error, the trial balance will agree because debits = credits, however the accounts are incorrect.

4 False. The omitted balance is an asset account and thus a debit so in the trial balance the total of credit balances will exceed the total of debit balances by £2,000.

Now try the questions below from the Exam Question Bank

Number	Level	Marks	Time
19	Exam	30	54 mins
20	Exam	2	3 mins
21	Exam	2	3 mins

Chapter 8

THE COST OF GOODS SOLD, ACCRUALS AND PREPAYMENTS

Topic List		Syllabus reference	Ability required
1	The accounting treatment of stocks and carriage costs	(iv)	Application
2	Accruals and prepayments	(iv)	Application

Introduction

Profit is the excess of income over expenses. But, it is not always immediately clear how much income and expenses are. A variety of difficulties can arise in measuring them. The purpose of this chapter is to describe some of these problems and their solutions.

We shall consider unsold goods in stock at the beginning and end of an accounting period, carriage costs, writing off or writing down stock values, and the accounting treatment of accruals and prepayments. Their common feature is that they are applications of the accruals concept or matching concept described in Chapter 2.

Learning outcomes covered in this chapter

- Explain, calculate and prepare accounts for stock
- Prepare accounts using accruals and prepayments

Syllabus content covered in this chapter

- Accounting for stocks (excluding long term contract work-in-progress)
- Accruals and prepayments

1 THE ACCOUNTING TREATMENT OF STOCKS AND CARRIAGE COSTS May 2001

1.1 The accruals concept requires us to match income with the expenses incurred in earning that income. Goods can be unsold at the end of an accounting period and so still be held in stock. The purchase cost of these goods should **not** be included in the cost of sales of the period.

1.2 EXAMPLE

Perry P Louis ends his financial year on 30 September each year. On 1 October 20X4 he had no goods in stock. During the year to 30 September 20X5, he purchased 30,000 umbrellas costing £60,000. He resold the umbrellas for £5 each, and sales for the year amounted to £100,000 (20,000 umbrellas). At 30 September there were 10,000 unsold umbrellas left in stock. What was Perry P Louis's gross profit for the year?

1.3 SOLUTION

Perry P Louis purchased 30,000 umbrellas, but only sold 20,000. Purchase costs of £60,000 and sales of £100,000 do not represent the same quantity of goods. The gross profit for the year is calculated by 'matching' the sales value of the 20,000 umbrellas sold with the cost of those 20,000 umbrellas.

	£	£
Sales (20,000 units)		100,000
Purchases (30,000 units)	60,000	
Less closing stock (10,000 units @ £2)	20,000	
Cost of sales (20,000 units)		40,000
Gross profit		60,000

1.4 EXAMPLE CONTINUED

The next accounting year is 1 October 20X5 to 30 September 20X6. During the course of this year, Perry P Louis purchased 40,000 umbrellas at a total cost of £95,000. During the year he sold 45,000 umbrellas for £230,000. At 30 September 20X6 he had 5,000 umbrellas left in stock, which had cost £12,000.

What was his gross profit for the year?

1.5 SOLUTION

In this accounting year, he purchased 40,000 umbrellas to add to the 10,000 he already had in stock at the start of the year. He sold 45,000, leaving 5,000 umbrellas in stock at the year end. Once again, gross profit should be calculated by matching the value of 45,000 units of sales with the cost of those 45,000 units.

The cost of sales is the value of the 10,000 umbrellas in stock at the beginning of the year, plus the cost of the 40,000 umbrellas purchased, less the value of the 5,000 umbrellas in stock at the year end.

	£	£
Sales (45,000 units)		230,000
Opening stock (10,000 units) *	20,000	
Add purchases (40,000 units)	95,000	
	115,000	
Less closing stock (5,000 units)	12,000	
Cost of sales (45,000 units)		103,000
Gross profit		127,000

*Taken from the closing stock value of the previous accounting year, see paragraph 1.3.

The cost of goods sold

FORMULA TO LEARN

	£
Opening stock value	X
Add cost of purchases (or, in the case of a manufacturing company, the cost of production)	X
	X
Less closing stock value	(X)
Equals cost of goods sold	X

Question 1

On 1 January 20X6, the Grand Union Food Stores had goods in stock valued at £6,000. During 20X6 it purchased supplies costing £50,000. Sales for the year to 31 December 20X6 amounted to £80,000. The cost of goods in stock at 31 December 20X6 was £12,500.

Calculate the gross profit for the year.

Answer

GRAND UNION FOOD STORES
TRADING ACCOUNT FOR THE YEAR ENDED 31 DECEMBER 20X6

	£	£
Sales		80,000
Opening stocks	6,000	
Add purchases	50,000	
	56,000	
Less closing stocks	12,500	
Cost of goods sold		43,500
Gross profit		36,500

Carriage inwards and outwards

KEY TERM

'**Carriage**' refers to the cost of transporting purchased goods from the supplier to the purchaser. Someone has to pay for these delivery costs: sometimes the supplier pays, and sometimes the purchaser pays. When the purchaser pays, the cost to the purchaser is **carriage inwards**. When the supplier pays, the cost to the supplier is **carriage outwards**.

1.6 The cost of carriage inwards is usually added to the cost of purchases, and is therefore included in the trading account. The cost of carriage outwards is a selling and distribution expense in the profit and loss account.

THE MAIN POINT

Carriage inwards is part of 'purchases'. Carriage outwards is part of selling and distribution expenses.

1.7 EXAMPLE

Gwyn Tring, trading as Clickety Clocks, imports and resells cuckoo clocks and grandfather clocks. He pays for the costs of delivering the clocks from his supplier in Switzerland to his shop in Wales. He resells the clocks to other traders throughout the country, paying the costs of carriage to his customers.

On 1 July 20X5, he had clocks in stock valued at £17,000. During the year to 30 June 20X6 he purchased more clocks at a cost of £75,000. Carriage inwards amounted to £2,000. Sales for the year were £162,100. Other expenses of the business amounted to £56,000 excluding carriage outwards which cost £2,500. Gwyn Tring took drawings of £20,000 from the business during the course of the year. The value of the goods in stock at the year end was £15,400.

Required

Prepare the trading, profit and loss account of Clickety Clocks for the year ended 30 June 20X6.

1.8 SOLUTION

CLICKETY CLOCKS
TRADING, PROFIT AND LOSS ACCOUNT FOR THE YEAR ENDED 30 JUNE 20X6

	£	£
Sales		162,100
Opening stock	17,000	
Purchases	75,000	
Carriage inwards	2,000	
	94,000	
Less closing stock	15,400	
Cost of goods sold		78,600
Gross profit		83,500
Carriage outwards	2,500	
Other expenses	56,000	
		58,500
Net profit (transferred to balance sheet)		25,000

Question 2

Sam's trial balance at 31.12.X6 was:

	Dr £	Cr £
Stock at 1.1.X6	500	
Sales		12,800
Purchases	6,000	
Carriage inwards	800	
Carriage outwards	500	
Selling expenses	1,200	
Administration expenses	1,000	
Fixtures and fittings	20,000	
Vans	10,000	
Debtors	900	
Creditors		600
Capital at 1.1.X6		27,500
	40,900	40,900

Stock at 31.12.X6 was valued at £1,500.

For the year ended 31.12.X6, calculate:

(a) The gross profit
(b) The cost of sales
(c) The net profit

Answer

(a) £7,000
(b) £5,800
(c) £4,300

Sales 12800
Opening stock 500
Purchase 6000
Carriage inwards 800
b) 7300
1500
(7300)
Gross profit a) 7000
Carriage outwards 500
Selling expenses 1200
1700
(1700)
Net profit 3800

	£	£
Sales		12,800
Cost of sales		
Opening stock	500	
Purchases	6,000	
Carriage inwards	800	
	7,300	
Closing stock	(1,500)	
		5,800
Gross profit		7,000
Selling and delivery expenses (500 + 1,200)		(1,700)
Administration expenses		(1,000)
Net profit		4,300

Goods written off or written down

1.9 A trader might be unable to sell all the goods that he purchases if they are:

- Lost or stolen
- Damaged
- Obsolete or out of fashion, and so thrown away or possibly sold off in a clearance sale

1.10 When goods are lost, stolen or thrown away as worthless, the business will make a loss on those goods because their 'sales value' will be nil.

Similarly, when goods lose value because they are obsolete or out of fashion, the business will make a loss if their clearance sales value is less than their cost. For example, if goods which originally cost £500 are now obsolete and can only be sold for £150, the business will suffer a loss of £350.

> **KEY TERM**
>
> **Net realisable value** is the sales value less any costs that will be incurred in making the sale.

1.11 If, at the end of an accounting period, a business still has goods in stock which are either worthless or worth less than their original cost, the value of the stocks should be written down to one of the following.

- Nothing, if they are worthless
- Their net realisable value, if this is less than their original cost

The loss will be reported as soon as it is foreseen, even if the goods have not yet been scrapped or sold off at a cheap price. This is an application of - the prudence concept.

1.12 The costs of stock written off or written down should not usually cause any problems in calculating the gross profit of a business, because the cost of goods sold will include the cost of stocks written off or written down, as the following example shows.

1.13 EXAMPLE: STOCKS WRITTEN OFF AND WRITTEN DOWN

Lucas Wagg, trading as Fairlock Fashions, ends his financial year on 31 March. At 1 April 20X5 he had goods in stock valued at £8,800. During the year to 31 March 20X6, he purchased goods costing £48,000. Fashion goods which cost £2,100, were still held in stock at 31 March 20X6 that can only be sold at a sale price of £400. The goods still held in stock at 31 March 20X6 (including the fashion goods) had an original purchase cost of £7,600. Sales for the year were £81,400.

Required

Calculate the gross profit of Fairlock Fashions for the year ended 31 March 20X6.

1.14 SOLUTION

STOCK COUNT

	At cost	*Realisable value*
	£	£
Fashion goods	2,100	400
Other goods (balancing figure)	5,500	5,500
	7,600	5,900

FAIRLOCK FASHIONS
TRADING ACCOUNT FOR THE YEAR ENDED 31 MARCH 20X6

	£	£
Sales		81,400
Value of opening stock	8,800	
Purchases	48,000	
	56,800	
Less closing stock	5,900	
Cost of goods sold		50,900
Gross profit		30,500

THE MAIN POINTS

(a) Cost of sales in the profit and loss account is the cost of goods actually sold in the period (not bought), which is opening stock add purchases less closing stock.

(b) Carriage in is part of cost of sales, and this affects gross profit. Carriage out is an expense and affects net profit.

(c) Stock is valued at the lower of cost and net realisable value.

Exam focus point

Stock valuation was examined in Section A of the May 2001 exam.

2 ACCRUALS AND PREPAYMENTS — Pilot Paper, May 2001

Introduction

REMEMBER

The accruals concept said the income and expenses should be included in the profit and loss account of the period in which they are earned or incurred, not paid or received.

2.1 Expenses might not be paid for during the period to which they relate. For example, a business rents a shop for £20,000 per annum, paid in full on 1 April each year. If we calculate the profit of the business for the first six months of the year 20X7, the correct charge for rent in the profit and loss account will be £10,000 even though the rent payment is £20,000 in that period. Similarly, the rent charge in the second six months of the year is £10,000, even though no rent payment is made in that period.

KEY TERM

Accruals or **accrued expenses** are expenses which are charged against the profit for a particular period, even though they have not yet been paid for. **Prepayments** are payments which have been made in one accounting period, but should not be charged against profit until a later period, because they relate to that later period.

Accruals are current liabilities, and prepayments are current assets in the balance sheet.

2.2 Accruals and prepayments can seem difficult at first, but the following examples will clarify the principle involved; that expenses are matched against the period to which they relate.

2.3 EXAMPLE: ACCRUALS

Horace Goodrunning, trading as Goodrunning Motor Spares, ends his financial year on 28 February each year. His telephone was installed on 1 April 20X6 and he receives his telephone account quarterly at the end of each quarter. He pays it promptly as soon as it is received. On the basis of the following data, calculate the telephone expense to be charged to the profit and loss account for the year ended 28 February 20X7.

Goodrunning Motor Spares - telephone expenses paid.

	£
30.6.20X6	23.50
30.9.20X6	27.20
31.12.20X6	33.40
31.3.20X7	36.00

2.4 SOLUTION

The telephone expenses for the year ended 28 February 20X7.

	£
1 March - 31 March 20X6 (no telephone)	0.00
1 April – 30 June 20X6	23.50
1 July – 30 September 20X6	27.20
1 October - 31 December 20X6	33.40
1 January - 28 February 20X7 (two months)	24.00
	108.10

The charge for the period 1 January - 28 February 20X7 is two-thirds of the quarterly bill received on 31 March. As at 28 February 20X7, no telephone bill has been received because it is not due for another month. However, it is inappropriate to ignore the telephone expenses for January and February, and so an accrual is charged of £24.

The accrued charge will also appear in the balance sheet of the business as at 28 February 20X7, as a current liability.

Question 3

Ratsnuffer deals in pest control. Its owner, Roy Dent, employs a team of eight who were paid £12,000 per annum each in the year to 31 December 20X5. At the start of 20X6 he raised salaries by 10% to £13,200 per annum each.

On 1 July 20X6, he hired a trainee at a salary of £8,400 per annum.

He pays his work force on the first working day of every month, one month in arrears, so that his employees receive their salary for January on the first working day in February, etc.

Required

(a) Calculate the cost of salaries charged in the profit and loss account for the year ended 31 December 20X6.

(b) Calculate the amount actually paid in salaries during the year.

(c) State the amount of accrued salaries in the balance sheet as at 31 December 20X6.

Answer

(a) Salaries cost in the profit and loss account

	£
Cost of 8 employees for a full year at £13,200 each	105,600
Cost of trainee for a half year	4,200
	109,800

(b) Salaries actually paid in 20X6

	£
December 20X5 salaries paid in January (8 employees × £1,000 per month)	8,000
Salaries of 8 employees for January - November 20X6 paid in February - December (8 employees × £1,100 per month × 11 months)	96,800
Salary of trainee (for July - November paid in August - December 20X6: 5 months × £700 per month)	3,500
Salaries actually paid	108,300

(c) Accrued salaries costs as at 31 December 20X6
(ie costs charged in the P & L account, but not yet paid)

	£
8 employees x 1 month x £1,100 per month	8,800
1 trainee x 1 month x £700 per month	700
	9,500

(d) Summary

	£
Accrued wages costs as at 31 December 20X5	8,000
Add salaries cost for 20X6 (P & L account)	109,800
	117,800
Less salaries paid	108,300
Equals accrued wages costs as at 31 December 20X6	9,500

2.5 EXAMPLE: PREPAYMENTS

The Square Wheels Garage pays fire insurance annually in advance on 1 June each year. From the following record of insurance payments, calculate the charge to profit and loss for the financial year to 28 February 20X8.

	Insurance paid
	£
1.6.20X6	600
1.6.20X7	700

2.6 Insurance cost for:

	£
(a) the 3 months, 1 March - 31 May 20X7 (3/12 × £600)	150
(b) the 9 months, 1 June 20X7 - 28 February 20X8 (9/12 × £700)	525
Insurance cost for the year, charged to the P & L account	675

At 28 February 20X8 there is a prepayment for fire insurance, covering the period 1 March - 31 May 20X8. This insurance premium was paid on 1 June 20X7, but only nine months worth of the full annual cost is charged in the accounting period ended 28 February 20X8. The prepayment of (3/12 × £700) £175 appears as a current asset in the balance sheet of the Square Wheels Garage.

In the same way, there was a prepayment of (3/12 × £600) £150 in the balance sheet one year earlier as at 28 February 20X7.

Summary	£
Prepaid insurance premiums as at 28 February 20X7	150
Add insurance premiums paid 1 June 20X7	700
	850
Less insurance costs charged to the P & L account for the year ended 28 February 20X8	675
Equals prepaid insurance premiums as at 28 February 20X8	175

Question 4

The Batley Print Shop rents a photocopying machine for which it makes a quarterly payment as follows.

- Three months rental in advance
- A further charge of 2 pence per copy made during the quarter just ended

The rental agreement began on 1 August 20X4 and the first six quarterly bills were as follows.

Bills dated and received	*Rental*	*Costs of copies taken*	*Total*
	£	£	£
1 August 20X4	2,100	0	2,100
1 November 20X4	2,100	1,500	3,600
1 February 20X5	2,100	1,400	3,500
1 May 20X5	2,100	1,800	3,900
1 August 20X5	2,700	1,650	4,350
1 November 20X5	2,700	1,950	4,650

The bills are paid promptly, as soon as they are received.

(a) Calculate the charge for photocopying expenses for the year to 31 August 20X4 and the amount of prepayments and/or accrued charges as at that date.

(b) Calculate the charge for photocopying expenses for the following year to 31 August 20X5, and the amount of prepayments and/or accrued charges as at that date.

Answer

(a) Year to 31 August 20X4

	£
One months' rental (1/3 x £2,100) *	700
Accrued copying charges (1/3 x £1,500) **	500
Photocopying expense (P & L account)	1,200

* From the quarterly bill dated 1 August 20X4

** From the quarterly bill dated 1 November 20X4

There is a prepayment for 2 months' rental (£1,400) and an accrual (£500) for copying charges as at 31 August 20X4.

(b) Year to 31 August 20X5

	£	£
Rental from 1 September 20X4 - 31 July 20X5 (11 months at £2,100 per quarter or £700 per month)		7,700
Rental from 1 August - 31 August 20X5 (1/3 × £2,700)		900
Rental charge for the year		8,600
Copying charges		
1 September - 31 October 20X4 (2/3 × £1,500)	1,000	
1 November 20X4 - 31 January 20X5	1,400	
1 February - 30 April 20X5	1,800	
1 May - 31 July 20X5	1,650	
Accrued charges for August 20X5 (1/3 × £1,950)	650	
		6,500
Total photocopying expenses (P & L account)		15,100

There is a prepayment for 2 months' rental (£1,800) and an accrual for copying charges (£650) as at 31 August 20X5.

Summary of year 1 September 20X4 - 31 August 20X5

	Rental charges	*Copying costs*
	£	£
Prepayments as at 31.8.20X4	1,400	
Accrued charges as at 31.8.20X4		(500)
Bills received during the year		
1 November 20X4	2,100	1,500
1 February 20X5	2,100	1,400
1 May 20X5	2,100	1,800
1 August 20X5	2,700	1,650
Prepayment as at 31.8.20X5	(1,800)	
Accrued charges as at 31.8.20X5		650
Charge to the P & L account for the year	8,600	6,500
Balance sheet items as at 31 August 20X5		
Prepaid rental (current asset)	1,800	
Accrued copying charges (current liability)		650

2.7 FURTHER EXAMPLE: ACCRUALS

Willie Woggle opens a shop on 1 May 20X6. The rent of the shop is £12,000 per annum, payable quarterly in arrears (with the first payment on 31 July 20X6). Willie decides that his accounting period should end on 31 December each year.

2.8 The rent account as at 31 December 20X6 will record only two rental payments (on 31 July and 31 October) and there will be two months' accrued rental expenses for November and December 20X6 (£2,000). The charge to the P & L account for the period to 31 December 20X6 will be for 8 months' rent (May-December inclusive) ie £8,000.

2.9 The rent account appears as follows.

RENT EXPENSE ACCOUNT

		£			£
20X6			*20X6*		
31 July	Cash	3,000			
31 Oct	Cash	3,000	31 Dec	P & L account	8,000

2.10 The accruals of £2,000 have to be put in, not only to balance the account, but also to have an opening balance of £2,000 ready for next year. So the accrued rent of £2,000 is debited to the rent account as a balance to be carried down, and credited as a balance brought down.

RENT EXPENSE ACCOUNT

		£			£
20X6			*20X6*		
31 July	Cash	3,000			
31 Oct	Cash	3,000			
31 Dec	Balance c/d (accruals)	2,000	31 Dec	P & L account	8,000
		8,000			8,000
			19X7		
			1 Jan	Balance b/d	2,000

2.11 The rent account for the **next** year to 31 December 20X7, assuming no increase in rent in that year, would be as follows.

RENT EXPENSE ACCOUNT

		£			£
20X7			*20X7*		
31 Jan	Cash	3,000	1 Jan	Balance b/d	2,000
30 Apr	Cash	3,000			
31 Jul	Cash	3,000			
31 Oct	Cash	3,000			
31 Dec	Balance c/d (accruals)	2,000	31 Dec	P & L account	12,000
		14,000			14,000
			20X8		
			1 Jan	Balance b/d	2,000

2.12 Here, you will see that for a full year, a full twelve months' rental charges are taken as an expense to the P & L account.

2.13 FURTHER EXAMPLE: PREPAYMENTS

Terry Trunk commences business as a landscape gardener on 1 September 20X5. He joins his local trade association, the Confederation of Luton Gardeners, at an annual membership subscription of £180, payable annually in advance. He paid this amount on 1 September. Terry decides that his account period should end on 30 June each year.

In the first period to 30 June 20X6 (10 months), a full year's membership will have been paid, but only ten twelfths of the subscription is charged to the period (ie $10/12 \times$ £180 = £150). There is a prepayment of two months of membership subscription (ie $2/12 \times$ £180 = £30).

2.14 The prepayment is recognised in the ledger account for subscriptions by using the balance carried down/brought down technique.

SUBSCRIPTIONS EXPENSE ACCOUNT

		£			£
20X5			*20X6*		
1 Sept	Cash	180	30 Jun	P & L account	150
			30 Jun	Balance c/d (prepayment)	30
		180			180
20X6					
1 Jul	Balance b/d	30			

2.15 The subscription account for the next year, assuming no increase in the annual charge and that Terry Trunk remains a member of the association, will be as follows.

SUBSCRIPTIONS EXPENSE ACCOUNT

		£			£
20X6			*20X7*		
1 Jul	Balance b/d	30	30 Jun	P & L account	180
1 Sep	Cash	180	30 Jun	Balance c/d	
				(prepayment)	30
		210			210
20X7					
1 Jul	Balance b/d	30			

2.16 Again, we see the charge to the P & L account is for a full year's subscriptions.

Exam focus point

The compulsory questions in Section B will almost certainly test your knowledge of accruals and prepayments. This may not be in a separate question, but as part of the preparation of a profit and loss account and balance sheet. In May 2001, this was examined in both Section A and B.

Chapter roundup

- This chapter has illustrated how the amount of profit is calculated when:
  - There are opening or closing stocks of goods in hand
  - There is carriage inwards and/or carriage outwards
  - Stocks are written off or written down in value
  - There are accrued charges
  - There are prepayments of expense
- The cost of goods sold is calculated by adding the value of opening stock in hand to the cost of purchases and subtracting the value of closing stock.
- Accrued expenses are expenses which relate to an accounting period but have not yet been paid for. They are a charge against the profit for the period and they are shown in the balance sheet as at the end of the period as a current liability.
- Prepayments are expenses which have already been paid but relate to a future accounting period. They are not charged against the profit of the current period, and they are shown in the balance sheet at the end of the period as a current asset.
- Accruals and prepayments are aspects of the accruals concept.

Quick quiz

1 Cost of sales is calculated as opening stock plus purchases less closing stock. (Fill in the blanks.)

2 Carriage inwards reduces gross profit and net profit. True or false? T

3 Carriage outwards reduces gross profit and net profit. True or false? F

4 Carriage inwards is added to cost of sales because?

A It is an expense of the business
B It is an expense connected with purchasing stock for resale T
C It is not a controllable expense of running the business
D If it appeared in the profit and loss account, net profit would be incorrect

5 If a business has paid rates of £1,000 for the year to 31 March 20X9, the prepayment in the accounts for the year to 31 December 20X8 is £ ___400___.

6 Stock is valued at the lower of ___write off___ and ___net realization___.

7 ___Accurals___ in the balance sheet are amounts incurred but not yet paid.

___Prepayment___ in the balance sheet are amounts paid but not yet incurred. (Fill in the blanks.)

1 600

8 A draft profit and loss account shows a gross profit of £2,000 and net profit of £1,000. It is then realised that £400 of carriage inwards has been incorrectly treated as carriage outwards. When this mistake is corrected what happens to gross and net profit?

	Gross profit	*Net profit*
A	No change	No change
B	Falls £400	Falls £400
C	Falls £400	Rises £400 ✓
D	Falls £400	No change

Answers to quick quiz

1 Opening stock + purchases (or cost of production) – closing stock

2 True

3 False. It affects net profit only.

4 B Correct.

A This is not a precise answer.

C It is controllable as a result of buying decisions.

D Net profit would be unchanged regardless of how it is reported. Gross profit would be affected however.

5 £250 (3/12 × £1,000)

6 Stock is valued at the lower of **cost** and **net realisable value**.

7 Accruals are amounts incurred but not yet paid. Prepayments are amounts paid but not yet incurred.

8 D Cost of sales increases, so gross profit falls by £400. There is no change in net profit.

Now try the questions below from the Question Bank

Number	Level	Marks	Time
22	Introductory	15	27 mins
23	Exam	2	3 mins
24	Introductory	5	9 mins

Chapter 9

DISCOUNTS, BAD DEBTS AND PROVISIONS

Topic List		Syllabus reference	Ability required
1	Discounts	(ii)	Application
2	Accounting for bad and doubtful debts	(iv)	Application

Introduction

The accounting problems discussed in this chapter are concerned with sales or purchases on credit. With credit transactions, the time when a sale or purchase is recognised in the accounts is not the same as the time when cash is eventually received or paid. There is a gap, during which something might happen which results in the amount of cash eventually paid (if any) being different from the original value of the sale or purchase on the invoice.

We shall consider three such events.

- Discounts allowed by the supplier for goods purchased
- Discounts allowed to customers for goods sold
- Bad debts, which arise when a credit customer does not pay the money he owes

Learning outcomes covered in this chapter

- Prepare accounts for sales and purchases
- Explain the difference between and prepare accounts for bad debts and provisions for doubtful debts

Syllabus content covered in this chapter

- Accounting for sales and purchases
- Bad debts and provisions for doubtful debts

1 DISCOUNTS

Types of discount

KEY TERM

A **discount** is a reduction in the price of goods.

1.1 There are two types of discount.

- Trade discount
- Cash discount, or settlement discount

KEY TERM

Trade discount is a reduction in the cost of goods owing to the nature of the trading transaction. It usually results from buying goods in bulk.

For example, a customer is quoted £1 per unit for a particular item, but a lower price of 95 pence per unit for 100 units or more at a time. An important or regular customer can be offered a discount on all goods, regardless of the order size, because the total volume of his purchases over time is so large.

KEY TERM

Cash discount is a reduction in the amount payable to the supplier in return for immediate payment rather than credit.

For example, a supplier charges £1,000 for goods, but offers a discount of 5% if the goods are paid for immediately in cash.

KEY TERM

Settlement discount is similar to cash discount. It is a discount on the price of the goods purchased for credit customers who pay their debts promptly.

For example, a discount of 5% for payment within 30 days of the invoice date.

Accounting for trade discount

1.2 Trade discount is a reduction in the amount of money demanded from a customer at the time of the sale. If trade discount is received by a business, the amount of money payable will be net of discount (ie it will be the normal sales value less the discount). Similarly, if a trade discount is given by a business to a customer, the amount of money due will be after deduction of the discount.

1.3 Trade discount is accounted for as follows.

(a) Trade discount received is deducted from the gross cost of purchases. Purchases are recorded at the net invoiced amount which is after deducting the discount.

(b) Trade discount allowed is deducted from the gross sales price, so that sales are recorded at net invoiced value which is after deducting the discount.

Cash discounts and settlement discounts received

1.4 When a business is given the opportunity to take advantage of a cash discount or a settlement discount for prompt payment, the decision as to whether or not to take the discount is a matter of financing policy, not trading policy, and the benefit is at the time of payment.

1.5 EXAMPLE

A buys goods from B, on the understanding that A will be allowed a period of credit before having to pay for the goods. The terms of the transaction are as follows.

- Date of sale: 1 July 20X6
- Credit period allowed: 30 days
- Invoice price of the goods: £2,000
- Discount offered: 4% for prompt payment

A has a choice between holding on to his money for 30 days and then paying the full £2,000, or paying £2,000 less 4% (£1,920) now. This is a financing decision whether it is worthwhile for A to save £80 by paying its debts sooner.

If A decides to take the cash discount, he will pay £1,920, instead of the invoiced amount £2,000. The cash discount received (£80) will be accounted for in the books of A as follows.

(a) In the trading account, the cost of purchases will be at the invoiced price of £2,000.

(b) In the profit and loss account, the cash discount received is shown as though it were income received.

We would have:

	£
Cost of purchase from B by A (trading account)	2,000
Discount received (income in the P & L account)	(80)
Net cost	1,920

Settlement discounts received are accounted for in exactly the same way as cash discounts received.

Cash discounts and settlement discounts allowed

1.6 The same principle is applied in accounting for cash discounts or settlement discounts allowed to customers. Goods are sold and the offer of a discount is a matter of financing policy for the business, and not trading policy.

1.7 EXAMPLE

X sells goods to Y at a price of £5,000. Y is allowed 60 days' credit before payment, but is also offered a settlement discount of 2% for payment within 10 days of the invoice date. X issues an invoice to Y for £5,000. X has no idea whether or not Y will take advantage of the discount. In trading terms Y is a debtor for £5,000.

If Y subsequently decides to take the discount, he will pay £5,000 less 2% (£4,900) ten days later. The discount allowed (£100) will be accounted for by X as follows.

(a) In the trading account, sales are valued at their full invoice price, £5,000.
(b) In the profit and loss account, the discount allowed will be shown as an expense.

We would have:

	£
Sales (trading account)	5,000
Discounts allowed (P & L account)	(100)
Net sales	4,900

Cash discounts allowed are accounted for in exactly the same way as settlement discounts allowed.

THE MAIN POINTS

(a) Trade discounts are received at the time of sale. Sales and purchases are recorded net of trade discounts (ie after deducting the discount).

(b) Cash and settlement discounts are received at the time of payment. Sales and purchases are recorded gross (ie before deducting the discount) when payment is made or received. Any discount received from suppliers is credited to a discounts received income account and any discount allowed to customers is debited to discounts allowed expense account.

Question 1

You are required to prepare the trading, profit and loss account of Seesaw Timber Merchants for the year ended 31 March 20X6, given the following information.

	£
Goods in stock, 1 April 20X5	18,000
Purchases at gross cost	120,000
Trade discounts received	4,000
Cash and settlement discounts received	1,500
Goods in stock, 31 March 20X6	25,000
Cash sales	34,000
Credit sales at invoice price	150,000
Cash and settlement discounts allowed	8,000
Selling expenses	32,000
Administrative expenses	40,000
Drawings by proprietor, Tim Burr	22,000

Answer

SEESAW TIMBER MERCHANTS
TRADING, PROFIT AND LOSS ACCOUNT
FOR THE YEAR ENDED 31 MARCH 20X6

	£	£
Sales (note 1)		184,000
Opening stocks	18,000	
Purchases (note 2)	116,000	
	134,000	
Less closing stocks	25,000	
Cost of goods sold		109,000
Gross profit		75,000
Discounts received		1,500
		76,500
Expenses		
Selling expenses	32,000	
Administrative expenses	40,000	
Discounts allowed	8,000	
		80,000
Net loss transferred to balance sheet		(3,500)

Notes

1 £(34,000 + 150,000)
2 £(120,000 – 4,000)
3 Drawings are not an expense, but an appropriation of profit.

Question 2

Fill in the blanks.

(a) Fred sells goods on special offer to Bert. The goods usually sell for £100 but Bert pays £90. The double entry to record this sale in Fred's books is:

DEBIT	Debtors/Cash	account	£ 90.	
CREDIT	Purchases	account		£ 90

(b) Fred sells goods to Tom for £100, but agrees to accept £95 if payment is within 30 days. The double entry to record this sale in Fred's books is:

DEBIT	Debtors	account	£ 100	
CREDIT	Purchases	account		£ 100

The double entry to record the receipt of £95 is:

DEBIT	Cash	account	£ 95	
DEBIT	Discounts/allow	account	£ 5	
CREDIT	Debtors	account		£ 10.5

Answer

(a)	DEBIT	Cash account	£90	
	CREDIT	Sales account		£90
(b)	DEBIT	Debtors account	£100	
	CREDIT	Sales account		£100
	Then:			
	DEBIT	Cash account	£95	
	DEBIT	Discounts allowed account	£5	
	CREDIT	Debtors account		£100

2 ACCOUNTING FOR BAD AND DOUBTFUL DEBTS Pilot Paper, May 2001

KEY TERM

A **bad or doubtful debt** is one that may not be paid.

2.1 Credit customers may fail to pay for goods, out of dishonesty or because they have gone bankrupt and cannot pay. Customers in another country may be prevented from paying by the unexpected introduction of foreign exchange control during the credit period. For whatever reason, a business may decide to write the debt off as a 'lost cause'.

Writing off bad debts

2.2 Bad debts written off are accounted for as follows.

(a) Sales are shown at their invoice value in the trading account. The sale has been made, and gross profit earned. The failure to collect the debt is a separate matter.

(b) Bad debts written off are shown as an expense in the profit and loss account.

If a sale of £300 became a bad debt:

	£
Sale (in the trading account)	300
Bad debt written off (expense in the P & L account)	300
Net profit on this transaction	0

2.3 When a debt is written off, the value of the debtor as a current asset falls to zero.

Bad debts written off: ledger accounting entries

2.4 Bad debts written off are posted to a bad debts account.

(a) When a particular debt will not be paid, the customer is no longer a debtor.

DEBIT Bad debts account (expense)
CREDIT Debtors account

(b) At the end of the accounting period, the balance on the bad debts account is transferred to the P & L ledger account (like all other expense accounts).

DEBIT P & L account
CREDIT Bad debts account

2.5 EXAMPLE: BAD DEBTS WRITTEN OFF

At 1 October 20X5 a business had total outstanding debts of £8,600. During the year to 30 September 20X6.

(a) Credit sales amounted to £44,000

(b) Payments from various debtors amounted to £49,000

(c) Two debts, for £180 and £420, are declared bad and these are to be written off

Required

Prepare the debtors account and the bad debts account for the year.

2.6 SOLUTION

DEBTORS

	£		£
Opening balance b/f	8,600	Cash	49,000
Sales	44,000	Bad debts	180
		Bad debts	420
		Closing balance c/d	3,000
	52,600		52,600
Opening balance b/d	3,000		

BAD DEBTS

	£		£
Debtors	180	P & L a/c: bad debts written off	600
Debtors	420		
	600		600

2.7 In the sales ledger, personal accounts of the customers whose debts are bad will be written off. The business should ensure it does not sell goods on credit to those customers again.

Bad debts written off and subsequently paid

2.8 A bad debt which has been written off may be unexpectedly paid. The only accounting problem arising is when a debt written off as bad in one accounting period is subsequently paid in a later period. The amount paid is recorded as income in the profit and loss account of the period in which payment is received. So the entry is:

DEBIT	Cash account
CREDIT	Debts paid previously written off as bad account

2.9 EXAMPLE

A trading, profit and loss account for the Blacksmith's Forge for the year to 31 December 20X5 is prepared from the following information.

	£
Stocks of goods in hand, 1 January 20X5	6,000
Purchases of goods	122,000
Stocks of goods in hand, 31 December 20X5	8,000
Cash sales	100,000
Credit sales	70,000
Discounts allowed	1,200
Discounts received	5,000
Bad debts written off	9,000
Debts paid in 20X5 which were previously written off as bad in 20X4	2,000
Other expenses	31,800

2.10 SOLUTION

BLACKSMITH'S FORGE
TRADING, PROFIT AND LOSS ACCOUNT FOR THE YEAR ENDED 31.12.20X5

	£	£
Sales		170,000
Opening stock	6,000	
Purchases	122,000	
	128,000	
Less closing stock	8,000	
Cost of goods sold		120,000
Gross profit		50,000
Add: discounts received		5,000
debts paid, previously written off as bad		2,000
		57,000
Expenses		
Discounts allowed	1,200	
Bad debts written off	9,000	
Other expenses	31,800	
		42,000
Net profit		15,000

THE MAIN POINTS

(a) To write off a bad debt:

DEBIT	Bad debts expense account
CREDIT	Debtors account

(b) To record a receipt from a debt previously written off:

DEBIT	Cash account
CREDIT	Debts paid, previously written off as bad account

A provision for doubtful debts

2.11 When bad debts are written off, specific debts owed to the business are identified as unlikely ever to be collected.

However, because of the risks involved in selling goods on credit, a certain percentage of outstanding debts at any time are unlikely to be collected. Although it might be estimated that 5% of debts will be bad, the business will not know which specific debts are bad.

2.12 When a business expects bad debts, it can make a provision for doubtful debts. The business is more likely to avoid claiming profits which subsequently fail to materialise because of bad debts (the prudence concept).

THE MAIN POINTS

(a) When a provision is first made, the amount is charged as an expense in the profit and loss account.

(b) When a provision already exists, but is subsequently increased in size, the amount of the **increase** in provision is charged as an expense in the profit and loss account.

(c) When a provision already exists, but is subsequently reduced in size, the amount of the **decrease** in provision is recorded as an item of 'income' in the profit and loss account.

2.13 The balance sheet must also be adjusted to show a provision for doubtful debts. **The value of debtors in the balance sheet must be shown after deducting the provision for doubtful debts.** This is because the net realisable value of all the debtors of the business is estimated to be less than their 'sales value'.

2.14 EXAMPLE

A business has debtors of £50,000 and creates a provision for doubtful debts at 30 June 20X5 of 5% (£2,500). Although total debtors are £50,000, eventual payment of only £47,500 is expected. What will be shown in the profit and loss account and balance sheet?

2.15 SOLUTION

(a) In the P & L account, the provision of £2,500 will be shown as an expense.

(b) In the balance sheet, debtors will be shown as

	£
Total debtors at 30 June 20X5	50,000
Less provision for doubtful debts	2,500
	47,500

2.16 Provision for doubtful debts: ledger accounting entries

The procedure is to leave the total debtors balances completely untouched, but to open up a provision account by the following entries.

DEBIT	Doubtful debts account (expense)
CREDIT	Provision for doubtful debts

When preparing a balance sheet, remember the credit balance on the provision account is deducted from the total debit balances in the debtors ledger.

2.17 **In subsequent years**, adjustments may be needed to the amount of the provision. The procedure to be followed then is as follows.

(a) Calculate the new provision required.

(b) Compare it with the existing balance on the provision account (ie the balance b/f from the previous accounting period).

(c) Calculate increase or decrease required.

(i) If a higher provision is required, post the **increase** as follows.

DEBIT	P & L account
CREDIT	Provision for doubtful debts

(ii) If a lower provision is needed, post the **decrease** as follows.

DEBIT	Provision for doubtful debts
CREDIT	P & L account

Exam focus point

If dealing with a movement on a provision account, be careful to include in the profit and loss account only the increase or decrease in the provision. A common error is to include the total provision figure.

2.18 EXAMPLE: ACCOUNTING ENTRIES FOR PROVISION FOR DOUBTFUL DEBTS

Alex Gullible has total debtors' balances outstanding at 31 December 20X2 of £28,000. He believes that about 1% of these balances will not be collected and wishes to make an appropriate provision. Before now, he has not made any provision for doubtful debts.

On 31 December 20X3 his debtors balances amount to £40,000. His experience during the year has convinced him that a provision of 5% should be made.

What accounting entries should Alex make on 31 December 20X2 and 31 December 20X3, and what figures for debtors will appear in his balance sheets as at those dates?

2.19 SOLUTION

At 31 December 20X2

Provision required = 1% × £28,000 = £280

Alex will make the following entries.

DEBIT	P & L account (doubtful debts)	£280	
CREDIT	Provision for doubtful debts		£280

In the balance sheet debtors will appear as follows under current assets.

	£
Sales ledger balances	28,000
Less provision for doubtful debts	280
	27,720

At 31 December 20X3

Following the procedure described above, Alex will calculate as follows.

	£
Provision required now (5% × £40,000)	2,000
Existing provision	(280)
∴ Additional provision required	1,720

He will make the following entries.

DEBIT	P & L account (doubtful debts)	£1,720	
CREDIT	Provision for doubtful debts		£1,720

The provision account will by now appear as follows.

PROVISION FOR DOUBTFUL DEBTS

		£			£
20X2			*20X2*		
31 Dec	Balance c/d	280	31 Dec	P & L account	280
20X3			*20X3*		
31 Dec	Balance c/d	2,000	1 Jan	Balance b/d	280
			31 Dec	P & L account	1,720
		2,000			2,000
			20X4		
			1 Jan	Balance b/d	2,000

For the balance sheet debtors will be valued as follows.

	£
Sales ledger balances	40,000
Less provision for doubtful debts	2,000
	38,000

2.20 In practice, it is unnecessary to show the total debtors balances and the provision as separate items in the balance sheet. A balance sheet would normally show only the net figure (£27,720 in 20X2, £38,000 in 20X3).

Question 3

Corin Flakes owns and runs the Aerobic Health Foods Shop in Dundee. He commenced trading on 1 January 20X1. Customers are allowed to purchase up to £200 of goods on credit but must repay a certain proportion of their outstanding debt every month.

This credit system gives rise to a large number of bad debts, and Corin Flake's results for his first three years of operations are as follows.

Year to 31 December 20X1	
Gross profit	£27,000
Bad debts written off	£8,000
Debts owed by customers as at 31 December 20X1	£40,000
Provision for doubtful debts	2½% of outstanding debtors
Other expenses	£20,000

Year to 31 December 20X2	
Gross profit	£45,000
Bad debts written off	£10,000
Debts owed by customers as at 31 December 20X2	£50,000
Provision for doubtful debts	2½% of outstanding debtors
Other expenses	£28,750
Year to 31 December 20X3	
Gross profit	£60,000
Bad debts written off	£11,000
Debts owed by customers as at 31 December 20X3	£30,000
Provision for doubtful debts	3% of outstanding debtors
Other expenses	£32,850

Required

For each of these three years, prepare the profit and loss account of the business, and state the value of debtors appearing in the balance sheet as at 31 December.

Answer

AEROBIC HEALTH FOOD SHOP
PROFIT AND LOSS ACCOUNTS FOR THE YEARS ENDED 31 DECEMBER

	20X1		*20X2*		*20X3*	
	£	£	£	£	£	£
Gross profit		27,000		45,000		60,000
Reduction in provision for doubtful debts*						350
						60,350
Expenses:						
Bad debts written off	8,000		10,000		11,000	
Increase in provision for doubtful debts*	1,000		250		-	
Other expenses	20,000		28,750		32,850	
		29,000		39,000		43,850
Net(loss)/profit		(2,000)		6,000		16,500

*At 1 January 20X1 the provision for doubtful debts was nil. At 31 December 20X1 the provision required was 2½% of £40,000 = £1,000. The increase in the provision is therefore £1,000. At 31 December 20X2 the provision required was 2½% of £50,000 = £1,250. The 20X1 provision must therefore be increased by £250. At 31 December 20X3 the provision required is 3% × £30,000 = £900. The 20X2 provision is therefore reduced by £350.

VALUE OF DEBTORS IN THE BALANCE SHEET

	As at 31.12.20X1	*As at 31.12.20X2*	*As at 31.12.20X3*
	£	£	£
Total value of debtors	40,000	50,000	30,000
Less provision for doubtful debts	1,000	1,250	900
Balance sheet value	39,000	48,750	29,100

Question 4

Horace Goodrunning decides to make a provision for doubtful debts of 2% of outstanding debtors at the balance sheet date from 28 February 20X6. On 28 February 20X8, Horace decides that the provision has been over-estimated and he reduces it to 1% of outstanding debtors. Outstanding debtors balances at the various balance sheet dates are as follows.

	£
28.2.20X6	15,200
28.2.20X7	17,100
28.2.20X8	21,400

You are required to show extracts from the following accounts for each of the three years above.

(a) Debtors
(b) Provision for doubtful debts
(c) Profit and loss

Show how debtors would appear in the balance sheet at the end of each year.

Answer

The entries for the three years are denoted by (a), (b) and (c) in each account.

DEBTORS (EXTRACT)

			£			£
(a)	28.2.20X6	Balance	15,200			
(b)	28.2.20X7	Balance	17,100			
(c)	28.2.20X8	Balance	21,400			

PROVISION FOR DOUBTFUL DEBTS

			£			£
(a)	28.2.20X6	Balance c/d		28.2.20X6	Profit and loss	304
		(2% of 15,200)	304			
			304			304
(b)	28.2.20X7	Balance c/d		1.3.20X6	Balance b/d	304
		(2% of 17,100)	342	28.2.20X7	Profit and loss (note (i))	38
			342			342
(c)	28.2.20X8	Profit and loss (note (ii))	128	1.3.20X7	Balance b/d	342
	28.2.20X8	Balance c/d				
		(1% of 21,400)	214			
			342			342
				1.3.20X8	Balance b/d	214

PROFIT AND LOSS (EXTRACT)

		£
28.2.20X6	Provision for doubtful debts	304
28.2.20X7	Provision for doubtful debts	38
28.2.20X8	Provision for doubtful debts	(128)

Notes

(i) The increase in the provision is £(342 - 304) = £38
(ii) The decrease in the provision is £(342 - 214) = £128
(iii) We calculate the net debtors figure for inclusion in the balance sheet as follows.

	20X6	*20X7*	*20X8*
	£	£	£
Current assets			
Debtors	15,200	17,100	21,400
Less provision for doubtful debts	304	342	214
	14,896	16,758	21,186

Exam focus point

In May 2001, bad and doubtful debts were examined in both Sections A and B.

Other provisions

KEY TERM

Companies legislation defines a **provision** as 'any amount written off or retained by way of providing for depreciation, renewals or diminution in value of assets or retained by way of providing for any known liability of which the amount cannot be determined with substantial accuracy'.

2.21 For most businesses, by far the largest provision in their accounts is the provision for depreciation which is described in a later chapter.

You should now use what you have learned to produce a solution to the following exercise, which involves preparing a trading, profit and loss account and balance sheet.

Question 5

The financial affairs of Newbegin Tools prior to the commencement of trading were as follows.

NEWBEGIN TOOLS
BALANCE SHEET AS AT 1 AUGUST 20X5

	£	£
Fixed assets		
Motor vehicle	2,000	
Shop fittings	3,000	
		5,000
Current assets		
Stocks	12,000	
Cash	1,000	
	13,000	
Current liabilities		
Bank overdraft	2,000	
Trade creditors	4,000	
	6,000	
Net current assets		7,000
		12,000
Financed by		
Capital		12,000

At the end of six months the business had made the following transactions.

(a) Goods were purchased on credit at a gross amount of £10,000.

(b) Trade discount received was 2% on this gross amount and there was a settlement discount received of 5% on settling debts to suppliers of £8,000. These were the only payments to suppliers in the period.

(c) Closing stocks of goods were valued at £5,450.

(d) Cash sales and credit sales together totalled £27,250.

(e) Outstanding debtors balances at 31 January 20X6 amounted to £3,250 of which £250 were to be written off. A further provision for doubtful debts is to be made amounting to 2% of the remaining outstanding debtors.

(f) Cash payments were made in respect of the following expenses.

		£
(i)	Stationery, postage and wrapping	500
(ii)	Telephone charges	200
(iii)	Electricity	600
(iv)	Cleaning and refreshments	150

(g) Cash drawings by the proprietor, Alf Newbegin, amounted to £6,000.

(h) The outstanding overdraft balance as at 1 August 20X5 was paid off. Interest charges and bank charges on the overdraft amounted to £40.

Prepare the trading, profit and loss account of Newbegin Tools for the six months to 31 January 20X6 and a balance sheet as at that date.

Answer

TRADING AND PROFIT AND LOSS ACCOUNT
FOR THE SIX MONTHS ENDED 31 JANUARY 20X6

	£	£
Sales		27,250
Opening stocks	12,000	
Purchases (note (a))	9,800	
	21,800	
Less closing stocks	5,450	
Cost of goods sold		16,350
Gross profit		10,900
Discounts received (note (b))		400
		11,300
Electricity (note (c))	600	
Stationery, postage and wrapping	500	
Bad debts written off	250	
Provision for doubtful debts (note (d))	60	
Telephone charges	200	
Cleaning and refreshments	150	
Interest and bank charges	40	
		1,800
Net profit		9,500

Notes

(a) Purchases at cost £10,000 less 2% trade discount.

(b) 5% of £8,000 = £400.

(c) Expenses are grouped into sales and distribution expenses (here assumed to be electricity, stationery and postage, bad debts and provision for doubtful debts) administration expenses (here assumed to be telephone charges and cleaning) and finance charges.

(d) 2% of £3,000 = £60.

The preparation of a balance sheet is not so easy, because we must calculate the value of creditors and cash in hand.

(a) Creditors as at 31 January 20X6

The amount owing to creditors is the sum of the amount owing at the beginning of the period, plus the cost of purchases during the period (net of all discounts), less the payments already made for purchases.

	£
Creditors as at 1 August 20X5	4,000
Add purchases during the period, net of trade discount	9,800
	13,800
Less settlement discounts received	(400)
	13,400
Less payments to creditors during the period*	(7,600)
	5,800

* £8,000 less cash discount of £400.

(b) Cash at bank and in hand at 31 January 20X6

You need to identify cash payments received and cash payments made.

		£
(i)	*Cash received from sales*	
	Total sales in the period	27,250
	Add debtors as at 1 August 20X5	0
		27,250
	Less unpaid debts as at 31 January 20X6	3,250
	Cash received	24,000

		£
(ii)	*Cash paid*	
	Trade creditors (see (a))	7,600
	Stationery, postage and wrapping	500
	Telephone charges	200
	Electricity	600
	Cleaning and refreshments	150
	Bank charges and interest	40
	Bank overdraft repaid	2,000
	Drawings by proprietor	6,000
		17,090

Note. It is easy to forget some of these payments, especially drawings.

		£
(iii)	Cash in hand at 1 August 20X5	1,000
	Cash received in the period	24,000
		25,000
	Cash paid in the period	(17,090)
	Cash at bank and in hand as at 31 January 20X6	7,910

(c) When bad debts are written off, the value of outstanding debtors must be reduced by the amount written off. Debtors in the balance sheet will be valued at £3,250 less bad debts £250 and the provision for doubtful debts of £60 - ie at £2,940.

(d) Fixed assets should be depreciated. However, in this exercise depreciation has been ignored.

NEWBEGIN TOOLS
BALANCE SHEET AS AT 31 JANUARY 20X6

	£	£
Fixed assets		
Motor vehicles	2,000	
Shop fittings	3,000	
		5,000
Current assets		
Stocks	5,450	
Debtors	2,940	
Cash	7,910	
		16,300
		21,300
Current liabilities		
Trade creditors		(5,800)
		15,500
Capital		
Capital at 1 August 20X5		12,000
Net profit for the period		9,500
		21,500
Less drawings		6,000
Capital at 31 January 20X6		15,500

The bank overdraft has now been repaid and is therefore not shown.

Chapter roundup

- In this chapter, the following terms were defined.
  - *Trade discount* is a reduction in the catalogue price of an article, given by a wholesaler or manufacturer to a retailer. It is often given in return for bulk purchase orders. The sale or purchase is recorded net.
  - *Cash discount* is a reduction in the amount payable for the purchase of goods or services in return for payment in cash rather than taking credit. The sale or purchase is recorded gross.
  - *Settlement discount* is a reduction in the amount payable for the purchase of goods or services in return for prompt payment within an agreed credit period. The sale or purchase is recorded gross.
  - *Bad debts* are specific debts owed to a business which are never going to be paid.
  - *Doubtful debts* are debts which might become bad in the future but are not yet bad.
  - A *provision* is an amount written off to provide for depreciation or the fall in value of an asset, or to provide for any known liability of uncertain value. The amount is written off by:
    - charging the amount of the extra provision as an expense in the P & L account
    - reducing the value of the asset in the balance sheet by the amount of the provision
- We looked at the accounting treatment of each of these items.
  - *Trade discounts received* are deducted from the cost of purchases. *Cash and settlement discounts received* are included as 'other income' of the period in the profit and loss account. Similarly, cash and settlement discounts allowed are shown as expenses in the profit and loss account.
  - *Bad debts written off* are an expense in the profit and loss account.
- An *increase* in the provision for doubtful debts is an expense in the profit and loss account whereas a decrease in the provision for doubtful debts is shown as 'other income' in the P & L account.
- *Debtors* are valued in the balance sheet after deducting any provision for doubtful debts.

Quick quiz

1 What is a trade discount received?

A An allowance given by a supplier to reduce the value of an invoice received.
B A reduction in invoice price as a result of (eg) buying in quantity.
C A suppliers response when a debit note is received.
D A discount for prompt payment.

2 Sam buys goods invoiced at £250 but is offered a 4% discount if she pays within 30 days which she does. What are the entries to record this payment in her books?

DEBIT ______________________ account £__________

CREDIT ______________________ account £__________

CREDIT ______________________ account £__________

3 The entry to record a bad debt is:

DEBIT ______________________ account

CREDIT ______________________ account

4 The entry to record money received from a debt previously written off is:

DEBIT ______________________ account

CREDIT ______________________ account

5 The entry to record the creation of a provision for doubtful debts is:

DEBIT ______________________ account

CREDIT ______________________ account

6 The entry to record an increase in a provision for doubtful debts is:

DEBIT ______________________ account

CREDIT ______________________ account

7 Which of the fundamental accounting concepts are being applied when a provision for bad debts is erected?

A Accruals and going concern
B Accruals and consistency
C Accruals and prudence
D Going concern and prudence

8 Y plc has a provision for doubtful of £20,000, this is to be changed to 3% of the sales ledger balance of £500,000. Which of the following entries records the transaction?

A	Dr	P&L a/c	£5,000
	Cr	Sales ledger control a/c	
B	Dr	Provision for bad debts a/c	£5,000
	Cr	P&L a/c	
C	Dr	P&L a/c	£5,000
	Cr	Provision for bad debts	
D	Dr	P&L a/c	£15,000
	Cr	Provision for bad debts	

Answers to quick quiz

1 B Correct

A Incorrect. Trade discounts are deducted from invoice prices before a purchase invoice is finalised.

C The response should be to issue a credit note if the debit note is accepted.

D This is a cash discount.

2	DEBIT	Creditor account	£250	
	CREDIT	Cash account		£240
	CREDIT	Discounts received (income) account		£10

3 DEBIT Bad debts expense account
CREDIT Debtors account

4 DEBIT Cash account
CREDIT Debts paid previously written off account

5 DEBIT Bad debts expense account
CREDIT Doubtful debts provision account

6 DEBIT Bad debts expense account
CREDIT Doubtful debts provision account

7 C This is correct because the accruals or matching concept requires bad debt expenses to be matched against related sales revenue on a prudent basis.

A Going concern is always presumed unless there are contrary indications.

B As the provision has just been created, there are no prior year provisions against which consistency can be judged.

D Incorrect for reasons stated in above explanations.

8 B Correct: the required provision is 3% of the sales ledger balance £500,000 = £15,000. So the required reduction is £5,000.

A Incorrect; this entry will write off debtor balances not make a provision.

C Incorrect; this entry will increase the provision.

D Incorrect; this entry will increase the provision a/c by the full amount of the provision required.

Now try the questions below from the Exam Question Bank

Number	Level	Marks	Time
25	Exam	15	27 mins
26	Exam	2	3 mins
27	Exam	2	3 mins

Chapter 10

ACCOUNTING FOR STOCKS

Topic List		Syllabus reference	Ability required
1	Accounting for opening and closing stocks	(iv)	Application
2	Stocktaking	(iv)	Application
3	Valuing stocks	(iv)	Application

Introduction

Stock is one of the most important assets in a company's balance sheet. As we have seen it also affects the profit and loss account.

In an earlier chapter, we saw that in order to calculate gross profit it is necessary to work out the cost of goods sold, and in order to calculate the cost of goods sold it is necessary to have values for the opening stock and closing stock.

You should remember that the trading part of a profit and loss account includes the following:

	£
Opening stock	X
Plus purchases	X
Less closing stock	(X)
Equals cost of goods sold	X

However this formula hides three basic problems.

(a) How do you manage to get a precise **count of stock** in hand at any one time?
(b) Once it has been counted, how do you **value** the stock?
(c) Assuming the stock is given a value, how does the **double entry** bookkeeping for stock work?

The purpose of this chapter is to answer all three of these questions. In order to make the presentation a little easier to follow, it is convenient to tackle the last question first.

Learning outcomes covered in this chapter

- Explain, calculate and prepare accounts for stock

Syllabus content covered in this chapter

- Accounting for stocks (excluding long term contract work-in-progress)
- Methods of stock valuation (FIFO, LIFO and average cost)

1 ACCOUNTING FOR OPENING AND CLOSING STOCKS

Ledger accounting for stocks

1.1 A stock account must be kept. This stock account is only ever used at the end of an accounting period, when the business counts up and values the stock in hand (a stocktake). To record this stock value:

DEBIT	Stock account (closing stock value)	£X	
CREDIT	Trading account		£X

1.2 The debit balance on stock account represents an asset, which will be shown as part of current assets in the balance sheet, and the credit in the trading account is **closing stock**, in cost of sales.

1.3 Closing stock at the end of one period becomes opening stock at the start of the next period. The stock account remains unchanged until the end of the next period, when the value of opening stock is taken to the trading account.

DEBIT	Trading account	£X	
CREDIT	Stock account (value of opening stock)		£X

Question 1

A business is established with capital of £2,000 and this amount is paid into a business bank account by the proprietor. During the first year's trading, the following transactions occurred:

	£
Purchases of goods for resale, on credit	4,300
Payments to trade creditors	3,600
Sales, all on credit	4,000
Payments from debtors	3,200
Fixed assets purchased for cash	1,500
Other expenses, all paid in cash	900

The bank has provided an overdraft facility of up to £3,000.

All 'other expenses' relate to the current year (ie no accruals or prepayments).

Closing stocks of goods are valued at £1,800. (This is the first year of the business, so there are no opening stocks.)

Ignore depreciation and drawings.

Required

Prepare the ledger accounts, a trading, profit and loss account for the year and a balance sheet as at the end of the year.

Answer

CASH

	£		£
Capital	2,000	Trade creditors	3,600
Debtors	3,200	Fixed assets	1,500
Balance c/d	800	Other expenses	900
	6,000		6,000
		Balance b/d	800

CAPITAL

	£		£
Balance c/d	2,600	Cash	2,000
		P & L a/c	600
	2,600		2,600
		Balance b/d	2,600

TRADE CREDITORS

	£		£
Cash	3,600	Purchases	4,300
Balance c/d	700		
	4,300		4,300
		Balance b/d	700

PURCHASES ACCOUNT

	£		£
Trade creditors	4,300	Trading a/c	4,300

FIXED ASSETS

	£		£
Cash	1,500	Balance c/d	1,500
Balance b/d	1,500		

SALES

	£		£
Trading a/c	4,000	Debtors	4,000

DEBTORS

	£		£
Sales	4,000	Cash	3,200
		Balance c/d	800
	4,000		4,000
Balance b/d	800		

OTHER EXPENSES

	£		£
Cash	900	P & L a/c	900

TRADING, PROFIT AND LOSS ACCOUNT

	£		£
Purchases account	4,300	Sales	4,000
Gross profit c/d	1,500	Closing stock (stock account)	1,800
	5,800		5,800
Other expenses	900	Gross profit b/d	1,500
Net profit (transferred to capital account)	600		
	1,500		1,500

STOCK ACCOUNT

	£		£
Trading account (closing stock)	1,800	B/S	1,800

BALANCE SHEET AS AT THE END OF THE PERIOD

	£	£
Fixed assets		1,500
Current assets		
Goods in stock	1,800	
Debtors	800	
	2,600	
Current liabilities		
Bank overdraft	800	
Trade creditors	700	
	1,500	
Net assets		1,100
		2,600
Capital		
At start of period		2,000
Profit for period		600
		2,600

Make sure you understand the entries. The balance on the stock account was £1,800, which appears in the balance sheet as a current asset. The transfer from the stock account to the trading account is the closing stock in the calculation of cost of sales. The £1,800 closing stock was the only entry in the stock account - there was no figure for opening stock.

If there had been, it would be eliminated by transferring it as a debit balance to the trading account.

DEBIT Trading account (with value of opening stock)
CREDIT Stock account (with value of opening stock)

The debit in the trading account would then have increased the cost of sales, ie opening stock is added to purchases in calculating cost of sales. Remember the formula: opening stock + purchases – closing stock = cost of sales.

1.4 EXAMPLE

A trader starts a business on 1 January 20X1.

On 31 December 20X1 stock is £2,000
31 December 20X2 stock is £2,500
31 December 20X3 stock is £3,000

Draw up the stock account for 20X1,20X2 and 20X3.

1.5 SOLUTION

STOCK ACCOUNT

		£			£
31.12.X1	Trading a/c (closing stock)	2,000	31.12.X1	Balance c/d	2,000
		2,000			2,000
1.1.X2	Balance b/d	2,000	31.12.X2	Trading a/c (opening stock)	2,000
31.12.X2	Trading a/c (closing stock)	2,500	31.12.X2	Balance c/d	2,500
		4,500			4,500
1.1X3	Balance b/d	2,500	31.12.X3	Trading a/c (opening stock)	2,500
31.12.X3	Trading a/c (closing stock)	3,000	31.12.X3	Balance c/d	3,000
		5,500			5,500
1.1.X4	Balance b/d	3,000			

THE MAIN POINTS

(a) Closing stock is an asset (a debit) in the balance sheet and a credit in the trading account.

(b) Opening stock is a debit in the trading account.

(c) At the year end

(i) Debit trading account / Credit stock account } with opening stock value

(ii) Debit stock account / Credit trading account } with closing stock valuation

(d) The balance on the stock account is the figure for the balance sheet.

2 STOCKTAKING

KEY TERM

Stocktaking means counting and valuing stock at a given moment.

2.1 The continuous nature of trading activity may cause a problem in that stock movements may continue during the physical stocktake. Two possible solutions are as follows.

- Close down the business while the count takes place
- Keep detailed records of stock movements during the course of the stocktake

2.2 Closing down the business for a short period for a stocktake (eg over a weekend or at Christmas) is considerably easier than trying to keep detailed records of stock movements during a stocktake. So most businesses prefer that method unless they happen to keep detailed records of stock movements anyway (for example, because they wish to keep strict control on stock movements).

2.3 In more complicated cases, an alternative approach to establishing stock quantities is to maintain continuous stock records. This means that a card is kept for every item of stock, showing receipts and issues from the stores, and a running total. A few stock items are counted each day to make sure the record cards are correct. This is called a 'continuous' stocktake because it is spread out over the year.

3 VALUING STOCKS — Pilot Paper, May 2001

THE BASIC RULE

Stock is valued in accordance with the prudence concept at the lower of cost and net realisable value.

Remember that net realisable value is what you can sell the stock for less any costs of sale such as advertising.

Applying the basic valuation rule

3.1 If a business has many stock items, on hand the comparison of cost and NRV should be carried out for each item separately. It is not sufficient to compare the total cost of all stock items with their total NRV.

3.2 EXAMPLE

A company has four items of stock and their cost and NRVs are as follows.

Stock item	*Cost*	*NRV*	*Lower of cost/NRV*
	£	£	£
1	27	32	27
2	14	8	8
3	43	55	43
4	29	40	29
	113	135	107

What is the value of closing stock?

3.3 SOLUTION

It would be incorrect to compare total costs (£113) with total NRV (£135) and to state stocks at £113 in the balance sheet. The company can foresee a loss of £6 on item 2 and this should be recognised. By performing the cost/NRV comparison for each item separately the prudent valuation of £107 can be derived. This is the value which should appear in the balance sheet.

3.4 However, for a company with large amounts of stock this procedure may be impracticable. In this case it is acceptable to group similar items into categories and perform the comparison of cost and NRV category by category, rather than item by item.

Exam focus point

There were 10 marks in Section C of the May 2001 exam, for explaining stock valuations.

Determining the purchase cost

3.5 Stock may be raw materials or components bought from suppliers, finished goods which have been made by the business but not yet sold, or work in the process of production, but only part-completed (this is called work in progress or WIP). It will simplify matters, however, if we think about the cost of purchased raw materials and components.

3.6 A business may be continually purchasing a particular component. As each consignment is received from suppliers they are stored in the appropriate bin, where they will be mingled with previous consignments. When the storekeeper issues components to production, he will simply pull out the nearest components to hand, which may have arrived in the latest consignment or in an earlier consignment or in several different consignments.

3.7 There are several techniques to attribute cost to the components.

KEY TERMS

(a) **FIFO (first in, first out).** We assume that components are used in the order in which they are received from suppliers, so that the issue is part of the oldest consignment still unused and is costed accordingly, stocks are themselves recent receipts.

(b) **Average cost.** Each component in the bin is assumed to have been purchased at the weighted average price of all components in the bin at that moment.

(c) **LIFO (last in, first out).** Components issued to production formed part of the most recent delivery, stocks are the oldest receipts.

(d) **Standard cost.** A pre-determined standard cost is applied to all stock items. If this standard price differs from prices actually paid during the period, the difference is written off as a 'variance' in the profit and loss account.

(e) **Replacement cost.** It is assumed that the cost at which a stock unit was purchased is the amount it would cost to replace it.

Exam focus point

Only the first three methods, FIFO, LIFO and average cost are examinable in your syllabus. In the May 2001 exam Section C had a 10 mark question on the effect on the financial statements of using FIFO rather than LIFO.

3.8 It is worth mentioning here that if you are preparing **financial** accounts you would normally expect to use FIFO or average costs for the balance sheet valuation of stock. SSAP 9 specifically discourages the use of LIFO and replacement costs. (CA 85 allows any method the directors think appropriate, so long as, under the historical cost accounting rules, stock is stated at production cost or purchase price.)

3.9 EXAMPLE

To illustrate the two pricing methods, the following transactions will be used in each case.

TRANSACTIONS DURING MAY 20X3

	Quantity	*Unit cost*	*Total cost*
	Units	£	£
Opening balance 1 May	100	2.00	200
Receipts 3 May	400	2.10	840
Issues 4 May	200		
Receipts 9 May	300	2.12	636
Issues 11 May	400		
Receipts 18 May	100	2.40	240
Issues 20 May	100		
Closing balance 31 May	200		
			1,916

Receipts mean goods received into store and issues the issue of goods from store.

How would issues and closing stock be valued using the following bases.

(a) FIFO?

(b) Average cost?

FIFO (first in, first out)

KEY TERM

FIFO assumes that materials are issued out of stock in the order in which they were delivered into stock, ie issues are priced at the cost of the earliest delivery remaining in stock.

3.10 SOLUTION

The cost of issues and closing stock value in the example, using FIFO would be as follows.

Date of issue	*Quantity*	*Value issued*	*Cost of issues*	
	Units		£	£
4 May	200	100 at £2	200	
		100 at £2.10	210	
				410

Date of issue	*Quantity* Units	*Value issued*	*Cost of issues* £	£
11 May	400	300 at £2.10	630	
		100 at £2.12	212	
				842
20 May	100	100 at £2.12		212
				1,464
Closing stock value	200	100 at £2.12	212	
		100 at £2.40	240	
				452
				1,916

Note that the cost of materials issued plus the value of closing stock equals the cost of purchases plus the value of opening stock (£1,916).

Average cost

KEY TERM

The **cumulative weighted average pricing method** calculates a weighted average price for all units in stock. Issues are priced at this average cost, and the balance of stock remaining would have the same unit valuation.

3.11 A new weighted average price is calculated whenever a new delivery of materials into store is received. This is the key feature of cumulative weighted average pricing.

3.12 SOLUTION CONTINUED

In our example, issue costs and closing stock values would be as follows.

Date	*Received* Units	*Issued* Units	*Balance* Units	*Total stock value* £	*Unit cost* £	*Price of issue* £
Opening stock			100	200	2.00	
3 May	400			840	2.10	
			500	1,040	2.08 *	
4 May		200		(416)	2.08 **	416
			300	624	2.08	
9 May	300			636	2.12	
			600	1,260	2.10 *	
11 May		400		(840)	2.10 **	840
			200	420	2.10	
18 May	100			240	2.40	
			300	660	2.20 *	
20 May		100		(220)	2.20 **	220
						1,476
Closing stock value			200	440	2.20	440
						1,916

* A new unit cost of stock is calculated whenever a new receipt of materials occurs.

** Whenever stocks are issued, the unit value of the items issued is the current weighted average cost per unit at the time of the issue.

For this method too, the cost of materials issued plus the value of closing stock equals the cost of purchases plus the value of opening stock (£1,916).

3.13 EXAMPLE: STOCK VALUATIONS AND PROFIT

On 1 November 20X2 a company held 300 units of finished goods item No 9639 in stock. These were valued at £12 each. During November 20X2 three batches of finished goods were received into store from the production department as follows.

Date	*Units received*	*Production cost per unit*
10 November	400	£12.50
20 November	400	£14
25 November	400	£15

Goods sold out of stock during November were as follows.

Date	*Units sold*	*Sale price per unit*
14 November	500	£20
21 November	500	£20
28 November	100	£20

What was the profit from selling stock item 9639 in November 20X2, applying the following principles of stock valuation.

(a) FIFO
(b) Cumulative weighted average costing
(c) LIFO

Ignore administration, sales and distribution costs.

3.14 SOLUTION

(a) FIFO

Date	*Issue costs*	*Issue cost Total* £	*Closing stock* £
14 November	300 units × £12 plus		
	200 units × £12.50	6,100	
21 November	200 units × £12.50 plus		
	300 units × £14	6,700	
28 November	100 units × £14	1,400	
Closing stock	400 units × £15		6,000
		14,200	6,000

(b) Cumulative weighted average costs

		Unit cost	*Balance in stock* £	*Total cost of issues* £	*Closing stock* £
1 November	Opening stock 300	12	3,600		
10 November	400	12.50	5,000		
	700	12.286	8,600		
14 November	500	12.286	6,143	6,143	
	200	12.286	2,457		
20 November	400	14	5,600		
	600	13.428	8,057		
21 November	500	13.428	6,714	6,714	
	100	13.428	1,343		
25 November	400	15	6,000		
	500	14.686	7,343		
28 November	100	14.686	1,469	1,469	
30 November	400	14.686	5,874	14,326	5,874

(c) LIFO

			Balance in stock £	Total cost of issues £	Closing stock £
1 November		Opening stock 300	3,600		
10 November		400	5,000		
		700	8,600		
14 November	(400: 10/11 + 100 o/s)	500	6,200	6,200	
		200	2,400		
20 November		400	5,600		
		600	8,000		
21 November	(400: 20/11 + 100 o/s)	500	6,800	6,800	
		100	1,200		
25 November		400	6,000		
		500	7,200		
28 November	(100: 25/11)	100	1,500	1,500	
30 November	(300: 25/11 + 100 o/s)	400	5,700	14,500	5,700

	FIFO £	Weighted average £	LIFO £
Opening stock	3,600	3,600	3,600
Cost of production	16,600	16,600	16,600
	20,200	20,200	20,200
Closing stock	6,000	5,874	5,700
Cost of sales	14,200	14,326	14,500
Sales (1,100 × £20)	22,000	22,000	22,000
Profit	7,800	7,674	7,500

3.15 Different stock valuations have produced different cost of sales figures, and therefore different profits.

3.16 The profit differences are only temporary. In our example, the opening stock in December 20X2 will be £6,000, £5,874 or £5,700, depending on the stock valuation used. Different opening stock values will affect the cost of sales and profits in December, so that in the long run inequalities in costs of sales each month will even themselves out.

Question 2

In times of inflation, changing from a FIFO method of stock valuation to a LIFO is likely to:

A Increase reported profit
B Reduce reported profit
C Have no effect on reported profit
D Have an unpredictable effect on reported profit

Answer

B is correct. Under FIFO, stock was the most recent purchases. Under LIFO, stock is the oldest (and cheapest) purchases. Thus, changing to LIFO puts up the cost of sales and reduces reported profits.

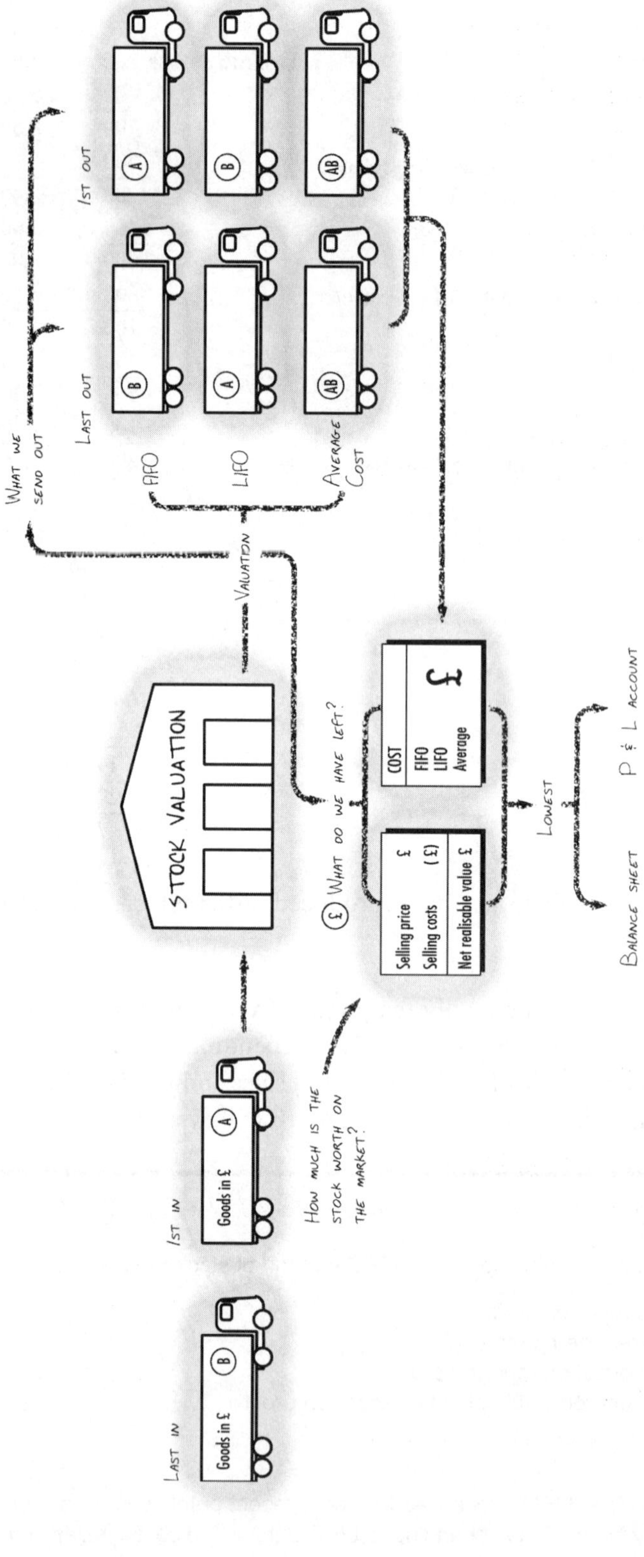
Last in
Goods in £
B
1st in
Goods in £
A
How much is the stock worth on the market?
Stock valuation
Valuation
What we send out
FIFO
LIFO
Average cost
Last out
1st out
What do we have left?
Selling price £
Selling costs (£)
Net realisable value £
COST
FIFO
LIFO
Average
£
Lowest
Balance sheet
P & L account

Chapter roundup

- The quantity of stocks held at the year end is established by means of a physical count of stock in an annual stocktaking exercise, or by a 'continuous' stocktake.
- The value of these stocks is then calculated, taking the lower of cost and net realisable value for each separate item or group of stock items.
- In order to value the stocks, some rule of thumb must be adopted. The possibilities include FIFO, LIFO, average costs and standard costs. But remember that in *financial* accounts FIFO or average cost should normally be used. For the purposes of your examination, you will need to know these two methods and LIFO.
- NRV is the selling price less all costs to completion and less selling costs.
- Cost comprises purchase costs and costs of conversion.
- The value of closing stocks is accounted for in the nominal ledger by debiting a stock account and crediting the trading account at the end of an accounting period. The stock will therefore always have a debit balance at the end of a period, and this balance will be shown in the balance sheet as a current asset for stocks.
- Opening stocks brought forward in the stock account are transferred to the trading account, and so at the end of the accounting year, the balance on the stock account ceases to be the opening stock value b/f, and becomes instead the closing stock value c/f.

Quick quiz

1 Put debit or credit in the blanks.

Closing stock is a ____________ in the balance sheet and a ____________ in the trading account.

2 Net realisable value is ____

____.

3 SSAP 9 requires stock to be valued using a consistent approach. Which of the following valuation methods describes the correct approach?

A At the higher of cost or net realisable value
B At cost
C At net realisable value
D At the lower of cost or net realisable value

4 SSAP 9 requires stock to be valued using acceptable methods.

Which of the following is an unacceptable method of valuing stock?

A 'First in First out'
B 'Average cost'
C 'Last in First out'
D Standard cost

5 At the year end a business has stocks of bags and bells.

	Bags	*Bells*
	£	£
Original purchase price (per unit)	10	12
Number in shock	100	80
Estimated future sales price (per unit)	9	15
Estimated selling costs (per unit)	1	1

The value of closing stock is £____________.

Answers to quick quiz

1 Closing stock is a **debit** in the balance sheet and a **credit** in the trading account.

2 Net realisable value is the expected selling price less any costs to be incurred in getting the stock ready for sale and any costs of sale.

3 D Correct.
A Incorrect, stock valuation must be prudent.
B Incorrect.
C Incorrect.

4 C Not acceptable according to SSAP 9, but it remains a permissible method under CA85.
A Acceptable.
B Acceptable.
D Acceptable provided that variances are appropriately treated.

5 Bags: Cost £10, NRV £8, value £8 × 100 = £800

Bells: Cost £12, NRV £14, value £12 × 80 = 960

∴ The value of closing stock is £(800 + 960) = £1,760)

Now try the questions below from the Exam Question Bank

Number	Level	Marks	Time
28	Exam	15	27 mins
29	Exam	2	3 mins
30	Exam	2	3 mins

Chapter 11

FIXED ASSETS – DEPRECIATION, REVALUATION AND DISPOSAL

Topic List		Syllabus reference	Ability required
1	Depreciation	(iv)	Application
2	Revaluation of fixed assets	(iv)	Application
3	Fixed asset disposals	(iv)	Application
4	The fixed assets register	(iv)	Application

Introduction

You are familiar with the distinction between fixed and current assets, a fixed asset being one bought for ongoing use in the business. (If you are unsure look back to Chapter 3.)

Fixed assets are held and used by a business for a number of years, but they wear out or lose their usefulness over time. Every tangible fixed asset has a limited life. The only exception is land held freehold or on a very long leasehold.

The accounts of a business recognise that the cost of a fixed asset is consumed as the asset wears out, by writing off the asset's cost in the profit and loss account over several accounting periods. For example, a machine costs £1,000 and is expected to wear out after ten years. We can reduce the balance sheet value by £100 each year. This process is known as depreciation. Depreciation is the subject of a *reporting standard* (FRS 15), which you will need to know for your exam. This is discussed in Section 1.

Generally the market value of a fixed asset, particularly land or buildings, will rise with time. The asset may then be **revalued**. The accounting treatment of revaluations and the effect on depreciation are considered in Section 2. Section 3 deals with disposals of fixed assets. A profit or loss may arise on the sale of a fixed asset.

Section 4 deals with a more practical issue: the fixed assets register. You are sure to encounter this in real life, nearly all organisations have one.

Learning outcomes covered in this chapter

- Explain and calculate the methods of depreciation including straight line, reducing balance and revaluation and prepare accounts using each method
- Prepare a fixed asset register

Syllabus content covered in this chapter

- Accounting treatment for depreciation (straight line, reducing balance and revaluation methods)
- Fixed asset register

1 DEPRECIATION

Pilot Paper, May 2001

> **KEY TERM**
>
> Since a fixed asset has a cost, a limited useful life and a declining value, a charge is made in the trading, profit and loss account to reflect the use. This charge is called **depreciation**. Depreciation is a means of spreading the cost of a fixed asset over its useful life. This matches the cost against the period over which it earns profits for the business (the accruals concept).

1.1 A **fixed asset** is acquired with a view to earning profits. Its life extends **over more** than one accounting period, and so it earns profits over more than one period. With the exception of land held on freehold or very long leasehold, every fixed asset eventually wears out over time. Machines, cars and other vehicles, fixtures and fittings, and even buildings do not last for ever. When a business acquires a fixed asset, it will have some idea about how long its useful life will be. Its policy may be one of the following.

- Use the fixed asset until it is worn out, useless, and worthless
- Sell off the fixed asset at the end of its useful life as second-hand or as scrap

1.2 EXAMPLE

A business buys a machine for £40,000. Its expected life is four years, and at the end of that time it is expected to be worthless. Calculate the annual depreciation charge.

1.3 SOLUTION

Since the fixed asset will earn profits for four years, it seems reasonable to charge the cost of the asset over those four years at £10,000 per annum. (By the end of the four years, the total cost will have been written off against profits.)

FRS 15 Tangible fixed assets

1.4 The CA 1985 requires that all fixed assets having a limited economic life should be depreciated. FRS 15 *Tangible fixed assets* gives a useful discussion of the purpose of depreciation and supplements the statutory requirements in important respects.

> **KEY TERMS**
>
> **Depreciation** is defined in FRS 15 as 'the measure of the cost or revalued amount of the economic benefits of the tangible fixed asset that have been consumed during the period. Consumption includes the wearing out, using up or other reduction in the useful economic life of a tangible fixed asset whether arising from use, effluxion (passing) of time or obsolescence through either changes in technology or demand for the goods and services produced by the asset'.
>
> **Net book value** is cost (or revalued amount) less depreciation to date.

Question 1

A business buys a machine on 1 January 20X2 for £10,000. It expects to use it for 4 years and then sell it for £2,000.

Calculate the annual depreciation charge and the net book value at 31 December 20X2, 20X3, 20X4 and 20X5 (the expected sale date).

Answer

The annual depreciation charge is $\frac{£10{,}000 - 2{,}000}{4} = £2{,}000$

	Cost	Depreciation to date	Net book value
	£	£	£
31 December 20X2	10,000	2,000	8,000
31 December 20X3	10,000	4,000	6,000
31 December 20X4	10,000	6,000	4,000
31 December 20X5	10,000	8,000	2,000

1.5 The net book value (NBV) of an asset is not equal to its net realisable value and so the object of depreciation is not to reflect the fall in value of an asset over its life.

1.6 Another misconception is that depreciation provides funds to replace the asset at the end of its useful life. This is not the case, there is no movement of cash when depreciation is calculated and charged in the profit and loss account.

Exam focus point

The definition and purpose of depreciation was examined for 6 marks in Section C of the May 2001 exam.

KEY TERM

The depreciable amount is the total amount to be charged over the life of a fixed asset, usually its cost less any expected 'residual' sales or disposal value at the end of its life.

Calculating depreciation

1.7 FRS 15 states factors that need to be considered in determining the useful economic life, residual value and depreciation method of an asset.

- **Expected usage** with reference to the asset's expected capacity or physical output
- **Expected physical deterioration** through use or passing of time
- **Economic or technological obsolescence** (eg typesetters replaced by word processors)
- **Legal or similar limits** on the use of the asset (eg the expiry date of a lease)

1.8 The cost at which fixed assets are to be stated in the accounts is defined by the CA1985 and is, broadly speaking, purchase price or manufacturing cost, plus incidental expenses.

1.9 The estimated residual value of an asset is a matter of judgement. If it is expected to be a relatively small amount in relation to the asset's cost, it is usually taken to be nil.

1.10 The expected life of an asset is again a matter of judgement. FRS 15 comments that an asset's useful life may be affected by the following points.

- Pre-determined (eg leaseholds)
- Directly governed by extraction or consumption (eg a mine or quarry)
- Dependent on the extent of use (eg a motor car)
- Reduced by economic or technological obsolescence (eg last year's fashions)

1.11 If the original estimate of an asset's useful life is incorrect, it should be revised. Normally, no adjustment is made in respect of the depreciation charged in previous years; but the remaining NBV of the asset should be depreciated over the new estimate of its remaining useful life. However, if future results could be **materially** distorted, the adjustment to accumulated depreciation should be recognised in the accounts.

1.12 EXAMPLES

(a) A fixed asset costing £20,000, with an expected life of five years and an expected residual value of nil, will be depreciated by £20,000 in total over the five year period.

(b) A fixed asset costing £20,000, with an expected life of five years and an expected residual value of £3,000, will be depreciated by £17,000 in total over the five years.

THE MAIN POINTS

(a) A depreciation charge (provision) is made in the profit and loss account in each accounting period for every depreciable fixed asset. Nearly all fixed assets are depreciable, the most important exceptions being freehold land and long-term investments.

(b) The total accumulated depreciation builds up as the asset gets older. Therefore, the total provision for depreciation increases until the fixed asset is fully depreciated (NBV is nil).

The ledger accounting entries for depreciation

1.13 (a) There is a provision for depreciation account for each separate category of fixed assets, eg plant and machinery, land and buildings, fixtures and fittings.

(b) The depreciation charge for an accounting period is a charge against profit and is recorded as:

DEBIT	Depreciation expense account
CREDIT	Provision for depreciation account

(c) The balance on the provision for depreciation account is the total accumulated depreciation. This is always a credit balance.

(d) The fixed asset accounts are unaffected by depreciation. Fixed assets are recorded in these accounts at cost (or, if they are revalued, at their revalued amount).

(e) In the balance sheet of the business, the accumulated depreciation is deducted from the cost of fixed assets (or revalued amount) to arrive at the net book value of the fixed assets.

1.14 EXAMPLE

Using the information in Question 1, write up the depreciation expense and provision for depreciation accounts for 20X2, 20X3, 20X4 and 20X5.

1.15 SOLUTION

PROVISION FOR DEPRECIATION

DEPRECIATION EXPENSE ACCOUNT

		£			£
31.12.X2	Provision	2,000	31.12.X2	Profit and loss a/c	2,000
31.12.X3	Provision	2,000	31.12.X3	Profit and loss a/c	2,000
31.12.X4	Provision	2,000	31.12.X4	Profit and loss a/c	2,000
31.12.X5	Provision	2,000	31.12.X5	Profit and loss a/c	2,000

PROVISION FOR DEPRECIATION ~~EXPENSE~~ ACCOUNT

		£			£
31.12.X2	Balance c/d	2,000	31.12.X2	Depreciation expense a/c	2,000
		2,000			2,000
			1.1.X3	Balance b/d	2,000
31.12.X3	Balance c/d	4,000	31.12.X3	Depreciation expense a/c	2,000
		4,000			4,000
			1.1.X4	Balance b/d	4,000
31.12.X4	Balance c/d	6,000	31.12.X4	Depreciation expense a/c	2,000
		6,000			6,000
			1.1.X5	Balance b/d	6,000
31.12.X5	Balance c/d	8,000	31.12.X5	Depreciation expense a/c	2,000
		8,000			8,000

Methods of depreciation

1.16 There are several different methods of depreciation. The ones you need to know about are:

- Straight-line method
- Reducing balance method

KEY TERM

The **straight line method** means that the total depreciable amount is charged in equal instalments to each accounting period over the expected useful life of the asset

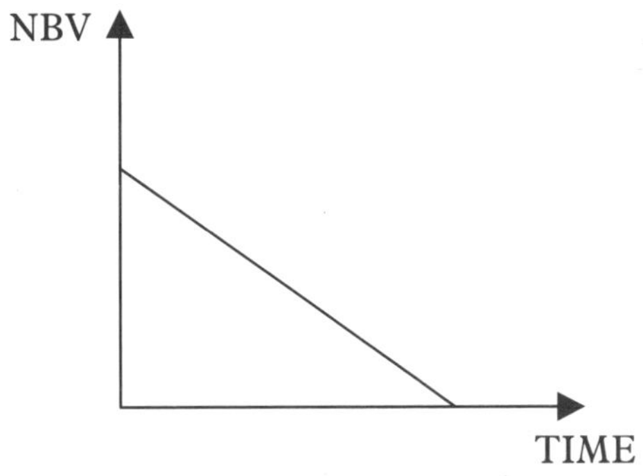

1.17 The straight line method is a fair allocation of the total depreciable amount, if it is reasonable to assume that the business enjoys equal benefits from the use of the asset throughout its life.

FORMULA TO LEARN

The annual depreciation charge is calculated as:

$$\frac{\text{Cost of asset minus residual value}}{\text{Expected useful life of the asset}}$$

1.18 EXAMPLE: STRAIGHT LINE DEPRECIATION

(a) A fixed asset costs £20,000 with an estimated life of 10 years and no residual value.

$$\text{Depreciation} = \frac{£20{,}000}{10 \text{ years}} = £2{,}000 \text{ per annum}$$

(b) A fixed asset costs £60,000 with an estimated life of 5 years and a residual value of £7,000.

$$\text{Depreciation} = \frac{£(60{,}000 - 7{,}000)}{5 \text{ years}} = £10{,}600 \text{ per annum}$$

The net book value of the fixed asset is calculated as follows.

	After 1 year	*After 2 years*	*After 3 years*	*After 4 years*	*After 5 years*
	£	£	£	£	£
Cost of the asset	60,000	60,000	60,000	60,000	60,000
Accumulated depreciation	10,600	21,200	31,800	42,400	53,000
Net book value	49,400	38,800	28,200	17,600	7,000 *

* ie its estimated residual value.

1.19 Since the depreciation charge per annum is the same amount every year, it is often stated that depreciation is charged at the rate of x per cent per annum on the cost of the asset. In the example in Paragraph 1.22(a) above, the depreciation charge per annum is 10% of cost (ie 10% of £20,000 = £2,000). **Examination questions** often describe straight line depreciation in this way.

KEY TERM

The **reducing balance method** of depreciation calculates the annual charge as a fixed percentage of the **net book value** of the asset, as at the end of the previous accounting period.

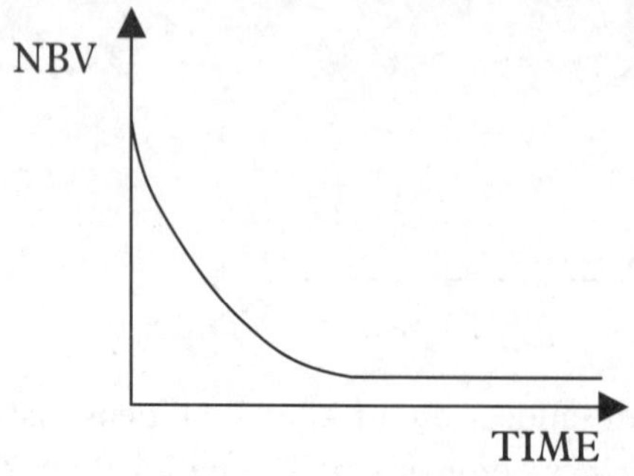

FORMULA TO LEARN

Reducing balance method = Net book value x X%.

1.20 EXAMPLE

A business purchases a fixed asset at a cost of £10,000. Its expected useful life is 3 years and its estimated residual value is £2,160. The business uses the reducing balance method and calculates that the rate of depreciation should be 40% of the reducing (net book) value of the asset. (The method of deciding that 40% is a suitable annual percentage is outside of the scope of your syllabus.)

Calculate the depreciation charge per annum and the net book value of the asset as at the end of each year.

1.21 SOLUTION

	£	*Accumulated depreciation* £	
Asset at cost	10,000		
Depreciation in year 1 (40%)	4,000	4,000	
Net book value at end of year 1	6,000		
Depreciation in year 2 (40% of reducing balance)	2,400	6,400	(4,000 + 2,400)
Net book value at end of year 2	3,600		
Depreciation in year 3 (40%)	1,440	7,840	(6,400 + 1,440)
Net book value at end of year 3	2,160		

1.22 With the reducing balance method, the annual charge for depreciation is higher in the earlier years of the asset's life, and lower in the later years. Therefore, it is used when it is considered fair to allocate a greater proportion of the total depreciable amount to the earlier years. The assumption is that the benefits obtained by the business from using the asset decline over time.

Question 2

A lorry bought for a business cost £17,000. It is expected to last for five years and then be sold for scrap for £2,000.

Required

Work out the depreciation to be charged each year under the following methods.

(a) The straight line method
(b) The reducing balance method (using a rate of 35%)

Answer

(a) Under the straight line method, depreciation for each of the five years is:

$$\text{Annual depreciation} = \frac{£17,000 - 2,000}{5} = £3,000$$

(b) Under the reducing balance method, depreciation for each of the five years is:

Year	*Depreciation*		
1	35% × £17,000	=	£5,950
2	35% × (£17,000 – £5,950) = 35% × £11,050	=	£3,868

Year	*Depreciation*		
3	35% × (£11,050 – £3,868) = 35% × £7,182	=	£2,514
4	35% × (£7,182 – £2,514) = 35% × £4,668	=	£1,634
5	Balance to bring book value down to £2,000 = £4,668 – £1,634 – £2,000	=	£1,034

Choice of method

1.23 Neither the CA 1985 nor FRS 15 states which method should be used. Management must exercise its judgement and FRS 15 states that:

> 'The depreciable amount of a tangible fixed asset should be allocated on a **systematic** basis over its useful economic life. The depreciation method used should reflect as fairly as possible the pattern in which the asset's economic benefits are consumed by the entity. The depreciation charge for each period should be recognised as an expense in the profit and loss account unless it is permitted to be included in the carrying amount of another asset.'
>
> 'A variety of methods can be used to allocate the depreciable amount of a tangible fixed asset on a systematic basis over its useful economic life. The method chosen should result in a **depreciation charge throughout the asset's useful** economic life and not just towards the end of its useful economic life or when the asset is falling in value.'

1.24 FRS 15 also states that a change from one method of providing depreciation to another is allowed only if the new method will give a fairer presentation of the company's results and financial position. Such a change is not a change of accounting policy and so no disclosure of a prior year adjustment is needed. Instead, the asset's net book amount is written off over its remaining useful life. The change of method, the reason for the change, and its quantitative effect, is disclosed by note to the accounts.

1.25 Many companies carry fixed assets in their balance sheets at revalued amounts, particularly in the case of freehold buildings. When this is done, the depreciation charge is calculated on the basis of the revalued amount (not the original cost).

Disclosure requirements of FRS 15

1.26 The following information should be disclosed separately in the financial statements for each class of tangible fixed assets.

- Depreciation methods used
- Useful economic lives or the depreciation rates used
- Total depreciation charged for the period
- Where material, the financial effect of a change during the period in either the estimate of useful economic lives or the estimate of residual values
- The cost or revalued amount at the beginning and end of the financial period
- The cumulative amount of depreciation at the beginning of and end the financial period
- A reconciliation of the movements (separately disclosing additions, disposals, revaluations, transfers, depreciation, impairment losses, and reversals of past impairment losses written back in the financial period)
- The NBV at the beginning and end of the financial period

Question 3

Brian Box set up his own computer software business on 1 March 20X6. He purchased a computer system, at a cost of £16,000. The system has an expected life of three years and a residual value of £2,500.

Using the straight line method of depreciation, produce the fixed asset account, provision for depreciation account, P & L account (extract) and balance sheet (extract) for each of the three years, 28 February 20X7, 20X8 and 20X9.

16000 – 2500 / 3
4500 per annum.

Answer

FIXED ASSET - COMPUTER EQUIPMENT

	Date		£	*Date*		£
(a)	1.3.X6	Creditor	16,000	28.2.X7	Balance c/d	16,000
(b)	1.3.X7	Balance b/d	16,000	28.2.X8	Balance c/d	16,000
(c)	1.3.X8	Balance b/d	16,000	28.2.X9	Balance c/d	16,000
(d)	1.3.X9	Balance b/d	16,000			

The fixed asset has now lasted its expected useful life. However, until it is sold or scrapped, the asset still appears in the balance sheet at cost (less accumulated depreciation) and it remains in the ledger account for computer equipment until disposal.

PROVISION FOR DEPRECIATION

	Date		£	*Date*		£
(a)	28.2.X7	Balance c/d	4,500	28.2.X7	P & L account	4,500
(b)	28.2.X8	Balance c/d	9,000	1.3.X7	Balance b/d	4,500
				28.2.X8	P & L account	4,500
			9,000			9,000
(c)	28.2.X9	Balance c/d	13,500	1.3.X8	Balance b/d	9,000
				28.2.X9	P & L account	4,500
			13,500			13,500
				1 Mar 20X9	Balance b/d	13,500

The annual depreciation charge is $\frac{(£16,000 - 2,500)}{3 \text{ years}} = £4,500$ pa

The asset is depreciated to its residual value. If it continues to be used, it will not be depreciated any further (unless its residual value is reduced).

P & L ACCOUNT (EXTRACT)

	Date		£
(a)	28 Feb 20X7	Provision for depreciation	4,500
(b)	28 Feb 20X8	Provision for depreciation	4,500
(c)	28 Feb 20X9	Provision for depreciation	4,500

BALANCE SHEET (EXTRACT) AS AT 28 FEBRUARY

	20X7	*20X8*	*20X9*
	£	£	£
Computer equipment at cost	16,000	16,000	16,000
Less accumulated depreciation	4,500	9,000	13,500
Net book value	11,500	7,000	2,500

Assets acquired in the middle of an accounting period

1.27 A business can purchase new fixed assets at any time during the course of an accounting period. So it may seem fair to charge depreciation in the period of purchase which reflects the limited amount of use the business has had in that period.

1.28 EXAMPLE

A business, with an accounting year ending on 31 December, purchases a new fixed asset on 1 April 20X1, at a cost of £24,000. The expected life of the asset is 4 years, and its residual value is nil. What is the depreciation charge for 20X1?

1.29 SOLUTION

The annual depreciation charge will be $\frac{24{,}000}{4 \text{ years}}$ = £6,000 per annum

However, since the asset was acquired on 1 April 20X1, the business has only benefited from the use of the asset for 9 months. Therefore it seems fair to charge depreciation in 20X1 for only 9 months.

$$\frac{9}{12} \times £6{,}000 = £4{,}500$$

1.30 In practice, however, many businesses ignore part-year depreciation, and charge a full year's depreciation in the year of purchase and none in the year of sale.

Exam focus point

If an examination question gives you the purchase date of a fixed asset, which is in the middle of an accounting period, unless told otherwise, you should assume that depreciation will be calculated on the basis of 'part year' use.

However, be sure to read the question carefully. A question may clearly state that depreciation on office equipment is charged at 20% per annum on the net book value at the year end. This means that any equipment introduced during the year will have a **full year's** depreciation charge.

1.31 EXAMPLE: PROVISION FOR DEPRECIATION WITH ASSETS ACQUIRED PART-WAY THROUGH THE YEAR

Brian Box purchases a car for himself and later for his chief assistant Bill Ockhead. Relevant data is as follows.

	Date of purchase	*Cost*	*Estimated life*	*Estimated residual value*
Brian Box car	1 June 20X6	£20,000	3 years	£2,000
Bill Ockhead car	1 June 20X7	£8,000	3 years	£2,000

The straight line method of depreciation is to be used.

Prepare the motor vehicles account and provision for depreciation of motor vehicle account for the years to 28 February 20X7 and 20X8. (You should allow for the part-year's use of a car in computing the annual charge for depreciation.) Calculate the net book value of the motor vehicles as at 28 February 20X8.

1.32 SOLUTION

(a) (i) Brian Box car Annual depreciation $\frac{£(20{,}000 - 2{,}000)}{3 \text{ years}}$ = £6,000 pa

Monthly depreciation £500

Depreciation	1 June 20X6 - 28 February 20X7 (9 months)	£4,500
	1 March 20X7 - 28 February 20X8	£6,000

(ii) Bill Ockhead car Annual depreciation $\frac{£(8{,}000 - 2{,}000)}{3 \text{ years}}$ = £2,000 pa

Depreciation	1 June 20X7 - 28 February 20X8 (9 months)	£1,500

(b)

MOTOR VEHICLES

Date		£	*Date*		£
1 Jun 20X6	Creditors (or cash)	20,000	28 Feb 20X7	Balance c/d	20,000
1 Mar 20X7	Balance b/d	20,000			
1 Jun 20X7	Creditors (or cash)	8,000	28 Feb 20X8	Balance c/d	28,000
		28,000			28,000
1 Mar 20X8	Balance b/d	28,000			

PROVISION FOR DEPRECIATION OF MOTOR VEHICLES

Date		£	*Date*		£
28 Feb 20X7	Balance c/d	4,500	28 Feb 20X7	P & L account	4,500
			1 Mar 20X7	Balance b/d	4,500
28 Feb 20X8	Balance c/d	12,000	28 Feb 20X8	P & L account (6,000+1,500)	7,500
		12,000			12,000
			1 March 20X8	Balance b/d	12,000

BALANCE SHEET (WORKINGS) AS AT 28 FEBRUARY 20X8

	Brian Box car		*Bill Ockhead car*		*Total*
	£	£	£	£	£
Asset at cost		20,000		8,000	28,000
Accumulated depreciation:					
Year to:					
28 Feb 20X7	4,500		-		
28 Feb 20X8	6,000		1,500		
		10,500		1,500	12,000
Net book value		9,500		6,500	16,000

Applying a depreciation method consistently

1.33 The business has to decide which method of depreciation to use. Once that decision is made, however, it should not be changed - the chosen method should be applied consistently from year to year. This is an example of the consistency concept.

1.34 Similarly, the business has to decide a sensible life span for a fixed asset. Once that life span is chosen, it should not be changed unless something unexpected happens to the fixed asset.

1.35 However a business can depreciate different categories of fixed assets in different ways. If a business owns three cars, then each car is depreciated in the same way (eg the straight line method) but another category of fixed asset (photocopiers) can be depreciated using a different method (eg by the reducing balance).

THE MAIN POINTS

(a) Depreciation is a measure of the 'wearing out' of a fixed asset.

(b) The accruals concept requires that depreciation be charged over the useful life of an asset.

(c) Two common methods of calculating depreciation are straight line and reducing balance.

(d) To record depreciation:

DEBIT	Depreciation expense account
CREDIT	Depreciation provision

Then to get the charge into the profit and loss account

DEBIT	Profit and loss account
CREDIT	Depreciation expense account

Exam focus point

The calculation and recording of depreciation was examined in Section C of the May 2001 exam.

2 REVALUATION OF FIXED ASSETS **Pilot Paper**

2.1 Due to inflation, it is now quite common for the market value of certain fixed assets to go up. The most obvious example of rising market values is land and buildings.

A business is not obliged to revalue fixed assets in its balance sheet. However, in order to give a 'true and fair view' it may decide to revalue some fixed assets upwards. When fixed assets are revalued, depreciation is charged on the revalued amount.

2.2 EXAMPLE: THE REVALUATION OF FIXED ASSETS

Ira Vann commenced trading on 1 January 20X1 and purchased freehold premises for £50,000.

For the purpose of accounting for depreciation, he decided that

(a) the freehold land part of the business premises was worth £20,000 and would not be depreciated.

(b) the building part of the business premises was worth the remaining £30,000. This would be depreciated by the straight-line method to a nil residual value over 30 years.

After five years, on 1 January 20X6, the business premise is now worth £150,000.

	£
Land	75,000
Building	75,000
	150,000

He estimates that the building still has a further 25 years of useful life remaining.

Calculate the annual charge for depreciation in each of the 30 years of its life, and the balance sheet value of the land and building as at the end of each year.

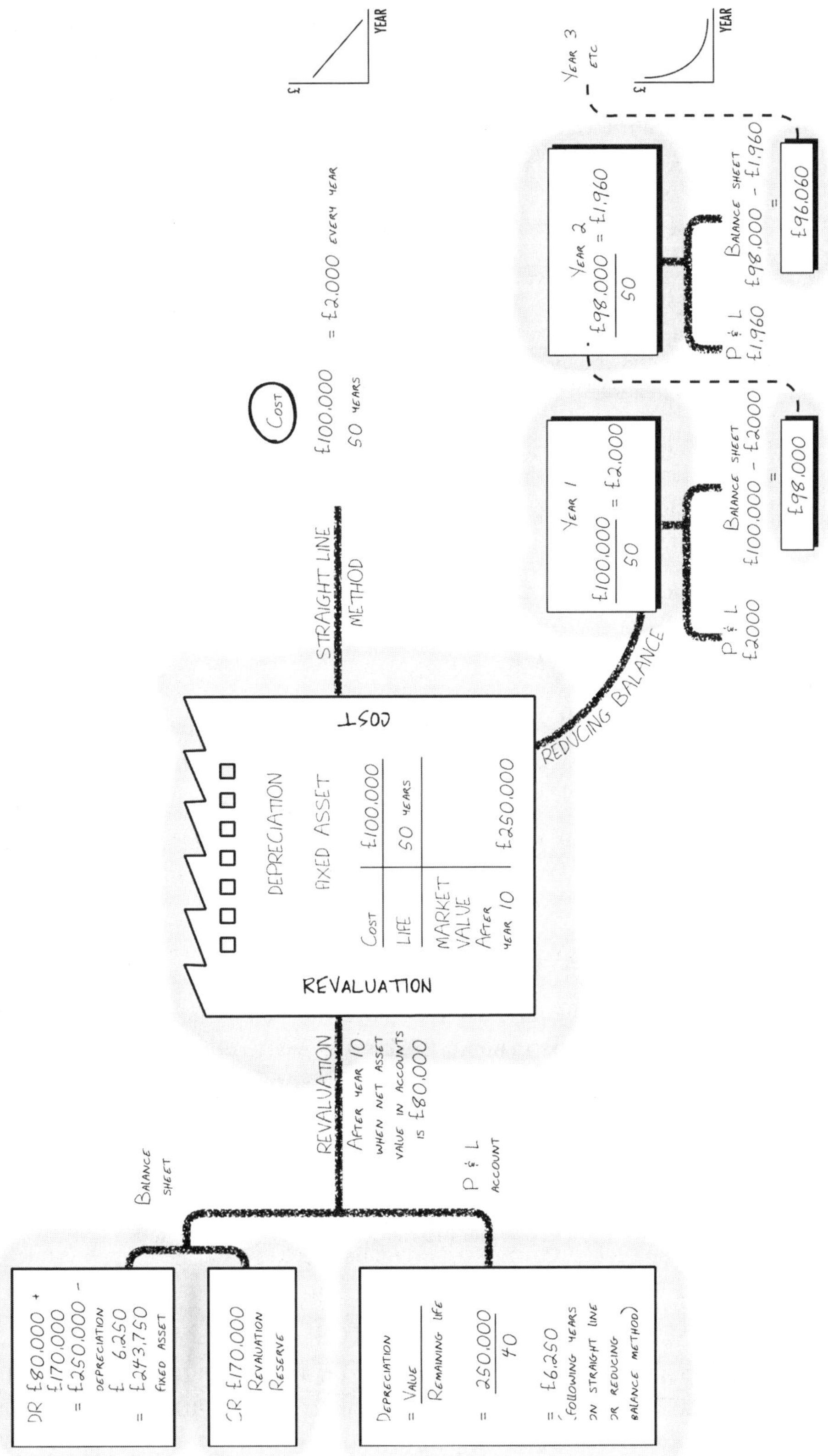

BPP PUBLISHING

2.3 SOLUTION

Before the revaluation, the annual depreciation charge is £1,000 (£30,000/30) per annum on the building. This charge is made in each of the first five years of the asset's life.

The net book value of the total asset will decline by £1,000 per annum.

(a) £49,000 as at 31.12.X1
(b) £48,000 as at 31.12.X2
(c) £47,000 as at 31.12.X3
(d) £46,000 as at 31.12.X4
(e) £45,000 as at 31.12.X5

When the revaluation takes place, the amount of the revaluation is:

	£
New asset value	150,000
Net book value as at end of 20X5	45,000
Amount of revaluation	105,000

The asset will be revalued by £105,000 to £150,000. If you remember the accounting equation, you will realise that if assets go up in value by £105,000, capital or liabilities must increase by the same amount. Since the increased value benefits the owner of the business, the amount of the revaluation is added to capital.

After the revaluation, depreciation will be charged on the building at a new rate.

$$\frac{£75{,}000}{25 \text{ years}} = £3{,}000 \text{ per annum}$$

The net book value of the property will then fall by £3,000 per annum over 25 years, from £150,000 as at 1 January 20X6 to only £75,000 at the end of the 25 years - ie the building part of the property value will be fully depreciated.

The consequence of an upwards revaluation is therefore a higher annual depreciation charge.

A fall in the value of a fixed asset

2.4 When the 'market' value of a fixed asset falls to below its net book value, and the fall in value is expected to be permanent, the asset is written down to its new market value. The charge in the profit and loss account for the impairment in the value of the asset during the accounting period is:

	£
Net book value at the beginning of the period	X
Less: new value	(X)
Equals: the charge for the impairment in the asset's value in the period.	X

2.5 EXAMPLE: FALL IN ASSET VALUE

A business purchased a leasehold property on 1 January 20X1 at a cost of £100,000. The lease has a 20 year life. After 5 years' use, on 1 January 20X6, the leasehold is now worth only £60,000 and the reduction is permanent.

2.6 SOLUTION

Before the asset is reduced in value, the annual depreciation charge is:

$\frac{£100,000}{20 \text{ years}}$ = £5,000 per annum (= 5% of £100,000)

After 5 years, the accumulated depreciation is £25,000 and the net book value £75,000, which is £15,000 more than the new asset value. This £15,000 is written off in year 5, so that the total charge in year 5 is

	£
Net book value of the leasehold after 4 years (£100,000 – 20,000)	80,000
Revised asset value at end of year 5	60,000
Charge against profit in year 5	20,000

An alternative method of calculation is

	£
'Normal' depreciation charge per annum	5,000
Further fall in value, from net book value at end of year 5 to revised value	15,000
Charge against profit in year 5	20,000

The leasehold has a further 15 years to run and its value is now £60,000. From year 6 to year 20, the annual charge for depreciation will be

$\frac{£60,000}{15 \text{ years}}$ = £4,000 per annum

Question 4

The following are possible methods of valuing the fixed assets of an organisation:

- Historical cost
- Replacement cost
- Realisable value
- Present value

Required

(a) Briefly describe each of the four methods of valuing fixed assets listed above.

(b) State the advantages of each of the asset valuation models listed above.

(c) PS Ltd acquired its premises on 1 January 20X5 at a cost of

Buildings	£140,000
Land	£60,000

The depreciation policy of the company is to write off assets having a finite life over their estimated useful life, using the straight-line method and assuming a nil residual value. Buildings are deemed to have a useful life of 25 years.

On 1 January 20X9 the buildings and land were revalued at:

Buildings	£200,000
Land	£100,000

Required

Calculate the following.

(i) The net book value of land and buildings at 31 December 20X8
(ii) The net book value of land and buildings at 31 December 20X9
(iii) The capital reserve at 31 December 20X9

Answer

(a) (i) *Historical cost* is the original purchase price of an asset as entered in the accounting records, less depreciation.

(ii) *Replacement cost* is the estimated amount that would have to be paid in order to replace an asset. The value to be entered in the balance sheet would be the cost of a new asset less estimated depreciation to date.

(iii) *Realisable value* is the estimated amount that would be received, net of disposal costs, from the sale of an asset. This should be a sale in the normal course of business, not a forced sale - for example, in a liquidation.

(iv) *Present value* is the future cash flow arising from an individual asset, discounted at an appropriate rate to its present value.

(b) (i) *Historical cost.* An organisation might adopt this method because it is objective. The depreciation charge is the allocation of the historical cost and is a measure of the resource consumed in a period. It provides information on the original cost of the asset and its estimated remaining life.

(ii) *Replacement cost.* An organisation might adopt this method because it uses up-to-date market values in the balance sheet and shows the current cost, via the depreciation charge in the profit and loss account, of the resources consumed in a period. It provides information on the estimated amount of finance that will be needed when the asset is replaced.

(iii) *Realisable value.* An organisation might adopt this method because it uses up-to-date market values in the balance sheet and shows the changes in value as gains and losses in the profit and loss account. It provides information on the estimated amount of finance that would be raised if the asset were sold (normally on a going-concern basis),and the business could consider the alternative use of that finance.

(iv) *Present value.* An organisation might adopt this method because it values an asset at its value to the business. The value of an asset is dependent on the cash flow arising from its use and this will fluctuate as there are changes in the cash flow forecast. The profit and loss account will reflect this change in the estimated value of future income. It provides information on the value of the asset to a business and this may be compared to alternative strategies for the asset, for example to buy another asset, or to sell the asset.

(c) (i) **Valuation of land and buildings at 31 December 20X8**

	£
Buildings (a finite life asset)	140,000
Depreciation	
£140,000 ÷ 25 years = £5,600 pa	
£5,600 × 5 years	28,000
	112,000
Land (an infinite asset)	60,000
	172,000

(ii) **Valuation of land and buildings at 31 December 20X9**

	£
Buildings at valuation	200,000
Depreciation	
£200,000 ÷ 20 years	(10,000)
	190,000
Land	100,000
	290,000

(iii) **Capital reserve**

	£
Buildings at valuation on 1 January 20X9	200,000
Land at valuation on 1 January 20X9	100,000
	300,000
Less book value at 31 December 20X8	(172,000)
Revaluation reserve	128,000

3 FIXED ASSET DISPOSALS

The disposal of fixed assets — Pilot Paper, May 2001

3.1 Fixed assets are not purchased by a business with the intention of reselling them in the normal course of trade. However, they may be sold either when their useful life is over or before then. A fixed asset could be sold early if it is no longer needed for the trade.

3.2 When fixed assets are sold, there will be a **profit or loss on disposal**. These gains or losses are reported in the profit and loss account of the business (and not in the trading account). They are commonly referred to as 'profit on disposal of fixed assets' or 'loss on disposal'.

KEY TERM

The **profit or loss on the disposal of a fixed asset** is the difference between:

- **Net book value** of the asset at the time of sale, and
- Net **sale price** (the price minus any costs of making the sale)

A profit is made when the sale price exceeds the NBV, and vice versa for a loss.

3.3 EXAMPLE: DISPOSAL OF A FIXED ASSET

A business purchased a fixed asset on 1 January 20X1 for £25,000, with an estimated life of six years and an estimated residual value of £7,000. The asset was sold after three years on 1 January 20X4, for £17,500.

What was the profit or loss on disposal, assuming that the business uses the straight line method for depreciation?

3.4 SOLUTION

$$\text{Annual depreciation} = \frac{£(25{,}000 - 7{,}000)}{6 \text{ years}}$$

$$= £3{,}000 \text{ per annum}$$

	£
Cost of asset	25,000
Less accumulated depreciation (three years)	9,000
Net book value at date of disposal	16,000
Sale price	17,500
Profit on disposal	1,500

This profit will be shown in the profit and loss account as other income added to the gross profit brought down from the trading account.

Question 5

A business purchased a machine on 1 July 20X1for £35,000. The machine had an estimated residual value of £3,000 and a life of eight years. The machine was sold for £18,600 on 31 December 20X4, the last day of the accounting year. The business incurred dismantling costs and transformation costs of £1,200.

The business uses the straight line method of depreciation. What was the profit or loss on disposal of the machine?

Answer

Annual depreciation $\frac{£(35,000 - 3,000)}{8 \text{ years}}$ = £4,000 per annum

It is assumed that in 20X1 only one-half year's depreciation was charged, because the asset was purchased six months into the year.

	£	£
Fixed asset at cost		35,000
Depreciation in 20X1 (6 months)	2,000	
20X2, 20X3 and 20X4	12,000	
Accumulated depreciation		14,000
Net book value at date of disposal		21,000
Sale price	18,600	
Costs incurred in making the sale	(1,200)	
Net sale price		17,400
Loss on disposal		(3,600)

This capital loss will be shown as an expense in the profit and loss account of the business.

The disposal of fixed assets: ledger accounting entries

3.5 The disposal of fixed assets is recorded in a **disposal of fixed assets** account.

(a) The following items appear in the disposal of fixed assets account.

- Value of the asset (cost or revalued amount)
- Accumulated depreciation up to the date of sale
- Sale price of the asset

(b) The ledger accounting entries are as follows.

(i) DEBIT Disposal of fixed asset account
CREDIT Fixed asset account

with the cost of the asset disposed of.

(ii) DEBIT Provision for depreciation account
CREDIT Disposal of fixed asset account

with the accumulated depreciation on the asset as at the date of sale.

(iii) DEBIT Debtor account or cash book
CREDIT Disposal of fixed asset account

with the sale price of the asset.

(iv) The balance on the disposal account is the profit or loss on disposal and the corresponding double entry is recorded in the P & L account.

3.6 EXAMPLE: DISPOSAL OF ASSETS: LEDGER ACCOUNTING ENTRIES

A business has machinery costing £110,000. Depreciation is provided at 20% per annum straight line. The total provision now stands at £70,000. The business sells for £19,000 a machine which it purchased exactly two years ago for £30,000.

Show the relevant ledger entries.

3.7 SOLUTION

PLANT AND MACHINERY ACCOUNT

	£		£
Balance b/d	110,000	Plant disposals account	30,000
		Balance c/d	80,000
	110,000		110,000
Balance b/d	80,000		

PLANT AND MACHINERY DEPRECIATION PROVISION

	£		£
Plant disposals (20% of £30,000 for 2 years)	12,000	Balance b/d	70,000
Balance c/d	58,000		
	70,000		70,000
		Balance b/d	58,000

PLANT DISPOSALS

	£		£
Plant and machinery account	30,000	Depreciation provision	12,000
Profit and loss a/c (profit on sale)	1,000	Cash	19,000
	31,000		31,000

Check:

	£
Asset at cost	30,000
Accumulated depreciation at time of sale	12,000
Net book value at time of sale	18,000
Sale price	19,000
Profit on sale	1,000

3.8 EXAMPLE CONTINUED: PART EXCHANGE

Taking the example above, assume that the machine was exchanged for a new machine costing £60,000. £19,000 is the trade-in received for the old machine. Now what are the relevant ledger account entries?

3.9 SOLUTION

PLANT AND MACHINERY ACCOUNT

	£		£
Balance b/d	110,000	Plant disposal	30,000
Cash (60,000 - 19,000)	41,000	Balance c/d	140,000
Plant disposals	19,000		
	170,000		170,000
Balance b/d	140,000		

The new asset is recorded in the fixed asset account at cost £(41,000 + 19,000) = £60,000.

PLANT AND MACHINERY DEPRECIATION PROVISION

	£		£
Plant disposals (20% of £30,000 for 2 years)	12,000	Balance b/d	70,000
Balance c/d	58,000		
	70,000		70,000
		Balance b/d	58,000

PLANT DISPOSALS

	£		£
Plant and machinery	30,000	Depreciation provision	12,000
Profit transferred to P & L	1,000	Plant and machinery	19,000
	31,000		31,000

THE MAIN POINTS

On disposal of fixed assets

(a)	DEBIT	Disposal account	original cost of the asset
	CREDIT	Fixed asset account	
(b)	DEBIT	Provision for depreciation account	depreciation charged to date
	CREDIT	Disposals account	
(c)	DEBIT	Cash (if money)	sales value
		Fixed asset (if part exchange)	
	CREDIT	Disposals account	

The balance on the disposals account is transferred to the profit and loss account.

Question 6

A business purchased two widget-making machines on 1 January 20X5 at a cost of £15,000 each. Each had an estimated life of five years and a nil residual value. The straight line method of depreciation is used.

Owing to an unforeseen slump in market demand for widgets, one widget-making machine was sold (on credit) for £8,000 on 31 March 20X7.

Later in the year, it was decided to abandon production of widgets altogether, and the second machine was sold on 1 December 20X7 for £2,500 cash.

Prepare the machinery account, provision for depreciation of machinery account and disposal of machinery account for the accounting year to 31 December 20X7.

Answer

MACHINERY ACCOUNT

		£			£
20X7			*20X7*		
1 Jan	Balance b/f	30,000	31 Mar	Disposal of machinery	15,000
			1 Dec	Disposal of machinery	15,000
		30,000			30,000

PROVISION FOR DEPRECIATION OF MACHINERY

		£			£
20X7			*20X7*		
31 Mar	Disposal of machinery*	6,750	1 Jan	Balance b/f (W1)	12,000
1 Dec	Disposal of machinery**	8,750	31 Dec	P & L account***	3,500
		15,500			15,500

* Depreciation at date of disposal (£3,000 × 2 + £750)

** Depreciation at date of disposal (£3,000 × 2 + £2,750)

*** Depreciation charge for the year (£750 + £2,750) (W2)

DISPOSAL OF MACHINERY

20X7		£	20X7		£
31 Mar	Machinery	15,000	31 Mar	Debtor account (sale price)	8,000
			31 Mar	Provision of depreciation	6,750
1 Dec	Machinery	15,000	1 Dec	Cash (sale price)	2,500
			1 Dec	Provision of depreciation	8,750
			31 Dec	P & L account (loss on disposal)	4,000
		30,000			30,000

You should be able to calculate that there was a loss on the first disposal of £250, and on the second disposal of £3,750, giving a total loss of £4,000.

Workings

1 At 1 January 20X7, accumulated depreciation on the machines will be 2 machines × 2 years × $\frac{£15,000}{5}$ per machine pa = £12,000, or £6,000 per machine

2 Monthly depreciation is $\frac{£3,000}{12}$ = £250 per machine per month. Therefore the machine disposed of on 31 March has 3 months' depreciation (£750) and the 1 December disposal has 11 months' depreciation (£2,750).

Exam focus point

The disposal of fixed assets including part exchange and ledger entries was examined in both Section A and C of the May 2001 exam.

4 THE FIXED ASSETS REGISTER **May 2001**

KEY TERM

The **fixed assets register** is a listing of all fixed assets owned by the organisation, broken down perhaps by department, location or asset type.

4.1 A fixed assets register is maintained primarily for internal purposes. It shows an organisation's investment in capital equipment. A fixed asset register is also part of the **internal control system.**

Data kept in a fixed assets register

4.2 Details likely to be kept about each fixed asset are:

- The internal reference number (for physical identification purposes)
- Manufacturer's serial number (for maintenance purposes)
- Description of asset
- Location of asset
- Department which 'owns' asset
- Purchase date (for calculation of depreciation)
- Cost
- Depreciation method and estimated useful life (for calculation of depreciation)
- Net book value (or written down value)

4.3 The following events give rise to entries in a fixed asset register.

- Purchase of an asset
- Sale of an asset
- Loss or destruction of an asset
- Transfer of assets between departments
- Revision of estimated useful life of an asset
- Scrapping of an asset
- Revaluation of an asset

4.4 'Outputs' from a fixed assets register include the following.

- Reconciliations of NBV to the nominal ledger
- Depreciation charges posted to the nominal ledger
- Physical verification/audit purposes

Control

4.5 It is important, for external reporting (ie the audit) and for internal purposes, that there are controls over fixed assets.

(a) **Purchase** of fixed assets must be authorised and must only be made by a responsible official. The purchaser should obtain several quotations. The person authorising the expenditure should not be the person using the asset.

(b) Procedures should exist and be enforced for **disposal** of fixed assets to ensure that the sales proceeds are not misappropriated.

(c) The fixed assets register must reconcile with the nominal ledger.

(d) The fixed assets register must reconcile with the physical presence of capital items.

The fixed assets register and the nominal ledger

4.6 The fixed assets register is not part of the double entry and is there for **memorandum** and **control** purposes. It must be reconciled to the nominal ledger to make sure that all additions, disposals and depreciation charges have been posted. For example, the total of all the 'cost' figures in the register for motor vehicles should equal the balance on the 'motor vehicles cost' account in the nominal ledger. The same goes for accumulated depreciation.

The fixed assets register and the physical assets

4.7 It is possible that the fixed assets register may not reconcile with the fixed assets actually present because:

- An asset has been stolen or damaged, which has not been noticed or recorded
- Excessive wear and tear or obsolescence has not been recorded
- New assets not yet recorded in the register because it has not been kept up to date
- Errors made in entering details in the register
- Improvement and modifications have not been recorded in the register

4.8 It is important that the company physically inspects all the items in the fixed assets register and keeps the fixed assets register up to date.

The nature of the inspection will vary between organisations. A large company could inspect 25% of assets by value each year, aiming to cover all categories every five years. A small company may inspect all its fixed assets very quickly, although this 'inspection' may not be formally recorded.

Dealing with discrepancies

4.9 As mentioned in 4.7 above, some assets may require an adjustment in their expected life due to excessive wear and tear or damage. The proper person must authorise any change to estimates of the life of an asset. The accounts department will need a copy of the authorised changes to make the right adjustments in the journal, the register and the ledger.

4.10 When discrepancies are discovered, it may be possible to resolve them by updating the fixed assets register and/or nominal ledger. It may not be possible for the person who discovers the discrepancy to resolve it himself. For example, if a fixed asset has to be revalued downwards due to wear and tear or obsolescence, it should be authorised by his superior.

Exam focus point

An examination question may ask for adjustment of the nominal ledger where it does not reconcile with the fixed assets register. In May 2001 there was a question in Section A on the use of a fixed asset register.

4.11 EXAMPLE: EXTRACT FROM A COMPUTERISED FIXED ASSETS REGISTER

Most fixed assets registers will be computerised. Below is an extract from a fixed asset register showing one item as it might appear when the details are printed out.

FASSET HOLDINGS PLC

Asset Code: 938		Next depreciation: 539.36
A	Description:	1 × Seisha Laser printer YCA40809
B	Date of purchase:	25/05/X6
C	Cost:	1618.25
D	Accumulated depreciation:	584.35
E	Depreciation %:	33.33%
F	Depreciation type:	straight line
G	Date of disposal:	NOT SET
H	Sale proceeds:	0.00
I	Accumulated depreciation amount:	55Q O/EQPT DEP CHARGE
J	Depreciation expense account:	34F DEPN O/EQPT
K	Depreciation period:	standard
L	Comments:	electronic office
M	Residual value:	0.00
N	Cost account:	65C O/E ADDITIONS

Chapter roundup

- There has been a lot to take in, so do not be surprised if it has taken you longer than expected. You should understand the following points.
- The cost of a fixed asset, less its estimated residual value, is allocated fairly between accounting periods by means of depreciation. The provision for depreciation is charged against profit and deducted from the value of the fixed asset in the balance sheet.
- There are several different methods of depreciation, but the straight line method and the reducing balance method are most commonly used in practice. Every method allocates the total depreciable amount between accounting periods, although in different ways.
- When a fixed asset is revalued, depreciation is charged on the revised amount.
- When a fixed asset is sold, there is likely to be a profit or loss on disposal. This is the difference between the net sale price of the asset and its net book value at the time of disposal.
- You should know the double entry bookkeeping for depreciation and the disposal of fixed assets.
- You should be aware of the provisions of FRS 15 *Tangible fixed assets.*
- Most organisations keep a fixed assets register. This is a listing of all fixed assets owned by the organisation broken down perhaps by department, location or asset type. This must be kept up to date.
- Discrepancies between the fixed assets register and the physical assets or the nominal ledger must be investigated and either resolved or referred to the appropriate person.

Quick quiz

1 Which of the following statements regarding fixed asset accounting is correct?

A All fixed assets should be revalued each year.

B Fixed assets may be revalued at the discretion of management. Once revaluation has occurred it must be repeated regularly for all fixed assets in a class.

C Management can choose which fixed assets in a class of fixed assets should be revalued.

D Fixed assets should be revalued to reflect rising prices.

2 Which of the following statements regarding depreciation is correct?

A All fixed assets must be depreciated.

B Straight line depreciation is usually the most appropriate method of depreciation.

C A change in the chosen depreciation method is a change in accounting policy which should be disclosed.

D Depreciation charges must be based upon the carrying value of an asset (less residual value if appropriate).

3 Fill in the blanks. Net book value is ______________ less ______________________________,

4 Two common depreciation methods are:

(1) ______________________

(2) ______________________

5 A fixed asset (cost £10,000, depreciation £7,500) is given in part exchange for a new asset costing £20,500. The agreed trade-in value was £3,500. The profit and loss account will include?

A A loss on disposal £1,000
B A profit on disposal £1,000
C A loss on purchase of a new asset £3,500
D A profit on disposal £3,500

6 The details about a fixed asset that would be included in a fixed assets register are:

(1) ____________________

(2) ____________________

(3) ____________________

(4) ____________________

(5) ____________________

(6) ____________________

Answers to quick quiz

1 B Correct.
A Fixed assets may be revalued, there is no requirement to do so in FRS 15.
C Incorrect, all fixed assets in a class must be revalued.
D Incorrect, fixed assets may be reduced in value as well as being increased.

2 D Correct.
A Incorrect, some fixed assets are not depreciated eg land.
B Incorrect, management should choose the most appropriate method.
C Incorrect, a method change is not a change in accounting policy.

3 Net book value is **cost** less **accumulated depreciation**.

4 (1) Straight-line
(2) Reducing balance

5 B Correct.

	£
Net book value at disposal	2,500
Trade-in allowance	3,500
Profit	1,000

6 (1) Date of purchase
(2) Description and location
(3) Original cost
(4) Depreciation rate and method
(5) Accumulated depreciation to date
(6) Date and amount of any revaluation

Now try the questions below from the Question Bank

Number	Level	Marks	Time
31	Exam	30	54 mins
32	Exam	2	3 mins
33	Exam	2	3 mins

Chapter 12

BANK RECONCILIATIONS

Topic List		Syllabus reference	Ability required
1	The bank reconciliation	(ii)	Application
2	Worked examples	(ii)	Application

Introduction

Tho cach book of a business is the record of how much cash the business believes that it has in the bank.

Why might the business' estimate of its bank balance be different from the amount shown on the bank statement? There are three common explanations.

(a) **Error**. Errors in calculation or recording transactions are more likely to be made by themselves than by the bank.

(b) **Bank charges or bank interest**. The bank usually only shows these on the bank statement.

(c) **Timing differences.** These include amounts banked, but not yet 'cleared' and added to the account. Similarly, payments by cheque not yet recorded by the bank.

The comparison of the cash book balance with the bank statements is called a bank reconciliation.

Learning outcomes covered in this chapter

- Prepare bank reconciliations

Syllabus content covered in this chapter

- Bank reconciliations

1 THE BANK RECONCILIATION — May 2001

KEY TERM

A **bank reconciliation** is a comparison of a bank statement (sent monthly, weekly or even daily by the bank) with the cash book. Differences between the balance on the bank statement and the balance in the cash book will be errors or timing differences, and they should be identified and satisfactorily explained.

The bank statement

1.1 It is a common practice for a business to issue a monthly statement to each credit customer. In the same way, a bank sends a statement to its short-term debtors and creditors - ie customers with bank overdrafts and those with money in their account - itemising the balance on the account at the beginning of the period, receipts and payments during the period, and the balance at the end of the period.

Remember, however, that if a customer has money in his account, the bank owes him that money and so the customer is a creditor of the bank (hence the phrase 'to be in credit' means to have money in your account). If a business has £8,000 cash in the bank, it will have a debit balance in its own cash book, but the bank statement will show a credit balance of £8,000. (The bank's records are a 'mirror image' of the customer's own records, with debits and credits reversed.)

Why is a bank reconciliation necessary?

1.2 A bank reconciliation identifies differences between the cash book and bank statement.

- **Errors**
- **Bank charges** or bank interest
- **Timing differences**

What to look for when doing a bank reconciliation

1.3 The cash book and bank statement will rarely agree at a given date. When doing a bank reconciliation, you need to look for the following items.

(a) *Correction of errors*

(b) *Adjustments to the cash book*

- Payments by standing order into or from the account, not yet entered into the cash book
- Dividends received direct into the bank account, not yet entered in the cash book
- Bank interest and bank charges, not yet entered in the cash book

(c) *Timing differences reconciling the corrected cash book balance to the bank statement*

- Cheques payments credited in the cash book, not yet on the bank statement
- Cheques received, paid into the bank and debited in the cash book, but not yet on the bank statement

KEY TERMS

Unpresented cheques are cheques sent out which do not yet appear on the statement.

Uncleared lodgements are cheques received and paid into the bank which do not yet appear on the statement. Unpresented cheques reduce the balance at the bank, uncleared lodgements increase it.

2 WORKED EXAMPLES

2.1 EXAMPLE: BANK RECONCILIATION

At 30 September 20X6, the cash book balance is £805.15 (debit). A bank statement on 30 September 20X6 shows a balance of £1,112.30.

On investigation of the difference between the two sums, the following points arise.

(a) The cash book had been undercast by £90.00 on the debit side*.
(b) Cheques paid in not yet credited by the bank amounted to £208.20.
(c) Cheques drawn not yet presented to the bank amounted to £425.35.

* 'Casting' is an accountant's term for adding up.

Required

(a) Show the correction to the cash book.
(b) Prepare a statement reconciling the bank statement and cash book balance.

2.2 SOLUTION

(a)

	£
Cash book balance brought forward	805.15
Add	
Correction of undercasting	90.00
Corrected balance	895.15

(b)

	£	£
Balance per bank statement		1,112.30
Add		
Outstanding lodgements	208.20	
Less		
Unpresented cheques	425.35	
		(217.15)
Balance per cash book		895.15

Question 1

Which two of the following statements are true?

(i) Unpresented cheques should be treated as a timing difference.
(ii) Unpresented cheques should be written back into the cash book.
(iii) Uncleared lodgements reduce the figure per the bank statement.
(iv) Uncleared lodgements increase the figure per bank statement.

Answer

(i) and (iv) are true.

2.3 EXAMPLE: MORE COMPLICATED BANK RECONCILIATION

On 30 June 20X0, Cook's cash book showed an overdraft of £300 on his current account. A bank statement as at the end of June 20X0 showed that Cook was in credit with the bank by £65.

On checking the cash book with the bank statement you find the following.

(a) Cheques drawn of £500, entered in the cash book but not yet presented.

(b) Cheques received of £400, entered in the cash book, but not yet credited by the bank.

(c) The bank had transferred interest received on deposit account of £60 to current account, recording the transfer on 5 July 20X0. This amount had been credited in the cash book as on 30 June 20X0.

(d) Bank charges of £35 in the bank statement had not been entered in the cash book.

(e) The payments side of the cash book had been undercast by £10.

(f) Dividends received amounting to £200 were paid direct to the bank and not entered in the cash book.

(g) A cheque for £50 drawn on deposit account had been shown in the cash book as drawn on current account.

(h) A cheque issued to Jones for £25 was replaced when out of date. It was entered again in the cash book, no other entry being made. Both cheques were included in the total of unpresented cheques shown above.

Required

(a) Indicate the appropriate adjustments in the cash book.

(b) Prepare a statement reconciling the amended balance with that shown in the bank statement.

2.4 SOLUTION

(a) The errors to correct are given in notes (c) (e) (f) (g) and (h). Bank charges (note (d)) also need adjustment.

		Adjustments in cash book	
		Debit (ie add to cash balance)	*Credit (ie deduct from cash balance)*
		£	£
Item			
(c)	Cash book incorrectly *credited* with interest on 30 June, should have been *debited* with the receipt	60	
(c)	Debit cash book (current a/c) with transfer of interest from deposit a/c (note 1)	60	
(d)	Bank charges		35
(e)	Undercast on payments (credit) side of cash book		10
(f)	Dividends received should be debited in the cash book	200	
(g)	Cheque drawn on deposit account, not current account. Add cash back to current account	50	
(h)	Cheque paid to Jones is out of date and so cancelled. Cash book should now be debited, since previous credit entry is no longer valid (note 2)	25	
		395	45

	£	£
Cash book: balance on current account as at 30 June 20X0		(300)
Adjustments and corrections:		
Debit entries (adding to cash)	395	
Credit entries (reducing cash balance)	(45)	
Net adjustments		350
Corrected balance in the cash book		50

Notes

1 Item (c) is rather complicated. The transfer of interest from the deposit to the current account was presumably given as an instruction to the bank on or before 30 June 20X0. Since the correct entry is to debit the current account (and credit the deposit account) the correction in the cash book is to debit the current account with 2 × £60 = £120 - ie to cancel out the incorrect credit entry in the

cash book and then to make the correct debit entry. However, the bank does not record the transfer until 5 July and so it will not appear in the bank statement.

2 Item (h). Two cheques have been paid to Jones, but one is now cancelled. Since the cash book is credited whenever a cheque is paid, it should be debited whenever a cheque is cancelled. The amount of unpresented cheques is reduced by the amount of the cancelled cheque.

(b) BANK RECONCILIATION STATEMENT AT 30 JUNE 20X0

	£	£
Balance per bank statement		65
Add: outstanding lodgements		
(ie cheques paid in but not yet credited)	400	
deposit interest not yet credited (note 1)	60	
		460
		525
Less: unpresented cheques	500	
less cheque to Jones cancelled (note 2)	25	
		475
Balance per corrected cash book		50

Exam focus point

Notice that in preparing a bank reconciliation it is good practice to begin with the balance shown by the bank statement and end with the balance shown by the cash book. It is this corrected cash book balance which will appear in the balance sheet as 'cash at bank'. Examination questions sometimes ask for the reverse order: as always, read the question carefully.

Question 2

From the information given below relating to PWW Ltd you are required:

(a) To make such additional entries in the cash account of PWW Ltd as you consider necessary to show the correct balance at 31 October 20X2.

(b) To prepare a statement reconciling the corrected cash account balance as shown in (a) above with the balance at 31 October 20X2 on the bank statement.

CASH AT BANK ACCOUNT IN THE LEDGER OF PWW LIMITED

20X2		£	*20X2*		£
October			*October*		
1	Balance b/f	274	1	Wages	3,146
8	Q Manufacturing	3,443	1	Petty Cash	55
8	R Cement	1,146	8	Wages	3,106
11	S Limited	638	8	Petty Cash	39
11	T & Sons	512	15	Wages	3,029
11	U & Co	4,174	15	Petty Cash	78
15	V plc	1,426	22	A & Sons	929
15	W Electrical	887	22	B Limited	134
22	X and Associates	1,202	22	C & Company	77
26	Y Limited	2,875	22	D & E	263
26	Z Limited	982	22	F Limited	1,782
29	ABC plc	1,003	22	G Associates	230
29	DEE Corporation	722	22	Wages	3,217
29	GHI Limited	2,461	22	Petty Cash	91
31	Balance c/f	14	25	H & Partners	26
			26	J Sons & Co Ltd	868
			26	K & Co	107

20X2 October		£	*20X2 October*		£
			26	L, M & N	666
			28	O Limited	112
			29	Wages	3,191
			29	Petty Cash	52
			29	P & Sons	561
		21,759			21,759

Z BANK PLC - STATEMENT OF ACCOUNT WITH PWW LIMITED

20X2 October		*Payments* £	*Receipts* £		*Balance* £
1					1,135
1	cheque	55			
1	cheque	3,146			
1	cheque	421		O/D	2,487
2	cheque	73			
2	cheque	155		O/D	2,715
6	cheque	212		O/D	2,927
8	sundry credit		4,589		
8	cheque	3,106			
8	cheque	39		O/D	1,483
11	sundry credit		5,324		3,841
15	sundry credit		2,313		
15	cheque	78			
15	cheque	3,029			3,047
22	sundry credit		1,202		
22	cheque	3,217			
22	cheque	91			941
25	cheque	1,782			
25	cheque	134		O/D	975
26	cheque	929			
26	sundry credit		3,857		
26	cheque	230			1,723
27	cheque	263			
27	cheque	77			1,383
29	sundry credit		4,186		
29	cheque	52			
29	cheque	3,191			
29	cheque	26			
29	dividends on investments		2,728		
29	cheque	666			4,362
31	bank charges	936			3,426

Answer

(a)

CASH BOOK

		£			£
31 Oct	Dividends received (W5)	2,728	31 Oct	Unadjusted balance b/f (overdraft)	14
			31 Oct	Bank charges (W4)	936
			31 Oct	Adjusted balance c/f	1,778
		2,728			2,728

(b) BANK RECONCILIATION STATEMENT
AT 31 OCTOBER 20X2

	£	£
Corrected balance as per cash book		1,778
Cheques paid out but not yet presented (W3)	1,648	
Cheques paid in but not yet cleared by bank (W7)	0	
		1,648
Balance as per bank statement		3,426

Workings

1	Payments shown on bank statement but not in cash book £(421 + 73 + 155 + 212)* * Presumably recorded in cash book before 1 October 20X2 but not yet presented for payment as at 30 September 20X2	£861
2	Payments in the cash book and on the bank statement £(3,146 + 55 + 3,106 + 39 + 78 + 3,029 + 3,217 + 91 + 1,782 + 134 + 929 + 230 + 263 + 77 + 52 + 3,191 + 26 + 666)	£20,111
3	Payments in the cash book but not on the bank statement (Total payments in cash book £21,759 minus £20,111)	£1,648

		£
Alternatively	J & Sons	868
	K & Co	107
	O Ltd	112
	P & Sons	561
		1,648

4	Bank charges, not in the cash book	£936
5	Receipts recorded by bank statement but not in cash book: dividends on investments	£2,728
6	Receipts in the cash book and also bank statement (8 Oct £4,589; 11 Oct £5,324; 15 Oct £2,313; 22 Oct £1,202; 26 Oct £3,857; 29 Oct £4,186)	£21,471
7	Receipts recorded in cash book but not bank statement	None

Exam focus point

In May 2001 there was a question in Section A on bank reconciliations.

Chapter roundup

- In theory, the entries appearing on a business's bank statement should be exactly the same as those in the business cash book. The balance shown by the bank statement as on a particular date should be the same as the cash book balance at the same date.
- It is common (and a very important financial control) to check this at regular intervals, say weekly or monthly. Invariably it will be found that the picture shown by the bank statement differs from that shown by the cash book. The reasons for this fall into three categories.
    - **Errors**. Entries on the bank statement may be incorrect, but more commonly, errors may be found in the cash book.
    - **Omissions**. Items may appear on the bank statement which have not yet been entered in the cash book. These may include bank changes and payments made by direct debit.
    - **Timing differences**. Cheques are entered in the cash book as soon as they are written, but there may be a delay before the payee receives them and a further delay while they are processed through the bank clearing system.
- When these discrepancies are noticed, appropriate adjustments must be made. Errors must be corrected and omissions from the cash book entered. The balance in the cash book will then be correct and up to date. Any remaining difference between the cash book balance and the statement balance should then be explained as the result of identifiable timing differences.

Quick quiz

1 The bank column of a cash book showed a closing balance of £550 (credit). Unpresented cheques amount to £1,500 and receipts undeposited at the bank were £500. The bank statement balance was? (Hint: prepare a bank reconciliation.)

A £1,550 (in hand)
B £450 (in hand)
C £1,450 (in hand)
D £2,550 (overdrawn)

2 The cash book balance was £1,500 (debit). The bank statement revealed an overdrawn balance of £500. Unpresented cheques were £1,200 and receipts undeposited were £3,000. The bank has incorrectly charged another customers cheque to the company account. How much was the incorrect cheque drawn for?

A £3,200
B £6,200
C £3,800
D £200

Answers to quick quiz

1 B

Cash book	(550)
Add unpresented cheques	1,500
Less undeposited receipts	(500)
B/S balance	450 (in hand)

A Incorrect, you have treated the opening balance as a debit in the reconciliation.

C Incorrect, you have treated the undeposited receipts incorrectly.

D Incorrect, because you have treated the unpresented cheques incorrectly.

2 D Correct.

	£
Cash book	1,500 (debit)
Add: unpresented cheques	1,200
	2,700
Less: undeposited receipts	(3,000)
	(300)
Bank error	(200)
Bank balance	(500) o/d

A Incorrect, you have omitted the undeposited receipts from the reconciliation.

B Incorrect, you have added back the undeposited receipts instead of deducting them from the cash book balance.

C Incorrect, you have reversed the treatments of the unpresented cheques and the undeposited receipts.

Now try the questions below from the Question Bank

Number	Level	Marks	Time
34	Exam	15	27 mins
35	Exam	2	3 mins
36	Exam	2	3 mins

Chapter 13

CONTROL ACCOUNTS

Topic List		Syllabus reference	Ability required
1	What are control accounts?	(ii)	Application
2	The purpose of control accounts	(ii)	Application
3	The operation of control accounts	(ii)	Application
4	Balancing and reconciling control accounts with sales and purchase ledgers	(ii)	Application

Introduction

In this chapter (and in Chapter 16) we explain how accounting errors can be detected, what kinds of error might exist, and how to post corrections and adjustments to produce final accounts.

Learning outcomes covered in this chapter

- Prepare accounts for sales and purchases including personal accounts and control accounts

Syllabus content covered in this chapter

- Accounting for sales and purchases including personal accounts and control accounts

1 WHAT ARE CONTROL ACCOUNTS?

KEY TERM

A **control account** is an account in the nominal ledger in which a record is kept of the total value of a number of similar but individual items.

1.1 A **debtors control account** is an account in which records are kept of transactions involving all debtors in total. The balance on the debtors control account at any time will be the total amount due to the business from its debtors.

1.2 A **creditors control account** is an account in which records are kept of transactions involving all creditors in total, and the balance on this account at any time will be the total amount owed by the business at that time to its creditors.

1.3 Control accounts can also be kept for other items, such as stocks of goods, wages and salaries and VAT.

Control accounts and personal accounts

1.4 The personal accounts of individual debtors are kept in the sales ledger. The amount owed by all the debtors added together is the balance on the debtors control account. At any time the balance on the debtors control account should be equal to the sum of the individual balances on the personal accounts in the sales ledger.

1.5 EXAMPLE

A business has three debtors, A Arnold who owes £80, B Bagshaw who owes £310 and C Cloning who owes £200, the debit balances on the various accounts would be

Sales ledger (personal accounts)

	£
A Arnold	80
B Bagshaw	310
C Cloning	200
Nominal ledger - debtors control account	590

REMEMBER!

When we looked at day books we said that individual amounts (eg invoices to customers in the sales day book) would be posted by single entry into personal account, and that day book totals would be posted by double entry to the nominal ledger accounts.

IMPORTANT POINT!

The balance on the debtors control account should be the same as the sum of all customers accounts in the sales ledger because they have been posted from the same day books.

2 THE PURPOSE OF CONTROL ACCOUNTS **Pilot Paper**

2.1 (a) They provide a check on the accuracy of entries made in the personal accounts in the sales and purchase ledgers. It is very easy to make a mistake in posting entries. Figures can get transposed. Some entries can be omitted altogether, so that an invoice or a payment does not appear in a personal account. Comparison of the balance on the debtors control account with the total of individual personal account balances in the sales ledger will show if any errors have occurred. Similarly the creditors control account provides a check on the purchase ledger.

(b) The control accounts also assist in the location of errors. If a clerk fails to record an invoice or a payment in a personal account, it would be difficult to locate the error or errors at the end of a year. By using the control account, a comparison with the individual balances in the sales or purchase ledger can be made daily or weekly and the error found much more quickly.

(c) Where there is separation of bookkeeping duties, the control account provides an **internal check**. The person posting entries to the control accounts will act as a check on a different person(s) posting entries to the sales and purchase ledger.

(d) Control accounts provide the total debtors and creditors balances more quickly for producing a trial balance or balance sheet.

2.2 In computerised systems, it may be possible to use sales and purchase ledgers as part of the double entry without needing separate control accounts. The sales or purchase ledger printouts provide the list of individual balances, as well as a total (control account) balance.

3 THE OPERATION OF CONTROL ACCOUNTS — Pilot Paper

3.1 EXAMPLE: ACCOUNTING FOR DEBTORS

The following example shows how transactions involving debtors are accounted for. Folio numbers are shown in the accounts to illustrate the cross-referencing that is needed.

(a) SDB refers to a page in the sales day book.
(b) SL refers to a particular account in the sales ledger.
(c) NL refers to a particular account in the nominal ledger.
(d) CB refers to a page in the cash book.

At 1 July 20X2, the Outer Business Company had no debtors at all. During July, the following credit sale transactions occurred.

(a)	July 3	invoiced A Arnold for the sale on credit of hardware goods: £100.
(b)	July 11	invoiced B Bagshaw for the sale on credit of electrical goods: £150.
(c)	July 15	invoiced C Cloning for the sale on credit of hardware goods: £250.
(d)	July 10	received payment from A Arnold of £90, in settlement of his debt in full, having taken a permitted discount of £10 for payment within seven days.
(e)	July 18	received a payment of £72 from B Bagshaw in part settlement of £80 of his debt. A discount of £8 was allowed for payment within seven days.
(f)	July 28	received a payment of £120 from C Cloning, who was unable to claim any discount.

Account numbers are:

SL 4	Personal account: A Arnold
SL 9	Personal account: B Bagshaw
SL 13	Personal account: C Cloning
NL 6	Debtors control account
NL 7	Discounts allowed
NL 21	Sales: hardware
NL 22	Sales: electrical
NL 1	Cash control account

Required

Write up the day books, nominal ledger postings and personal account postings to record these transactions.

3.2 SOLUTION

The accounting entries are:

SALES DAY BOOK — SDB 35

Date	Name	Folio	Total	Hardware	Electrical
20X2			£	£	£
July 3	A Arnold	SL 4	100.00	100.00	
11	B Bagshaw	SL 9	150.00		150.00
15	C Cloning	SL13	250.00	250.00	
			500.00	350.00	150.00
			NL 6	NL 21	NL 22

Note. The personal accounts in the sales ledger are debited on the day the invoices are sent out. The double entry in the ledger accounts is made when the day book is totalled. Here it is made at the end of the month, by posting as follows.

			£	£
DEBIT	NL 6	Debtors control account	500	
CREDIT	NL 21	Sales: hardware		350
	NL 22	Sales: electrical		150

CASH BOOK EXTRACT
RECEIPTS CASH BOOK JULY 20X2

CB 23

Date	Narrative	Folio	Total	Discount	Debtors
20X2			£	£	£
July 10	A Arnold	SL 4	90.00	10.00	100.00
18	B Bagshaw	SL 9	72.00	8.00	80.00
28	C Cloning	SL13	120.00	-	120.00
			282.00	18.00	300.00
			NL 1 Dr	NL 7 Dr	NL 6 Cr

MEMORANDUM SALES LEDGER

ARNOLD — A/c no: SL 4

Date	Narrative	Folio	£	Date	Narrative	Folio	£
20X2				20X2			
July 3	Sales	SDB 35	100.00	July 10	Cash	CB 23	90.00
					Discount	CB 23	10.00
			100.00				100.00

B BAGSHAW — A/c no: SL 9

Date	Narrative	Folio	£	Date	Narrative	Folio	£
20X2				20X2			
July 11	Sales	SDB 35	150.00	July 18	Cash	CB 23	72.00
					Discount	CB 23	8.00
				July 31	Balance	c/d	70.00
			150.00				150.00
Aug 1	Balance	b/d	70.00				

C CLONING — A/c no: SL 13

Date	Narrative	Folio	£	Date	Narrative	Folio	£
20X2				20X2			
July 15	Sales	SDB 35	250.00	July 28	Cash	CB 23	120.00
				July 31	Balance	c/d	130.00
			250.00				250.00
Aug 1	Balance	b/d	130.00				

NOMINAL LEDGER (EXTRACT)
TOTAL DEBTORS (SALES LEDGER) CONTROL ACCOUNT

A/c no: NL 6

Date	*Narrative*	*Folio*	£	*Date*	*Narrative*	*Folio*	£
20X2				*20X2*			
July 31	Sales	SDB 35	500.00	July 31	Cash and discount	CB 23	300.00
				July 31	Balance	c/d	200.00
			500.00				500.00
Aug 1	Balance	b/d	200.00				

Note. At 31 July the closing balance on the debtors control account (£200) is the same as the total of the individual balances on the personal accounts in the sales ledger (£0 + £70 + £130).

DISCOUNT ALLOWED

A/c no: NL 7

Date	*Narrative*	*Folio*	£	*Date*	*Narrative*	*Folio*	£
20X2							
July 31	Debtors	CB 23	18.00				

CASH CONTROL ACCOUNT

A/c no: NL 1

Date	*Narrative*	*Folio*	£	*Date*	*Narrative*	*Folio*	£
20X2							
July 31	Cash received	CB 23	282.00				

SALES - HARDWARE

A/c no: NL 21

Date	*Narrative*	*Folio*	£	*Date*	*Narrative*	*Folio*	£
				20X2			
				July 31	Debtors	SDB 35	350.00

SALES - ELECTRICAL

A/c no: NL 22

Date	*Narrative*	*Folio*	£	*Date*	*Narrative*	*Folio*	£
				20X2			
				July 31	Debtors	SDB 35	150.00

If we took the balance on the accounts as at 31 July 20X2, the trial balance would be as follows.

TRIAL BALANCE

	Debit	*Credit*
	£	£
Cash (all receipts)	282	
Debtors	200	
Discount allowed	18	
Sales: hardware		350
Sales: electrical		150
	500	500

The trial balance emphasises the point that it includes the balances on control accounts, but excludes the personal account balances in the sales and purchase ledgers.

Accounting for creditors

3.3 If you were able to follow the above example, you should have no difficulty in dealing with similar examples relating to purchases/creditors. If necessary revise the entries in the purchase day book and purchase ledger personal accounts.

Entries in control accounts

3.4 Typical entries in the control accounts are shown below. Folio reference Jnl indicates that the transaction is first lodged in the journal before posting to the control account and other accounts indicated. References SRDB and PRDB are to sales returns and purchase returns day books.

SALES LEDGER (DEBTORS) CONTROL

	Folio	£		*Folio*	£
Opening debit balances	b/d	7,000	Opening credit balances (if any)	b/d	200
Sales	SDB	52,390	Cash received	CB	52,250
Dishonoured bills or cheques	Jnl	1,000	Discounts allowed	CB	1,250
Cash paid to clear credit balances	CB	110	Returns inwards from debtors	SRDB	800
Closing credit balances	c/d	120	Bad debts	Jnl	300
			Closing debit balances	c/d	5,820
		60,620			60,620
Debit balances b/d		5,820	Credit balances b/d		120

Note. Opening credit balances are unusual in the debtors control account. They represent debtors to whom the business owes money, probably as a result of the over payment of debts or for advance payments of debts for which no invoices have yet been sent.

BOUGHT LEDGER (CREDITORS) CONTROL

	Folio	£		*Folio*	£
Opening debit balances (if any)	b/d	70	Opening credit balances	b/d	8,300
			Purchases	PDB	31,000
Cash paid	CB	29,840	Cash received clearing debit balances	CB	20
Discounts received	CB	30			
Returns outwards to suppliers	PRDB	60	Closing debit balances (if any)	c/d	80
Closing credit balances	c/d	9,400			
		39,400			39,400
Debit balances	b/d	80	Credit balances	b/d	9,400

Note. Opening debit balances in the creditors control account represent suppliers who owe the business money, perhaps because debts have been overpaid or because debts have been prepaid before the supplier has sent an invoice.

3.5 Posting from the journal is shown in the following example, where C Cloning has returned goods with a sales value of £50.

Journal entry	*Folio*	*Dr*	*Cr*
		£	£
Sales	NL 21	50	
To debtors' control	NL 6		50
To C Cloning (memorandum)	SL 13	-	50

Return of electrical goods inwards.

3.6 A flowchart follows to show how the debtors ledger and debtors (control) account are used.

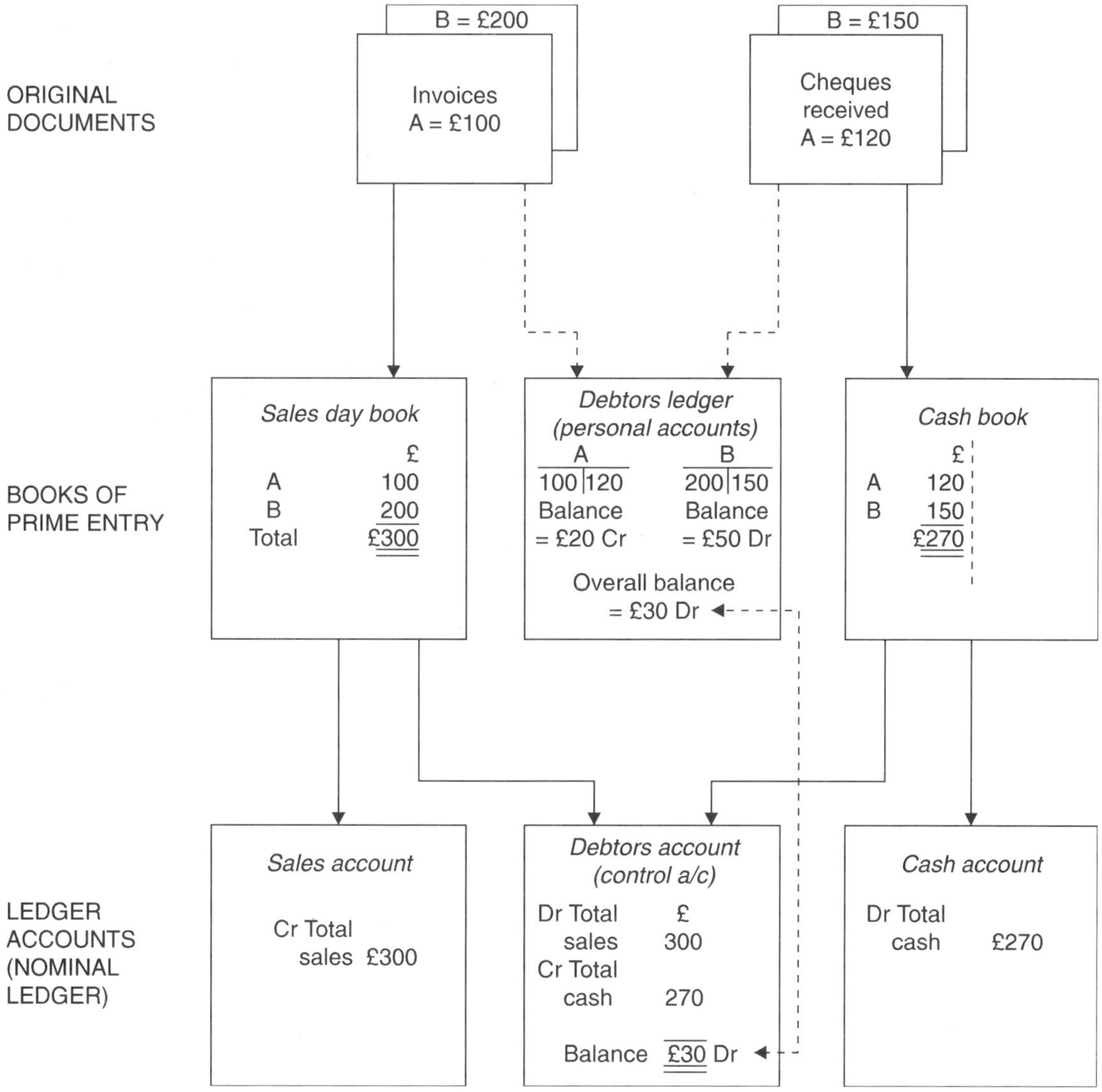

IMPORTANT POINTS

(a) The debtors ledger is **not** part of the double entry system.

(b) The total balance on the debtors ledger (ie all the personal account balances added up) should equal the balance on the debtors (control) account.

(c) This diagram implies that the memorandum accounts (sales or purchase ledger) are written up from the original documents rather than from the sales day book. This is CIMA's official line, although the other treatment is possible in practice.

Question 1

On 1 October 20X8 the debtors' ledger balances were £8,024 debit and £57 credit, and the creditors' ledger balances on the same date were £6,235 credit and £105 debit.

For the year ended 30 September 20X9 the following particulars are available.

	£
Sales	63,728
Purchases	39,974
Cash received from debtors	55,212
Cash paid to creditors	37,307
Discount received	1,475
Discount allowed	2,328
Returns inwards	1,002
Returns outwards	535
Bad debts written off	326
Cash received in respect of debit balances in creditors' ledger	105
Amount due from customer as shown by debtors' ledger, offset against amount due to the same firm as shown by creditors' ledger (settlement by contra)	434
Cash received in respect of debt previously written off as bad	94
Allowances to customers on goods damaged in transit	212

On 30 September 20X9 there were no credit balances in the debtors' ledger except those outstanding on 1 October 20X8, and no debit balances in the creditors' ledger.

You are required to write up the following accounts recording the above transactions and bringing down the balances as on 30 September 20X9.

(a) Debtors control account
(b) Creditors control account

Answer

(a)

DEBTORS CONTROL ACCOUNT

20X8		£	*20X8*		£
Oct 1	Balances b/f	8,024	Oct 1	Balances b/f	57
20X9			*20X9*		
Sept 30	Sales	63,728	Sept 30	Cash received from debtors	55,212
	Balances c/f	57		Discount allowed	2,328
				Returns	1,002
				Bad debts written off	326
				Transfer creditors control account	434
				Allowances on goods damaged	212
				Balances c/f	12,238
		71,809			71,809

(b)

CREDITORS CONTROL ACCOUNT

		£			£
20X8			*20X8*		
Oct 1	Balances b/f	105	Oct 1	Balances b/f	6,235
20X9			*20X9*		
Sept 30	Cash paid to creditors	37,307	Sept 30	Purchases	39,974
	Discount received	1,475		Cash	105
	Returns outwards	535			
	Transfer debtors control account	434			
	Balances c/f	6,458			
		46,314			46,314

Note. The double entry in respect of cash received for the bad debt previously written off is:

DEBIT	Cash	£94	
CREDIT	Profit and loss account		£94

4 BALANCING AND RECONCILING CONTROL ACCOUNTS WITH SALES AND PURCHASE LEDGERS May 2001

4.1 The control accounts should be balanced regularly (at least monthly) and the balance agreed with the sum of the individual debtors' or creditors' balances in the sales or bought ledgers respectively. The balance on the control account may not agree with the sum of balances extracted, for one or more of the following reasons.

(a) An **incorrect amount** may be posted to the control account because of a miscast of the book of prime entry (ie adding up incorrectly the total value of invoices or payments). The nominal ledger debit and credit postings will balance, but the control account balance will not agree with the sum of individual balances extracted from the sales ledger or purchase ledger. A journal entry must then be made in the nominal ledger to correct the control account and the corresponding sales or expense account.

(b) A **transposition error** may occur in posting an individual's balance eg the sale to C Cloning of £250 might be posted to his account as £520. This means that the sum of balances extracted from the memorandum ledger must be corrected. No accounting entry is required except to alter the figure in C Cloning's account.

(c) A transaction may be recorded in the control account and **not** in the memorandum ledger, or vice versa. This requires a double posting if the control account has to be corrected, or a single posting to the individual's balance in the memorandum ledger.

(d) The sum of balances extracted from the memorandum ledger may be incorrectly extracted or **miscast**. This would involve simply correcting the total of the balances.

Exam focus point

In May 2001 there was a question on control accounts in Section A of the exam.

4.2 EXAMPLE: AGREEING CONTROL ACCOUNT BALANCES WITH THE SALES AND BOUGHT LEDGERS

The balance on the debtors control account is £15,091. The total of the list of balances taken from the sales ledger is £15,320. It is discovered that:

(i) £10 received from a debtor and put in the petty cash tin was correctly recorded in his personal account but excluded from the nominal ledger. NL LP ✓

(ii) The sales day book for March was undercast by £100. NL DP ✓

(iii) When posting an invoice for £95 to a customers account it was recorded as £59 by mistake. Sales ledger. ✓

(iv) A credit balance in the sales ledger was treated as a debit balance when adding up the list of balances. x2 credit x2 debit

(v) The list of balances has been overcast by £90.

(vi) The returns inwards for June totalling £35 have been correctly recorded in the sales ledger, but no entries have been made in the nominal ledger.

Required

Show the adjustments necessary to the list of balances and to the debtors control account.

4.3 SOLUTION

	£	£
Sales ledger total		
Original total extracted		15,320
Add difference arising from transposition error (£95 written as £59)		36
		15,356
Less		
Credit balance of £60 extracted as a debit balance (£60 × 2)	120	
Overcast of list of balances	90	
		210
		15,146

DEBTORS CONTROL

	£		£
Balance before adjustments	15,091	Petty cash - posting omitted	10
		Returns inwards - individual posting omitted from control account	35
Undercast of total invoices issued in sales day book	100	Balance c/d (now in agreement with the corrected total of individual balances in (a))	15,146
	15,191		15,191
Balance b/d	15,146		

Question 2

(i) An invoice for £39 is recorded in the sales day book as £93.
(ii) The sales day book is overcast by £100.

To correct these errors we will need to adjust:

	Debtors control a/c	*Sales ledger*
A	For (i) and (ii)	For (i) and (ii)
B	No adjustment necessary	No adjustment necessary
C	For (i) and (ii)	For (i) only
D	For (i) only	For (i) and (ii)

Answer

C is correct. Both affect the control account and because totals are not posted to the sales ledger, (ii) does not affect the sales ledger.

Chapter roundup

- The two most important control accounts are those for debtors and creditors. They are part of the double entry system.
- Cash books and day books are totalled periodically (say once a month) and the appropriate totals are posted to the control accounts.
- The individual entries in cash and day books will have been entered one by one in the appropriate personal accounts contained in the sales ledger and purchase ledger. These personal accounts are not part of the double entry system: they are memorandum only.
- At suitable intervals the balances on personal accounts are extracted from the ledgers, listed and totalled. The total of the outstanding balances can then be reconciled to the balance on the appropriate control account and any errors located and corrected.

Quick quiz

1 XYZ Ltd has a sales ledger control account containing the following. Balances b/f £12,200, credit sales £87,000, receipts from debtors £56,000, bad debts written off £1,800, refunds to credit customers £500, discounts allowed £1,500. The closing debtors balance is?

A £42,700
B £44,000
C £38,400
D £40,400

2 Which of the following items will not appear in a debtors control account?

A Discount allowed
B Bad debts written off
C Increases in the provision of doubtful debts
D Allowances to credit customers

3 Four reasons to maintain a control account as well as a sales ledger are:

(1) ________________

(2) ________________

(3) ________________

(4) ________________

Answers to quick quiz

1 D Correct.

Sales ledger control

Balance b/d	12,200	Bank: receipts	56,000
Sales	87,000	Bad debts	1,800
Bank: refunds	500	Discount allowed	1,500
		Balance c/d	40,400
	99,700		99,700

A Incorrect: you have transposed the figures for bad debts and refunds in the control account.

B Incorrect: you have not recorded bad debts correctly – as a credit in the sales ledger control account.

C Incorrect: you have recorded refunds as a credit entry in the sales ledger control account.

2 C Correct. Will not appear, the debts are not actually written off
  A Will appear – credit entry.
  B Will appear – credit entry.
  D Will appear – credit entry.

3 (1) To provide a check on the accuracy of entries in the personal accounts
  (2) To assist in the location of errors
  (3) To provide separation of duties
  (4) Control accounts provide the balance sheet debtors figure

Now try the questions below from the Question Bank

Number	Level	Marks	Time
37	Exam	10	18 mins
38	Exam	2	3 mins
39	Exam	2	3 mins

Chapter 14

ACCOUNTING FOR VALUE ADDED TAX

Topic List		Syllabus reference	Ability required
1	The nature of VAT and how it is collected	(ii)	Application
2	Accounting for VAT	(ii)	Application

Introduction

Many business transactions involve **VAT (value added tax)**. Invoices and bills show any VAT charged separately.

VAT is charged on the supply of goods and services. It is a **general consumer expenditure tax**.

Section 1 explains how VAT works.

Section 2 deals with the accounting treatment of VAT. If you understand the principle behind the tax and how it is collected, you will understand the accounting treatment.

Learning outcomes covered in this chapter

- Prepare accounts for indirect taxes (eg VAT)

Syllabus content covered in this chapter

- Accounting for indirect taxes (eg VAT)

1 THE NATURE OF VAT AND HOW IT IS COLLECTED — Pilot Paper

KEY TERM

Value added tax is an indirect tax levied on the sale of goods and services. It is administered by Customs and Excise rather than the Inland Revenue.

1.1 VAT is a cumulative tax, collected at various stages of a product's life. In the illustrative example below, a manufacturer of a television buys materials and components and then sells the television to a wholesaler, who in turn sells it to a retailer, who then sells it to a customer. It is assumed that the rate for VAT is 17.5% on all items. All the other figures are for illustration only.

1.2 EXAMPLE

			Price net of VAT	*VAT 17.5%*	*Total price*
			£	£	£
(a)	(i)	Manufacturer purchases raw materials and components	40	7	47
	(ii)	Manufacturer sells the completed television to a wholesaler	200	35	235
		The manufacturer hands over to Customs and Excise		28	
(b)	(i)	Wholesaler purchases television for	200	35	235
	(ii)	Wholesaler sells television to a retailer	320	56	376
		Wholesaler hands over to Customs and Excise		21	
(c)	(i)	Retailer purchases television for	320	56	376
	(ii)	Retailer sells television	480	84	564
		Retailer hands over to Customs and Excise		28	
(d)		Customer purchases television for	480	84	564

The total tax of £84 is borne by the ultimate consumer. However, the tax is handed over to the authorities in stages. If we assume that the VAT of £7 on the initial supplies to the manufacturer is paid by the supplier, Customs and Excise would collect the VAT as follows.

	£
Supplier of materials and components	7
Manufacturer	28
Wholesaler	21
Retailer	28
Total VAT paid	84

Input and output VAT

KEY TERM

VAT charged on goods and services sold by a business is referred to as **output VAT.** VAT paid on goods and services 'bought in' by a business is referred to as **input VAT.**

1.3 The example above assumes that the supplier, manufacturer, wholesaler and retailer are all VAT-registered traders.

A VAT-registered trader must carry out the following tasks.

(a) Charge VAT on the goods and services sold at the rate prescribed by the government. This is output VAT.

(b) Pay VAT on goods and services purchased from other businesses. This is input VAT.

(c) Pay to Customs and Excise the difference between the VAT collected on sales and the VAT paid to suppliers for purchases. Payments are made at quarterly intervals.

1.4 If output VAT exceeds input VAT, the business pays the difference in tax to the authorities. If output VAT is less than input VAT in a period, Customs and Excise will refund the difference to the business.

Irrecoverable VAT

1.5 There are some circumstances in which traders are not allowed to reclaim VAT paid on their inputs. In these cases the trader must bear the cost of VAT and account for it accordingly. Three such cases need to be considered.

(a) Non-registered persons
(b) Registered persons carrying on exempted activities
(c) Non-deductible inputs

Non-registered persons

1.6 Traders whose sales (outputs) are below a certain minimum level need not register for VAT. Non-registered persons will pay VAT on their inputs and, because they are not registered, they cannot reclaim it. The VAT paid will effectively increase the cost of their P & L expenses and the cost of any fixed assets they may purchase. Non-registered persons do not charge VAT on their outputs.

Registered persons carrying on exempted activities

1.7 All outputs of registered traders are either taxable or exempt. Taxable outputs are charged to VAT either at zero per cent (zero-rated items) or at 17.5% (standard-rated items).

1.8 Traders carrying on exempt activities (such as banks) cannot reclaim VAT paid on their inputs, even though they may be VAT-registered. Some traders and companies carry on a mixture of taxable and exempt activities. Such traders need to apportion the VAT paid on inputs. Only VAT relating to taxable outputs may be reclaimed.

Non-deductible inputs

1.9 There are a few special cases where the input tax is not deductible even for a taxable person with taxable outputs. These are as follows.

(a) VAT on motor cars is never reclaimable unless a car is acquired new for resale, ie by a car dealer. VAT on a car used wholly for business purposes is reclaimable. However, company cars usually have some private use, so you should assume that the VAT is not reclaimable unless told otherwise. VAT on accessories such as car radios is deductible if ordered on a separate purchase order and fitted after delivery. The VAT charged when a car is hired is reclaimable if all use is business use. If there is some non-business use and the leasing company reclaimed VAT, the hirer can only reclaim 50% of the VAT on the hire charge.

(b) VAT on business entertaining is not deductible other than VAT on entertaining staff.

(c) VAT on expenses incurred on domestic accommodation for directors.

(d) VAT on non-business items passed through the business accounts with limited relief where the goods are used partly in the business.

(e) VAT which does not relate to the making of supplies in the course of a business.

THE MAIN POINT!

Where VAT is not recoverable, for any of the reasons described above, it must be regarded as part of the cost of the items purchased and included in the P & L charge or in the balance sheet as appropriate.

Relief for bad debts

1.10 Relief is available for VAT on bad debts if the debt is over six months old (measured from the date of the supply) and has been written off in the creditor's accounts. Where a supplier of goods or services has accounted for VAT on the supply and the customer does not pay, the supplier may claim a refund of VAT on the amount unpaid.

1.11 Where payments on account have been received, they are attributed to debts in date order. The consideration must be money and ownership of goods must have passed.

1.12 If the debtor later pays all or part of the amount owed, a corresponding part of the VAT repaid must be paid back to HM Customs & Excise.

1.13 In order to claim the relief, the creditor must have a copy of the tax invoice and records to show that the VAT has been accounted for and the debt has been written off. The VAT is reclaimed on the creditor's VAT return.

THE IMPORTANT POINTS

Registered businesses charge output VAT on sales and suffer input VAT on purchases. VAT does not affect the profit and loss account, but is simply being collected on behalf of Customs and Excise to whom a quarterly payment is made.

2 ACCOUNTING FOR VAT — Pilot Paper, May 2001

Profit and loss account

2.1 A business does not make any profit out of the VAT it charges. It therefore follows that its profit and loss figures should not include VAT. For example, if a business sells goods for £600 + VAT £105, ie for £705 total price, the sales account should only record the £600 excluding VAT. The accounting entries to record the sale would be as follows.

DEBIT	Cash or trade debtors	£705	
CREDIT	Sales		£600
CREDIT	VAT creditor (output VAT)		£105

(a) If input VAT is recoverable, the cost of purchases should exclude the VAT and be recorded net of tax. For example, if a business purchases goods on credit for £400 + VAT £70, the transaction would be recorded as follows.

DEBIT	Purchases	£400	
DEBIT	VAT creditor (input VAT recoverable)	£70	
CREDIT	Trade creditors		£470

(b) If the input VAT is not recoverable, the cost of purchases must include the tax, because it is the business itself which must bear the cost of the tax.

REMEMBER!

	Purchases	Sales
Profit and Loss Account	Irrecoverable input VAT: include Recoverable input VAT: exclude	Exclude VAT

VAT in the cash book, sales day book and purchase day book

2.2 When a business makes a credit sale the total amount invoiced, including VAT, will be recorded in the sales day book. The analysis columns will then separate the VAT from the sales income of the business as follows.

Date	*Total*	*Sales income*	*VAT*
	£	£	£
A Detter and Sons	235	200	35

2.3 When a business is invoiced by a supplier the total amount payable, including VAT, will be recorded in the purchase day book. The analysis columns will then separate the recoverable input VAT from the net purchase cost to the business as follows.

Date	*Total*	*Purchase*	*VAT*
	£	£	£
A Splier (Merchants)	188	160	28

2.4 When debtors pay what they owe, or creditors are paid, there is **no need to show** the VAT in an analysis column of the cash book, because input and output VAT arise when the sale is made, not when the debt is settled.

2.5 However, VAT charged on **cash sales** or VAT paid on **cash purchases** will be analysed in a separate column of the cash book. This is because output VAT has just arisen from the cash sale and must be credited to the VAT creditor in the ledger accounts. Similarly input VAT paid on cash purchases, having just arisen, must be debited to the VAT creditor.

2.6 For example, the receipts side of a cash book might be written up as follows.

Date	*Narrative*	*Folio*	*Total*	*Analysis columns*		
				Sales ledger (debtors)	*Cash sales*	*Output VAT on cash sales*
			£	£	£	£
	A Detter & Sons		235	235		
	Owen Ltd		660	660		
	Cash sales		329		280	49
	Newgate Merchants		184	184		
	Cash sales		94		80	14
			1,502	1,079	360	63

The payments side of a cash book might be written up as follows.

Date	*Narrative*	*Folio*	*Total*	*Analysis columns*		
				Purchase ledger (creditors)	*Cash purchases and sundry items*	*Input VAT on cash purchases*
			£	£	£	£
	A Splier (Merchants)		188	188		
	Telephone bill paid		141		120	21
	Cash purchase of stationery		47		40	7
	VAT paid to Customs and Excise		1,400		1,400	
			1,776	188	1,560	28

Exam focus point

Section A of the May 2001 exam had a question on recording transactions subject to VAT.

Question 1

Are trade debtors and trade creditors shown in the accounts inclusive of VAT or exclusive of VAT?

Answer

Paragraph 2.1 will tell you.

Exam focus point

A small element of VAT is quite likely in questions. It is worth spending a bit of time ensuring that you understand the logic behind the way VAT is accounted for, rather than trying to learn the rules by rote. This will ensure that even if you forget the rules, you will be able to work out what should be done.

Creditor for VAT

2.7 The VAT paid to the authorities each quarter is the difference between recoverable input VAT on purchases and output VAT on sales. For example, if a business is invoiced for input VAT of £8,000 and charges VAT of £15,000 on its credit sales and VAT of £2,000 on its cash sales, the VAT creditor account would be as follows.

VAT CREDITOR

	£		£
Creditors (input VAT)	8,000	Debtors (output VAT invoiced)	15,000
Cash (payment to authorities)	9,000	Cash (output VAT on cash sales)	2,000
	17,000		17,000

2.8 Payments to the authorities do not coincide with the end of the accounting period of a business, and so at the balance sheet date there will be a balance on the VAT creditor account. If this balance is for an amount payable to the authorities, the outstanding creditor for VAT will appear as a current liability in the balance sheet.

2.9 Occasionally, a business will be owed money back by the authorities, and in such a situation, the VAT refund owed by the authorities would be a current asset in the balance sheet.

Question 2

A business in its first period of trading charges £4,000 of VAT on its sales and suffers £3,500 of VAT on its purchases which included £250 VAT on business entertaining. Prepare the VAT creditor account.

Answer

VAT CREDITOR ACCOUNT

	£		£
Creditors	3,250	Debtors	4,000
Balance c/d (owed to C+E)	750		
	4,000		4,000
		Balance b/d	750

THE MAIN POINTS

(a)	**Credit sales**	**(b)**	**Credit purchases**
(i)	Include VAT in sales day book; show it separately	(i)	Include VAT in purchases day book; show it separately
(ii)	Include gross receipts from debtors in cashbook; no need to show VAT separately	(ii)	Include gross payments in cashbook; no need to show VAT separately
(iii)	Exclude VAT element from profit and loss account	(iii)	Exclude recoverable VAT from profit and loss account
(iv)	Credit VAT creditor with output VAT element of debtors invoiced	(iv)	Include irrecoverable VAT in profit and loss account
		(v)	Debit VAT creditor with recoverable input VAT element of credit purchases
(c)	**Cash sales**	**(d)**	**Cash purchases**
(i)	Include gross receipts in cashbook; show VAT separately	(i)	Include gross payments in cashbook: show VAT separately
(ii)	Exclude VAT element from profit and loss account	(ii)	Exclude recoverable VAT from profit and loss account
(iii)	Credit VAT creditor with output VAT element of cash sales	(iii)	Include irrecoverable VAT in profit and loss account
		(iv)	Debit VAT creditor with recoverable input VAT element of cash purchases

Chapter roundup

- VAT is an indirect tax levied on the sale of goods and services. Output VAT is charged on the sales made by a business. Input VAT is paid by a business on its purchases.
- The difference between input VAT and output VAT is paid to or reclaimed from Customs and Excise.
- If input VAT is recoverable it is excluded from the cost of purchases in the profit and loss account. VAT charged on sales to customers is also excluded from the profit and loss account.
- An outstanding creditor for VAT will appear as a current liability in the balance sheet.
- Some inputs are described as non-deductible, for example, cars unless they are bought for resale by a person trading in cars. Exam questions may try to catch you out with this.

Quick quiz

1 Value added tax is:

A A direct tax levied on sales of goods and services
B An indirect tax levied on the sales of goods and services
C Administered by the Inland Revenue
D Charged by businesses on taxable supplies

2 What are the two rates of VAT which may be applicable to taxable outputs?

(1) ____________________

(2) ____________________

3 When VAT is not recoverable on the cost of a motor car, it should be treated in which of the following ways?

A Deducted from the cost of the asset capitalised
B Included in the cost of the asset capitalised
C Deducted from output tax for the period
D Written off to P&L as an expense

4 Purchases of goods costing £500 subject to VAT at 17.5% occur. Which of the following correctly records the **credit purchase**?

A	Dr	Purchases	£500.00	
	Dr	VAT	£87.50	
	Cr	Creditors		£587.50
B	Dr	Purchases	£587.50	
	Cr	Creditors		£587.50
C	Dr	Purchases	£412.50	
	Dr	VAT	£87.50	
	Cr	Creditors		£500.00
D	Dr	Purchases	£500.00	
	Cr	VAT		£87.50
	Cr	Creditors		£412.50

5 A business purchases goods valued at £400. VAT is charged at 17.5%. The double entry to record the purchase is:

DEBIT ____________________ £________
DEBIT ____________________ £________
CREDIT ____________________ £________

6 Fill in the blanks.

Input VAT is ____,

output VAT is ____.

7 When a cash sale is made for £117.50 (including VAT) the entries made are:

DEBIT ____________________ account £________
CREDIT ____________________ account £________
CREDIT ____________________ account £________

8 When a cash purchase of £117.50 is made (including VAT) the entries are:

DEBIT ____________________ account £________
DEBIT ____________________ account £________
CREDIT ____________________ account £________

9 The VAT paid to Customs and Excise each quarter is the difference between ____________________

____________________ and ____________________

____________________.

Answers to quick quiz

1 B Correct

A Incorrect, the consumer has a choice as to whether or not to consume so VAT is only chargeable when this choice is exercised.

C Incorrect, VAT is administrated by Customs and Excise.

D Only VAT registered traders can charge VAT.

2 Zero-rate and standard-rate (17.5%).

3 B Correct the balance sheet value will therefore include VAT and the depreciation charge will rise accordingly

A Incorrect, it must be added.

C Incorrect.

D Incorrect, the motor car is a fixed asset not an expense, VAT will form part of the depreciable amount of the asset.

4 A Correct, recoverable input tax is debited to the VAT a/c and the purchases account is debited net of VAT.

B Incorrect, the VAT has not been reclaimed.

C Incorrect, the £500 is subject to VAT.

D Incorrect, reversal of the VAT transaction has occurred.

5

DEBIT:	PURCHASES	£400	
	VAT	£70	
CREDIT:	CASH or CREDITORS		£470

6 Input VAT is **VAT suffered on goods and services brought by a business**, output VAT is **the VAT collected on sales.**

7

DEBIT	Cash account	£117.50	
DEBIT	Sales account	£100	
CREDIT	VAT account		£17.50

8

DEBIT	Purchases account	£100	
CREDIT	VAT account		£17.50
CREDIT	Cash account		£117.50

9 The VAT paid to Customs & Excise each quarter is the difference between **output VAT collected on sales** and **input VAT suffered on purchases and expenses**.

Now try the questions below from the Question Bank

Number	Level	Marks	Time
40	Introductory	15	27 mins
41	Exam	2	3 mins
42	Exam	2	3 mins

Chapter 15

ACCOUNTING FOR WAGES AND SALARIES

Topic List		Syllabus reference	Ability required
1	Gross pay and deductions	(ii)	Application
2	Accounting for wages and salaries	(ii)	Application

Introduction

The salary paid to the bank or the jangle of coins in the wages packet is the final result of a long process of recording and calculation. This is often referred to as payroll processing and payroll accounting, a payroll being simply a list of employees and what they are to be paid. Being on the payroll of an organisation means that you are selling your labour to it for an agreed price.

From an employer's point of view, too, the wages and salaries bill is of great importance. It is often one of the largest items of expenditure an employer has to incur.

Most people have to pay some of what they earn to the government as taxation (Income Tax) which pays for general social benefits, eg the Health Service. In addition, people pay National Insurance Contributions (NIC), which, in practice, is similar to a tax. The tax and NIC is collected by the employer when the employee is paid. The system is called PAYE (Pay As You Earn). This system is the subject of Section 1.

While you might think that the employer is doing the government a favour by acting as a tax collector, the legal apparatus surrounding PAYE is quite strict. It is vital therefore, that proper accounting records are kept. This is covered in Section 2 of the chapter.

Learning outcomes covered in this chapter

- Prepare accounts for payroll

Syllabus content covered in this chapter

- Accounting for payroll

1 GROSS PAY AND DEDUCTIONS — May 2001

KEY TERMS

Gross pay is the full amount that an employee earns.

Deductions are the amounts taken from gross pay for income tax, National Insurance contributions and any other reasons agreed by employer and employee such as pension contributions.

Net pay is gross pay less deductions, ie the amount actually received by the employee.

1.1 The government requires that businesses should act as collecting agents on behalf of the Inland Revenue. When a business makes a wages or salary payment to an employee, it calculates the amount of tax and NIC due. These amounts are deducted from the employee's gross remuneration and paid by the business to the Inland Revenue. The employee receives only the net amount remaining after these deductions.

1.2 An employee effectively pays his income tax liability in instalments each time he receives a wages payment. This system of income tax collection is called PAYE or pay-as-you-earn.

1.3 Apart from these compulsory deductions, which all businesses must operate, there may be other voluntary deductions from an employee's pay.

(a) **Savings schemes**. An employee agrees to save £5 a week. Each week the £5 is deducted from his gross pay and held for him by his employer until he decides to withdraw it.

(b) **Contributions to charity**. An employee might agree to a weekly deduction of 50p as a contribution to Oxfam. The employer deducts the agreed amount each week and at suitable intervals hands over the money collected to the charity.

(c) **Pension schemes**.

1.4 EXAMPLE: ACCOUNTING FOR DEDUCTIONS FROM GROSS PAY

Mr Little's gross pay for the week ending 31 October 20X6 is £140. His employer, Mr Big, calculates that income tax of £20 and NIC of £13 are due on that level of earnings. In addition, Little received a loan from the business in June 20X6 which he is repaying by weekly deductions of £5. He also voluntarily contributes 20p per week to a local charity, again by deduction from his gross wages.

How should these amounts be accounted for?

1.5 SOLUTION

The cost to Mr Big is the gross pay of £140 and this is charged in his profit and loss account. The amount actually paid to Little is only £101.80 (£140 – £20 – £13 – £5 – 20p).

The deductions should be accounted for as follows.

(a) PAYE of £20 and NIC of £13 are paid over to the Inland Revenue. In practice, this payment would not be made every week. Mr Big would accumulate the amounts due in respect of all his employees and would make a single payment to Inland Revenue once a month.

(b) The £5 deduction is applied to reduce the amount of the loan outstanding from Little.

(c) The 20p deduction is handed over to the local charity. Again, it would probably be convenient to accumulate these amounts for a number of weeks before payment.

Employer's National Insurance contributions and pension contributions

1.6 Employees are normally obliged to pay NIC which is deducted from their gross pay and paid over by their employer on their behalf. But employers also have to make a contribution themselves in respect of each of their employees. This is **not** a deduction from the employee's gross pay, it is an **extra** cost borne by the employer. Also, the employer is likely to make contributions to pension schemes. The employer's profit and loss account must show the total cost of employing staff and this includes not only the gross pay, but also the employer's NIC and any employer's pension contributions.

1.7 An employer's monthly payment to the Inland Revenue therefore includes the following.

- **PAYE** income tax for each employee (deducted from the employees' gross pay)
- **Employees**' NIC (deducted from the employees' gross pay)
- **Employer's** NIC, paid from the employer's own funds

IMPORTANT POINT

The cost to a business of employing its workforce is gross pay plus employer's NIC and any employer's pension contributions.

Question 1

An employee earns £10 an hour gross and has worked 48 hours this week. His income tax liability is £58 and his NIC is £12. Voluntary deductions are £5 sports club subscription and pension contributions of £40. The employer's NIC is £25 and pension contribution is £20.

The employee's net pay is £ 365 . 10×48 = 480 - 58 12 - 5 - 40 = 365

The gross payroll cost to the employer is £ 525 .

Answer

The employee's net pay is £365. ((£10 × 48) = £480 – £58 – £12 – £5 – £40 = £365)

The gross payroll cost to the employer is £525. (£480 + £25 + £20 = £525)

National Insurance contributions

1.8 Calculating NIC is easy. An employee pays a fixed percentage of his gross income, the percentage depending on the level of his income. For the employer's contribution, again a fixed percentage is applied to the employee's gross pay, but the percentage may differ from that used in calculating the employee's contribution.

1.9 Employees' NIC is subject to a maximum amount. There is no limit on the amount of an employer's contributions.

1.10 The government publishes tables detailing the amount of NIC payable at all levels of income. Therefore employers simply extract the amounts due from the tables.

Calculating PAYE deductions

1.11 PAYE contributions are more complicated, but again the use of Inland Revenue tables simplifies matters in practice.

1.12 First add the amount of the employee's gross pay for the current period to the previous total of gross pay. This gives his gross pay for the tax year to date. (Tax years run from 6 April to 5 April.) Next calculate the amount of tax due for the year to date. This will depend on the employee's tax code, which reflects the amount of tax free pay he can earn.

1.13 The tax due for the year to date is then compared with the tax actually paid by the employee up to and including the previous week/month. The difference is the amount of tax due from the employee in the current week/month, and is the amount deducted from his gross pay.

1.14 Sometimes the tax due for the year to date is less than the tax already paid by the employee. In that case the employee will be entitled to a tax refund as an **addition** to his gross pay.

Exam focus point

The calculation of the P+L charge for wages was examined in Section A of the May 2001 exam.

2 ACCOUNTING FOR WAGES AND SALARIES **Pilot Paper**

2.1 Three accounts are needed.

- Wages control account
- PAYE control account
- NIC control account

2.2 First calculate the total costs of employment to be borne by the business. These consist of employees' gross pay plus employer's NIC. The following accounting entries are made.

DEBIT	P & L account - wages/salaries (gross pay + employer's NIC)
CREDIT	Wages control account (gross pay)
CREDIT	NIC control account (employer's NIC)

2..3 Then the amount of deductions are calculated for PAYE and employee's NIC.

DEBIT	Wages control account (total deductions)
CREDIT	PAYE control account (PAYE)
CREDIT	NIC control account (employee's NIC)

2.4 Then pay employees their net pay.

DEBIT	Wages control account
CREDIT	Cash account

2.5 In due course, the credit balances on PAYE control and NIC control are eliminated by making payments to Inland Revenue.

2.6 Any voluntary deductions permitted by employees must be debited to wages control account and credited to a liability account until they are eventually paid over by the employer as appropriate.

2.7 EXAMPLE: LEDGER ACCOUNTS FOR WAGES AND SALARIES

At 1 November 20X5 Netpay Ltd had the following credit balances on ledger accounts.

	£
PAYE control account	4,782
NIC control account	2,594
Employee savings account	1,373

The company's wages records for the month of November 20X5 showed the following.

	£
Total gross pay	27,294
PAYE	6,101
Employer's NIC	2,612
Employees' NIC	2,240
Employees' savings deductions	875
Net amounts paid to employees	18,078

The company paid £9,340 to Inland Revenue during the month, being £4,750 PAYE and £4,590 NIC.

Show the ledger accounts recording these transactions.

2.8 SOLUTION

WAGES CONTROL ACCOUNT

	£		£
PAYE control	6,101	Wages expense a/c - gross pay	27,294
NIC control - employees' contributions	2,240		
Employee savings a/c	875		
Bank - net pay	18,078		
	27,294		27,294

PAYE CONTROL ACCOUNT

	£		£
Bank	4,750	Balance b/f	4,782
Balance c/d	6,133	Wages control	6,101
	10,883		10,883
		Balance b/d	6,133

NIC CONTROL ACCOUNT

	£		£
Bank	4,590	Balance b/f	2,594
Balance c/d	2,856	Wages control - employees' NIC	2,240
		Wages expense a/c - employer's NIC	2,612
	7,446		7,446
		Balance b/d	2,856

EMPLOYEE SAVINGS ACCOUNT

	£		£
Balance c/d	2,248	Balance b/f	1,373
		Wages control	875
	2,248		2,248
		Balance	2,248

Note. This account shows the company's liability to employees, who may wish to withdraw their savings at any time.

Question 2

At 1 March 20X3 Brubeck Ltd had the following credit balances on ledger accounts.

	£
PAYE control account	23,000
NIC control account	12,500
Employee savings account	26,250

The company's wages records for the month of March 20X3 showed the following.

	£
PAYE	30,505
Employer's NIC	13,060
Employees' NIC	11,200
Employees' savings deductions	4,375
Net amounts paid to employees	90,390

The company paid £46,700 to the Inland Revenue during the month, being £23,750 PAYE and £22,950 NIC.

(a) How much was gross pay for the month?
(b) What is the balance c/d on the PAYE control account, if any?
(c) What is the balance c/d on the NIC control account, if any?
(d) What is the balance c/d on the Employee Savings account, if any?

Answer

(a) £136,470 (£90,390 + £30,505 + £11,200 + £4,375)
(b) £29,755 credit (£23,000 + £20,505 – £23,750)
(c) £13,810 credit (£12,500 + £13,060 + £11,200 – £22,950)
(d) £30,625 credit (£26,250 + £4,375)

Exam focus point

As long as you understand the principles of control accounts and logically follow through the double entry, you should not experience too many difficulties. Do not be put off by the 'tax' content. PAYE is just another creditor.

Chapter roundup

- The cost of employing staff must be shown in a business's profit and loss account. It comprises the gross pay earned by employees, plus employer's NIC.
- A business must deduct PAYE income tax and employees' NIC from employees' gross pay. Only the net amount is then paid to employees. The amounts deducted are paid over every month by the employer to the Inland Revenue.

Quick quiz

1 PAYE stands for? (In relation to income tax issues.)

A Payroll and your earnings
B Pay as you earn
C Pay after you earn
D Payroll accounting year end

2 Three voluntary deductions that an employee might permit from his gross pay are:

(1) ____________________ (2) ____________________

(3) ____________________

3 The total cost of employing staff shown in an employer's profit and loss account is ________________ ________________.

4 At 31.12.20X0 a company had the following balance in its records: PAYE control a/c £15,800. NIC control a/c £7,600. Deductions from pay in January 20X1 were: income tax £8,600, NIC £3,400. Employer's NIC were £2,800. PAYE payments were £6,800. NI payments were £3,400. Calculate the PAYE and NI control account balances as at 31.1.20X1.

A PAYE £19,400 (cr) NIC £13,200 (cr)
B PAYE £17,600 (cr) NIC £7,600 (cr)
C PAYE £17,600 (dr) NIC £10,400 (dr)
D PAYE £17,600 (cr) NIC £10,400 (cr)

5 An employee has a gross pay of £150, a bonus of £25, income tax and NIC amount to £30 and pension contributions are made totalling £15. The employers NIC and pension contributions amount to £55. The gross payroll cost to the employer is?

A £230
B £175
C £130
D £185

6 What ledger accounting entries are made in respect of voluntary deductions permitted by employees?

DEBIT ________________

CREDIT ________________

Answers to quick quiz

1 B The employer is responsible for deducting income tax from employees and accounting for these deductions to the Inland Revenue.

2
- Savings scheme
- Charity contributions
- Pension scheme

3 The gross salary, plus employer's NIC

4 D Correct.

PAYE Control A/C

Bank	6,800	Balance b/d	15,800
Balance c/d	17,600	Wages control	8,600
	24,400		24,400

NIC Control A/C

Bank	3,400	Balance b/d	7,600
Balance c/d	10,400	Wages control	3,400
		Wages control	2,800
	13,800		13,800

A Incorrect, you have reversed the opening and closing balances.

B Incorrect, you have omitted the employers NI contribution.

C Incorrect, these are liabilities not assets.

5 A Correct, employees wage plus bonus plus employers contributions.
B Incorrect, this is the total gross pay.
C Incorrect, this is the employees net pay.
D Incorrect, this is net pay plus employers contributions.

6 DEBIT Wages control
CREDIT Deduction liability account

Now try the questions below from the Question Bank

Number	Level	Marks	Time
43	Exam	15	27 mins
44	Exam	2	3 mins
45	Exam	2	3 mins

Chapter 16

CORRECTION OF ERRORS. PREPARATION OF FINAL ACCOUNTS

Topic List		Syllabus reference	Ability required
1	Types of error in accounting	(iii)	Comprehension
2	The correction of errors	(iii)	Comprehension
3	Suspense accounts	(iii)	Comprehension
4	Preparation of final accounts	(iv)	Comprehension

Introduction

We have nearly reached our goal of preparing of the final accounts of a sole trader.

This chapter continues the subject of errors in accounts. You have already learned about errors which arise in the context of the cash book or the sales and purchase ledgers and debtors and creditors control account. Here we deal with errors that may be corrected by means of the journal or a suspense account.

Learning outcomes covered in this chapter

- Explain the nature of errors and to be able to make accounting entries for them
- Prepare journal entries

Syllabus content covered in this chapter

- Errors
- Adjustments to the trial balance

WARNING!

To understand the correction of errors you must really understand the accounting process, ie the use of day books, nominal ledger accounts and the sales and purchase ledger.

1 TYPES OF ERROR IN ACCOUNTING — Pilot Paper

1.1 It is not possible to draw up a complete list of all the errors which might be made by bookkeepers and accountants. However, it is possible to describe five **types** of error which cover most of the errors as:

- Errors of **transposition**
- Errors of **omission**
- Errors of **principle**

- Errors of **commission**
- **Compensating** errors

1.2 Once an error has been detected, it needs to be put right.

(a) If the correction involves a double entry in the ledger accounts, then it is done by using a journal entry.

(b) When the error breaks the rule of double entry and prevents the trial balance balancing, it is corrected by the use of a suspense account as well as a journal entry.

KEY TERM

An **error of transposition** is when **a number of digits** in an amount are accidentally recorded the **wrong way round**.

1.3 For example, suppose that a sale is recorded in the sales account as £6,843, but it is incorrectly recorded in the total debtors account as £6,483. The error is the transposition of the 4 and the 8. The consequence is that total debits will not be equal to total credits. You can often detect a transposition error by checking whether the difference between debits and credits can be divided exactly by 9. For example, £6,843 – £6,483 = £360; £360 ÷ 9 = 40. Such an error will stop the trial balance balancing, but if the sale of £6,843 had been recorded in both the sales and the debtors account as £6,483, the trial balance should balance.

KEY TERM

An **error of omission** means **failing to record** a transaction at all, or making one entry but not the corresponding double entry.

1.4 For example:

(a) A business receives an invoice from a supplier for £250. The transaction might be omitted from the books entirely. As a result, both the total debits and the total credits of the business will be out by £250, and the trial balance still balances.

(b) A business receives an invoice from a supplier for £300. The purchase ledger control account is credited, but the debit entry in the purchases account is omitted. In this case, the total credits would not equal total debits (total debits are £300 less than they ought to be), and the trial balance still balances.

KEY TERM

An **error of principle** involves making a double entry in the belief that the transaction is being entered in the correct accounts, but subsequently finding out that the accounting entry **breaks the 'rules'** of an accounting principle or concept. A typical example of such an error is to treat revenue expenditure incorrectly as capital expenditure.

1.5 For example, £100 spent repairing a car is recorded as debit fixed assets (cars), credit cash; when it should be debit motor expenses, credit cash. This error does not stop the trial balance balancing.

KEY TERM

Errors of commission are where the bookkeeper makes a mistake in recording transactions in the accounts.

1.6 For example:

(a) **Putting a debit entry or a credit entry in the wrong account** eg telephone expenses of £540 are debited to the electricity expenses account.

(b) **Errors of casting (adding up)** eg the total of the sales day book should add up to £28,425, but is incorrectly added up as £28,825.

These type of errors will not stop the trial balance balancing.

KEY TERM

Compensating errors are errors which are, coincidentally, **equal and opposite** to one another.

1.7 For example, two transposition errors of £540 occur in extracting ledger balances, one on each side of the double entry. In the administration expenses account, £2,282 is written instead of £2,822. While in the sundry income account, £8,391 is written instead of £8,931. Both the debits and the credits are £540 too low and the mistake is not apparent when the trial balance is cast.

Exam focus point

You could be given a number of scenarios and asked to identify the type of error that has occurred in each case.

Question 1

Which of the following errors would stop the trial balance balancing? And by how much?

(i) A cheque is written out for £96, but is incorrectly recorded in the cash book as £69.

(ii) The sales day book is correctly totalled as £324 but is recorded in the nominal ledger as £342 in both the sales account and the debtors control account.

(iii) The sale day book is correctly totalled as £324 and correctly posted to the debtors control account, but is recorded as £234 in the sales account.

(iv) An invoice from a supplier for £200 is not entered in the purchases day book.

(v) The only posting made from the purchases day book to the nominal ledger is to debit purchases account with the total of £3,000.

(vi) Goods costing £100 bought for a proprietors private use are recorded in the purchases day book, which is then correctly posted to the nominal ledger.

Answer

(i) The trial balance will balance.

(ii) The trial balance will balance.

(iii) The trial balance will not balance. Debtors control account has been debited with £324. Sales has been debited with £234. So the trial balance will exceed credits by £90.

(iv) The trial balance will balance.

(v) The trial balance will not balance. Purchases has been debited £3,000. No credit entry has been made. So in the trial balance debits will exceed credits by £3,000.

(vi) The trial balance will balance.

2 THE CORRECTION OF ERRORS — Pilot Paper, May 2001

Journal entries

2.1 Errors are corrected by journal entries. The format of a journal entry is:

Date	*Folio*	*Debit*	*Credit*
		£	£
Account to be debited		X	
Account to be credited			X
(Narrative to explain the transaction)			

2.2 EXAMPLE

Suppose a bookkeeper accidentally posts a bill for £40 to the rates account instead of to the electricity account. A trial balance is drawn up, and total debits are £40,000 and total credits are £40,000.

Show the journal entry made to correct the misposting error.

2.3 SOLUTION

1.7.20X7

DEBIT	Electricity account	£40	
CREDIT	Rates account		£40

To correct a misposting of £40 from the rates account to electricity account.

After the journal has been posted, total debits will still be £40,000 and total credits will be £40,000. Total debits and totals credits are still equal.

Question 2

Write out the journal entries which would correct the following errors.

(a) A business receives an invoice for £250 from a supplier which was omitted from the books entirely.

(b) Repairs worth £150 were incorrectly debited to the fixed asset (machinery) account instead of the repairs account.

(c) Telephone expenses of £540 are incorrectly debited to the electricity account.

(d) A page in the sales day book has been added up to £28,425 when it should be £28,825.

Answer

(a)	DEBIT	Purchases	£250	
	CREDIT	Creditors		£250

A transaction previously omitted.

(b)	DEBIT	Repairs account	£150	
	CREDIT	Fixed asset (machinery) a/c		£150

The correction of an error of principle. Repairs costs incorrectly added to fixed asset costs.

(c)	DEBIT	Telephone expenses	£540	
	CREDIT	Electricity expenses		£540

Correction of an error of commission. Telephone expenses wrongly charged to the electricity account.

(d)	DEBIT	Debtors	£400	
	CREDIT	Sales		£400

The correction of a casting error in the sales day book.
(£28,825 – £28,425 = £400)

Use of journal entries in examinations

2.4 Occasionally an examination question will ask you to 'journalise' a transaction (ie write it out in the form of a journal entry), **even** though the transaction is perfectly normal and not an error.

Question: A business sells £500 of goods on credit. Journalise the transaction.

Answer:

DEBIT	Debtors	£500	
CREDIT	Sales		£500

Goods to the value of £500 sold on credit.

2.5 No error has occurred, just a normal credit sale of £500. By asking you to put it in the form of a journal, the examiner can see if you understand the double-entry bookkeeping involved.

Exam focus point

Think about the effect of each journal entry on net profit. You might be asked to journalise some transactions and then to recalculate net profit accordingly. There were four marks in Section B of the May 2001 exam for writing out journals to correct errors.

3 SUSPENSE ACCOUNTS

KEY TERM

A **suspense** account is a **temporary** account which is opened because either:

- A trial balance does not balance
- The bookkeeper does not know where to post one side of a transaction (eg a cash payment is credited to cash, but the bookkeeper does not know what the payment is for and so will not know which account to debit).

Use of suspense account: when the trial balance does not balance

3.1 When an error has occurred which results in an imbalance between total debits and total credits in the ledger accounts, the first step is to open a suspense account.

3.2 EXAMPLE

Suppose an accountant draws up a trial balance and finds that, for some as yet unknown reason, total debits exceed total credits by £162.

There is an error somewhere, and for the time being, open a suspense account and enter a credit of £162 in it. This serves two purposes.

- A reminder of an outstanding error
- The suspense account balances the trial balance

3.3 SOLUTION

When the cause of the £162 discrepancy is tracked down, it is corrected by means of a journal entry. For example, suppose it turned out that the accountant had accidentally failed to record a credit of £162 to creditors control. The journal entry would be:

DEBIT	Suspense a/c	£162	
CREDIT	Creditors control a/c		£162

To close off suspense a/c and correct error.

THE MAIN POINT!

Whenever an error occurs which results in total debits not being equal to total credits, the first step an accountant makes is to open up a suspense account.

3.4 EXAMPLE: TRANSPOSITION ERROR

The bookkeeper of Mixem Gladly Ltd made a transposition error when entering an amount for sales in the sales account. Instead of entering the correct amount of £37,453.60 he entered £37,543.60, transposing the 4 and 5. The debtors were posted correctly, and so when total debits and credits on the ledger accounts were compared, it was found that credits exceeded debits by £(37,543.60 – 37,453.60) = £90.

3.5 SOLUTION

The initial step is to equalise the total debits and credits by posting a debit of £90 to a suspense account.

When the cause of the error is discovered, the double entry to correct it should be logged in the journal as:

DEBIT	Sales	£90	
CREDIT	Suspense a/c		£90

To close off suspense a/c and correct transposition error.

3.6 EXAMPLE: ERROR OF OMISSION

When Guttersnipe Builders paid the monthly salary cheques to its office staff, the payment of £5,250 was correctly entered in the cash account, but the bookkeeper omitted to debit the office salaries account. As a consequence, the total debit and credit balances on the ledger accounts were not equal, and credits exceeded debits by £5,250.

3.7 SOLUTION

The initial step in correcting the situation is to debit £5,250 to a suspense account.

When the cause of the error is discovered, the double entry to correct it should be logged in the journal.

DEBIT	Office salaries account	£5,250	
CREDIT	Suspense account		£5,250

To close off suspense account and correct error of omission.

3.8 EXAMPLE: ERROR OF COMMISSION

A bookkeeper makes a mistake by entering what should be a debit entry as a credit, or vice versa. For example, a credit customer pays £460 of the £660 he owes, but the bookkeeper has debited £460 on the debtors account in the nominal ledger by mistake.

The total debit balances in Ashdown's ledger accounts would now exceed the total credits by 2 × £460 = £920.

3.9 SOLUTION

The initial step in correcting the error would be to make a credit entry of £920 in a suspense account. When the cause of the error is discovered, it should be corrected as follows.

DEBIT	Suspense account	£920	
CREDIT	Debtors		£920

To close off suspense account and correct error of commission.

In the debtors account in the nominal ledger, the correction would appear therefore as follows.

DEBTORS ACCOUNT

	£		£
Balance b/f	660	Suspense account: error corrected	920
Payment incorrectly debited	460	Balance c/f	200
	1,120		1,120

Use of suspense account: not knowing where to post a transaction

3.10 Suspense accounts are also used when a bookkeeper does not know in which account to post one side of a transaction. Until the mystery is sorted out, the entry is recorded in a suspense account. A typical example is when the business receives cash through the post from a source which cannot be determined. The double entry in the accounts would be a debit in the cash book, and a credit to a suspense account.

3.11 EXAMPLE: NOT KNOWING WHERE TO POST A TRANSACTION

Windfall Garments received a cheque in the post for £620. The name on the cheque is R J Beasley Esq, but Windfall Garments have no idea who this person is, nor why he should be sending £620. The bookkeeper decides to open a suspense account.

DEBIT	Cash	£620	
CREDIT	Suspense account		£620

Eventually, it transpires that the cheque was in payment for a debt owed by the Haute Couture Corner Shop and paid out of the proprietor's personal bank account.

DEBIT	Suspense account	£620	
CREDIT	Debtors		£620

Suspense accounts might contain several items

3.12 If more than one error or unidentifiable posting to a ledger account arises during an accounting period, they will all be merged together in the same suspense account. Indeed, until the causes of the errors are discovered, the bookkeepers are unlikely to know exactly how many errors there are.

Exam focus point

An examination question might give you a balance on a suspense account, together with enough information to make the necessary corrections, leaving a nil balance on the suspense account and correct balances on various other accounts. In practice, of course, finding these errors is far from easy!

REMEMBER

Not all corrections will affect the suspense account. If the original error did not stop the trial balance balancing, its correction will not involve the suspense account.

3.13 EXAMPLE: SUSPENSE ACCOUNT WITH SEVERAL ITEMS

Chi Knitwear Ltd is an old fashioned firm with a hand-written set of books. A trial balance is extracted at the end of each month, and a profit and loss account and balance sheet are computed. This month however the trial balance will not balance, the credits exceeding debits by £1,536.

You are asked to help and after inspection of the ledgers discover the following errors.

(a) A balance of £87 on a debtors account has been omitted from the schedule of debtors, the total of which was entered as debtors in the trial balance.

(b) A small piece of machinery purchased for £1,200 had been written off to repairs.

(c) The receipts side of the cash book had been undercast by £720.

(d) The total of one page of the sales day book had been carried forward as £8,154, whereas the correct amount was £8,514.

(e) A credit note for £179 received from a supplier had been posted to the wrong side of his account.

(f) An electricity bill in the sum of £152, not yet accrued for, is discovered in a filing tray.

(g) Mr Smith whose past debts to the company had been the subject of a provision, at last paid £731 to clear his account. His personal account has been credited but the cheques has not yet been entered in the cash book.

Required

(a) Write up the suspense account to clear the trial balance difference.
(b) State the effect on the accounts of correcting each error.

3.14 SOLUTION

(a)

SUSPENSE ACCOUNT

	£		£
Opening balance	1,536	Debtors - balance omitted	87
Sales - under-recorded	360	Cash book - receipts undercast	720
		Creditors: credit note posted to wrong side	358
		Cash book: Mr Smith's debt paid but cash receipt not recorded	731
	1,896		1,896

Notes

(i) Error (b) is an error of principle, whereby a fixed asset item (capital expenditure) has been accounted for as revenue expenditure. The correction will be logged in the journal, but since the error did not result in an inequality between debits and credits, the suspense account would not have been used.

(ii) The electricity bill has been omitted from the accounts entirely. The error of omission means that both debits and credits will be logged in the journal, but the suspense account will not be involved, since there is equality between debits and credits in the error.

(b) (i) The error means that debtors are understated. The correction of the error will increase the total amount for debtors to be shown in the balance sheet.

(ii) The correction of this error will add £1,200 to fixed assets at cost (balance sheet item) and reduce repair costs by £1,200. The P & L account will therefore show an increased profit of £1,200, less any depreciation now charged on the fixed asset.

(iii) The undercasting (ie under-adding) of £720 on the receipts side of the cash book means that debits of cash will be £720 less than they should have been. The correction of the error will add £720 to the cash balance in the balance sheet.

(iv) This transposition error means that total sales would be under-recorded by £8,514 - £8,154 = £360 in the sales account. The correction of the error will add £360 to total sales, and thus add £360 to the profits in the P & L account.

(v) The credit note must have been issued for a purchase return to the supplier by the business. It should have been debited to the creditor's account, but instead has been credited. Assuming that the purchase returns account was credited correctly, the effect of the error has been to overstate total creditors by 2 × £179 = £358, and this amount should be credited from the suspense account and debited to the creditors account. The effect will be to reduce the total for creditors in the balance sheet by £358.

(vi) The electricity bill, when entered in the accounts, will increase creditors by £152, and reduce profits (by adding to electricity expenses) by £152, assuming that none of this cost is a prepayment of electricity charges.

(vii) Since the cheque has not yet been recorded in the cash book, the correction of the error will add £731 to the cash balance in the balance sheet. At the same time, the provision for doubtful debts can be reduced, which will increase the net amount for debtors in the balance sheet by £731 (ie debtors less provision for doubtful debts, although the reduction in gross debtors by £731 has already been accounted for, due to the cash received) and increase profits by £731.

Suspense accounts are temporary

3.15 It must be stressed that a suspense account can only be temporary. Postings to a suspense account are only made when the bookkeeper doesn't know yet what to do or when an error has occurred. Mysteries must be solved, and errors must be corrected. Under no circumstances should there still be a suspense account when it comes to preparing the balance sheet of a business. The suspense account must be cleared and all the correcting entries made before the final accounts are drawn up.

Question 3

When the trial balance was prepared a suspense account was opened. These errors were discovered:

(i) Opening stock of £2,000 was omitted from the trial balance.

(ii) £400 was received from a customer whose debt had been written off and the bookkeeper credited the bad debts expense account and the debtors control account and debited cash.

What was the balance on the suspense account?

A £1,600 debit
B £2,400 debit
C £1,600 credit
D £2,400 credit

Answer

B is correct.

Opening stock is a debit, so omitting it puts £2,000 debit into suspense. Then, when cash was received from the written off debtor the entry made were debits of £400 and credits of £800, putting another £400 debit into suspense.

---

4 PREPARATION OF FINAL ACCOUNTS — Pilot Paper

4.1 Once the suspense account is cleared and all known errors corrected, the final accounts are prepared. You have already prepared a profit and loss account and balance sheet from a simple trial balance. Now see if you can do the same thing but at a more advanced level, taking account of adjustments for depreciation, stock, accruals, prepayments and bad and doubtful debts.

4.2 EXAMPLE: ACCOUNTS PREPARATION

The following trial balance was extracted from the ledger of Stephen Chee, a sole trader, as at 31 May 20X1 - the end of his financial year.

STEPHEN CHEE
TRIAL BALANCE AS AT 31 MAY 20X1

	Dr	*Cr*
	£	£
Property, at cost	120,000	
Equipment, at cost	80,000	
Provisions for depreciation (as at 1 June 20X0)		
- on property		20,000
- on equipment		38,000
Purchases	250,000	
Sales		402,200
Stock, as at 1 June 20X0	50,000	
Discounts allowed	18,000	
Discounts received		4,800
Returns out		15,000
Wages and salaries	58,800	
Bad debts	4,600	
Loan interest	5,100	
Other operating expenses	17,700	
Trade creditors		36,000
Trade debtors	38,000	
Cash in hand	300	
Bank	1,300	
Drawings	24,000	
Provision for bad debts		500
17% long term loan		30,000
Capital, as at 1 June 20X0		121,300
	667,800	667,800

The following additional information as at 31 May 20X1 is available.

(a) Stock as at the close of business has been valued at cost at £42,000.
(b) Wages and salaries need to be accrued by £800.
(c) Other operating expenses are prepaid by £300.
(d) The provision for bad debts is to be adjusted so that it is 2% of trade debtors.
(e) Depreciation for the year ended 31 May 20X1 has still to be provided for as follows.

Property: 1.5% per annum using the straight line method; and
Equipment: 25% per annum using the diminishing balance method.

Required

Prepare Stephen Chee's trading and profit and loss account for the year ended 31 May 20X1 and his balance sheet as at that date.

4.3 SOLUTION

STEPHEN CHEE
TRADING AND PROFIT AND LOSS ACCOUNT
FOR THE YEAR ENDED 31 MAY 20X1

	£	£
Sales		
Cost of sales		402,200
Opening stock	50,000	
Purchases	250,000	
Purchases returns	(15,000)	
	285,000	
Closing stock	42,000	
		243,000
Gross profit		159,200
Other income - discounts received		4,800
		164,000
Expenses		
Operating expenses		
Wages and salaries (£58,800 + £800)	59,600	
Discounts allowed	18,000	
Bad debts (W1)	4,860	
Loan interest	5,100	
Depreciation	12,300	
Other operating expenses (£17,700 - £300)	17,400	
		117,260
Net profit for the year		46,740

STEPHEN CHEE
BALANCE SHEET AS AT 31 MAY 20X0

	Cost	Accumulated depn.	Net book value
Fixed assets	£	£	£
Property	120,000	21,800	98,200
Equipment	80,000	48,500	31,500
	200,000	70,300	129,700
Current assets			
Stock		42,000	
Trade debtors net of provision for bad debts (£38,000 less 2%)		37,240	
Prepayments		300	
Bank		1,300	
Cash in hand		300	
		81,140	
Current liabilities			
Trade creditors		36,000	
Accruals		800	
		36,800	
Net current assets			44,340
Less 17% loan			30,000
Net assets			144,040
Capital			
Balance at 1 June 20X0			121,300
Net profit for the year			46,740
			168,040
Drawings			24,000
			144,040

Workings

		£
1	*Provision for bad debts*	
	Previous provision	500
	New provision (2% × 38,000)	760
	Increase	260
	Per trial balance	4,600
	Profit and loss account	4,860
2	*Depreciation*	
	Property	
	Opening provision	20,000
	Provision for the year (1.5% × 120,000)	1,800
	Closing provision	21,800
	Equipment	
	Opening provision	38,000
	Provision for the year (25% × 42,000)	10,500
	Closing provision	48,500

Tips for final accounts questions

4.4 Whatever form the final accounts question takes, you should bear in mind the following tips.

(a) **Annotate the trial balance** with the final destination of each item.

T = Trading account
P/L = Profit and loss account
M = Manufacturing account
I/E = Income and expenditure account
B/S = Balance sheet

(b) **Show workings clearly**. The workings should be clearly referenced to the final accounts and should enable the marker to follow through your calculations. This is particularly important if you make minor arithmetical mistakes. You will not be heavily penalised if the marker can see that you have used the right method.

(c) **Present a clear, logical layout of financial accounts.** Allow plenty of space, better too much than too little. Underline any totals for columns and figures and, if you make a mistake, cross it out neatly and clearly. You do not have time to wait for Tippex to dry.

Question 4

Donald Brown, a sole trader, extracted the following trial balance on 31 December 20X0.

TRIAL BALANCE AS AT 31 DECEMBER 20X0

	Debit	*Credit*
	£	£
Capital at 1 January 20X0		26,094
Debtors	42,737	
Cash in hand	1,411	
Creditors		35,404
Fixtures and fittings at cost	42,200	
Discounts allowed	1,304	
Discounts received		1,175
Stock at 1 January 20X0	18,460	
Sales		491,620
Purchases	387,936	
Motor vehicles at cost	45,730	
Lighting and heating	6,184	
Motor expenses	2,862	
Rent	8,841	
General expenses	7,413	
Balance at bank		19,861
Provision for deprecation		
Fixtures and fittings		2,200
Motor vehicles		15,292
Drawings	26,568	
	591,646	591,646

The following information as at 31 December is also available.

(a) £218 is owing for motor expenses.

(b) £680 has been prepaid for rent.

(c) Depreciation is to be provided of the year as follows.

Motor vehicles: 20% on cost
Fixtures and fittings: 10% reducing balance method

(d) Stock at the close of business was valued at £19,926.

Required

Prepare Donald Brown's trading and profit and loss account for the year ended 31 December 20X0 and his balance sheet at that date.

Answer

Tutorial note. You should note these points.

(a) Discounts allowed are an expense of the business and should be shown as a deduction from gross profit. Similarly, discounts received is a revenue item and should be added to gross profit.

(b) The figure for depreciation in the trial balance represents accumulated depreciation up to and including 20W9. You have to calculate the charge for the year 20X0 for the profit and loss account and add this to the trial balance figure to arrive at the accumulated depreciation figure to be included in the balance sheet.

DONALD BROWN
TRADING AND PROFIT AND LOSS ACCOUNT
FOR THE YEAR ENDED 31 DECEMBER 20X0

	£	£
Sales		491,620
Less cost of sales		
Opening stock	18,460	
Purchases	387,936	
	406,396	
Closing stock	19,926	
		386,470
Gross profit		105,150
Discounts received		1,175
		106,325
Less expenses:		
discounts allowed	1,304	
lighting and heating	6,184	
motor expenses	3,080	
rent	8,161	
general expenses	7,413	
depreciation (W)	13,146	
		39,288
Net profit		67,037

Working: depreciation charge

Motor vehicles: £45,730 × 20% = £9,146
Fixtures and fittings: 10% × £(42,200 – 2,200) = £4,000
Total: £4,000 + £9,146 = £13,146.

DONALD BROWN
BALANCE SHEET AS AT 31 DECEMBER 20X0

	Cost	*Depreciation*	*Net*
	£	£	£
Fixed assets			
Fixtures and fittings	42,200	6,200	36,000
Motor vehicles	45,730	24,438	21,292
	87,930	30,638	57,292
Current assets			
Stock		19,926	
Debtors		42,737	
Prepayments		680	
Cash in hand		1,411	
		64,754	
Current liabilities			
Creditors	35,404		
Accruals	218		
Bank overdraft	19,861		
		55,483	
Net current assets			9,271
Net assets			66,563
Represented by:			
Capital			26,094
Net profit for year			67,037
			93,131
Less drawings			26,568
			66,563

Chapter roundup

- There are five types of error.
  - Errors of transposition
  - Errors of omission
  - Errors of principle
  - Errors of commission
  - Compensating errors
- Errors which leave total debits and total credits in balance can be corrected by using journal entries. Otherwise, a suspense account has to be opened first (and a journal entry used later to record the correction of the error and clear the suspense account in the process).
- Suspense accounts, as well as being used to correct some errors, are also opened when it is not known immediately where to post an amount. When the mystery is solved, the suspense account is closed and the amount correctly posted using a journal entry.
- Suspense accounts are only temporary. None should exist when it comes to drawing up the financial statements at the end of the accounting period.
- You should now be able to prepare a set of final accounts for a sole trader from a trial balance after incorporating period end adjustments for depreciation, stock, prepayments, accruals and bad and doubtful debts.

Quick quiz

1 Which of the following is an error of principle?

A Recording the income from selling a fixed asset as a miscellaneous receipt in the profit and loss account

B Petty cash expense £50 credited to expense and debited to cash

C Failing to record an invoice in the sales ledger

D Recording a stock purchase invoice for £500 as
Dr purchases £500
Cr purchase ledger control a/c

2 A business incurred an expense costing £600. The expense was <u>only</u> entered in the company cash book as a debit. Which of the following journal entries is required to correct the error? (Assume a suspense account has been used to clear the imbalance.)

A	Dr Expense	600	Cr Bank	600
B	Dr Suspense	600	Cr Bank	1,200
	Dr Expense	600		
C	Dr Suspense	600	Cr Bank	600
D	Dr Bank	1,200	Cr Suspense	600
			Cr Expense	600

3 What is the function of a suspense account?

A A device used to enable the production of the financial statements, when required, despite the presence of errors.
B A method of ensuring the trial balance will agree.
C A way of focussing attention upon the corrective action required to ensure the trial balance does agree and the integrity of the accounting system is maintained.
D A way of recording transactions when the ultimate accounting treatment required in unclear.

4 Correction of an error will only involve an entry to a suspense account if the original error ______________

____. (Complete the sentence.)

Answers to quick quiz

1 A Correct, the sale of a fixed asset must not be confused with a revenue item – gross profit will be overstated.

B This is a reversal error.

C This is an error of omission.

D This entry has been correctly recorded, there is no error.

2 B Correct, it is necessary to correct the error and record the transactions hence the duplication of the £600 posting to bank.

A Incorrect, you have not cleared the suspense account balance which will arise as a result of the incomplete but incorrect entry.

C Incorrect, this will clear the suspense account but will not record the transaction.

D Incorrect, the entry is reversed.

3 C This is the correct answer.

A A suspense account can be used, expediently, to allow the production of accounts provided it is acknowledgod thc accounts may be flawed.

B Opening a suspense account will ensure the trial balance agrees, but the function of a trial balance is to reveal errors. The suspense account focuses attention upon those errors.

D Whilst suspense accounts are often used for this purpose, the transactions 'in suspense' must be journalised out when the treatment has been clarified.

4 Correction of an error will only involve an entry to a suspense account if the original error prevented the trial balance from balancing.

Now try the questions below from the Question Bank

Number	Level	Marks	Time
46	Exam	15	27 mins
47	Exam	2	3 mins
48	Exam	2	3 mins

Part C

Final accounts and audit

Chapter 17

THE ACCOUNTS OF UNINCORPORATED ORGANISATIONS (INCOME AND EXPENDITURE ACCOUNTS)

Introduction

This part of the Study Text is concerned with the preparation of final accounts.

So far you have dealt with the accounts of businesses. This chapter considers non-trading organisations, that is organisations which are not incorporated under the Companies Act and whose objectives are to provide services to their members or the pursuit of one or a number of activities rather than the earning of profit.

If subscriptions are charged, there will be a need for some financial records the minimum possible being a cash book and petty cash book. Clubs, which rely on this minimum package often, confine their annual accounts to a **receipts and payments account**. This is simply a summary of cash received and paid for a period, and is discussed in Section 2 of this chapter.

A receipts and payments account may be adequate for some clubs but has important deficiencies when used by clubs which have substantial assets (in addition to cash) and liabilities. The arguments in favour of accruals based accounting applying to clubs as well as profit making entities. Most large clubs do produce financial statements based on accruals accounting. In particular many clubs produce what is basically a profit and loss account but they call it an **income and expenditure account.** This is the subject of Section 3 of this chapter.

Learning outcomes covered in this chapter

- Prepare income and expenditure accounts

Syllabus content covered in this chapter

- Income and expenditure accounts

1 THE RECEIPTS AND PAYMENTS ACCOUNT

KEY TERM

The **receipts and payments** account is effectively a summary of an organisation's cash book.

1.1 Many charities and clubs keep records only of cash paid and received. To facilitate production of the financial statement, an analysed cash book may be used. No balance sheet is produced with a receipts and payments account.

1.2 EXAMPLE: RECEIPTS AND PAYMENTS ACCOUNT

HIGH LEE STRONG TENNIS CLUB
RECEIPTS AND PAYMENTS ACCOUNT
FOR THE YEAR ENDED 30 APRIL 20X0

Receipts	£	*Payments*	£
Balance b/f	16	Bar expenses	106
Bar takings	160	Rent	50
Subscriptions	328	Wages	140
		Postage	10
		Printing	12
		Affiliation fees to LTS	18
		Lawn mower*	50
		Heat and light	60
		Balance c/f	58
	504		504

*Item of capital expenditure

1.3 The table lists **advantages** and **disadvantages** of this type of financial statement.

Advantages		Disadvantages	
(a)	Very easy to produce and understand.	(a)	Takes no account of any amounts owing or prepaid.
(b)	Serves as a basis for the preparation of the income and expenditure account and balance sheet.	(b)	Includes items of capital expenditure and makes no distinction between capital and revenue items.
		(c)	Takes no account of depreciation of fixed assets.

2 INCOME AND EXPENDITURE ACCOUNT

KEY TERM

An **income and expenditure account** is the name given to what is effectively the profit and loss account of a non-trading organisation, eg sports clubs, social clubs, societies, charities and so on. The principles of 'accruals' accounting (the matching concept) are applied to income and expenditure accounts in the same way as for profit and loss accounts.

2.1 There are a few differences between the final accounts of a non-trading organisation and those of a business.

(a) Since non-trading organisations do not exist to make profits, the difference between income and matching expenditure in the **income and expenditure account** is referred to as a **surplus** or a **deficit** rather than a profit or loss.

(b) The capital or proprietorship of the organisation is referred to as the **accumulated fund**, rather than the capital account. In addition, other separate funds might be kept by the organisation.

(c) There is usually no separate trading account. Instead, it is usual to net off expenditure against income for like items.

Exam focus point

The definition of an income and expenditure account was examined in Section A of the May 2001 exam.

Sources of income for non-trading organisations

2.2 Non-trading organisations differ in purpose and character, but we shall concentrate here on sports clubs, social clubs or societies. These will obtain their income from various sources which include the following.

- Membership subscriptions
- Payments for life membership
- 'Profits' from bar sales
- 'Profits' from the sale of food in the club restaurant or cafeteria
- 'Profits' from social events, such as dinner-dances
- Interest received on investments

KEY TERM

Netting off expenditure against income for like items means that where some sources of income have associated costs, the net surplus or deficit should be shown in the income and expenditure account.

2.3 For example:

(a) If a club holds an annual dinner-dance the income and expenditure account will net off the costs of the event against the revenue to show the surplus or deficit.

(b) If a club has a bar, the income and expenditure account will show the surplus or deficit on its trading. Although the organisation itself does not trade, the bar does and so it is correct to refer to 'profits' from the bar.

2.4 Where there is trading activity within a non-trading organisation (eg bar sales, cafeteria sales etc) so that the organisation must hold stocks of drink or food etc it is usual to prepare a trading account for that particular activity, and then to record the surplus or deficit from trading in the income and expenditure account. An example is shown below.

FOOLSMATE CHESS CLUB
BAR TRADING ACCOUNT FOR THE YEAR TO 31 DECEMBER 20X5

	£	£
Sales		18,000
Less cost of goods sold		
Bar stocks 1 January 20X5	1,200	
Purchases	15,400	
	16,600	
Less bar stocks at 31 December 20X5	1,600	
		15,000
Bar profit (taken to income and expenditure account)		3,000

Funds of non-trading organisations

2.5 Although the capital of a non-trading organisation is generally accounted for as the accumulated fund, some separate funds might be set up for particular purposes.

(a) A life membership fund is a fund for the money subscribed for life membership by various members of the organisation. The money paid for life membership is commonly invested outside the organisation (for example in a building society account). The investment then earns interest for the organisation.

(b) A building fund might be set up whereby the organisation sets aside money to save for the cost of a new building extension. The money put into the fund will be invested outside the organisation, earning interest, until it is needed for the building work. It might take several years to create a large enough fund.

Accounting for special funds

2.6 The double entry is:

(a) When money is put into the fund

DEBIT Cash
CREDIT Special-purpose fund

(b) When the cash is invested

DEBIT Investments (eg building society account)
CREDIT Cash

(c) When the investments earn interest

DEBIT Cash

CREDIT Interest received (special-purpose fund) account

3 PREPARING INCOME AND EXPENDITURE ACCOUNTS

Exam focus point

Examination questions may provide a receipts and payments account, balances of assets and liabilities at the beginning of the period, and details of accruals and prepayments at the end of the period. You would be required typically to perform any of the following tasks.

(a) Calculate the balance on the accumulated fund at the beginning of the period.
(b) Prepare a trading account for a particular activity for the period.
(c) Prepare an income and expenditure account for the period.
(d) Prepare a balance sheet at the end of the period.

3.1 Before looking at an example of an income and expenditure account we need to look at each of the following items in some detail.

- Membership subscriptions
- Bar trading account
- Life membership

These are items which we have not come across previously because they are not found in the accounts of businesses. Remember, however, that in many respects the accounts of non-trading organisations are similar to those of businesses with fixed assets, depreciation, current assets and current liabilities, expense accounts, accruals and prepayments.

Membership subscriptions

3.2 Annual membership subscriptions of clubs and societies are usually payable one year in advance.

A club or society therefore receives payments from members for benefits which the members have yet to enjoy. They are receipts in advance and are shown in the balance sheet of the society as a current liability.

3.3 EXAMPLE: SUBSCRIPTIONS IN ADVANCE

The Mudflannels Cricket Club charges an annual membership of £50 payable in advance on 1 October each year. All 40 members pay their subscriptions promptly on 1 October 20X4. The club's accounting year ends on 31 December

3.4 SOLUTION

Total subscriptions of 40 × £50 = £2,000 would be treated as follows.

(a) $\frac{9\text{ months}}{12\text{ months}} \times £2{,}000 = £1{,}500$ appears in the balance sheet of the club as a current liability 'subscriptions in advance' (1 January to 30 September 20X5).

(b) $\frac{3\text{ months}}{12\text{ months}} \times £2{,}000 = £500$ appears as income in the income and expenditure account for the period 1 October to 31 December 20X4.

3.5 When members are in arrears with subscriptions and owe money to the club or society, they are 'debtors' of the organisation and so appear as current assets under the heading 'subscriptions in arrears'. These should be shown as a separate item and should not be netted off against subscriptions in advance.

3.6 EXAMPLE: WHEN SUBSCRIPTIONS ARE IN ARREARS

Bluespot Squash Club has 100 members, each of whom pays an annual membership of £60 on 1 November. Of those 100 members, 90 pay their subscriptions before 31 December 20X5 (for the 20X5/X6 year) but 10 have still not paid.

3.7 SOLUTION

As at 31 December 20X5 the balance sheet of the club would include the following items.

(a) *Subscriptions in advance (current liability)*

$$90 \text{ members} \times \frac{10 \text{ months}}{12 \text{ months}} \times £60 = £4{,}500$$

(b) *Subscriptions in arrears (current asset)*

$$10 \text{ members} \times \frac{2 \text{ months}}{12 \text{ months}} \times £60 = £100$$

It is common for clubs to take no credit for subscription income until the money is received. In such a case, subscriptions in arrears are **not** credited to income and **not** shown as a current asset. It is essential to read the question carefully.

3.8 EXAMPLE: SUBSCRIPTIONS ACCOUNT

At 1 January 20X8, the Little Blithering Debating Society had membership subscriptions paid in advance of £1,600, and subscriptions in arrears of £250. During the year to 31 December 20X8 receipts of subscription payments amounted to £18,400. At 31 December 20X8 subscriptions in advance amounted to £1,750 and subscriptions in arrears to £240.

What is the income from subscriptions to be shown in the income and expenditure account for the year to 31 December 20X8?

3.9 SOLUTION

The question does not say that subscriptions are only accounted for when received. You may therefore assume that the society takes credit for subscriptions as they become due.

The income for the income and expenditure account would be calculated as follows.

		£	£
Payments received in the year			18,400
Add:	subscriptions due but not yet received (ie subscriptions in arrears 31 Dec 20X8)	240	
	subscriptions received last year relating to current year (ie subscriptions in advance 1 Jan 20X8)	1,600	
			1,840
			20,240
Less:	subscriptions received in current year relating to last year (ie subscriptions in arrears 1 Jan 20X8)	250	
	subscriptions received in current year relating to next year (ie subscriptions in advance 31 Dec 20X8)	1,750	
			2,000
Income from subscriptions for the year			18,240

3.10 You may find it simpler to do this calculation as a ledger account.

SUBSCRIPTIONS ACCOUNT

	£		£
Subscriptions in arrears b/f	250	Subscriptions in advance b/f	1,600
I & E a/c (balancing figure)	18,240	Cash	18,400
Subscriptions in advance c/d	1,750	Subscriptions in arrears c/d	240
	20,240		20,240
Subscriptions in arrears b/d	240	Subscriptions in advance b/d	1,750

Question 1

The following information relates to a sports club.

	£
20X4 subscriptions unpaid at beginning of 20X5	410
20X4 subscriptions received during 20X5	370
20X5 subscriptions received during 20X5	6,730
20X6 subscriptions received during 20X5	1,180
20X5 subscriptions unpaid at end of 20X5	470

The club takes credit for subscription income when it becomes due, but takes a prudent view of overdue subscriptions. What amount is credited to the income and expenditure account for 20X5?

Answer

SUBSCRIPTIONS

	£		£
Balance b/f	410	Bank: 20X4	370
		20X5	6,730
∴ I & E account	7,200	20X6	1,180
		20X4 subs written off	40
Balance c/f	1,180	Balance c/f	470
	8,790		8,790

Note that the net figure taken to the income and expenditure account will be £7,160 (£7,200 - £40) as the 20X4 subs write off will be netted off against the income and expenditure figure.

Bar trading account

3.11 If a club has a bar or cafeteria a separate trading account will be prepared for its trading activities. A bar trading account will contain the following items.

- Bar takings
- Opening stocks of goods, purchases and closing stocks of goods (cost of bar sales)
- Gross profit (takings less cost of bar takings)
- Other expenses directly related to the running of the bar (if any)
- Net profit (gross profit less any expenses)

The net bar profit is then included under income in the income and expenditure account. A loss on the bar would be included under expenditure.

Life membership

3.12 Some clubs offer membership for life in return for a given lump sum subscription. Life members, having paid this lump sum, do not pay any further annual subscriptions. The club receives a sum of money, which it can then invest, with the annual interest from these investments being accounted for as income in the income and expenditure account.

3.13 The payments from life members are not income relating to the year in which they are received by the club, because the payment is for the life of the members, which can be a very long time to come. As they are long-term payments, they are recorded in the club accounts as an addition to a life membership fund as follows.

DEBIT Cash
CREDIT Life membership fund

3.14 The life membership fund is shown in the balance sheet of the club or society immediately after the accumulated fund.

3.15 Life members enjoy the benefits of membership over their life, and so their payment to the club is 'rewarded' as time goes by. Accounting for life membership over time can be explained with an example.

3.16 Suppose that Annette Cord pays a life membership fee of £300 to the Tumbledown Tennis Club. The £300 will initially be put into the club's life membership fund. We will suppose that this money is invested by the club, and earns interest of £30 per annum.

3.17 There are two ways of accounting for the life membership fee.

(a) To keep the £300 in the life membership fund until Annette Cord dies. (Since the £300 earns interest of £30 pa this interest can be said to represent income for the club in lieu of an annual subscription.) When Annette eventually dies, the £300 she contributed can then be transferred out of the life membership fund and directly into the accumulated fund.

(b) To write off subscriptions to the life membership fund by transferring a 'fair' amount from the fund into the income and expenditure account. A 'fair' amount will represent the proportion of the total life membership payment which relates to the current year. We do not know how long any life member will live, but use an estimated average life say 20 years. In each year, one-twentieth of life membership fees would be deducted from the fund and added as income in the income and expenditure account.

3.18 In the case of Annette Cord, the annual transfer under (b) is £15 and, after 20 years, her contribution to the fund has been written off in full and transferred to the income and expenditure accounts of those 20 years. This transfer of £15 is in addition to the annual interest of £30 earned by the club each year from investing the fee of £300.

3.19 If method (b) is selected in preference to method (a), the life membership fund can be written down by either a straight line method or a reducing balance method, in much the same way as fixed assets are depreciated. However it is a capital fund being written off and the amount of the annual write-off is **income** to the club, and not an expense.

3.20 A further feature of method (b) is that there is no need to record the death of individual members (unlike method (a)). The annual write off is based on an average expected life of members and it does not matter when any individual member dies.

3.21 A possible reason for preferring method (b) to method (a) is that life membership subscriptions regularly pass through the income and expenditure account as income of the club.

3.22 In spite of the logical reasons why method (b) should perhaps be preferable, method (a) is still commonly used.

Exam focus point

In an examination question, unless you are told about a rate for 'writing off' the life membership fund annually, you should assume that method (a) should be used, where the question gives you information about the death of club life members.

3.23 EXAMPLE: LIFE MEMBERSHIP FUND

The Coxless Rowing Club has a scheme where members can opt to pay a lump sum which gives them membership for life. Lump sum payments received for life membership are held in a life membership fund but then credited to the income and expenditure account in equal instalments over a ten year period, beginning in the year when the lump sum payment is made and life membership is acquired.

The treasurer of the club, Beau Trace, establishes the following information.

(a) At 31 December 20X4, the balance on the life membership fund was £8,250.

(b) Of this opening balance, £1,220 should be credited as income for the year to 31 December 20X5.

(c) During the year to 31 December 20X5, new life members made lump sum payments totalling £1,500.

Required

Show the movements in the life membership fund for the year to 31 December 20X5, and in doing so, calculate how much should be transferred as income from life membership fund to the income and expenditure account.

3.24 SOLUTION

LIFE MEMBERSHIP FUND

	£	£
As at 31 December 20X4		8,250
New life membership payments received in 20X5		1,500
		9,750
Less transfer to income and expenditure account:		
out of balance as at 31 December 20X4	1,220	
out of new payments in 20X5 (10% of £1,500)	150	
		1,370
Fund as at 31 December 20X5		8,380
The income and expenditure account for the year would show:		
Income from life membership		1,370

Accounting for the sale of investments and fixed assets

3.25 In accounting for clubs and societies, the income and expenditure account is used to record the surplus or deficit in the transactions for the year. Occasionally a club or society might sell off some of its investments or fixed assets, and in doing so might make a profit or loss on the sale.

(a) The profit/loss on the sale of an investment is simply the difference between the sale price and the balance sheet value (usually cost) of the investment.

(b) The profit/loss on the sale of a fixed asset is the difference between the sale price and the net book value of the asset at the date of sale.

3.26 There is nothing different or unusual about the accounts of non-trading organisations in computing the amount of such profits or losses. What is different, however, is how the profit or losses should be recorded in the accounts.

(a) The profit or loss on the sale of investments is not shown in the income and expenditure account. Instead, the profit is directly added to (or loss subtracted from) the accumulated fund.

(b) The profit or loss on the sale of a fixed asset which is not subject to depreciation charges in the income and expenditure account, is also taken directly to the accumulated fund.

(c) The profit or loss on the sale of fixed assets which have been subject to depreciation charges is recorded in the income and expenditure account.

3.27 The point of difference in (c) compared with (a) and (b) is that since depreciation on the asset has been charged in the income and expenditure account in the past, it is appropriate that a profit or loss on sale should also be reported through the account.

3.28 EXAMPLE: INCOME AND EXPENDITURE ACCOUNTS

The assets and liabilities of the Berley Sports Club at 31 December 20X4 were as follows.

	£
Pavilion at cost less depreciation	13,098
Bank and cash	1,067
Bar stock	291
Bar debtors	231
Rates prepaid	68
Contributions owing to sports club by users of sports club facilities	778
Bar creditors	427
Loans to sports club	1,080
Accruals: water	13
electricity	130
miscellaneous	75
loan interest	33
Contributions paid in advance by users of sports club facilities	398

A receipts and payments account for the year ended 31 December 20X5 was produced as follows.

	£		£
Opening balance	1,067	Bar purchases	2,937
Bar sales	4,030	Repayment of loan capital	170
Telephone	34	Rent of ground	79
Contributions from users of club facilities	1,780	Rates	320
		Water	38
Socials	177	Electricity	506
Miscellaneous	56	Insurance	221
		Repairs to equipment	326
		Expenses of socials	67
		Maintenance of ground	133
		Wages of groundsman	140
		Telephone	103
		Bar sundries	144
		Loan interest	97
		Miscellaneous	163
		Closing balance	1,700
	7,144		7,144

The following information as at 31 December 20X5 was also provided.

	£
Bar stock	394
Bar debtors	50
Bar creditors	901
Rent prepaid	16
Water charges owing	23
Electricity owing	35
Creditors for bar sundries	65
Contributions by users of sports club facilities:	
owing to sports club	425
paid in advance to sports club	657
Rates prepaid	76

Depreciation on the pavilion for the year was £498.

You are asked to prepare a statement showing the gross and net profits earned by the bar, an income and expenditure account for the year ended 31 December 20X5 and a balance sheet as at that date.

3.29 SOLUTION

We are not given the size of the accumulated fund as at the beginning of the year, but it can be calculated as the balancing figure to make total liabilities plus capital equal to total assets (as at 31 December 20X4).

Calculation of accumulated fund at 1 January 20X5

	£	£
Assets		
Pavilion at cost less depreciation		13,098
Bank and cash		1,067
Bar stock		291
Bar debtors		231
Rates prepaid		68
Contributions in arrears		778
		15,533
Liabilities		
Bar creditors	427	
Loans	1,080	
Accrued charges £(13 + 130 + 75 + 33)	251	
Contributions received in advance	398	
		2,156
∴ Accumulated fund at 1 January 20X5		13,377

The next step is to analyse the various items of income and expenditure.

(a) There is a bar, and so a bar trading account can be prepared.
(b) Income from the telephone can be netted off against telephone expenditure.
(c) The revenue from socials has associated expenses to net off against it.
(d) There is also miscellaneous income and contributions from club members.

The bar trading account can only be put together after we have calculated bar sales and purchases.

(a) We are given bar debtors as at 1 January 20X5 and 31 December 20X5 and also cash received from bar sales. The bar sales for the year can therefore be calculated.

BAR DEBTORS

		£			£
1.1.20X5	Balance b/f	231	31.12.20X5	Cash	4,030
31.12.20X5	∴Bar sales	3,849	31.12.20X5	Balance c/f	50
		4,080			4,080

(b) Similarly, purchases for the bar are calculated from opening and closing amounts for bar creditors, and payments for bar purchases.

BAR CREDITORS

		£			£
31.12.20X5	Cash	2,937	1.1.20X5	Balance b/f	427
31.12.20X5	Balance c/f	901	31.12.20X5	∴ Bar purchases	3,411
		3,838			3,838

(c) Understand that cash receipts from bar sales and cash payments for bar supplies are not the bar sales and cost of bar sales that we want. Cash receipts and payments in the year are not for matching quantities of goods, nor do they relate to the actual goods sold in the year.

(d) Other bar trading expenses are bar sundries.

	£
Cash payments for bar sundries	144
Add creditors for bar sundries as at 31.12.20X5	65
	209
Less creditors for bar sundries as at 1.1.20X5	0
Expenses for bar sundries for the year	209

BAR TRADING ACCOUNT
FOR THE YEAR ENDED 31 DECEMBER 20X5

	£	£
Sales		3,849
Cost of sales		
Opening stock	291	
Purchases	3,411	
	3,702	
Less closing stock	394	
		3,308
Gross profit		541
Sundry expenses		209
Net profit		332

Contributions to the sports club for the year should be calculated in the same way as membership subscriptions. Using a T account format below, the income from contributions (for the income and expenditure account) is the balancing figure. Contributions in advance brought forward are liabilities (credit balance b/f) and contributions in arrears brought forward are assets (debit balance b/f).

CONTRIBUTIONS

		£			£
1.1.20X5	Balance in arrears b/f	778	1.1.20X5	Balance in advance b/f	398
31.12.20X5	∴Income and expenditure	1,168	31.12.20X5	Cash	1,780
31.12.20X5	Balance in advance c/f	657	31.12.20X5	Balance in arrears c/f	425
		2,603			2,603

BERLEY SPORTS CLUB - INCOME AND EXPENDITURE ACCOUNT
FOR THE YEAR ENDED 31 DECEMBER 20X5

		£	£
Income			
Contributions			1,168
Net income from bar trading			332
Income from socials:	receipts	177	
	less expenses	67	
			110
Miscellaneous			56
			1,666
Expenses			
Ground rent (79 – 16)		63	
Rates (320 + 68 – 76)		312	
Water (38 – 13 + 23)		48	
Electricity (506 – 130 + 35)		411	
Insurance		221	
Equipment repairs		326	
Ground maintenance		133	
Wages		140	
Telephone (103 – 34)		69	
Loan interest (97 –33)		64	
Miscellaneous expenses (163 – 75)		88	
Depreciation		498	
			2,373
			(707)

BERLEY SPORTS CLUB
BALANCE SHEET AS AT 31 DECEMBER 20X5

	£	£
Fixed assets		
Pavilion at NBV £(13,098 – 498)		12,600
Current assets		
Bar stock	394	
Bar debtors	50	
Contributions in arrears	425	
Prepayments £(16+76)	92	
Cash at bank	1,700	
	2,661	
Current liabilities		
Bar creditors £(901+65)	966	
Accrued charges	58	
Contributions in advance	657	
	1,681	
Net current assets		980
		13,580
Long-term liability		
Loan £(1,080-170)		910
		12,670
Accumulated fund		
Balance at 1 January 20X5		13,377
Less deficit for year		(707)
		12,670

Chapter roundup

- The **receipts and payments account is**, in effect, a summary of the cash book. For small clubs with a few straightforward transactions, this statement may be sufficient. For larger concerns, however, the receipts and payments account will form the basis for the preparation of the income and expenditure account and balance sheet.
- **Income and expenditure accounts** are the equivalent of profit and loss accounts for non-trading organisations. In the examination it is usually easy to recognise such questions because they always refer to the accounts of a club or society.
- You should remember to do the following when presenting income and expenditure accounts.
  - Match the sources of revenue with related costs to show net income from the organisation's various activities.
  - Treat subscriptions received in advance as a current liability and (unless the question states the contrary) treat subscriptions in arrears as a current asset.
  - Describe the result for the year as surplus or deficit, not as profit or loss.
  - Describe the capital of the organisation as the accumulated fund but remember that capital may also include other funds such as a life membership fund.

Quick quiz

1 Three differences between the accounts of a non-trading organisation and those of a business are:

(1) ______________________________

(2) ______________________________

(3) ______________________________

2 If a 'not for profit' organisation does make a surplus it will be?

A Credit to capital
B Credit to the accumulated fund
C Repaid to the contributions or members
D Added to the bank account balance

3 A club has 150 members who pay £10 each for membership. The opening subscription debtor was £70 and 5 members had paid subscriptions in advance at the year end. How much money was collected from members?

A £1,500
B £1,740
C £1,620
D £1,520

4 The assets and liabilities of a social club were (at 31.12.20X1) equipment £1,500, premises £16,000, bar stock £1,300, bar creditors £1,100, managers wage owing £250, subscriptions in arrears £500, prepaid subscriptions £350, cash £1,900. The accumulated fund is?

A £21,200
B £19,650
C £19,500
D £200,000

Answers to quick quiz

1 (1) A non-trading organisation does not make profits, so the profit and loss account is replaced by an income and expenditure account

(2) The 'capital' account is the accumulated fund

(3) There is no separate trading account

2 B Correct.

A Non trading organisations such as clubs and societies refer to their capital as 'accumulated funds'.

C Incorrect, unless in the unlikely event of the club or society specifying this is to happen.

D Incorrect.

3 C Correct.

Subscriptions A/C

Balance b/f	70	Bank	1,620
I&E (subscriptions)			
150 × £10	1,500		
Bal c/f 5 × £10	50		
	1,620		1,620

A Incorrect, you have not adjusted for opening subscriptions in arrears or closing prepaid subscriptions.

B Incorrect, you have posted subscription income to the credit of the subscription a/c incorrectly.

D Incorrect, the closing prepayment of subscriptions must be treated as a creditor.

4 C Correct, £1,500 + £16,000 + £1,300 - £1,100 - £250 + £500 - £350 + £1,900 = 19,500.
A Incorrect, this is the amount of the total assets of the club.
B Incorrect, you have treated the subscriptions incorrectly.
D Incorrect, you have treated the outstanding wages as an asset.

Now try the questions below from the Question Bank

Number	Level	Marks	Time
49	Exam	20	36 mins
50	Exam	2	3 mins
51	Exam	2	3 mins

Chapter 18

INCOMPLETE RECORDS

Introduction

So far in your work on preparing the final accounts for a sole trader we have assumed that a full set of records are kept. In practice many sole traders do not keep a full set of records and you must apply certain techniques to arrive at the necessary figures.

Incomplete records questions are a very good test of your understanding of the way in which a set of accounts is built up.

Limited companies are obliged by law to keep proper accounting records. They will be considered in Chapter 19.

Learning outcomes covered in this chapter

- Prepare accounts from incomplete records

Syllabus content covered in this chapter

- Production of accounting statements from incomplete data

1 INCOMPLETE RECORDS QUESTIONS

KEY TERM

Incomplete records occur when a business does not have a full set of accounting records because:

(a) The proprietor of the business does not keep a full set of accounts.
(b) Some of the business accounts are accidentally lost or destroyed.

1.1 The accountant must prepare a set of year-end accounts for the business ie a trading, profit and loss account, and a balance sheet. Since the business does not have a full set of accounts, it is not a simple matter of closing off accounts and transferring balances to the trading, P&L account, or showing outstanding balances in the balance sheet. The task of preparing the final accounts involves establishing the following.

- Cost of purchases and other expenses
- Total amount of sales
- Amount of creditors, accruals, debtors and prepayments at the end of the year

Exam focus point

Examination questions may take incomplete records problems a stage further, by introducing an 'incident' - such as fire or burglary - which leaves the owner of the business uncertain about how much stock has been destroyed or stolen. This happened in Section A of the May 2001 exam.

KEY TERM

The final accounts you are asked to prepare a may include a **statement of affairs.** This simply means a balance sheet in summary form because there is insufficient data for a full one, or one which is not in a standard format.

1.2 To understand what incomplete records are about, it will obviously be useful now to look at what exactly might be incomplete. The items we shall consider in turn are:

(a) The opening balance sheet.
(b) Credit sales and debtors.
(c) Purchases and trade creditors.
(d) Purchases, stocks and the cost of sales.
(e) Stolen goods or goods destroyed.
(f) The cash book.
(g) Accruals and prepayments.
(h) Drawings.

2 THE OPENING BALANCE SHEET

Exam focus point

In practice there should not be any missing items in the opening balance sheet of the business, because it should be available from the preparation of the previous year's final accounts. However, an examination problem might provide information about the assets and liabilities of the business at the beginning of the period under review, but then leave the balancing figure - ie the proprietor's business capital - unspecified.

2.1 EXAMPLE: OPENING BALANCE SHEET

A business has the following assets and liabilities as at 1 January 20X3.

	£
Fixtures and fittings at cost	7,000
Provision for depreciation, fixtures and fittings	4,000
Motor vehicles at cost	12,000
Provision for depreciation, motor vehicles	6,800
Stock in trade	4,500
Trade debtors	5,200
Cash at bank and in hand	1,230
Trade creditors	3,700
Prepayment	450
Accrued rent	2,000

You are required to prepare a balance sheet for the business, inserting a balancing figure for proprietor's capital.

2.2 SOLUTION

Balance sheet as at 1 January 20X3

	£	£
Fixed assets		
Fixtures and fittings at cost	7,000	
Less accumulated depreciation	4,000	
		3,000
Motor vehicles at cost	12,000	
Less accumulated depreciation	6,800	
		5,200
		8,200
Current assets		
Stock in trade	4,500	
Trade debtors	5,200	
Prepayment	450	
Cash	1,230	
	11,380	
Current liabilities		
Trade creditors	3,700	
Accrual	2,000	
	5,700	
Net current assets		5,680
		13,880
Proprietor's capital as at 1 January 20X3 (balancing figure)		13,880

3 CREDIT SALES AND DEBTORS

3.1 If a business does not keep a record of its sales on credit, the value of these sales can be derived from the opening balance of trade debtors, the closing balance of trade debtors, and the payments received from trade debtors during the period.

FORMULA TO LEARN

	£
Credit sales are:	
Payments received from trade debtors	X
Plus closing balance of trade debtors (since these represent sales in the current period for which cash payment has not yet been received)	X
Less opening balance of trade debtors (unless these become bad debts, they will pay what they owe in the current period for sales in a previous period)	(X)
	X

3.2 EXAMPLE: SALES AND DEBTORS

A business had trade debtors of £1,750 on 1 April 20X4 and £3,140 on 31 March 20X5. If payments received from trade debtors during the year to 31 March 20X5 were £28,490, and there were no bad debts, calculate credit sales for the period.

3.3 SOLUTION

	£
Cash received from debtors	28,490
Plus closing debtors	3,140
Less opening debtors	(1,750)
Credit sales	29,880

3.4 The same calculation could be made in a T account, with credit sales being the balancing figure to complete the account.

DEBTORS

	£		£
Opening balance b/f	1,750	Cash received	28,490
Credit sales (balancing fig)	29,880	Closing balance c/f	3,140
	31,630		31,630

3.5 The same interrelationship between balances can be used to derive a missing figure for cash from debtors (or opening or closing debtors), given the values for the three other items.

3.6 EXAMPLE: TO FIND CASH RECEIVED

Opening debtors are £6,700, closing debtors are £3,200 and credit sales for the period are £69,400. What was cash received from debtors during the period?

3.7 SOLUTION

DEBTORS

	£		£
Opening balance	6,700	Cash received (balancing figure)	72,900
Sales (on credit)	69,400	Closing balance c/f	3,200
	76,100		76,100

3.8 If there are bad debts during the period, the value of sales will be increased by the amount of bad debts written off, no matter whether they relate to opening debtors or credit sales during the current period.

Question 1

Opening debtors are £1,500, closing debtors are £1,800. During the year £45,800 was received from debtors including £800 in respect of debts written off in an earlier period. £3,200 of debts were written off and the doubtful debts provision increased by £700.

What are the credit sales for the year?

Answer

£48,500.

DEBTORS ACCOUNT

	£		£
B/d	1,500	Cash	45,000
Credit sales (balance)	48,500	Bad debts expense	3,200
		C/d	1,800
	50,000		50,000

Remember that cash received from debts written off in an earlier period is not credited to debtors, and that the movement in the doubtful debts provision does not go through debtors.

4 PURCHASES AND TRADE CREDITORS

4.1 A similar relationship exists between purchases of stock during a period, the opening and closing balances for trade creditors, and amounts paid to trade creditors during the period.

FORMULA TO LEARN

	£
Payments to trade creditors during the period	X
Plus closing balance of trade creditors	X
(since these represent purchases in the current period for which payment has not yet been made)	
Less opening balance of trade creditors	(X)
(these debts, paid in the current period, relate to purchases in a previous period)	
Purchases during the period	X

4.2 EXAMPLE: PURCHASES AND TRADE CREDITORS

A business had trade creditors of £3,728 on 1 October 20X5 and £2,645 on 30 September 20X6. If payments to trade creditors during the year to 30 September 20X6 were £31,479, what was purchases during the year?

4.3 SOLUTION

	£
Payments to trade creditors	31,479
Plus closing balance of trade creditors	2,645
Less opening balance of trade creditors	(3,728)
Purchases	30,396

4.4 The same calculation could be made in a T account, with purchases being the balancing figure to complete the account.

CREDITORS

	£		£
Cash payments	31,479	Opening balance b/f	3,728
Closing balance c/f	2,645	Purchases (balancing figure)	30,396
	34,124		34,124

5 ESTABLISHING PURCHASES, STOCKS, OR COST OF SALES

5.1 In some questions you must use the information in the trading account rather than the trade creditors account to find the cost of purchases. This information could also be used to find stocks or cost of sales.

FORMULA TO LEARN

		£
Since	opening stocks	X
	plus purchases	X
	less closing stocks	(X)
	equals the cost of goods sold	X
then	the cost of goods sold	X
	plus closing stocks	X
	less opening stocks	(X)
	equals purchases	X

5.2 EXAMPLE: USING A TRADING ACCOUNT

The stock in trade of a business on 1 July 20X6 was £8,400, and a stock taking exercise at 30 June 20X7 showed stock to be valued at £9,350. Sales for the year to 30 June 20X7 are £80,000, and the cost of goods sold was £60,000. What were the purchases during the year?

5.3 SOLUTION

The cost of goods sold is 75% of sales value.

	£
Cost of goods sold	60,000
Plus closing stock	9,350
Less opening stocks	(8,400)
Purchases	60,950

6 USING GROSS PROFIT MARGIN AND MARK-UP TO FIND FIGURES IN THE TRADING ACCOUNT

6.1 A question may ask you to use profit percentages to calculate sales or cost of sales.

FORMULAS TO LEARN

Gross margin is: $\dfrac{\text{Gross profit}}{\text{Sales}}$

Mark-up is: $\dfrac{\text{Gross profit}}{\text{Cost of goods sold}}$

6.2 EXAMPLE

Sales are £1,000 and cost of goods sold are £600. What are the profit margin and mark-up?

6.3 SOLUTION

	£
Sales	1,000
Cost of goods sold	600
Gross profit	400

Profit margin is: $\dfrac{£400}{£1{,}000} = 40\%$

Mark-up is: $\dfrac{£400}{£600} = 67\%$

Question 2

At 1 May 20X3 stock was £4,000, at 30 April 20X4 it was £3,000. Sales for the year were £80,000 and the business always has a mark up of $33^1/_3$%. What were purchases for the year?

Answer

		£	
	Sales	80,000	= $133^1/_3$%
	Cost of sales	(60,000)	= 100
	Mark up or gross profit	20,000	= $33^1/_3$%
So,	Cost of goods sold	60,000	
	plus opening stock	4,000	
	less closing stock	(3,000)	
=	purchases	61,000	

7 STOLEN GOODS OR GOODS DESTROYED

7.1 A similar type of calculation can derive the value of goods stolen or destroyed.

7.2 EXAMPLE: COST OF GOODS DESTROYED

Orlean Flames is a shop which sells fashion clothes. On 1 January 20X5, it had stock in trade which cost £7,345. During the 9 months to 30 September 20X5, the business purchased goods from suppliers costing £106,420. Sales during the same period were £154,000. The shop makes a gross profit of 40% on **cost** (mark-up) for everything it sells. On 30 September 20X5, there was a fire in the shop which destroyed most of the stock in it. Only a small amount of stock, known to have cost £350, was undamaged and still fit for sale.

How much stock was lost in the fire?

7.3 SOLUTION

(a)

	£
Sales (140%)	154,000
Gross profit (40%)	44,000
Cost of goods sold (100%)	110,000

(b)

	£
Opening stock, at cost	7,345
Plus purchases	106,420
	113,765
Less closing stock, at cost	350
Equals cost of goods sold and goods lost	113,415

(c)

	£
Cost of goods sold and lost	113,415
Cost of goods sold	110,000
Cost of goods lost	3,415

Accounting for stock destroyed, stolen or otherwise lost

7.4 When stock is stolen, destroyed or otherwise lost, the loss must be accounted for somehow.

7.5 The account that is to be debited is one of two possibilities, depending on whether or not the lost goods were insured.

(a) If the lost goods were not insured, the business must bear the loss, and the loss is shown in the P & L account.

DEBIT	Profit and loss
CREDIT	Trading account

(b) If the lost goods were insured, the business will not suffer a loss, because the insurance will pay back the cost of the lost goods. There is no charge in the P&L account.

DEBIT	Insurance claim account (debtor account)
CREDIT	Trading account

with the cost of the loss. The insurance claim will then be a current asset, and shown in the balance sheet of the business as such. When the claim is paid, the account is then closed by

DEBIT	Cash
CREDIT	Insurance claim account

Question 3

Beau Gullard runs a jewellery shop in the High Street. On 1 January 20X9, his stock in trade, at cost, amounted to £4,700 and his trade creditors were £3,950.

During the six months to 30 June 20X9, sales were £42,000. Beau Gullard makes a gross profit of $33^1/3$% on the **sales value** (margin) of everything he sells.

On 30 June, there was a burglary at the shop, and all the stock was stolen.

In trying to establish how much stock had been taken, Beau Gullard was only able to say that

(a) he knew from his bank statements that he had paid £28,400 to creditors in the 6 month period to 30 June 20X9.

(b) he currently owed creditors £5,550.

Required

(a) Calculate the amount of stock stolen.
(b) Prepare a trading account for the 6 months to 30 June 20X9.

Answer

(a) The first 'unknown' is the amount of purchases during the period. This is established by writing up a creditors account.

CREDITORS

	£		£
Payments to creditors	28,400	Opening balance b/f	3,950
Closing balance c/f	5,550	Purchases (balancing figure)	30,000
	33,950		33,950

(b) The cost of goods sold is also unknown, but this can be established from the **gross profit margin** and the sales for the period.

		£
Sales	(100%)	42,000
Gross profit	($33^1/3$%)	14,000
Cost of goods sold	($66^2/3$%)	28,000

(c) The cost of the goods stolen is

	£
Opening stock at cost	4,700
Purchases	30,000
	34,700
Less closing stock (after burglary)	0
Cost of goods sold and goods stolen	34,700
Cost of goods sold (see (b) above)	28,000
Cost of goods stolen	6,700

(d) The cost of the goods stolen is a charge in the profit and loss account, and so the trading account for the period is as follows.

BEAU GULLARD
TRADING ACCOUNT FOR THE SIX MONTHS TO 30 JUNE 20X9

	£	£
Sales		42,000
Less cost of goods sold		
Opening stock	4,700	
Purchases	30,000	
	34,700	
Less stock stolen	(6,700)	
		28,000
Gross profit		14,000

8 THE CASH BOOK

Exam focus point

The construction of a cash book, largely from bank statements showing receipts and payments of a business during a given period, is often an important feature of incomplete records problems. In an examination, the purpose of an incomplete records question is largely to test the understanding of candidates about how various items of receipts or payments relate to the preparation of a final set of accounts for a business.

8.1 We have already seen in this chapter that information about cash receipts or payments might be needed to establish:

- Purchases during a period
- Credit sales during a period

Other items of receipts or payments might be relevant to establishing

- Cash sales
- Certain expenses in the P & L account
- Drawings by the business proprietor

8.2 Often, to answer a question, we need to write up a cash book. Where there appears to be a sizeable volume of receipts and payments in cash (ie notes and coins), then it is helpful to construct a two column cash book. This is a cash book with one column for cash receipts and payments, and one column for money paid into and out of the business bank account.

8.3 EXAMPLE: TWO COLUMN CASH BOOK

Jonathan Slugg owns and runs a shop selling fishing tackle, making a gross profit of 25% on the cost of everything he sells. He does not keep a cash book.

On 1 January 20X7 the balance sheet of his business was as follows.

	£	£
Net fixed assets		20,000
Stock	10,000	
Cash in the bank	3,000	
Cash in the till	200	
	13,200	
Trade creditors	1,200	
		12,000
		32,000
Proprietor's capital		32,000

In the year to 31 December 20X7

(a) there were no sales on credit.

(b) £41,750 in receipts were banked.

(c) the bank statements of the period show the following payments.

		£
(i)	to trade creditors	36,000
(ii)	sundry expenses	5,600
(iii)	in drawings	4,400

(d) payments were also made in cash out of the till.

		£
(i)	to trade creditors	800
(ii)	sundry expenses	1,500
(iii)	in drawings	3,700

At 31 December 20X7, the business had cash in the till of £450 and trade creditors of £1,400. The cash balance in the bank was not known and the value of closing stock has not yet been calculated. There were no accruals or prepayments. No further fixed assets were purchased during the year. The depreciation charge for the year is £900.

Required

(a) Prepare a two column cash book for the period.

(b) Prepare the trading, profit and loss account for the year to 31 December 20X7 and the balance sheet as at 31 December 20X7.

8.4 DISCUSSION AND SOLUTION

A two column cash book is completed as follows.

(a) Enter the opening cash balances.

(b) Enter the information given about cash payments (and any cash receipts, if there had been any such items given in the problem).

(c) The cash receipts banked are a 'contra' entry, being both a debit (bank column) and a credit (cash in hand column) in the same account.

(d) Enter the closing cash in hand (cash in the bank at the end of the period is not known).

CASH BOOK

	Cash in hand	*Bank*		*Cash in hand*	*Bank*
	£	£		£	£
Balance b/f	200	3,000	Trade creditors	800	36,000
Cash receipts banked (contra)		41,750	Sundry expenses	1,500	5,600
Sales*	48,000		Drawings	3,700	4,400
			Cash receipts banked (contra)	41,750	
Balance c/f		*1,250	Balance c/f	450	
	48,200	46,000		48,200	46,000

* Balancing figure

(e) The closing balance of money in the bank is a balancing figure.

(f) Since all sales are for cash, a balancing figure that can be entered in the cash book is sales, in the cash in hand (debit) column.

8.5 It is important to notice that since not all receipts from cash sales are banked, the value of cash sales during the period is the balance on the cash account or it could be calculated as:

	£
Receipts banked	41,750
Plus expenses and drawings paid out of the till in cash £(800 + 1,500 + 3,700)	6,000
Plus any cash stolen (here there is none)	0
Plus the closing balance of cash in hand	450
	48,200
Less the opening balance of cash in hand	(200)
Equals cash sales	48,000

8.6 The cash book has enabled us to establish both the closing balance for cash in the bank and also the volume of cash sales. Now calculate purchases.

CREDITORS

	£		£
Cash book:		Balance b/f	1,200
Payments from bank	36,000	Purchases (balancing figure)	37,000
Cash book:			
Payments in cash	800		
Balance c/f	1,400		
	38,200		38,200

The gross profit margin of 25% on cost indicates that the cost of the goods sold is £38,400.

	£
Sales (125%)	48,000
Gross profit (25%)	9,600
Cost of goods sold (100%)	38,400

The closing stock amount is now a balancing figure in the trading account.

JONATHAN SLUGG
TRADING, PROFIT AND LOSS ACCOUNT
FOR THE YEAR ENDED 31 DECEMBER 20X7

	£	£
Sales		48,000
Less cost of goods sold		
Opening stock	10,000	
Purchases	37,000	
	47,000	
Less closing stock (balancing figure)	8,600	
		38,400
Gross profit (25/125 × £48,000)		9,600
Expenses		
Sundry £(1,500 + 5,600)	7,100	
Depreciation	900	
		8,000
Net profit		1,600

JONATHAN SLUGG
BALANCE SHEET AS AT 31 DECEMBER 20X7

	£	£
Net fixed assets £(20,000 – 900)		19,100
Stock	8,600	
Cash in the till	450	
	9,050	
Bank overdraft	1,250	
Trade creditors	1,400	
	2,650	
Net current assets		6,400
		25,500
Proprietor's capital		
Balance b/f		32,000
Net profit for the year		1,600
		33,600
Drawings £(3,700 + 4,400)		(8,100)
Balance c/f		25,500

Theft of cash from the till

8.7 When cash is stolen from the till, the amount stolen will be a credit entry in the cash book, and a debit in either the P&L account or insurance claim account, depending on whether the business is insured.

9 ACCRUALS AND PREPAYMENTS

9.1 Where there is an accrued expense or a prepayment, the charge to be made in the P&L account for the item concerned should be found from the opening balance b/f, the closing balance c/f, and cash payments for the item during the period. The charge in the P&L account is perhaps most easily found as the balancing figure in a T account.

9.2 EXAMPLE: PREPAYMENTS

On 1 April 20X6 a business had prepaid rent of £700. During the year to 31 March 20X7 it pays £9,300 in rent and at 31 March 20X7 the prepayment of rent is £1,000.

Calculate the P+L figure for rent expense.

9.3 SOLUTION

The cost of rent in the P&L account for the year to 31 March 20X7 is the balancing figure in the following T account. (Remember that a prepayment is a current asset, and so is a debit balance b/f.)

RENT EXPENSE

	£		£
Prepayment: balance b/f	700	P & L account (balancing figure)	9,000
Cash	9,300	Prepayment: balance c/f	1,000
	10,000		10,000
Balance b/f	1,000		

9.4 EXAMPLE: ACCRUAL

Similarly, if a business has accrued telephone expenses as at 1 July 20X6 of £850, pays £6,720 in telephone bills during the year to 30 June 20X7, and has accrued telephone expenses of £1,140 as at 30 June 20X7.

Calculate the P+L figure for telephone expense.

9.5 SOLUTION

The telephone expense to be shown in the P&L account for the year to 30 June 20X7 is the balancing figure in the following T account. (Remember that an accrual is a current liability, and so is a credit balance b/f.)

TELEPHONE EXPENSES

	£		£
Cash	6,720	Balance b/f (accrual)	850
Balance c/f (accrual)	1,140	P&L a/c (balancing figure)	7,010
	7,860		7,860
		Balance b/f	1,140

10 DRAWINGS

Exam focus point

Drawings would normally represent no particular problem at all in preparing a set of final accounts from incomplete records, but it is not unusual for examination questions to introduce a situation in which:

(a) the business owner pays income into his bank account which has nothing whatever to do with the business operations. For example, the owner might pay dividend income, or other income from personal investments into the bank.

(b) the business owner pays money out of the business bank account for items which are not business expenses, eg life insurance premiums or holidays.

10.1 Where such personal items of receipts or payments are made.

(a) Receipts should be set off against drawings. For example, if a business owner receives £600 in personal dividend income and pays it into his business bank account then the accounting entry is

DEBIT Cash
CREDIT Drawings

(b) Payments should be charged to drawings.

DEBIT Drawings
CREDIT Cash

Drawings: beware of the wording in an examination question

10.2 You should note the following.

(a) If a question states that a proprietor's drawings during the year are 'approximately £40 per week', you should assume that drawings for the year are £40 × 52 weeks = £2,080.

(b) If a question states that drawings in the year are 'between £35 and £45 per week', do **not** assume that the drawings average £40 per week and so amount to £2,080 for the year. You could not be certain that the actual drawings did average £40, and so you should treat the drawings figure as a missing item that needs to be calculated.

11 DEALING WITH INCOMPLETE RECORDS PROBLEMS IN THE EXAMINATION

11.1 A suggested approach to dealing with incomplete records problems brings together the various points described so far in this chapter. The nature of the 'incompleteness' in the records will vary from problem to problem, but the approach should be successful in arriving at the final accounts whatever the particular characteristics of the problem.

NOTE!

Even if you know that you will have only MCQ questions in your exam, it is worthwhile studying this section as it covers all areas of incomplete records.

Exam focus point

Following the approach below should ensure that if an incomplete records question does come up in your examination, you will be well equipped to deal with it successfully.

11.2 The approach is as follows.

Step 1. If it is not already known, establish the opening balance sheet and the proprietor's interest.

Step 2. Open up four accounts.

(i) Trading account (if you wish, leave space underneath for entering the P&L account later)

(ii) A cash book, with two columns if cash sales are significant and there are payments in cash out of the till

(iii) A debtors account

(iv) A creditors account

Step 3. Enter the opening balances in these accounts.

Step 4. Work through the information you are given line by line. Each item should be entered into the relevant account, as appropriate.

You should also try to recognise each item as a 'P&L account income or expense item' or a 'closing balance sheet item'.

It may be necessary to calculate an amount for drawings and an amount for fixed asset depreciation.

Step 5. Look for the balancing figures in your accounts. In particular you might be looking for a value for credit sales, cash sales, purchases, the cost of goods sold, the cost of goods stolen or destroyed, or the closing bank balance. Calculate these missing figures, and make any necessary double entry (eg to the trading account from the creditors account for purchases).

Step 6. Now complete the P&L account and balance sheet. Working T accounts might be needed where there are accruals or prepayments.

11.3 EXAMPLE: AN INCOMPLETE RECORDS PROBLEM

John Snow is the sole distribution agent in the Branton area for Diamond floor tiles. Under an agreement with the manufacturers, John Snow purchases the Diamond floor tiles at a trade discount of 20% off list price and annually in May receives an agency commission of 1% of his purchases for the year ended on the previous 31 March.

For several years, John Snow has obtained a gross profit of 40% on all sales. In a burglary in January 20X1 John Snow lost stock costing £4,000 as well as many of his accounting records. However, after careful investigations, the following information has been obtained covering the year ended 31 March 20X1.

(a) Assets and liabilities at 31 March 20X0 were as follows.

		£
Buildings:	at cost	10,000
	provision for depreciation	6,000
Motor vehicles:	at cost	5,000
	provision for depreciation	2,000
Stock: at cost		3,200
Trade debtors (for sales)		6,300
Agency commission due		300
Prepayments (trade expenses)		120
Balance at bank		4,310
Trade creditors		4,200
Accrued vehicle expenses		230

(b) John Snow will receive an agency commission of £440 on 1 May 20X1.

(c) Stock, at cost, at 31 March 20X1 was valued at £3,000 more than a year previously.

(d) In October 20X0 stock costing £1,000 was damaged by damp and had to be scrapped.

(e) Trade creditors at 31 March 20X1 related entirely to goods received whose list prices totalled £9,500.

(f) Discounts allowed amounted to £1,620 whilst discounts received were £1,200.

(g) Trade expenses prepaid at 31 March 20X1 totalled £80.

(h) Vehicle expenses for the year ended 31 March 20X1 amounted to £7,020.

(i) Trade debtors (for sales) at 31 March 20X1 were £6,700.

(j) All receipts are passed through the bank account.

(k) Depreciation is provided annually at the following rates.

Buildings 5% on cost
Motor vehicles 20% on cost

(l) Commissions received are paid directly to the bank account.

(m) In addition to the payments for purchases, the bank payments were

	£
Vehicle expenses	6,720
Drawings	4,300
Trade expenses	7,360

(n) John Snow is not insured against loss of stock owing to burglary or damage by damp.

Required

Prepare John Snow's trading and profit and loss account for the year ended 31 March 20X1 and a balance sheet on that date.

11.4 DISCUSSION AND SOLUTION

This is an incomplete records problem because we are told that John Snow has lost many of his accounting records. In particular we do not know sales for the year, purchases during the year, or all the cash receipts and payments.

11.5 The first step is to find the opening balance sheet. The proprietor's capital is the balancing figure.

JOHN SNOW
BALANCE SHEET AS AT 31 MARCH 20X0

	Cost	*Dep'n*	*NBV*
	£	£	£
Fixed assets			
Buildings	10,000	6,000	4,000
Motor vehicles	5,000	2,000	3,000
	15,000	8,000	7,000
Current assets			
Stock		3,200	
Trade debtors		6,300	
Commission due		300	
Prepayments		120	
Balance at hand		4,310	
		14,230	
Current liabilities			
Trade creditors		4,200	
Accrued expenses		230	
		4,430	
			9,800
			16,800
Proprietor's capital as at 31 March 20X0			16,800

11.6 The next step is to open up a trading account, cash book, debtors account and creditors account and to insert the opening balances, if known. Cash sales and payments in cash are not a feature of the problem, and so a single column cash book is sufficient.

11.7 Identify any transactions affecting those accounts.

TRADING ACCOUNT

	£	£
Sales (note (f))		60,000
Opening stock	3,200	
Purchases (note (a))	44,000	
	47,200	
Less: damaged stock written off (note (c))	(1,000)	
stock stolen (note (e))	(4,000)	
	42,200	
Less closing stock (note (b))	6,200	
Cost of goods sold		36,000
Gross profit (note (f))		24,000

CASH BOOK

	£		£
Opening balance	4,310	Trade creditors	
Trade debtors (see below)	57,980	(see creditors a/c)	39,400
Agency commission (note (g))	300	Trade expenses	7,360
		Vehicle expenses	6,720
		Drawings	4,300
		Balance c/f	4,810
	62,590		62,590

TRADE DEBTORS

	£		£
Opening balance b/f	6,300	Discounts allowed (note (d))	1,620
Sales (note (f))	60,000	Cash received (balancing figure)	57,980
		Closing balance c/f	6,700
	66,300		66,300

TRADE CREDITORS

	£		£
Discounts received (note (d))	1,200	Opening balance b/f	4,200
Cash paid (balancing figure)	39,400	Purchases (note (a))	44,000
Closing balance c/f	7,600		
	48,200		48,200

VEHICLE EXPENSES

	£		£
Cash	6,720	Accrual b/f	230
Accrual c/f (balancing figure)	530	P & L account	7,020
	7,250		7,250

11.8 The trading account is complete already, but now the P&L account and balance sheet can be prepared. Remember not to forget items such as the stock losses, commission earned on purchases, discounts allowed and discounts received.

JOHN SNOW
TRADING, PROFIT AND LOSS ACCOUNT
FOR THE YEAR ENDED 31 MARCH 20X1

	£	£
Sales (note (f))		60,000
Opening stock	3,200	
Purchases (note (a))	44,000	
	47,200	
Less: damaged stock written off (note (c))	(1,000)	
stock stolen	(4,000)	
	42,200	
Less closing stock (note (b))	6,200	
Cost of goods sold		36,000
Gross profit (note (f))		24,000
Add: commission on purchases		440
discounts received		1,200
		25,640
Expenses		
Trade expenses (note (h))	7,400	
Stock damaged	1,000	
Stock stolen	4,000	
Vehicle expenses	7,020	
Discounts allowed	1,620	
Depreciation		
Buildings	500	
Motor vehicles	1,000	
		22,540
Net profit (to capital account)		3,100

JOHN SNOW
BALANCE SHEET AS AT 31 MARCH 20X1

	Cost	*Dep'n*	*NBV*
	£	£	£
Fixed assets			
Buildings	10,000	6,500	3,500
Motor vehicles	5,000	3,000	2,000
	15,000	9,500	5,500
Current assets			
Stock		6,200	
Trade debtors		6,700	
Commission due		440	
Prepayments (trade expenses)		80	
Balance at bank		4,810	
		18,230	
Current liabilities			
Trade creditors		7,600	
Accrued expenses		530	
		8,130	
			10,100
			15,600
Proprietor's capital			
As at 31 March 20X0			16,800
Net profit for year to 31 March 20X1		3,100	
Less drawings		(4,300)	
Retained deficit			(1,200)
As at 31 March 20X1			15,600

Notes

(a) The agency commission due on 1 May 20X1 indicates that purchases for the year to 31 March 20X1 were

100%/1% × £440 = £44,000

(b) Closing stock at cost on 31 March 20X1 was £(3,200 + 3,000) = £6,200.

(c) Stock scrapped (£1,000) is accounted for as follows.

CREDIT	Trading account
DEBIT	P&L account

(d) Discounts allowed are accounted for.

DEBIT	Discounts allowed account
CREDIT	Debtors

Similarly, discounts received are

DEBIT	Creditors
CREDIT	Discounts received

Note. Discounts received represents settlement discounts, not *trade* discounts, which are not usually accounted for as they are given automatically at source.

(e) Stocks lost in the burglary are accounted for.

CREDIT	Trading account
DEBIT	P&L account

(f) The trade discount of 20% has already been deducted in arriving at the value of the purchases. The gross profit is 40% on sales, so with cost of sales = £36,000.

		£
Cost	(60%)	36,000
Profit	(40%)	24,000
Sales	(100%)	60,000

(It is assumed that trade expenses are not included in the trading account, and so should be ignored in this calculation.)

(g) The agency commission of £300 due on 1 May 20X0 is paid on that date.

(h) The P&L account expenditure for trade expenses and closing balance on vehicle expenses account are as follows.

TRADE EXPENSES

	£		£
Prepayment	120	P&L account (balancing figure)	7,400
Cash	7,360	Prepayment c/f	80
	7,480		7,480

12 USING A DEBTORS ACCOUNT TO CALCULATE BOTH CASH SALES AND CREDIT SALES

12.1 A final point which needs to be considered is how a missing value can be found for cash sales and credit sales, when a business has both, but takings banked by the business are not divided between takings from cash sales and takings from credit sales.

12.2 EXAMPLE: USING A DEBTORS ACCOUNT TO FIND TOTAL SALES

A business had, on 1 January 20X8, trade debtors of £2,000, cash in the bank of £3,000, and cash in hand of £300.

During the year to 31 December 20X8 the business banked £95,000 in takings.

It also paid out the following expenses in cash from the till.

Drawings	£1,200
Sundry expenses	£800

On 29 August 20X8 a thief broke into the shop and stole £400 from the till.

At 31 December 20X8 trade debtors amounted to £3,500, cash in the bank £2,500 and cash in the till £150.

What was the value of sales during the year?

12.3 SOLUTION

If we tried to prepare a debtors account and a two column cash book, we would have insufficient information, in particular about whether the takings which were banked related to cash sales or credit sales. All we do know is that the combined sums from debtors and cash takings banked is £95,000.

The value of sales can be found instead by using the debtors account, which should be used to record cash takings banked as well as payments by debtors. The balancing figure in the debtors account will then be a combination of credit sales and some cash sales. The cash book only needs to be a single column.

DEBTORS

	£		£
Balance b/f	2,000	Cash banked	95,000
Sales-to trading account	96,500	Balance c/f	3,500
	98,500		98,500

CASH (EXTRACT)

	£		£
Balance in hand b/f	300	Payments in cash:	
Balance in bank b/f	3,000	Drawings	1,200
Debtors a/c	95,000	Expenses	800
		Other payments	?
		Cash stolen	400
		Balance in hand c/f	150
		Balance in bank c/f	2,500

The remaining 'undiscovered' amount of cash sales is now found as follows.

	£	£
Payments in cash out of the till		
Drawings	1,200	
Expenses	800	
		2,000
Cash stolen		400
Closing balance of cash in hand		150
		2,550
Less opening balance of cash in hand		(300)
Further cash sales		2,250

(This calculation is similar to the one described above for calculating cash sales.)

Total sales for the year are

	£
From debtors account	96,500
From cash book	2,250
Total sales	98,750

A similar technique can be used to find cash and credit purchases using a creditors account.

Question 4

Mary Grimes, retail fruit and vegetable merchant, does not keep a full set of accounting records. However, the following information has been produced from the business's records.

(a) Summary of the bank account for the year ended 31 August 20X8

	£		£
1 Sept 20X7 balance brought forward	1,970	Payment to suppliers	72,000
		Purchase of motor van (E471 KBR)	13,000
Receipts from trade debtors	96,000	Rent and rates	2,600
Sale of private yacht	20,000	Wages	15,100
Sale of motor van (A123 BWA)	2,100	Motor vehicle expenses	3,350
		Postages and stationery	1,360
		Drawings	9,200
		Repairs and renewals	650
		Insurances	800
		31 August 20X8 balance c/fwd	2,010
	120,070		120,070
1 Sept 20X8 balance b/fwd	2,010		

(b) Assets and liabilities, other than balance at bank as at:

			1 Sept 20X7	*31 Aug 20X8*
			£	£
Trade creditors			4,700	2,590
Trade debtors			7,320	9,500
Rent and rates accruals			200	260
Motor vans:				
	A123 BWA:	At cost	10,000	-
		Provision for depreciation	8,000	-
	E471 KBR:	At cost	-	13,000
		Provision for depreciation	-	To be determined
Stock in trade			4,900	5,900
Insurance prepaid			160	200

(c) All receipts are banked and all payments are made from the business bank account.

(d) A trade debt of £300 owing by John Blunt and included in the trade debtors at 31 August 20X8 (see (b) above), is to be written off as a bad debt.

(e) It is Mary Grimes' policy to provide depreciation at the rate of 20% on the cost of motor vans held at the end of each financial year; no depreciation is provided in the year of sale or disposal of a motor van.

(f) Discounts received during the year ended 31 August 20X8 from trade creditors was to £1,100.

Required

(a) Prepare Mary Grimes' trading and profit and loss account for the year ended 31 August 20X8.

(b) Prepare Mary Grimes' balance sheet as at 31 August 20X8.

Answer

(a) TRADING AND PROFIT AND LOSS ACCOUNT
FOR THE YEAR ENDED 31 AUGUST 20X8

	£	£
Sales (W1)		98,180
Opening stock	4,900	
Purchases (W2)	70,990	
	75,890	
Less closing stock	5,900	
		69,990
Gross profit		28,190
Discounts received		1,100
Profit on sale of motor vehicle £2,100 - £(10,000 - 8,000)		100
		29,390
Rent and rates (W3)	2,660	
Wages	15,100	
Motor vehicle expenses	3,350	
Postages and stationery	1,360	
Repairs and renewals	650	
Insurances (W4)	760	
Bad debt	300	
Depreciation of van (20% × £13,000)	2,600	
		26,780
		2,610

(b) BALANCE SHEET AS AT 31 AUGUST 20X8

	£	£
Fixed assets		
Motor van: cost	13,000	
depreciation	2,600	
		10,400
Current assets		
Stock	5,900	
Debtors (£9,500 - £300 bad debt)	9,200	
Prepayment	200	
Cash at bank	2,010	
	17,310	
Current liabilities		
Creditors	2,590	
Accrual	260	
	2,850	
Net current assets		14,460
		24,860
Capital account		
Balance at 1 September 20X7 (W5)		11,450
Additional capital: proceeds on sale of yacht		20,000
Net profit for the year	2,610	
Less drawings	9,200	
Retained loss for the year		(6,590)
Balance at 31 August 20X8		24,860

Workings

1 *Sales*

	£
Cash received from customers	96,000
Add debtors balances at 31 August 20X8	9,500
	105,500
Less debtors balances at 1 September 20X7	7,320
Sales in year	98,180

2 Purchases

	£	£
Payments to suppliers		72,000
Add: creditors balances at 31 August 20X8	2,590	
discounts granted by creditors	1,100	
		3,690
		75,690
Less creditors balances at 1 September 20X7		4,700
		70,990

3 Rent and rates

	£
Cash paid in year	2,600
Add accrual at 31 August 20X8	260
	2,860
Less accrual at 1 September 20X7	v200
Charge for the year	2,660

4 Insurances

	£
Cash paid in year	800
Add prepayment at 1 September 20X7	160
	960
Less prepayment at 31 August 20X8	200
	760

(Workings 1-4 could also be presented in a T account format as follows.)

TOTAL DEBTORS

	£		£
Balance b/f	7,320	Bank	96,000
∴ Sales	98,180	Balance c/f	9,500
	105,500		105,500

TOTAL CREDITORS

	£		£
Bank	72,000	Balance b/f	4,700
Discounts received	1,100	∴ Purchases	70,990
Balance c/f	2,590		
	75,690		75,690

RENT AND RATES

	£		£
Bank	2,600	Balance b/f	200
Balance c/f	260	∴ P & L charge	2,660
	2,860		2,860

INSURANCES

	£		£
Balance b/f	160	∴ P & L charge	760
Bank	800	Balance c/f	200
	960		960

5 Capital at 1 September 20X7

	£	£
Assets		
Bank balance		1,970
Debtors		7,320
Motor van £(10,000 - 8,000)		2,000
Stock		4,900
Prepayment		160
		16,350
Liabilities		
Trade creditors	4,700	
Accrual	200	
		4,900
		11,450

Chapter roundup

- Incomplete records questions may test your ability to prepare accounts in the following situations.
  - A trader does not maintain a ledger and therefore has no continuous double entry record.
  - Accounting records are destroyed by accident, such as fire.
  - Some essential figure is unknown and must be calculated as a balancing figure. This may occur as a result of stock being damaged or destroyed, or because of misappropriation of assets.
- The approach to incomplete records questions is to build up the information given so as to complete the necessary double entry. This may involve reconstructing control accounts for.
  - Cash and bank (often in columnar format)
  - Debtors and creditors
- Where stock, sales or purchases is the unknown figure it will be necessary to use information on gross profit percentages so as to construct a trading account in which the unknown figure can be inserted as a balance.

Quick quiz

1 Given cash sales £15,000, receipts from credit customers £23,000, opening debtors (1.1.X1) £7,500 and closing debtors (at 31.12.X1) £9,500, calculate the total sales for a business, which does not keep full records, for 20X1.

A £36,000
B £38,000
C £40,000
D £25,000

2 A business has opening creditors (1.7.20X1) £5,000, closing creditors (30.6.20X2) £7,000, cash purchases £1,500, cash payments to credit suppliers £28,000. Calculate the total purchases figure for inclusion in the trading account.

A £27,500
B £29,500
C £31,500
D £30,000

3 The term 'incomplete records' means that?

- A The business has not kept a full set of accounting records
- B The records have been lost
- C Small limited companies are not under an obligation to keep full accounts
- D The business is unable to complete its financial statements

4 A business has the following assets and liabilities at 1.1.X1, calculate the owners capital at 1.1.X1. Premises £15,000, van £5,000, stock £2,000, creditors £8,000, debtors £6,000, accruals £1,000, bank loan £10,000, bank overdraft £1,200.

- A £10,200
- B £9,800
- C £7,800
- D £23,800

Answers to quick quiz

1 C Correct: £23,000 + £9,500 - £7,500 + £15,000.

A Incorrect, you have reversed opening and closing debtor balances.

B Incorrect, this is cash sales plus receipts from debtors which must be adjusted for opening and closing debtors.

D Incorrect, this is credit sales, you were asked for total sales.

2 C Correct, 28,000 + 7,000 – 5,000 = £30,000 credit purchases + £1,500 cash purchases.

A Incorrect, you have transposed opening and closing creditors.

B Incorrect, payments to credit suppliers must be adjusted for creditor changes.

D This is the credit, not total, purchase figure.

3 A Correct.

B If records have been lost, it will be necessary to create financial statements from the data which remains.

C Small limited companies must keep 'proper accounting records'.

D This is a consequence of not keeping proper records, the business accountant will work from incomplete data which will make the task more difficult and expensive.

4 C Correct: 15,000 + 5,000 + 2,000 – 8,000 + 6,000 – 1,000 – 10,000 – 1,200 = 7,800 = net assets = capital.

A Incorrect you have treated the bank overdraft as an asset.

B Incorrect, you have treated both debtors and creditors incorrectly.

D Incorrect, you have included creditors as an asset – be careful how you extract data from lists of items given in questions.

Now try the questions below from the Exam Question Bank

Number	Level	Marks	Time
52	Exam	20	36 mins
53	Exam	2	3 mins
54	Exam	2	3 mins

Chapter 19

LIMITED COMPANIES

Topic List		Syllabus reference	Required ability
1	Limited companies	(i), (iv)	Application
2	Share capital and reserves	(iv)	Application
3	The final accounts of limited companies	(i), (iv)	Application
4	The ledger accounts of limited companies	(iv)	Application

Introduction

In this chapter we study the accounts of **limited companies**. The accounting rules and conventions for recording the business transactions of limited companies and then preparing their final accounts, are much the same as for sole traders. For example, companies will have a cash book, sales day book, purchase day book, journal, sales ledger, purchase ledger and nominal ledger etc. They also prepare a profit and loss account annually, and a balance sheet at the end of the accounting year.

We shall see that, in the balance sheet, the treatment of assets and liabilities is basically the same but the particular nature of limited companies calls for changes in the owners' equity section. Similarly, in the profit and loss account, the principal differences are found in the appropriation account - that part of the profit and loss account which shows how the profit or loss for the period has been divided.

One important difference is the legal requirement that limited companies must publish their accounts. The relevant legislation specifies certain information which must be included in the published financial statements of a limited company.

It should be stressed that, while you do not have to learn the published accounts formats by heart at this stage, it is important for you to have an overall awareness of the form of company accounts. In Chapter 20 you will learn about interpretation of accounts and this will include items in company accounts formats.

Learning outcomes covered in this chapter

- Explain the influence of legislation (eg Companies Acts) and accounting standards on the production of published accounting information for organisations
- Prepare trading accounts, profit and loss accounts, appropriations of profit and balance sheets from trial balance

Syllabus content covered in this chapter

- Regulatory influence of company law and accounting standards
- Items in formats for published accounts
- Trading, profit and loss accounts and balance sheets from trial balance
- Accounting for appropriations of profit

1 LIMITED COMPANIES

KEY TERMS

There are two classes of limited company.

(a) **Private companies**. These have the word 'limited' at the end of their name. Being private, they cannot invite members of the public to invest in their equity (shares).

(b) **Public companies.** These are much fewer in number than private companies, but are generally much larger in size. They have the words 'public limited company' - shortened to PLC or plc (or the Welsh language equivalent) at the end of their name. Public limited companies can invite members of the general public to invest in their equity, and the 'shares' of these companies are traded on a Stock Exchange.

Limited liability

KEY TERM

Limited companies offer **limited liability** to their owners. This means that the maximum amount that an owner stands to lose in the event that the company becomes insolvent and cannot pay off its debts, is the capital in the business. This limited liability is therefore a major advantage of turning a business into a limited company because an investor knows the maximum amount that they stand to lose when they buy shares in a company.

THE MAIN POINTS!

1 Company accounts preparation is governed by the Companies Act.
2 Companies issue shares to shareholders who enjoy limited liability.

2 SHARE CAPITAL AND RESERVES

Share capital

KEY TERM

The proprietors' capital in a limited company consists of **share capital**. A company issues **shares**, which are paid for by investors, who then become shareholders of the company.

2.1 When a company is set up with a **share capital** of, say, £100,000, it may be decided to issue

- 100,000 shares of £1 each nominal value
- 200,000 shares of 50p each
- 400,000 shares of 25p each
- 250,000 shares of 40p each

£1, 50p, 25p or 40p is the nominal value of the share. The nominal value is not the same as the market value, which is the price someone is prepared to pay for the share.

KEY TERM

The **authorised share capital** is the maximum amount of share capital that the company is empowered to issue. **Issued** share capital is the nominal amount of share capital that has been issued to shareholders. This cannot exceed the authorised share capital. **Called up share capital** is the total amount of issued share capital for which the shareholders are required to pay. **Paid up share capital** is the amount of share capital paid by the shareholders.

Dividends

KEY TERM

Profits paid out to shareholders are called **dividends.**

- An **interim** dividend is a dividend paid partway through the year
- At the end of the year, the company might pay a further **final** dividend.

The **total dividend** for the year is the sum of the interim and final dividends. (Not all companies pay an interim dividend. Interim dividends are commonly paid by public limited companies.)

2.2 Usually, at the end of an accounting year, a company's directors will propose a final dividend payment, but this will not yet have been paid. This means that the final dividend will be shown as a current liability in the balance sheet.

The terminology of dividend

2.3 The terminology of dividend payments can be confusing, since they may be expressed either in the form, as 'x pence per share' or as 'y per cent'. In the latter case, the meaning is always 'y per cent of the **nominal** value of the shares in issue'. For example, suppose a company's issued share capital consists of 100,000 50p ordinary shares. The company's balance sheet would include the following.

Called up share capital:	100,000 50p ordinary shares	£50,000

If the directors wish to pay a dividend of £5,000, they may propose any of the following.

- A dividend of 5p per share (100,000 × 5p = £5,000)
- A dividend of 10% (10% × £50,000 = £5,000)
- A dividend of 10p in the (£50,000 × 10p = £5,000)

Any profits not paid out as dividends are put in reserves (see below).

Ordinary shares and preference shares

2.4 The two types of shares most often encountered are preference shares and ordinary shares.

KEY TERM

Preference shares carry the right to a fixed dividend which is expressed as a percentage of their nominal value: eg a 6% £1 preference share carries a right to an annual dividend of 6p.

2.5 Preference dividends have priority over ordinary dividends. If the directors of a company wish to pay a dividend (which they are not obliged to do) they must pay any preference dividend first. Otherwise, no ordinary dividend may be paid.

KEY TERM

Ordinary shares are by far the most common. They carry no right to a fixed dividend but are entitled to all profits left after payment of any preference dividend. In most companies only ordinary shares carry voting rights.

2.6 Should the company be wound up, any surplus is shared between the ordinary shareholders.

Question 1

At the year-end, the trial balance for KT Limited shows a debit balance of £20,000 in respect of dividends. The Share Capital account of £1m comprises 200,000 5% preference shares of £1 with the balance made up of 50p ordinary shares. The dividends account represents a half-year's preference dividend and an interim ordinary dividend. A final dividend of 5p per ordinary share is proposed.

Calculate the interim and final dividends for each category of share.

Answer

A full year's dividend on the preference shares is 200,000 @ 5% = £10,000, therefore a half-year's dividend was £5,000, with a final dividend of the same amount.

The interim ordinary dividend was therefore £15,000 (£20,000 - £5,000).

As the share capital account amounts to £1m, £800,000 (£1m - £200k) must relate to ordinary shares. However, the ordinary shares are only 50p each, meaning that there are 1.6 million of them. The final dividend is therefore £80,000 (1.6m × 5p)

Exam focus point

It is worth spending a few minutes getting to grips with dividend calculations, as they are a likely exam topic. You are unlikely to get a calculation more difficult than that involved in the exercise above.

Question 2

A company's share capital is:

50p	Ordinary shares	£2m
£1	6% preference shares	£1m

Dividends to ordinary shareholders have been:

		Amount	*Date paid*
20X2	Final dividend	4p per share	31 Jan 20X3
20X3	Interim dividend	3p per share	13 July 20X3
20X3	Final dividend	5p per share	20 Jan 20X4

What is the figure for dividends in the profit and loss account to 31 December 20X3?

A £160,000
B £220,000
C £320,000
D 380,000

Answer

D is correct.

	£
1m 6% preference shares	60,000
20X3 interim (3p × 4m shares)	120,000
20X3 final (5p × 4m shares)	200,000
Total	380,000

Reserves

KEY TERMS

Reserves are profits that have not been distributed (paid out) to shareholders.

The ordinary shareholders' total investment in a limited company is called the **equity** and consists of ordinary share capital plus **reserves.**

Shareholders' funds is the total of all share capital, both ordinary and preference, and the reserves.

The important point to note is that all reserves are **owned** by the ordinary shareholders.

2.7 A distinction should be made between the two types of reserves.

KEY TERMS

Statutory reserves are reserves which a company is required to set up by law and which are not available for the distribution of dividends.

Non-statutory reserves are reserves consisting of profits which are distributable as dividends, if the company so wishes.

Profit and loss reserve (retained profits)

KEY TERM

These are profits earned by the company and **not appropriated** by dividends, taxation or transfer to another reserve account. This reserve generally increases from year to year, as most companies do not distribute all their profits as dividends. If a loss is made in one particular year, a dividend can still be paid from previous years' retained profits.

2.8 For example, if a company makes a loss of £100,000 in one year, yet has unappropriated profits from previous years totalling £250,000, it can pay a dividend not exceeding £150,000.

2.9 Very occasionally, you come across a debit balance on the profit and loss account. This indicates that the company has accumulated losses.

2.10 This is the most significant non-statutory reserve, and it is described in many different ways.

- Revenue reserve
- Retained profits
- Retained earnings
- Undistributed profits
- Profit and loss account
- Unappropriated profits

Other non-statutory reserves

2.11 The company directors may choose to set up other reserves. These may have a specific purpose (for example plant and machinery replacement reserve) or not (for example general reserve). The creation of these reserves usually indicates a general intention not to distribute the profits involved at any future date, although legally any such reserves, being non-statutory, remain available for the payment of dividends.

2.12 Profits are transferred to these reserves by making an appropriation out of profits, usually profits for the year. Typically, you might come across the following.

	£	£
Profit after taxation		100,000
Appropriations of profit		
Dividend	60,000	
Transfer to general reserve	10,000	
		70,000
Retained profits for the year		30,000
Profit and loss reserve b/f		250,000
Profit and loss reserve c/f		280,000

2.13 There is no real significance about the creation of separate non-statutory reserves. After all, there is little difference between the following two balance sheet extracts.

			£	£
(a)	Net assets			3,500
	Financed by			
	Share capital			2,000
	Reserves:	general (distributable as dividend)	1,000	
		retained profits (distributable)	500	
				1,500
				3,500

		£
(b)	Net assets	3,500
	Financed by	
	Share capital	2,000
	Reserves: retained profit (distributable)	1,500
		3,500

2.14 The establishment of a 'plant and machinery replacement reserve' (or something similar) indicates an intention by a company to keep funds in the business to replace its plant and machinery. However, the reserve would still (legally) represent distributable profits. The existence of such a reserve no more guarantees the company's ability to replace its fixed assets in the future, than the accumulated provision for depreciation in the balance sheet.

The share premium account

KEY TERM

The **share premium account** is a statutory reserve created if shares are issued for more than their nominal value.

2.15 When a company is first incorporated (set up) the issue price of its shares will probably be the same as their nominal value and so there would be no share premium. If the company does well the market value of its shares will increase, but not the nominal value. The price of any new shares issued will be approximately their market value. The difference between cash received by the company and the nominal value of the new shares issued is transferred to the share premium account.

2.16 EXAMPLE

X Ltd issues 1,000 £1 ordinary shares at £2.60. What entries record this issue?

2.17 SOLUTION

		£	£
DEBIT	Cash	2,600	
CREDIT	Ordinary share capital		1,000
CREDIT	Share premium account		1,600

2.18 A share premium account only comes into being when a company issues shares at a price in excess of their nominal value. The market price of the shares, once they have been issued, has no bearing at all on the company's accounts, and so if their market price goes up or down, the share premium account would remain unaltered.

Revaluation reserve

KEY TERM

A **revaluation reserve** is a statutory reserve which must be created when a company revalues its fixed assets.

2.19 Revaluations frequently occur with freehold property, as the market value of property rises. The directors might wish to show a more 'reasonable' value of the asset in their balance sheet to avoid giving a misleading impression about the financial position of the company.

2.20 When an asset is revalued the revaluation reserve is credited with the difference between the revalued amount of the asset, and its net book value before the revaluation took place. Depreciation is subsequently charged on the revalued amount.

2.21 EXAMPLE: REVALUATION RESERVE

X Ltd bought freehold land and buildings for £20,000 ten years ago; their net book value (after depreciation of the buildings) is now £19,300. A professional valuation of £390,000 has been given, and the directors wish to reflect this in the accounts. Show the entries to record this revaluation.

2.22 SOLUTION

The revaluation surplus is £390,000 – £19,300 = £370,700. The entry to be made is thus.

		£	£
DEBIT	Freehold property	370,700	
CREDIT	Revaluation reserve		370,700

The balance sheet will then include the following.

Reserves	
Revaluation reserve	370,700
Fixed assets	
Freehold property (at valuation)	390,000

2.23 An unrealised capital profit (such as the £370,700 above) is generally not distributable, whereas a realised capital profit (ie if the property is actually sold for £390,000) usually is distributable.

Distinction between reserves and provisions

KEY TERM

A **reserve** is an appropriation of distributable profits for a specific purpose (eg plant replacement) while a **provision** is an amount charged against revenue as an expense.

2.24 A provision relates either to a diminution in the value of an asset (eg doubtful debtors) or a known liability (eg audit fees), the amount of which cannot be established with any accuracy. Provisions (for depreciation, doubtful debts etc) are dealt with in company accounts in the same way as in the accounts of other types of business.

Question 3

(a) A public company has 10,000,000 25p shares in issue and their current value on the stock market is £4.97 per share. What is the value of share capital in the company's nominal ledger?

(b The profit and loss reserve of a limited company the same thing as the trading account of a sole trader. True or false?

(c) A freehold property is revalued from £180,000 to £500,000. What is the balance on the revaluation reserve after this revaluation?

Answer

(a) £2.5m.

(b) False. The reserve is for *retained* profits, not profits of the current year only.

(c) £320,000 (ie £500,000 – £180,000).

3 THE FINAL ACCOUNTS OF LIMITED COMPANIES

3.1 The preparation and publication of the final accounts of limited companies in the UK are governed by the CA 1985 as amended by the CA 1989. At this stage in your studies, you do not have to learn the detailed regulations laid down by these Acts. However, the general format of the balance sheet and profit and loss account of a limited company is important.

3.2 TYPICAL COMPANY LIMITED BALANCE SHEET AS AT.....

Fixed assets	£	£	£
Intangible assets			
Development costs		X	
Concessions, patents, licences, trademarks		X	
Goodwill		X	
			X
Tangible assets			
Land and buildings		X	
Plant and machinery		X	
Fixtures, fittings, tools and equipment		X	
Motor vehicles		X	
			X
Investments			X
			X
Current assets			
Stocks		X	
Debtors and prepayments		X	
Investments		X	
Cash at bank and in hand		X	
		X	
Creditors: amounts falling due within one year (ie current liabilities)			
Debenture loans			
(nearing their redemption date)	X		
Bank loans and overdrafts	X		
Trade creditors	X		
Bills of exchange payable	X		
Taxation	X		
Accruals	X		
Proposed dividend	X		
		(X)	
Net current assets			X
	£	£	£
Total assets less current liabilities			X
Creditors : amounts falling due after more than one year			
Debenture loans		X	
Taxation		X	
			(X)
			X
Capital and reserves			
Called up share capital			
Ordinary shares		X	
Preference shares		X	
			X
Reserves			
Share premium account		X	
Revaluation reserve		X	
Other reserves		X	
Profit and loss account (retained profits)		X	
			X
			X

3.3 TYPICAL COMPANY LIMITED
PROFIT AND LOSS ACCOUNT FOR THE YEAR ENDED...

	£	£
Turnover		X
Cost of sales		(X)
Gross profit		X
Distribution costs	X	
Administrative expenses	X	
		(X)
		X
Other operating income	X	
Income from fixed asset investments	X	
Other interest receivable and similar income	X	
		X
		X
Interest payable		(X)
Profit before taxation		X
Tax		(X)
Profit after tax		X
Dividends: preference	X	
ordinary	X	
		(X)
Retained profit for the year		X
Profit and loss account as at the beginning of the year		X
Profit and loss account as at the end of the year		X

NOTE

Investments are fixed assets if the company intends to hold on to them for a long time, and current assets if they are only likely to be held for a short time before being sold.

The term 'creditors: amounts falling due within one year' was introduced by the CA 1981 as an alternative phrase meaning 'current liabilities'.

4 DEBENTURE LOANS

KEY TERM

Debenture stock ('debentures') or loan stock are long-term liabilities described on the balance sheet as loan capital. They are different from share capital for the following reasons.

(a) Shareholders are members of a company, while providers of loan capital are creditors.

(b) Shareholders receive dividends (appropriations of profit) whereas the holders of loan capital are entitled to a fixed rate of interest (an expense charged against revenue).

(c) Loan capital holders can take legal action against a company if their interest is not paid when due, whereas shareholders cannot enforce the payment of dividends.

(d) Debentures or loan stock are often secured on company assets, whereas shares are not.

4.1 Interest is calculated on the nominal value of loan capital, regardless of its market value. If a company has £700,000 (nominal value) 12% debentures in issue, interest of £84,000 will be charged in the profit and loss account per year. Interest is usually paid half-yearly and examination questions often require an accrual to be made for interest due at the year end. Accrued interest is shown as a current liability in the year-end balance sheet.

4.2 For example, if a company has £700,000 of 12% debentures in issue, pays interest on 30 June and 31 December each year, and ends its accounting year on 30 September, there would be an accrual of three months' unpaid interest ($3/12 \times$ £84,000) = £21,000 at the end of each accounting year that the debentures are still in issue.

5 PROFIT AND LOSS APPROPRIATION ACCOUNT

KEY TERM

The **profit and loss appropriation statement** shows those items which reduce profits but which are not expenses incurred in the day to day running of the business. In other words, it shows how profits are set apart for particular purposes.

5.1 Essentially, profits are set aside (appropriated) for three purposes.

- Pay tax
- Pay dividends to shareholders
- Reinvest in the business

5.2 The amount reinvested in the business is the amount left after the tax and dividends have been paid. This amount is called retained profit for the year.

5.3 The profit and loss account at the beginning of the year is the profit and loss reserve as described in paragraph 2.15. The retained profit for the current year is added to this opening balance to give the profit and loss account balance at the end of the year.

Exam focus point

Profit and loss appropriation accounts are a very likely examination topic. Common errors include putting dividends in the main profit and loss account and putting debenture interest into the appropriation account.

6 TAXATION

6.1 Companies pay **corporation tax** on the profits they earn. The charge for corporation tax on profits for the year is shown as a deduction from net profit, before appropriations. In the balance sheet, tax payable to the government is generally shown as a current liability (ie it has not yet been paid out at the year end).

6.2 When corporation tax on profits is calculated for the profit and loss account the calculation is only an estimate of what the company thinks its tax liability will be. In subsequent dealings with the Inland Revenue, a different corporation tax charge might eventually be agreed. Any difference is adjusted in the estimated taxation charge for the following year.

6.3 EXAMPLE: TAXATION

Urals Ltd made a profit before tax of £150,000 in the year to 30 September 20X3 and of £180,000 in the following year (to 30 September 20X4).

The estimated corporation tax for the first year was £60,000 and in the second year was £75,000. The actual tax charge in the year to 30 September 20X3 was finally agreed with the Inland Revenue at £55,000.

Required

Compute the charge for taxation in the year to 30 September 20X4.

6.4 SOLUTION

	To 30 September	
	20X3	*20X4*
	£	£
Estimate of tax on profits	60,000	75,000
Actual tax charge	55,000	
Overestimate of tax in 20X3	5,000	
		(5,000)
Tax charge in year to 30 September 20X4		70,000

The effect will be to increase profits in 20X4 by £5,000, to correct the 'error' in 20X3 when profits were reduced by £5,000 due to the overestimate of the tax charge.

Exam focus point

We can now draw together several of the items described in this chapter into an illustrative example. Study it carefully because it is typical of the type of problems encountered in the examination. Even if you know that your exam will be MCQs only, this example is worth studying to ensure your understanding.

6.5 EXAMPLE

The accountant of Wislon Ltd has prepared the following trial balance as at 31 December 20X7.

	£'000
50p ordinary shares (fully paid)	350
7% £1 preference shares (fully paid)	100
10% debentures (secured)	200
Retained profit 1 January 20X7	242
General reserve 1 January 20X7	171
Freehold land and buildings 1 January 20X7 (cost)	430
Plant and machinery 1 January 20X7 (cost)	830
Provision for depreciation	
Freehold buildings 1 January 20X7	20
Plant and machinery 1 January 20X7	222
Stock 1 January 20X7	190
Sales	2,695
Purchases	2,152
Preference dividend	7
Ordinary dividend (interim)	8
Debenture interest	10
Wages and salaries	254
Light and heat	31
Sundry expenses	113
Suspense account	135
Debtors	179
Creditors	195
Cash	126

Notes

(a) Sundry expenses include £9,000 paid in respect of insurance for the year ending 1 September 20X8. Light and heat does not include an invoice of £3,000 for electricity for the three months ending 2 January 20X8, which was paid in February 20X8. Light and heat also includes £20,000 relating to salesmen's commission.

(b) The suspense account is in respect of the following items.

	£'000
Proceeds from the issue of 100,000 ordinary shares	120
Proceeds from the sale of plant	300
	420
Less paid to acquire Mary & Co	285
	135

(c) The net assets of Mary & Co were purchased on 3 March 20X7. Assets were valued as follows.

	£'000
Investments	230
Stock	34
	264

All the stock acquired was sold during 20X7. The investments were still held by Wislon at 31 December 20X7.

(d) The freehold property was acquired some years ago. The buildings element of the cost was estimated at £100,000 and the estimated useful life of the assets was fifty years. As at 31 December 20X7 the property is to be revalued at £800,000.

(e) The plant which was sold had cost £350,000 and had a net book value of £274,000 as on 1 January 20X7. £36,000 depreciation is to be charged on plant and machinery for 20X7.

(f) The debentures have been in issue for some years. The 50p ordinary shares all rank for dividends at the end of the year.

(g) The directors wish to provide for

- (i) debenture interest due
- (ii) a final ordinary dividend of 2p per share
- (iii) a transfer to general reserve of £16,000
- (iv) audit fees of £4,000

(h) Stock as at 31 December 20X7 was valued at £220,000 (cost).

(i) Taxation is to be ignored.

Required

Prepare the final accounts of Wislon Ltd.

6.6 APPROACH AND SUGGESTED SOLUTION

(a) The usual adjustments are needed for accruals and prepayments (insurance, light and heat, debenture interest and audit fees). The debenture interest accrued is calculated as follows.

	£'000
Charge needed in P & L account (10% × £200,000)	20
Amount paid so far, as shown in trial balance	10
Accrual - presumably six months' interest now payable	10

The accrued expenses shown in the balance sheet comprise

	£'000
Debenture interest	10
Light and heat	3
Audit fee	4
	17

(b) The misposting of £20,000 to light and heat is also adjusted, by reducing the light and heat expense, but charging £20,000 to salesmen's commission.

(c) Depreciation on the freehold building is calculated as $\frac{£100{,}000}{50} = £2{,}000$.

The net book value of the freehold property is then £430,000 – £20,000 – £2,000 = £408,000 at the end of the year. When the property is revalued a reserve of £800,000 – £408,000 = £392,000 is then created.

(d) The profit on disposal of plant is calculated as proceeds £300,000 (per suspense account) less NBV £274,000 ie £26,000. The cost of the remaining plant is calculated at £830,000 – £350,000 = £480,000. The depreciation provision at the year end is made up of the following.

	£'000
Balance 1 January 20X7	222
Charge for 20X7	36
Less depreciation on disposals (350 – 274)	(76)
	182

(e) Goodwill arising on the purchase of Mary & Co is calculated as follows.

	£'000
Paid (per suspense account)	285
Assets at valuation	264
Goodwill	21

In the absence of other instructions, this is shown as an asset on the balance sheet. The investments, being owned by Wislon at the year end, are also shown on the balance sheet, whereas Mary's stock, acquired and then sold, is added to the purchases figure for the year.

(f) The other item in the suspense account is dealt with as follows.

	£'000
Proceeds of issue of 100,000 ordinary shares	120
Less nominal value 100,000 × 50p	50
Excess of consideration over nominal value (= share premium)	70

(g) Appropriations of profit must be considered. The final ordinary dividend, shown as a current liability in the balance sheet, is calculated as follows.

(700,000 + 100,000 ordinary shares) × 2p = £16,000

(h) The transfer to general reserve increases that reserve to £171,000 + £16,000 = £187,000.

6.7 WISLON LIMITED
TRADING AND PROFIT AND LOSS ACCOUNT
FOR THE YEAR ENDING 31 DECEMBER 20X7

	£'000	£'000	£'000	
Sales			2,695	
Less cost of sales				
Opening stock		190		
Purchases		2,186		2152 + (e) 34
		2,376		
Less closing stock		220		
			2,156	
Gross profit			539	
Profit on disposal of plant			26	(d)
			565	
Less expenses				
Wages, salaries and commission		274		
Sundry expenses		107		
Light and heat		14		
Depreciation: freehold buildings		2		
plant		36		
Audit fees		4		
Debenture interest		20		
			457	
Net profit			108	
Appropriations				
Transfer to general reserve		16		
Dividends				
Preference (paid)	7			
Ordinary: interim (paid)	8			
final (proposed)	16			
		31		
			47	
Retained profit for the year			61	
Retained profit brought forward			242	
Retained profit carried forward			303	

6.8 WISLON LIMITED
BALANCE SHEET AS AT 31 DECEMBER 20X7

			£'000
Fixed assets			
Intangible assets			
Goodwill			21
Tangible assets	*Cost/ val'n*	*Dep'n*	
	£'000	£'000	
Freehold property	800	-	800
Plant and machinery	480	182	298
	1,280	182	
Investments			230
			1,349
Current assets			
Stock		220	
Debtors		179	
Prepayment		6	
Cash		126	
		531	
Creditors: amounts falling due within one year			
Creditors	195		
Accrued expenses	17		
Proposed dividend	16		
		228	
Net current assets			303
Total assets less current liabilities			1,652
Creditors: amounts falling due after more than one year			
10% debentures (secured)			(200)
			1,452
Capital and reserves			
Called up share capital			
50p ordinary shares		400	
7% £1 preference shares		100	
			500
Reserves			
Share premium		70	
Revaluation reserve		392	
General reserve		187	
Profit and loss account		303	
			952
			1,452

7 THE LEDGER ACCOUNTS OF LIMITED COMPANIES

7.1 Limited companies keep ledger accounts and the only difference from the ledger accounts of sole traders is that some additional accounts need to be kept.

7.2 There will be an account for each of the following items.

(a) *Taxation*

(i) Tax charged against profits will be accounted for as follows.

DEBIT P & L account
CREDIT Taxation account

(ii) The outstanding balance on the taxation account will be a liability in the balance sheet, until eventually paid, when the accounting entry would be as follows.

DEBIT	Taxation account
CREDIT	Cash

(b) *Dividends*

A separate account will be kept for the dividends for each different class of shares (eg preference, ordinary).

(i) Dividends declared out of profits will be accounted for as follows.

DEBIT	P & L appropriation account
CREDIT	Dividends payable account

Dividends payable (but not yet paid) are a current liability.

(ii) When dividends are paid the following entries would be made.

DEBIT	Dividends payable account
CREDIT	Cash

(c) *Debenture loans*

Debenture loans are a long term liability and will be shown as a credit balance in a debenture loan account. Interest payable on such loans is not credited to the loan account, but is credited to a separate creditors account for interest until it is eventually paid.

DEBIT	Interest account (an expense, chargeable against profits)
CREDIT	Interest payable (a current liability until eventually paid).

(d) *Share capital and reserves*

There will be a separate account for each different class of share capital and for each different type of reserve. The balance on the share capital account will always be a credit and the balance on the reserve account will nearly always be a credit.

Chapter roundup

- This chapter has explained some important differences between the accounts of a limited company and those of sole traders.
- The accounting records and financial statements of a limited company are strictly regulated by statute.
- A company is recognised in law as a person, with its own identity quite separate from that of its owners. One important consequence of this is the concept of limited liability: a company's shareholders have no liability for the company's debts, beyond what they have contributed as capital.
- To reflect the difference in ownership, the capital of companies is shown differently from that of sole traders.
- Profits paid out to shareholders are called dividends.
- Preference shares carry the right to a fixed dividend which is expressed as a percentage of their nominal value.
- Ordinary shares normally carry voting rights. They carry no right to a fixed dividend but are entitled to all profits left after payment of any preference dividend.
- Statutory reserves are reserves which a company must set up by law. They are not distributable.
- Non statutory reserves are distributable.
- The difference between the price paid for a new issue of shares and their nominal value is the premium, which is credited to a share premium account.
- A revaluation reserve must be created when a company revalues one or more of its fixed assets.
- The preparation and publication of final accounts of limited companies is governed by the Companies Act 1985.

Quick quiz

1 The nominal value of a share is?

A Its market price
B The price at which it was issued
C The price which it can be purchased for
D The 'face value' of a share

2 What does the phrase 'called up share capital' mean?

A The total amount of issued share capital which the shareholders are required to pay for
B The share capital actually issued
C The amount of share capital paid by the shareholders
D The amount of capital which is company has decided to issue

3 A provision is an amount charged as an expense, while a reserve is an appropriation of profit for a specific purpose. True or false?

4 At the year end a proposed dividend may be declared. Which of the following statements is correct regarding the proposed dividend?

A Treated as an expense in the P&L account
B Shown in the balance sheet as a long term liability
C It is an appropriation of the company's profit
D It is always the total profit which the company has agreed to distribute for the year

Answers to quick quiz

1 D This is correct, the nominal value can be any value.
A Incorrect, the quoted price bears no relationship to the nominal value.
B This will be nominal value plus a premium on issue which in total equals the issue price.
C This is the market price.

2 A Correct. Called up share capital means the capital which has been paid for plus current 'calls' outstanding

B This is issued capital

C This is paid up capital

D This capital has not yet been issued and must be less than authorised capital

3 True. A provision is an amount charged as an expense, while a reserve is an appropriation of profit for a specific purpose.

4 C Correct.

A Dividends are appropriations of profit not expenses.

B Proposed dividends are current liabilities.

D There may be an interim dividend as well, so the total distribution equals interim dividend paid plus proposed final dividend.

Now try the question below from the Exam Question Bank

Number	Level	Marks	Time
55	Exam	30	54 mins
56	Exam	2	3 mins
57	Exam	2	3 mins

Chapter 20

MANUFACTURING ACCOUNTS AND CASH FLOW STATEMENTS

Topic List		Syllabus reference	Ability required
1	**Manufacturing accounts**	(iv)	Application
2	**Profits and cash flow**	(iv)	Application
3	**Cash flow statements**	(iv)	Application

Introduction

So far in our studies of accounts preparation we have confined ourselves to the accounts of trading organisations. Britain has been called a nation of shopkeepers, but we would be a very hungry nation if no one actually made things. In Section 1 of this chapter we consider the problems of preparing accounting statements for manufacturing firms.

The most obvious difference between a manufacturing and a trading firm is that the former has many more different types of expense. The **purchases** of the trading firm are replaced by the myriad expenses that arise when, for example, a willow tree is converted into a cricket bat. The traditional way of showing the cost of goods produced is the **manufacturing account**.

Another type of statement is introduced in Sections 2 and 3: the cash flow statement.

In the short run, the making of a profit will not necessarily result in an increased cash balance. This observation leads us to two questions. The first relates to the importance of the distinction between cash and profit. The second is concerned with the usefulness of the information provided by the balance sheet and profit and loss account in the problem of deciding whether the company has, or will be able to generate, sufficient cash to finance its operations.

The importance of the distinction between cash and profit and the scant attention paid to this by the profit and loss account has resulted in the development of cash flow statements.

Learning outcomes covered in this chapter

- Prepare manufacturing accounts
- Prepare cash flow statements

Syllabus content covered in this chapter

- Manufacturing accounts
- Cash flow statements

1 MANUFACTURING ACCOUNTS — May 2001

1.1 A company's trading account will usually include a cost of goods sold derived as the total of opening stock plus purchases, less closing stock. This is particularly suitable for a retail business which buys in goods and sells them on to customers without altering their condition. But for a manufacturing company it would be truer to say that the cost of goods sold is as follows.

	£
Opening stock of finished goods	X
Plus cost of finished goods produced in the period	X
	X
Less closing stock of finished goods	(X)
Cost of finished goods sold	X

KEY TERMS

A **manufacturing account** is an account in which the costs of producing finished goods are calculated.

Direct factory costs are factory costs which change every time an extra unit is made. For example, direct factory wages are wages paid to production workers who are paid per unit made.

Production overheads or **indirect factory costs** are factory costs which do not change every time an extra unit is made. For example, indirect factory wages are wages paid to production managers who are paid the same each month regardless of how many units are made.

Prime cost is raw material costs plus direct factory costs.

1.2 A pro-forma manufacturing account is set out below with illustrative figures.

MANUFACTURING ACCOUNT
FOR THE YEAR ENDED 31 DECEMBER 20X6

	£	£
Raw materials		
Opening stock	4,000	
Purchases (net of returns)	207,000	
	211,000	
Less closing stock	23,000	
		188,000
Direct factory wages		21,000
Prime cost		209,000
Production overhead		
Factory power	4,000	
Plant depreciation	3,000	
Plant maintenance	1,500	
Rates and insurance	2,500	
Light and heat	3,000	
Sundry expenses	5,000	
Factory manager's salary	9,000	
Building depreciation	1,000	
		29,000
Production cost of resources consumed		238,000
Work in progress		
Opening stocks	8,000	
Closing stocks	(17,000)	
Increase in work in progress stocks		(9,000)
Production cost of finished goods produced		229,000

Work in progress

1.3 At the balance sheet date, there will be work in progress in the production departments, ie work which has been partly converted but which has not yet reached the stage of being finished goods.

1.4 The value of this work in progress is the cost of the raw materials, the wages of employees who have worked on it plus a share of overheads. To arrive at the cost of finished goods produced, an increase in work in progress must be deducted from the total production costs. Of course, if the value of work in progress had **fallen** during the period, this fall would be an **increase** in the cost of finished goods produced.

1.5 EXAMPLE: MANUFACTURING, TRADING AND PROFIT AND LOSS ACCOUNT

A manufacturing company has its factory and offices at the same site. Its results for the year to 31 December 20X5 were:

	£
Sales	179,000
Purchases of raw materials	60,000
Direct labour	70,000
Depreciation of equipment	10,000
Rates	5,000
Depreciation of building	2,000
Heating and lighting	3,000
Telephone	2,000
Other manufacturing overheads	2,300
Other administration expenses	2,550
Other selling expenses	1,150

Shared overhead costs are to be apportioned as follows.

	Manufacturing	*Administration*	*Selling*
Depreciation of equipment	80%	5%	15%
Rates	50%	30%	20%
Depreciation of building	50%	30%	20%
Heating and lighting	40%	35%	25%
Telephone	-	40%	60%

The values of stocks are as follows.

	At 1 January 20X5	*At 31 December 20X5*
	£	£
Raw materials	5,000	3,000
Work in progress	4,000	3,000
Finished goods	16,000	18,000

Required

Prepare the manufacturing, trading and profit and loss account of the company for the period to 31 December 20X5.

1.6 SOLUTION

MANUFACTURING ACCOUNT FOR THE YEAR ENDED 31 DECEMBER 20X5

	£	£
Opening stock of raw materials		5,000
Purchases		60,000
		65,000
Closing stock of raw materials		3,000
Raw materials used in production		62,000
Direct labour		70,000
Prime cost		132,000
Manufacturing overheads		
Depreciation of equipment (80% of £10,000)	8,000	
Rates (50% of £5,000)	2,500	
Depreciation of building (50% of £2,000)	1,000	
Heating and lighting (40% of £3,000)	1,200	
Other expenses	2,300	
		15,000
Manufacturing costs during the year		147,000
Add opening stock of work in progress	4,000	
Less closing stock of work in progress	(3,000)	
Reduction in stock of work in progress		1,000
Cost of finished goods fully produced, transferred to trading account		148,000

TRADING AND PROFIT AND LOSS ACCOUNT
FOR THE YEAR ENDED 31 DECEMBER 20X5

	£	£	£
Sales			179,000
Opening stock of finished goods		16,000	
Cost of finished goods produced		148,000	
		164,000	
Closing stock of finished goods		18,000	
Cost of goods sold			146,000
Gross profit			33,000
Selling expenses			
Depreciation of equipment (15% of £10,000)	1,500		
UBR (20% of £5,000)	1,000		
Depreciation of building (20% of £2,000)	400		
Heating and lighting (25% of £3,000)	750		
Telephone (60% of £2,000)	1,200		
Other expenses	1,150		
		6,000	
Administration expenses			
Depreciation of equipment (5% of £10,000)	500		
Rates (30% of £5,000)	1,500		
Depreciation of building (30% of £2,000)	600		
Heating and lighting (35% of £3,000)	1,050		
Telephone (40% of £2,000)	800		
Other expenses	2,550		
		7,000	
			13,000
Net profit			20,000

Exam focus point

Calculation of prime cost was in Section A of the May 2001 exam.

Q

Question 1

The following information has been extracted from the books of account of the Marsden Manufacturing Company for the year to 30 September 20X4.

	£
Advertising	2,000
Depreciation for the year to 30 September 20X4	
Factory equipment	7,000
Office equipment	4,000
Direct wages	40,000
Factory: insurance	1,000
heat	15,000
indirect materials	5,000
power	20,000
salaries	25,000
Finished goods (at 1 October 20X3)	24,000
Office: electricity	15,000
general expenses	9,000
postage and telephones	2,900
salaries	70,000
Raw material purchases	202,000
Raw material stock (at 1 October 20X3)	8,000
Sales	512,400
Work in progress (at 1 October 20X3)	12,000

Notes

(a) At 30 September 20X4 the following stocks were on hand.

	£
Raw materials	10,000
Work in progress	9,000
Finished goods	30,000

(b) At 30 September 20X4 there was an accrual for advertising of £1,000, and it was estimated that £1,500 had been paid in advance for electricity. These items had not been included in the books of account for the year to 30 September 20X4.

Required

Prepare Marsden's manufacturing, trading and profit and loss account for the year to 30 September 20X4.

Answer

MANUFACTURING, TRADING AND PROFIT AND LOSS ACCOUNT
FOR THE YEAR ENDED 30 SEPTEMBER 20X4

	£	£
Raw materials		
Opening stock	8,000	
Purchases	202,000	
	210,000	
Less closing stock	10,000	
		200,000
Factory wages		40,000
Prime cost		240,000
Indirect production expenses		
Insurance	1,000	
Heat	15,000	
Indirect materials	5,000	
Power	20,000	
Salaries	25,000	
Depreciation of factory equipment	7,000	
		73,000
		313,000
Work in progress		
Opening stock	12,000	
Less closing stock	9,000	
		3,000
Factory cost of goods produced		316,000

	£	£
Sales		512,400
Less cost of goods sold		
Opening stock of finished goods	24,000	
Factory cost of goods produced	316,000	
	340,000	
Less closing stock of finished goods	30,000	
		310,000
Gross profit		202,400
Expenses		
Advertising £(2,000 + 1,000)	3,000	
Depreciation of office equipment	4,000	
Electricity £(15,000 – 1,500)	13,500	
General expenses	9,000	
Postage and telephones	2,900	
Salaries	70,000	
		102,400
Net profit		100,000

2 PROFITS AND CASH FLOW **Pilot Paper**

The importance of profit

2.1 To be successful in business, an enterprise must make a profit. Profits are needed for dividends to shareholders (and shareholders expect to receive dividends as a return on their investment in ownership of the business) and to allow partners or proprietors to make drawings.

2.2 A loss means that the value of sales in a period is less than the value of resources used up in making the sales, so that a loss causes a reduction in the overall value of a business. Long-term losses will lead to the eventual collapse of a firm.

The importance of cash

2.3 In addition to being **profitable** in order to survive and grow, a firm must have cash to **pay** for the goods and services and capital equipment it buys, the workforce it employs and the other expenses (such as rent, rates and taxation) that it incurs, and to pay dividends and drawings.

2.4 If a firm does not pay its bills when they are due, it will lose the goodwill of its suppliers or workforce and may then be driven into liquidation. A business must be not just profitable, but also capable of obtaining cash to meet demands for payment.

Profit does not mean cash

2.5 Profits and cash surpluses are **not** the same thing, for a number of reasons.

(a) Cash may be obtained from a transaction which has nothing to do with profit or loss. For example, an issue of shares or loan stock for cash has no effect on profit (except for subsequent interest charges on a loan) but is obviously a source of cash. Similarly, an increase in bank overdraft provides a source of cash for payments, but it is not reported in the profit and loss account.

(b) Cash may be paid for the purchase of fixed assets, but the charge in the profit and loss account is depreciation, which is only a part of an asset's cost. For example, a company may have existing fixed assets which originally cost £300,000. If it buys a new asset for £20,000 on 1 January and if depreciation is charged at a rate of 10% of cost.

(i) The charge for depreciation for the year to 31 December would be 10% of £320,000 or £32,000.

(ii) The cash payments during the year would be £20,000 - the purchase cost of the new asset.

(c) When a fixed asset is sold there is a profit or loss on sale equal to the difference between the sale proceeds and the 'net book value' of the asset in the balance sheet at the time it is sold. For example, if an asset originally cost £50,000 and depreciation of £35,000 has been charged since its purchase, its net book value will be £15,000. If it is now sold for £11,000, there will be a loss on disposal of £4,000. This loss would be recorded in the profit and loss account, but the effect of the sale would be to increase the firm's cash by £11,000 (the sale price).

(d) The profit and loss account reports the total value of sales in a year. If goods are sold on credit, the cash receipts will differ from the value of sales. The relationship between sales and receipts is as follows (excluding increases or decreases in the provision for doubtful debts and writing-off bad debts).

	£
Debtors owing money at the start of the year	X
Sales during the year	X
Total money due from customers	X
Less debtors owing money at the end of the year	(X)
Cash receipts from debtors during the year	X

(e) Similarly, the profit and loss account reports the cost of goods sold during the year.

(i) If materials are bought on credit, the cash payments to suppliers will be different from the value of materials purchased.

(ii) If some materials are bought and added to stocks rather than sold (ie if there is an increase in stocks during the year) total purchases will be different from the materials cost of sales. (In the same way, a firm may decide to run down its stocks and sell goods without making good the stocks used up by purchasing replacement items.)

The relationship between the cost of materials in the materials cost of sales and cash payments for materials purchased is as follows.

	£
Opening stocks (at the start of the year)	X
Add purchases during the year	X
	X
Less closing stocks at the end of the year	(X)
Equals materials cost in the cost of sales	Y
Payments still owing to creditors at the start of the year	X
Add materials cost in the cost of sales	Y
	X
Less payments still owing to creditors at the end of the year	(X)
Equals cash payments to creditors during the year	X

The need for information about cash flow

2.6 Information about cash receipts and payments adds to our understanding of a firm's operations and financial stability. Whereas a profit and loss statement reports on profitability, cash flow statements report on liquidity.

THE MAIN POINTS

(a) To survive, a business needs both profit and cash.

(b) To make decisions about a business, interested parties need information about both profitability and cash flow.

Exam focus point

The Pilot Paper included a discussion question on profit versus cash flow.

3 CASH FLOW STATEMENTS — Pilot Paper

KEY TERM

A cash flow statement can be a historical statement or a forecast. It shows the sources and uses of cash over a period of time.

3.1 'Profit' does not always give a useful or meaningful picture of a company's operations. Readers of a company's financial statements might even be misled by a reported profit figure.

(a) Shareholders might believe that if a company makes a profit after tax, of say, £100,000 then this is the amount which it could afford to pay as a dividend. Unless the company has sufficient cash available to stay in business and also to pay a dividend, the shareholders' expectations would be wrong.

(b) Employees might believe that if a company makes profits, it can afford to pay higher wages next year. This opinion may not be correct: the ability to pay wages depends on the availability of cash.

(c) Creditors might consider that a profitable company is a going concern.

    (i) If a company builds up large amounts of unsold stocks of goods, their cost would not be chargeable against profits, but cash would have been used up in making them, thus weakening the company's liquid resources.

    (ii) A company might capitalise large development costs, having spent considerable amounts of money on R & D, but only charge small amounts against current profits. As a result, the company might show reasonable profits, but get into severe difficulties with its liquidity position. (This is roughly the problem that led to the collapse of the old Rolls Royce company in 1971.)

(d) Management might suppose that if their company makes a profit, and reinvests some of those profits, then the company must be expanding. This is not the case: in a period of inflation, a company might have insufficient retained profits to prevent the operating capability of the firm from declining.

(e) Survival of a business entity depends not so much on profits as on its ability to pay its debts when they fall due. Such payments might include 'profit and loss' items such as material purchases, wages, interest and taxation etc, but also capital payments for new fixed assets and the repayment of loan capital when this falls due (eg on the redemption of debentures).

3.2 A statement of cash flows is unambiguous and provides information which is additional to that provided in the rest of the accounts. It also lends itself to organisation by activity and not by balance sheet classification. In September 1991 the Accounting Standards Board (ASB) published FRS 1 *Cash flow statements*. The FRS was revised in October 1996.

Exam focus point

You do not need to know the prescribed format in detail, but you should know how to construct a cash flow statement and what its aims are. In the Pilot Paper, preparation of a cash flow statement was an optional question. However the examiner has indicated that this could be a compulsory question in future examinations. There were two cash flow questions in Section A of the May 2001 exam.

3.3 The aims of a cashflow statement are to assist users to assess.

(a) The enterprise's ability to generate positive net cash flows in the future.
(b) Its ability to meet its obligations to service loans, pay dividends etc.
(c) The reasons for difference between reported profit and related cash flows.
(d) The effect on its finances of major transactions in the year.

3.4 The statement shows changes in cash. The opening and closing figures given for cash etc are those shown in the balance sheet. Receipts and payments are not netted off. Non-cash transactions are reported separately by note (eg purchasing an asset with lease finance) and a reconciliation of net income to net cash flow from operating activities should be given.

3.5 The statement classifies cash receipts and payments as resulting from investing, financing or operating activities.

> **KEY TERMS**
>
> - **Investing**: making loans, acquiring/disposing of fixed assets
> - **Financing**: borrowing/repaying money, making an issue of shares, paying dividends
> - **Operating**: receipts from customers, payments to employees and suppliers, any other cash flows from transactions not classified as investing or financing

3.6 A cash budget shows expected sources and uses of cash daily, weekly or monthly, to help in management of working capital.

3.7 EXAMPLE: CASH FLOW STATEMENT

Flail Ltd commenced trading on 1 January 20X1 with a medium-term loan of £21,000 and a share issue which raised £35,000. The company purchased fixed assets for £21,000 cash, and during the year to 31 December 20X1 entered into the following transactions.

(a) Purchases from suppliers were £19,500, of which £2,550 was unpaid at the year end.

(b) Wages and salaries amounted to £10,500, of which £750 was unpaid at the year end.

(c) Interest on the loan of £2,100 was fully paid in the year and a repayment of £5,250 was made.

(d) Sales turnover was £29,400, including £900 debtors at the year end.

(e) Interest on cash deposits at the bank amounted to £75.

(f) A dividend of £4,000 was proposed as at 31 December 20X1.

You are required to prepare a historical cash flow statement for the year ended 31 December 20X1.

3.8 SOLUTION

FLAIL LIMITED
STATEMENT OF CASH FLOWS FOR
THE YEAR ENDED 31 DECEMBER 20X1

	£	£
Operating activities		
Cash received from customers (£29,400 – £900)	28,500	
Cash paid to suppliers (£19,500 – £2,550)	(16,950)	
Cash paid to and on behalf of employees (£10,500 – £750)	(9,750)	
Cash flow from operating activities		1,800
Returns on investment and servicing of finance		
Interest paid	(2,100)	
Interest received	75	
		(2,025)
Capital expenditure		
Purchase of fixed assets	(21,000)	
Cash flow from investing activities		(21,000)

Financing		
Issue of shares	35,000	
Proceeds from medium-term loan	21,000	
Repayment of medium-term loan	(5,250)	
Cash flow from financing activities		50,750
Net increase in cash		29,525
Cash at 1 January 20X1		-
Cash at 31 December 20X1		29,525

Note that the dividend is only proposed and so there is no related cash flow in 20X1.

Question 2

The directors of Flail Ltd obtain the following information in respect of projected cash flows for the year to 31 December 20X2.

(a) Fixed asset purchases for cash will be £3,000.

(b) Further expenses will be:

 (i) Purchases from suppliers - £18,750 (£4,125 owed at the year end)
 (ii) Wages and salaries - £11,250 (£600 owed at the year end)
 (iii) Loan interest - £1,575

(c) Turnover will be £36,000 (£450 debtors at the year end).

(d) Interest on bank deposits will be £150.

(e) A further capital repayment of £5,250 will be made on the loan.

(f) A dividend of £5,000 will be proposed and last year's final dividend paid.

(g) Corporation tax of £2,300 will be paid in respect of 20X1.

Prepare the cash flow forecast for the year to 31 December 20X2.

Answer

FLAIL LIMITED
STATEMENT OF FORECAST CASH FLOWS FOR
THE YEAR ENDING 31 DECEMBER 20X2

	£	£
Operating activities		
Cash received from customers (£36,000 + £900 – £450)	36,450	
Cash paid to suppliers (£18,750 + £2,550 – £4,125)	(17,175)	
Cash paid to and on behalf of employees (£11,250 + £750 – £600)	(11,400)	
Net cash flow from operating activities		7,875
Returns on investments and servicing of finance		
Interest paid	(1,575)	
Interest received	150	
		(1,425)
Taxation		(2,300)
Capital expenditure		
Purchase of fixed assets		(3,000)
		1,150
Equity dividends paid		(4,000)
Financing		
Repayment of medium-term loan		(5,250)
Forecast net decrease in cash at 31 December 20X2		(8,100)
Cash as at 31 December 20X1		29,525
Forecast cash as at 31 December 20X2		21,425

Exam focus point

Remember that a loss on disposal of fixed assets is calculated as net book value less proceeds, not original cost less proceeds. Do not forget to calculate the accumulated depreciation on the disposed asset. With respect to dividends, remember that dividends paid should be deducted as a cash outflow whereas dividends proposed are not yet a cash flow and should be added back to the retained profit.

Indirect method

3.9 Another way of arriving at net cash flows from operating activities is to start from operating profit and adjust for non-cash items, such as depreciation, debtors etc. This is known as the **indirect method**. A proforma calculation is given below.

FORMULA TO LEARN

	£
Operating profit (P&L)	X
Add depreciation	X
Loss (profit) on sale of fixed assets	X
(Increase)/decrease in stocks	(X)/X
(Increase)/decrease in debtors	(X)/X
Increase/(decrease) in creditors	X/(X)
Net cash flow from operating activities	X

REMEMBER!

(a) **Depreciation** is not a cash expense, but is deducted in arriving at the profit figure in the profit and loss account. It makes sense, therefore, to eliminate it by adding it back.

(b) By the same logic, a **loss on a disposal of a fixed asset** (arising through underprovision of depreciation) needs to be added back and a profit deducted.

(c) An increase in **stocks** means less cash - you have spent cash on buying stock.

(d) An increase in **debtors** means debtors have not paid as much, therefore less cash.

(e) If we pay off **creditors**, causing the figure to decrease, again we have less cash.

Question 3

Over a year, a business had net cash flow from operating activities of £50,000. The operating profit in the profit and loss account was £60,000, depreciation was £10,000, a fixed asset was sold for a profit of £15,000. Stocks fell by £5,000 and debtors increased by £4,000.

What was the change in creditors?

A Decrease by £14,000
B Decrease of £6,000
C Increase of £4,000
D Increase of £14,000

Answer

B is correct.

	£
Operating profit	60,000
Add depreciation	10,000
Less profit on sale of fixed assets	(15,000)
Add decrease in stocks	5,000
Less increase in debtors	(4,000)
	56,000
Net cash flow from operating activities	50,000
Decrease in creditors	6,000

Exam focus point

Note that, in an examination question, you may not be given the profit figure; instead you may be required to calculate it by finding the difference between the capital figures in two consecutive years' balance sheets.

The advantages of cash flow accounting

3.10 The advantages of cash flow accounting are as follows.

(a) Survival in business depends on the ability to generate cash. Cash flow accounting directs attention towards this critical issue.

(b) Cash flow is more comprehensive than 'profit' which is dependent on accounting conventions and concepts.

(c) Creditors (long and short-term) are more interested in an entity's ability to repay them than in its profitability. Whereas 'profits' might indicate that cash is likely to be available, cash flow accounting is more direct with its message.

(d) Cash flow reporting provides a better means of comparing the results of different companies than traditional profit reporting.

(e) Cash flow reporting satisfies the needs of all users better.

(i) For management, it provides the sort of information on which decisions should be taken: (in management accounting, 'relevant costs' to a decision are future cash flows); traditional profit accounting does not help with decision-making.

(ii) For shareholders and auditors, cash flow accounting can provide a satisfactory basis for stewardship accounting.

(iii) As described previously, the information needs of creditors and employees will be better served by cash flow accounting.

(f) Cash flow forecasts are easier to prepare, as well as more useful, than profit forecasts.

Question 4

You should give some thought to the possible **disadvantages** of cashflow accounting which are essentially the advantages of accruals accounting. There is also the practical problem that few businesses keep historical cash flow information in the form needed to prepare a historical cash flow statement and so extra record keeping is likely to be necessary.

Chapter roundup

- Manufacturing accounts are prepared for internal management use only. Their purpose is to distinguish between the costs and profitability associated with manufacturing operations and those associated with trading (which are shown in the trading account).
- Manufacturing accounts highlight the following.
  - **Prime cost.** The cost of raw materials and direct labour employed in production.
  - **Factory cost of goods produced**. Equal to prime cost plus indirect factory expenses and plus or minus any movement over the period in the cost of work in progress.
- Profit does not always give a useful or meaningful picture of a company's operations.
- Survival in business depends on the ability to generate cash. Cash flow accounting directs attention towards this critical issue.
- Cash flow statements concentrate on the sources and uses of cash, and are a useful indicator of a company's liquidity and solvency.

Quick quiz

1 The production cost of finished goods is?

A Prime cost plus production overheads plus opening WIP less closing WIP

B Prime cost plus production overheads

C Prime cost plus opening WIP less closing WIP

D Prime cost plus opening stock of materials less closing stock of materials plus production overheads

2 Prime cost comprises several elements of costs, excluding which of the following?

A Purchases of raw materials
B Direct wages
C Opening and closing stocks of raw materials
D Factory overheads

3 Calculate the operating cash flow for a company from the following information. Receipts from customers £391,000, paid to suppliers £156,000, wages paid £78,000, fixed assets purchased £17,000, interest paid £23,000, loan received £25,000.

A £157,000
B £140,000
C £134,000
D £182,000

4 Which of the following is <u>not</u> an advantage of cash flow accounting?

A Cash flows are an objective measure of business performance

B Cash flow accounting helps users to understand what makes a business profitable

C Cash flow accounting and reporting statements are more useful for business decision making

D Cash flow is an understandable concept, whereas accruals accounting can be confusing to non financially orientated managers

Answers to quick quiz

1 A Correct.
  B Incorrect, no adjustment for work in progress has been made.
  C This excludes production overheads.
  D Prime cost has already been adjusted for changes in raw material stock levels.

2 D Not part of prime cost.

3 A Correct, receipts £391,000 less payments to suppliers £156,000 less wages £78,000.
  B Incorrect, fixed asset purchases are not included in operating cash flows.
  C Incorrect, interest paid is not included in operating cash flows.
  D Incorrect, the loan received is not included in operating cash flows.

4 B Correct, cash flows are explained, not reasons for profitability.

Now try the questions below from the Exam Question Bank

Number	Level	Marks	Time
58	Exam	30	54 mins
59	Exam	20	36 mins
60	Exam	2	3 mins
61	Exam	2	3 mins

Chapter 21

INTERNAL AND EXTERNAL AUDIT

Topic List		Syllabus reference	Ability required
1	Ownership v stewardship	(i)	Knowledge
2	External audit	(iii)	Comprehension
3	Internal audit	(iii)	Comprehension
4	Internal control systems	(iii)	Comprehension
5	Controls over sales and debtors	(iii)	Comprehension
6	Controls over purchases and creditors	(iii)	Comprehension
7	Evaluation of internal controls	(iii)	Comprehension
8	Audit trail	(iii)	Comprehension
9	The detection and prevention of fraud	(iii)	Comprehension

Introduction

So far you have been concerned with the preparation of accounts. The syllabus also includes an appreciation of the purpose of external and internal audit.

It is a requirement of the Companies Act that all companies must appoint **external auditors** who will report to the **members** of the company on whether in their opinion, the annual statutory accounts give a true and fair view. The duties of the external auditor are imposed by statute and cannot be limited, either by the directors or by the members of the company. External auditors are not employees of the company.

Internal auditors are employees of the company whose duties are fixed by management, and who report ultimately to **management**. In recent years it has become increasingly common for large companies to set up internal audit departments and for the external auditors to alter their audit approach to take account of the work done by the internal auditors.

Learning outcomes covered in this chapter

- Identify the requirements for external audit and the basic processes undertaken
- Explain the purpose and basic procedures of internal audit
- Explain the meaning of true and fair view
- Explain the need for financial controls
- Explain the purpose of audit checks and audit trails
- Explain the nature of fraud and basic ideas of prevention

Syllabus content covered in this chapter

- Stewardship
- The purpose of external audit and the meaning of true and fair view
- Internal audit
- Financial controls
- Audit checks on financial controls
- Audit trails
- Errors or fraud

1 OWNERSHIP V STEWARDSHIP

KEY TERMS

Stewardship is the primary function of managers who are responsible for the running of the business on a day to day basis, it means the safeguarding of the business' assets.

An **audit** assures proprietors that the stewardship of the organisation was effectively carried out.

1.1 The stewardship concept is wider than ensuring that the assets of an organisation are properly recorded, valued and insured. It also includes the control of costs, the improvement of efficiency and the optimisation of profits. Additionally whilst management's stewardship responsibilities extend primarily to the owners of the business it also includes all other users of the accounts.

2 EXTERNAL AUDIT — Pilot Paper, May 2001

KEY TERM

An **external audit** is an independent examination of, and expression of opinion on the financial statements of an enterprise.

2.1 If the 'enterprise' is a limited company, 'external audit' means statutory audit, that is, under the Companies Act 1985. The statutory audit requirement, arose as discussed in Section 1, because of the separation of owners (shareholders) and managers (directors).

2.2 External auditors are generally firms of chartered or certified accountants. They summarise their conclusions on the company's financial statements by issuing an audit report, addressed to the shareholders. The report must state whether in the auditors opinion.

(a) The balance sheet gives a true and fair view of the state of affairs of the company at the end of the financial year.

(b) The profit and loss account gives a true and fair view of the profit or loss of the company for the financial year.

(c) The financial statements have been properly prepared in accordance with the Companies Act 1985.

Exam focus point

There was a question in Section A of the May 2001 exam on the objectives of an external audit.

KEY TERM

'**True and fair**' is not defined in company law or accounting standards. The words are used together rather than separately and the term is generally taken to mean 'reasonably accurate and free from bias or distortion'.

2.3 Although there is no official definition of 'true and fair', the Companies Act 1985 states that the directors may depart from any provisions of company law or accounting standards if these are inconsistent with the requirement to give a true and fair view. This 'true and fair override' has been treated as an important loophole in the law and has been the cause of much argument and dissatisfaction within the accounting profession.

2.4 In June 1993 Mary Arden QC stated that the Courts are more likely than ever to rule that compliance with accounting standards is necessary for accounts to give a true and fair view as required by the Companies Act 1985.

Exam focus point

You may be asked to explain the meaning of a 'true and fair view' of an organisation's accounts and how this view might be affected by the concept of materiality. The exam in May 2001 had a question in Section A on the meaning of 'true and fair'.

Other statutory audits

2.5 Limited company audits are by far the most important external audits for your purposes. However you should be aware that audits are compulsory under statute in the case of a large number of undertakings. Examples include the following.

(a) Building societies must be audited under the Building Society Act 1986

(b) Trade unions and employers' associations must be audited under the Trade Union and Labour Relations Act 1974.

(c) Various acts, including the Housing Association Act 1985 set out requirements for the audit of housing associations.

Non-statutory audits

2.6 Non-statutory audits are performed by independent auditors because the owners, members, trustees, governing bodies or other interested parties desire them, not because the law requires them. Auditing may therefore extend to any kind of undertaking which produces accounts (eg clubs, sole traders, charities, partnerships), and may extend to forms of financial statements other than the annual report and accounts. An example might be an audit of a statement of expenditure in support of an application for a regional development grant.

2.7 The term 'audit' is often applied to non-financial matters. Examples include the following.

- The circulation figures of a newspaper or magazine used when soliciting advertising
- Environmental audit reports, for example those produced by the Body Shop

Question 1

James Johnson is a sole trader. His business has grown rapidly over the last few years and he has asked John Jameson to become a partner in his firm. Jameson has agreed, but he has said that he will only become a partner if the books are properly audited every year. James asks you why John might want an audit and what advantages it could bring to the business.

Required

Answer the queries raised by James Johnson.

Answer

(a) John might decide that an audit is desirable because James has been in charge alone for a long time. John needs someone who is objective and can understand the accounting records to reassure him that the business is producing the results claimed by James. The other reasons for such a request are reflected in part (b).

(b) The advantages of an audit for a partnership include the following.

(i) Any weaknesses in the accounting system of the business would be highlighted and improvements to the system would be suggested by the auditor. These could save both time and money.

(ii) Arguments between the partners would be avoided if the accounts are checked by an independent auditor. This will be case particularly in the calculation of the partners' profit shares.

(iii) Third parties who have an interest in the accounts will find them more convincing if they are audited. Examples of such third parties will include Customs and Excise, the Inland Revenue and bankers and other potential sources of finance or credit.

---

3 INTERNAL AUDIT

KEY TERM

'**Internal auditing** is an independent appraisal function established within an organisation to examine and evaluate its activities as a service to the organisation. The objective of internal auditing is to assist members of the organisation in the effective discharge of their responsibilities. To this end internal auditing furnishes them with analysis, appraisals, recommendations, counsel and information concerning the activities reviewed.' (*Institute of Internal Auditors*)

The CIMA's Official Terminology defines an audit as a systematic examination of the activities and status of an entity based primarily on investigation and analysis of its systems, controls and records. Internal audit is now defined as per the Institute of Internal Auditors, and the CIMA's own definition is currently:

> 'an independent appraisal function established within a organisation to examine and evaluate its activities as a service to the organisation'.

3.1 Internal audit has a much wider scope than external audit. External auditors need **only** consider whether a company's accounts give a true and fair view of its financial position. They need not comment in their audit reports on ways in which the company's results or controls could be improved.

Functions of an internal audit department

3.2 The functions of an internal audit department are well summarised in a Statement of Auditing Standards *Considering the Work of Internal Audit,* issued by the Auditing Practices Board in March 1995.

> 'The scope and objectives of internal audit vary widely and depend on the size and structure of the entity and the requirements of its management and directors. Generally internal audit activities include one or more of the following:
>
> (a) review of the accounting and internal control systems: the establishment of adequate accounting and internal control systems is a responsibility of management and the directors which demands proper attention on a continuous basis. Often, internal audit is assigned

specific responsibility for reviewing the design of the systems, monitoring their operation and recommending improvements thereto;

(b) examination of financial and operating information: this may include review of the means used to identify, measure, classify and report such information and specific enquiry into individual items including detailed testing of transactions, balances and procedures;

(c) review of the economy, efficiency and effectiveness of operations including non-financial controls of an organisation;

(d) review of compliance with laws, regulations and other external requirements and with internal policies and directives and other requirements including appropriate authorisation of transactions; and

(e) special investigations into particular areas, for example suspected fraud.'

3.3 From the definitions of the internal audit the two main features of internal audit emerge.

(a) **Independence**. Although an internal audit department is part of an organisation, it should be independent of the line management whose sphere of authority it may audit. The department should therefore report to the board or to a special internal audit committee and not to the finance director. The reason for this is best seen by thinking about what could happen if the internal audit department reported some kind of irregularity to a finance director without realising that the finance director was actually involved. The director would take the report and decide that it was all very interesting, but not worth pursuing. A very different line might be taken by another, independent director!

It is also important that internal auditors should have appropriate scope in carrying out their responsibilities, and unrestricted access to records, assets and personnel.

'In the ideal situation, the internal audit function reports to the highest level of management but also has a direct line of communication to the entity's main board or audit committee and is free of any other operating responsibility.'

(b) **Appraisal**. Internal audit is concerned with the appraisal of work done by other people in the organisation, and internal auditors should not themselves carry out any of the work being audited. The appraisal of operations provides a service to management, providing information on strengths and weaknesses throughout the organisation. Such information is invaluable to management when it comes to taking action to improve performance, or planning future activities of the company.

Objectives of internal audit

3.4 After giving its broad definition, the Institute of Internal Auditors goes on to state the following.

'The objective of internal auditing is to assist members of the organisation in the effective discharge of their responsibilities. To this end internal auditing furnishes them with analyses, appraisals, recommendations, counsel and information concerning the activities reviewed.'

Internal audit is an important element of management control, as it is a tool used to ensure that all financial and any other internal controls are working satisfactorily. Internal auditors will investigate systems within the organisation, identify any weaknesses or scope for improvement, and make recommendations to the 'line' managers responsible for the system that they have audited.

Differences between internal and external audit

3.5 There are three main differences between internal and external audit.

(a) **Appointment**. External auditors are appointed by the shareholders (although they are usually only ratifying the directors' choice) and must be independent of the company, whereas internal auditors are employees of the organisation.

(b) **Responsibility**. External auditors are responsible to the owners (ie shareholders, the public or Parliament), whereas internal auditors are responsible to senior management.

(c) **Objectives**. The objectives for external auditors are defined by statute, whereas those for internal auditors are set by management. In other words, management - perhaps the internal auditors themselves - decide what parts of the organisation or what systems they are going to look at, and what type of audit should be carried out for example a systems audit, or a value for money audit.

3.6 Contrary to popular belief, it is not the responsibility of external auditors to detect fraud; they are merely obliged to plan their audit tests so that they have a reasonable expectation of detecting fraud. It is the responsibility of the **directors** to set up an adequate system of internal control to deter and expose fraud. Internal audit is one type of internal control.

Essential elements of internal audit

3.7 In addition to the need for ***independence*** several other essential elements of internal audit have been identified.

(a) **Staffing and training**

(i) The internal audit department should possess or have access to all the necessary skills for performing its function. It must be adequately staffed, and staff are likely to be drawn from a variety of disciplines.

(ii) Internal audit staff should be given the training to carry out their work competently.

(b) **Relationships**

Without surrendering their objectivity, internal auditors should try to establish good working relationships and mutual understanding with

- Management
- External auditors
- If there is one, the organisation's auditing committee

Internal audit plans should be discussed with senior management, individual audits should be arranged in consultation with the management concerned, and audit reports should be discussed with the management when they are being prepared.

Internal auditors should have regular meetings with the external auditors (who may be able to place reliance on some of the work done by the internal auditors). They should discuss their audit plans, so as to avoid unnecessary overlaps in their work.

(c) **Due care**

Internal auditors should exercise due care in fulfilling their responsibilities. The chief internal auditor should ensure that his staff maintain standards of integrity and of adequate quality in their work.

(d) **Planning, controlling and recording**

Internal auditors should plan, control and record their work.

(e) **Evidence**

Internal auditors should obtain sufficient, relevant and reliable evidence on which to base reasonable conclusions and recommendations.

Deciding just what evidence will be needed for any particular audit work calls for judgement by the auditors.

- The scope of the audit assignment
- The significance of the matters under review
- Just what evidence is available and obtainable
- What it would cost and how long it would take to obtain

(f) **Reporting**

Internal auditors should report their findings, conclusions and recommendations promptly to management.

'The chief internal auditor should ensure that reports are sent to managers who have a direct responsibility for the unit or function being audited and who have the authority to take corrective action.'

If the internal auditors find evidence of a serious weakness or malpractice, this should be reported immediately, orally or in writing, as soon as it is discovered, in an 'interim report'.

The internal auditors, having made recommendations in their report, should subsequently follow up their work by checking to see whether their recommendations have been implemented by management.

Auditing standards and guidelines

KEY TERM

Auditing standards and guidelines have been issued by the Auditing Practices Board (APB) and its forerunner the Auditing Practices Committee (APC), largely for the benefit of external auditors. However, many can be applied to internal audit and used to define 'best practice'. For example, a guideline on internal control will tell a business what type of internal control they should have, and external auditors what type of internal control they should expect to find.

Exam focus point

Do not worry about remembering the names of specific auditing standards or guidelines, or whether they were produced by the APB or the APC. The examiner has said quite categorically that you do not need to know the detailed content of auditing standards and guidelines. However, to understand internal auditing you will need a general understanding of the principles contained in such standards and guidelines.

4 INTERNAL CONTROL SYSTEMS — May 2001

4.1 One of the main tasks of the internal auditors is to check the operational 'systems' within their organisation, to find out whether the system's **internal controls** are sufficient and are working properly. If they are not, it is the auditors' task to recommend improvements.

An **internal control system** is defined by guidance of the Committee on the Financial Aspects of Corporate Governance (Cadbury Committee) as:

KEY TERM

'The whole system of **controls**, financial and otherwise, established in order to provide reasonable assurance of:

(a) effective and efficient operations;
(b) internal financial control; and
(c) compliance with laws and regulations.'

Exam focus point

The exam in May 2001 had a 6 mark question in Section B on financial controls.

4.2 The Cadbury Code is concerned with the financial aspects of corporate governance and thus principally with 'internal financial control'. This is defined as:

> 'the internal controls established in order to provide reasonable assurance of:
>
> (a) the safeguarding of assets against unauthorised use or disposition; and
>
> (b) the maintenance of proper accounting records and the reliability of financial information used within the business or for publication.'

4.3 These definitions are fairly broad, and a more comprehensive list of the range of internal controls which may exist in an organisation is given in the appendix to the old guideline of the Auditing Practices Committee *Internal Controls*. There are eight types of control listed (one way of remembering them is to use the mnemonic SPAM SOAP).

S egregation of duties
P hysical
A uthorisation and approval
M anagement
S upervision
O rganisation
A rithmetical and accounting
P ersonnel

Segregation of duties

4.4 The APC stated: 'one of the prime means of control is the separation of those responsibilities or duties which would, if combined, enable one individual to record and process a complete transaction. Segregation of duties reduces the risk of intentional manipulation or error and increases the element of checking. Functions which should be separated include those of authorisation, execution, custody, recording and, in the case of a computer-based accounting system, systems development and daily operations.'

4.5 A classic example of segregation of duties, which both internal and external auditors look for, concerns the receipt, recording and banking of cash. It is not a good idea for the person who opens the post (and 'receives' the cash) to be the person responsible for recording that the cash has arrived - and even poorer practice for him to be the person responsible for taking the cash to the bank. If these duties are not segregated, there is always the chance that he will simply pocket the cash, and nobody would be any the wiser. Dividing the duties so that no one person carries all these responsibilities is therefore a form of internal control, in this case helping to safeguard cash receipts.

Physical

4.6 These internal controls were defined by the APC as being 'concerned mainly with the custody of assets and involve procedures and security measures designed to ensure that access to assets is limited to authorised personnel. This includes both direct access and indirect access via documentation. These controls assume importance in the case of valuable, portable, exchangeable or desirable assets.' An example of a physical control is locking the cash box.

Authorisation and approval

4.7 The APC stated: 'all transactions should require authorisation or approval by an appropriate responsible person. The limits for these authorisations should be specified.'

For example, a company might set the rule that the head of a particular department may authorise revenue expenditure up to £500, but that for anything more expensive he must seek the approval of a director. Such authorisation limits will vary from company to company: £500 could be quite a large amount for a small company, but seem insignificant to a big one.

Management

4.8 The APC stated: 'these are the controls exercised by management outside the day-to-day routine of the system. They include the overall supervisory controls exercised by management, the review of management accounts and comparison thereof with budgets, the internal audit function and any other special review procedures.'

Supervision

4.9 The APC stated: 'any system of internal control should include the supervision by responsible officials of day-to-day transactions and the recording thereof.' For example, the chief accountant may review and sign a bank reconciliation each month.

Organisation

4.10 As stated by the APC: 'enterprises should have a plan of their organisation, defining and allocating responsibilities and identifying lines of reporting for all aspects of the enterprise's operations, including the controls. The delegation of authority and responsibility should be clearly specified.'

4.11 For example, it could happen that an employee in a company finds himself working for two masters, say a product manager (who is responsible for the production, marketing and profitability of one particular product) and a sales manager (who supervises the company sales policy for all products). A company which is organised in this overlapping fashion is said to have a matrix organisation. The point here is that the employee might be confused. He might not know who he is supposed to be working for at any one time; he might not know his priorities; he might work harder for one manager at the expense of the other. Such a state of affairs would be detrimental to the company, so it is sensible to set clear lines of authority and responsibility - in short, the company should utilise organisational controls.

Arithmetical and accounting

4.12 The APC stated: 'these are the controls within the recording function which check that the transactions to be recorded and processed have been authorised, that they are all included and that they are correctly recorded and accurately processed. Such controls include checking the arithmetical accuracy of the records, the maintenance and checking of totals, reconciliations, control accounts and trial balances, and accounting for documents.'

Personnel

4.13 This last type of internal control was defined by APC as:

> 'procedures to ensure that personnel have capabilities commensurate with their responsibilities. Inevitably, the proper functioning of any system depends on the competence and integrity of those operating it. The qualifications, selection and training as well as the innate personal characteristics of the personnel involved are important features to be considered in setting up any control system.'

4.14 As an example, a company accountant should be suitably qualified. It is no good asking somebody to produce a set of financial statements if he does not know a profit and loss account from a balance sheet. Nowadays, 'qualified' tends to mean someone who possesses a professional qualification of some sort, but it is important to remember that others are still able to do a job because of work experience - they are 'qualified' through that experience.

Question 2

The chief accountant reviewing and signing a bank reconciliation is what type of internal control?

A Authorisation and approval
B Management
C Segregation of duties
D Supervision

Answer

D is correct.

Internal control system

4.15 A company's operational systems (eg its purchasing system, its stock control system, its sales system, its capital expenditure planning system, its computerised management information systems etc) will incorporate some internal controls from the SPAM SOAP list above. The controls that there are will depend on the particular circumstances of the company, but the range of internal controls it ends up with is called the company's or the system's **internal control system.**

4.16 An operational system need not possess **all** of the SPAM SOAP internal controls - or indeed the organisation may not be able to implement all of them, perhaps because they would be too expensive and so not worth having. For example, a very small organisation may have insufficient staff to be able to organise a desirable level of segregation of duties.

4.17 Management has the responsibility for deciding what internal controls there should be. The internal auditors contribute to internal controls by measuring and evaluating the other internal controls installed by management and reporting to management on their effectiveness.

Administrative controls and accounting controls

4.18 It is useful to distinguish between administrative controls and accounting controls.

KEY TERMS

(a) **Administrative controls** are concerned with achieving the objectives of the organisation and with implementing policies. The controls relate to the following.

- Establishing a suitable organisation structure
- The division of managerial authority
- Reporting responsibilities
- Channels of communication

(b) **Accounting controls** aim to provide accurate accounting records and to achieve accountability.

- The recording of transactions
- Establishing responsibilities for records, transactions and assets

4.19 Accounting controls are applied to procedures/assets and liabilities such as cash and cheques, stocks, sales and debtors, purchases and creditors, fixed assets, investments, capital expenditure, and debt capital and equity.

Detect controls and prevent controls

4.20 Yet another way of analysing internal controls is to distinguish between detect controls and prevent controls.

KEY TERMS

(a) **Detect controls** are controls that are designed to detect errors once they have happened.

(b) **Prevent controls** are controls that are designed to prevent errors from happening in the first place.

4.21 Examples of detect controls in an accounting system are bank reconciliations and regular checks of physical stocks against book records of stocks.

4.22 Examples of prevent controls are:

(a) Checking invoices from suppliers against goods received notes before paying the invoices.

(b) Regular checking of delivery notes against invoices, to ensure that all deliveries have been invoiced.

(c) Signing of goods received notes, credit notes, overtime records etc, to confirm that goods have actually been received, credit notes properly issued, overtime actually authorised and worked etc.

Auditing internal controls

4.23 Internal auditors should check internal controls in two ways.

(a) First, they should establish what internal controls there are, and whether these are sufficient or whether they should be improved.

(b) Secondly, they should check whether the internal controls that exist are working properly. They will obtain evidence that controls exist and are working properly by means of verification procedures.

4.24 If an internal auditors notice that a control is absent or weak or not properly applied, then they should report it to senior management, who will probably ask for an assessment of the risk involved. It is then the responsibility of management to decide whether the risk is acceptable, or whether to take action on the missing or inadequate control.

4.25 No internal control system is foolproof. In fact, Statement of Auditing Standards 300, issued by the APB in March 1995, specifically makes this point.

> 'An internal control system can only provide the directors with reasonable confidence that their objectives are reached because of inherent limitations such as:
>
> (a) the usual requirement that the cost of an internal control is not disproportionate to the potential loss which may result from its absence;
>
> (b) most systematic internal controls tend to be directed at routine transactions rather than non-routine transactions;
>
> (c) the potential for human error due to carelessness, distraction, mistakes of judgement and the misunderstanding of instructions;
>
> (d) the possibility of circumvention of internal controls through collusion with parties outside or inside the entity;
>
> (e) the possibility that a person responsible for exercising an internal control could abuse that responsibility, for example by overriding an internal control; and
>
> (f) the possibility that procedures may become inadequate due to changes in conditions or that compliance with procedures may deteriorate over time.'

Exam focus point

For the purpose of your examination, you might need to specify the types of controls you would expect to find in certain areas of operations, for example:

(a) cash and cheques
(b) wages and salaries
(c) purchases and creditors
(d) sales and debtors
(e) fixed assets
(f) investments

These are all financial systems, but internal audit can apply to any other system, eg management information systems or decision making systems. Controls over sales/debtors and purchases/creditors will be considered below.

5 CONTROLS OVER SALES AND DEBTORS

There are three separate elements into which accounting controls may be divided. They are selling (authorisation), goods outwards (custody) and accounting (recording).

Selling

5.1 (a) What arrangements are to be made to ensure that goods are sold at their correct price and to deal with and check exchanges, discounts and special reductions including those in connection with cash sales.

(b) Who is to be responsible for, and how control is to be maintained over, the granting of credit terms to customers.

(c) Who is to be responsible for accepting customers' orders and what procedure is to be adopted for issuing production orders and despatch notes.

(d) Who is to be responsible for the preparation of invoices and credit notes and what controls are to be instituted to prevent errors and irregularities (for instance, how selling prices are to be ascertained and authorised, how the issue of credit notes is to be controlled and checked, what checks there should be on prices, quantities, extensions and totals shown on invoices and credit notes, and how such documents in blank or completed form are to be protected against loss or misuse).

(e) What special controls are to be exercised over the despatch of goods free of charge or on special terms.

Goods outwards

5.2 (a) Who may authorise the despatch of goods and how is such authority evidenced.

(b) What arrangements are to be made to examine and record goods outwards (preferably this should be done by a person who has no access to stocks and has no accounting or invoicing duties).

(c) The procedure to be instituted for agreeing goods outwards records with customers' orders, despatch notes and invoices.

Accounting

5.3 So far as possible sales ledger staff should have no access to cash, cash books or stocks, and should not be responsible for invoicing and other duties normally assigned to sales staff. The following are amongst matters which should be considered.

(a) The appointment of persons as far as possible separately responsible for the following.

(i) Recording sales and sales returns
(ii) Maintaining customers' accounts
(iii) Preparing debtors' statements

(b) The establishment of appropriate control procedures in connection with sales returns, price adjustments and similar matters.

(c) Arrangements to ensure that goods dispatched but not invoiced (or vice versa) during an accounting period are properly dealt with in the accounts of the periods concerned (cut-off procedures).

(d) The establishment of arrangements to deal with sales to companies or branches forming part of the same group.

(e) What procedures are to be adopted for the preparation, checking and despatch of debtors' statements and for ensuring that they are not subject to interference before despatch.

(f) How discounts granted and special terms are to be authorised and evidenced.

(g) Who is to deal with customers' queries arising in connection with statements.

(h) What procedure is to be adopted for reviewing and following up overdue accounts.

(i) Who is to authorise the writing off of bad debts, and how such authority is to be evidenced.

(j) The institution of a sales control account and its regular checking preferably by an independent official against customers' balances on the sales ledger.

6 CONTROLS OVER PURCHASES AND CREDITORS

6.1 There are also three separate elements into which accounting controls may be divided in the consideration of purchase procedures. They are buying (authorisation), receipt of goods (custody) and accounting (recording).

Buying

6.2 Factors to be considered include the following.

(a) The procedure to be followed when issuing requisitions for additions to and replacement of stocks, and the persons to be responsible for such requisitions.

(b) The preparation and authorisation of purchase orders (including procedures for authorising acceptance where tenders have been submitted or prices quoted).

(c) The institution of checks for the safe-keeping of order forms and safeguarding their use.

(d) As regards capital items, any special arrangements as to authorisations required.

Goods inwards

6.3 Factors to be considered include the following.

(a) Arrangements for examining goods inwards as to quantity, quality and condition; and for evidencing such examination.

(b) The appointment of a person responsible for accepting goods, and the procedure for recording and evidencing their arrival and acceptance.

(c) The procedure to be instituted for checking goods inwards records against authorised purchase orders.

Accounting

6.4 Factors to be considered include the following.

(a) The appointment of persons so far as possible separately responsible for

- (i) Checking suppliers' invoices.
- (ii) Recording purchases and purchase returns.
- (iii) Maintaining suppliers' ledger accounts or similar records.
- (iv) Checking suppliers' statements.
- (v) Authorising payment.

(b) Arrangements to ensure that before accounts are paid.

- (i) The goods concerned have been received, accord with the purchase order, are properly priced and correctly invoiced.

(ii) The expenditure has been properly allocated.

(iii) Payment has been duly authorised by the official responsible.

Question 3

You should get into the habit of thinking about the accounting and other systems you have come across at work (or which your friends and colleagues have worked with) and trying to spot the internal controls.

Ask yourself two questions.

(a) What could go wrong?
(b) How could these problems be prevented and, if not prevented, detected (cost-effectively)?

---

7 EVALUATION OF INTERNAL CONTROLS

7.1 The evaluation of internal controls within a system comes from the following sources.

(a) **System documentation**: ie deciding how the system works, and describing this 'on paper'.

(b) **Identification of potential errors**: ie recognising what can go wrong in this system.

Potential errors can arise whenever there is a chance that one of the following objectives might not be achieved or satisfied.

(i) Existence or occurrence - ie proof that something exists or has happened.
(ii) Completeness - ie that an account balance contains every item that it should.
(iii) Valuation or measurement - ie that a proper system of valuation has been used.
(iv) Ownership - ie proof of ownership of assets.
(v) Disclosure - ie that items are disclosed whenever disclosure is appropriate.

(c) **Identification of controls:** ie recognising the controls within the system that are designed to detect or prevent errors in the system.

7.2 Having identified potential errors and the controls to detect or prevent them, the auditors can assess whether the controls appear to be good enough to do their job sufficiently well.

7.3 When a control is evaluated, the auditors must assess the level of 'risk' that the control is inadequate or might not be properly applied. Factors to consider include the following.

(a) The nature of the control itself.

(b) The timing and frequency of the control check.

(c) Who performs the control, taking into consideration the competence, experience and integrity of staff, and the degree of supervision.

(d) What errors the control has succeeded in identifying and eliminating in the past.

(e) Whether there have been changes in the system or in staff, bearing in mind that control procedures might weaken and become slack in the early period of a new system or just after a change of staff.

8 AUDIT TRAIL **Pilot Paper**

KEY TERM

In general terms an **audit trail** is a means by which an auditor can follow through a transaction from its origin to its ultimate location or vice versa.

8.1 In a manual accounting system an audit trail is created by preserving hard copy evidence of transactions with the hard copy of various documents being preserved and stored for future checking or evidence if required.

8.2 An example of an audit trail for purchases would be the purchase order, the goods received note, the purchase invoice, the purchase day book and the purchases account.

8.3 An audit trail can be used by both internal and external auditors 'in both directions', depending on the auditors' objective. Thus the auditors can start with a sales order and trace it through to 'sales' in the profit and loss account or can trace a sale from the profit and loss account back through the sales account, the sales day book, the sales invoice and the despatch note to the sales order.

8.4 Special considerations apply to computerised accounting systems which are, of course, the majority. For the purposes of computerised systems an audit trail may be defined slightly differently as:

> '...a record of the file updating which takes place during a specific transaction. It enables a trace to be kept of all operations on files'
>
> *(Glossary of Computing Terms of the British Computer Society)*

8.5 An audit trail should ideally be provided so that every transaction on a file contains a unique reference back to the original source of the input, for example, a sales system transaction record should hold a reference to the customer order, delivery note and invoice.

8.6 Where master file records are updated several times, or from several sources, the provision of a satisfactory audit trail is more difficult but some attempt should nevertheless be made to provide one.

8.7 CIPFA, in its *Computer audit guidelines*, comments as follows.

> 'In a computer system the audit trail will not always be apparent as it would be in a manual system, as the data is often retained only on magnetic media and is a form that is intelligible only to the computer programs designed to access it.
>
> There may be occasions when the audit trail is not readily visible.
>
> (a) Output may be limited to a summary of items processed, thus making it impossible to trace an individual transaction right through the system from input to final resting place.
>
> (b) Magnetic storage devices may be updated by over-writing the equivalent record with the result brought about by the newly input data, thus making visible reconciliation of start, change and finish position impossible.
>
> (c) Reports may be on an exception basis only.
>
> Though such occasions may arise it should be remembered that though individual transactions are not visibly traceable through the system, the existence of adequate processing controls will ensure that at least an overall reconciliation of records/transactions input and processed can be made....

The auditor may therefore have to be satisfied with a trail which, while not visible in detail, is nevertheless reconcilable throughout the system.'

9 THE DETECTION AND PREVENTION OF FRAUD

KEY TERM

In *Derry v Peek*, **fraud** was defined as: 'a false representation of fact made with the knowledge of its falsity, or without belief in its truth, or recklessly careless, whether it be true or false'.

The auditing guideline concerns financial fraud, and the definition runs as follows:

> 'The word 'irregularities' is used to refer to intentional distortions of financial statements, for whatever purpose, and to misappropriations of assets, whether or not accompanied by distortions of financial statements. Fraud is one type of irregularity. The word 'fraud' is used to refer to irregularities involving the use of criminal deception to obtain an unjust or illegal advantage.'

9.1 Give an employee responsibility, and he may manage the resources under his control dishonestly. The incidence of financial fraud, particularly in a computer environment, is increasing fast. This trend, together with the increasing sophistication of fraudsters, creates difficult problems for management and for internal auditors.

9.2 The mere presence of internal auditors will serve to discourage fraudsters for fear of being discovered, but the public's expectations go much further.

9.3 The profession has responded in a number of ways, not least the issue of the Auditing Practices Board's Statement of Auditing Standards SAS 110 *Fraud and error* (January 1995).

9.4 The auditors will best be able to detect frauds if they are knowledgeable (not experienced!) in the most common methods of fraud. These are as follows.

- Ghost employees on the payroll
- Miscasting of the payroll
- Stealing unclaimed wages
- Collusion with external parties
- Teeming and lading
- Altering cheques after signature
- Inflating expense claims
- Using the company's assets for personal gain
- Stealing fully depreciated assets
- Issuing false credit notes or fraudulently writing off debts
- Failing to record all sales

9.5 **Ghost employees**. These are imaginary employees for whom the wages department prepare wage packets which are distributed amongst the fraudsters. This type of fraud arises when there is extensive reliance on casual workers, and minimal record keeping for such workers. Inflated overtime claims can also result from poor time recording systems. Such frauds can be detected from a review of the numbers of employees required to achieve a standard amount of work. If at some times of the year, a larger number appear to be required, there may be something amiss. Scrutiny of signatures given as proof of receipt of wages should also be made.

9.6 **Miscasting of the payroll**. This fraud often succeeds due to its simplicity. If there are twenty employees, each to be paid £100, then the computer program for the payroll could be adjusted so that an extra £50 is added to the total added up for the amounts to be paid. Thus management approve a payment of £2,050 for the period's wages, each employee gets his £100 and the fraudster collects his extra £50. Manual payroll systems can be manipulated in a similar way. When employees are paid in cash, this type of fraud can be hard to trace and all too easy to perpetrate.

9.7 Stealing **unclaimed wages** is also common. This is effectively confined to wages paid in cash and can occur when an employee leaves without notice or is away sick. In the case of a subsequent claim for unpaid wages, it could be claimed that the cash in the original pay packet was paid back into the bank.

9.8 **Collusion with external parties** could involve suppliers, customers or their staff. Possible frauds are overcharging on purchase invoices, undercharging on sales invoices or the sale of confidential information (eg customer lists, expansion plans) to a competitor. Management should watch out for unusual discounts or commissions being given or taken, or for an excessive zeal on the part of an employee to handle all business with a particular company.

9.9 **Teeming and lading** is a 'rolling' fraud rather than a 'one-off' fraud. It occurs when a clerk has the chance to misappropriate payments from debtors or to creditors. Cash received by the company is borrowed by the cashier rather than being kept as petty cash or banked. (It is also possible, although riskier and more difficult to organise, to misappropriate cheques made payable to the company.) When the cashier knows that a reconciliation is to be performed, or audit visit planned, he pays the money back so that everything appears satisfactory at that point, but after the audit the teeming and lading starts again. Surprise visits by auditors and independent checking of cash balances should discourage this fraud.

9.10 A common fraud arising when one employee has sole control of the sales ledger and recording debtors' cheques is to pay cheques into a separate bank account, either by forged endorsement or by opening an account in a name similar to the employer's.

9.11 The clerk has to allocate cheques or cash received from other debtors against the account of the debtor whose payment was misappropriated. This prevents other staff from asking why the account is still overdue or from sending statements etc to the debtors. However, the misallocation has to continue as long as the money is missing. This fraud, therefore, never really stops. It can be detected by independent verification of debtors balances (eg by writing to them) and by looking at unallocated payments, if the sales ledger is organised to show this. In addition, sending out itemised monthly statements to debtors should act as a deterrent, although in a really elaborate fraud the clerk may be keeping two sets of books, so that the statements show the debtor's own analysis of amounts due and paid off in the month, but do not agree with the books.

9.12 **Altering cheques** and **inflating expense claims** are self-explanatory.

9.13 **Using the company's assets for personal gain and stealing fully depreciated assets** are both encountered in practice. Whether or not the private use of company telephones and photocopiers is a serious matter is up to the company to judge, but it may still be fraudulent. More serious examples include the sale by employees of unused time on the computer, which is a growing fraud.

9.14 Another way of avoiding detection when cash and cheques received from debtors have been misappropriated is to **issue a credit note** which is not sent to the customer (who has paid his account) but is recorded in the books. Again, the issue of itemised statements monthly should show this up, as the customer would query the credit note. However, any company with sufficiently lax controls to allow one clerk both to receive and record cash and additionally to authorise and issue credit notes is unlikely to ensure that someone else issues and follows up statements. A similar tactic is to **write a debt off** as bad to cover up the disappearance of the payment.

9.15 A very elaborate fraud may be perpetrated in a business with extremely poor controls over sales recording and minimal segregation of duties. In such circumstances, a dishonest bookkeeper may invoice customers but fail to record the invoices so that the customer's payments never have to be recorded and the misappropriation is not missed.

9.16 This type of fraud can occur where a customer is receiving large numbers of invoices from the business every month and so the bookkeeper's failure to record one or two invoices (if detected by auditors or his superiors) is simply put down to incompetence rather than fraud.

91.7 A warning sign here is the perception by customers that 'your accounts department is a mess ... always getting things wrong ... we've given up trying to get our account right...'.

The role of the internal auditors

9.18 The internal auditors should start their work by identifying the areas of the business most susceptible to fraud. These will include areas where cash is involved, and the other areas where the auditors' judgement is that the internal controls are insufficient to safeguard the assets.

9.19 The existence of a properly functioning system of internal controls will diminish the incidence of frauds, so the auditors' opinion on the internal control system is of fundamental importance.

9.20 Whenever a fraud is discovered, they should judge whether a weakness in internal controls has been highlighted, and if so what changes are needed.

Prevention of fraud

9.21 Fraud will only be prevented successfully if potential fraudsters perceive the risk of detection as being high, and if personnel are adequately screened before employment and given no incentive to turn against the company once employed. The following safeguards should therefore be implemented.

(a) A good internal control system.
(b) Continuous supervision of all employees.
(c) Surprise audit visits.
(d) Thorough personnel procedures.

9.22 The work of employees must be monitored as this will increase the perceived risk of being discovered. Actual results must regularly be compared against budgeted results, and employees should be asked to explain significant variances.

9.23 Surprise audit visits are a valuable contribution to preventing fraud. If a cashier is carrying out a teeming and lading fraud and is told that an audit visit is due the following week, he may be able to square up the books before the visit so that the auditors will find nothing wrong. But if the threat of a surprise visit is constantly present, the cashier will not be able to carry out a teeming and lading fraud without the risk of being discovered, and this risk is usually sufficient to prevent the fraud.

9.24 The auditors do not need to carry out any sophisticated audit tests during their surprise visit. There are stories of internal auditors arriving without warning, and taking all the books into a room of their own to read the newspaper for an hour - but the fraud deterrent effect on the employee is highly significant, because the employee thinks that every figure is being checked.

9.25 Finally, personnel procedures must be adequate to prevent the occurrence of frauds.

(a) Whenever a fraud is discovered, the fraudster should be dismissed and the police should be informed. Too often an employee is 'asked to resign' and then moves on to a similar job where the fraud is repeated, often because management fear loss of face or investor confidence. This is a self-defeating policy.

(b) All new employees should be required to produce adequate references from their previous employers.

(c) If an employee's lifestyle changes dramatically, explanations should be sought.

(d) Every employee must be made to take his annual holiday entitlement. Sometimes in practice the employee who is 'so dedicated that he never takes a holiday' is in fact not taking his leave for fear of his fraud being discovered by his replacement worker while he is away.

(e) Pay levels should be adequate and working conditions of a reasonable standard. If employees feel that they are being paid an unfairly low amount or 'exploited', they may look for ways to supplement their pay dishonestly.

Management fraud

9.26 So far, this chapter has concentrated on employee fraud. However, arguably more serious (and very much more difficult to prevent and detect) is the growing problem of management fraud.

9.27 While employee fraud is usually undertaken purely for the employee's financial gain, management fraud is often undertaken to improve the company's apparent performance, to reduce tax liabilities or to improve manager's promotion prospects.

9.28 Managers are often in a position to override internal controls and to intimidate their subordinates into collusion or turning a blind eye. This makes it difficult to detect such frauds. In addition, where the company is benefiting financially rather than the manager, it can be difficult to persuade staff that any dishonesty is involved.

9.29 This clash of interest between loyalty to an employer and professional integrity can be difficult to resolve and can compromise an internal auditor's independence.

9.30 Management fraud often comes to light after a take-over or on a change of audit staff or practices. Its consequences can be far reaching for the employing company in damaging its reputation or because it results in legal action. Because management usually have access to much larger sums of money than more lowly employees, the financial loss to the company can be immense.

Chapter roundup

- It is important to distinguish between external and internal auditors.
- **External auditors** report to the members of the company on whether in their opinion, the annual statutory accounts give a true and fair view. Their duties are imposed by statute and they are not employees of the company.
- **Internal auditors** are employees of the company whose duties are fixed by management and who report to management.
- Financial statements are obliged by the Companies Act 1985 to give a true and fair view. This phrase has proved problematic on occasions and is not clearly defined.
- The scope of an internal audit varies widely and may range from systems review to implementation of corporate policies, plans and processes.
- The essential elements of internal audit are as follows.
  - Independence
  - Staffing and training
  - Relationships
  - Due care
  - Planning, controlling and recording
  - Reporting
- Eight types of internal control have been identified. They can be remembered by using the mnemonic SPAM SOAP.
- An audit trail enables auditors to trace a transaction from beginning to end to verify that it has been processed completely and correctly.
- In auditing, detection of fraud is an important objective (but by no means the only objective). Auditors should be aware of the common types of fraud and should be particularly watchful when internal controls are poor, especially if an employee's expenditure appears to be inconsistent with his salary or if a department is performing unexpectedly badly.

Quick quiz

1 The auditor's report states whether the financial statements give a 'true and fair' view. True and fair has never been statutorily defined. True or false?

2 To whom should the head of internal audit report in a large company?

A The finance director
B The chief accountant
C The chairman of the board of directors
D The external auditors

3 Which of the following statements concerning the status of an external auditor is incorrect?

A All companies must appoint external auditors
B The duties of an auditor are defined by the Companies Act 1985
C The auditor gives an opinion on the financial statements
D The auditor reports to the members of the company

4 Which of the following procedures is unlikely to be encountered in following through an 'audit trail' in a computerised accounting system?

A The authorisation of input documents

B One for one checking of master file amendments

C Output being completely checked against input data in a system producing budgetary control reports

D Authorisation of changes to a computer program

5 What is a 'teeming and lading fraud'?

A Stealing cash

B Colluding with external partners to submit false invoices

C Stealing cash, concealing the theft by delaying bankings or making good the shortage by transfers from other sources

D Altering cheques and cash receipt records to record lesser amounts and pocketing the difference

Answers to quick quiz

1 True

2 C Correct. This is ideal, an alternative would be to report to the board or an audit committee.

A Independence will be compromised and recommendations possibly diluted.

B The chief accountant may lack authority to implement the needed changes following an internal audit review and independence may be compromised.

D The external auditors must not be involved in executive decisions within a client, otherwise their independence could be compromised.

3 A Correct. Small limited companies and unincorporated businesses or partnerships need not have an external audit.

4 C Correct. It is more usual to find output on a exceptions basis, such as the investigation of significant variances in the example given.

A A key element of control over input, difficult to achieve in on-line or real-time systems.

B An important procedure to preserve the integrity of master file data.

D This would be present in the systems documentation.

5 C Correct. The characteristics of this type of fraud are theft (or 'borrowing') coupled with a scheme to conceal typically involving delayed bankings.

A The objective of a teeming and lading fraud is to misappropriate cash, it is how it is concealed which is unique.

B This is not a teeming and fraud, although it is a common type of fraud.

D This is a straightforward receipts fraud.

Now try the questions below from the Question Bank

Number	Level	Marks	Time
62	Exam	15	27 mins
63	Exam	2	3 mins
64	Exam	2	3 mins

Part D
Interpretation of accounts

Chapter 22

INTERPRETING COMPANY ACCOUNTS

Topic List		Syllabus reference	Ability required
1	Ratio analysis	(iv)	Application
2	Profit margin, asset turnover and return on capital employed	(iv)	Application
3	Working capital	(iv)	Application
4	Liquidity	(iv)	Application
5	Gearing	(iv)	Application
6	Items in company accounts formats	(iv)	Application
7	Planning your answers	(iv)	Application

Introduction

So far your studies have concentrated on the **preparation** of accounts. This chapter focuses on **interpretation** primarily by means of ratio analysis.

The purpose of financial statement analysis is to aid decision making. The financial statements help interested persons decide on questions such as whether to lend a business money or invest in its shares.

It has already been mentioned (in Chapter 1) that the users of financial statements extend beyond present and potential shareholders and creditors and include such groups as employees, government bodies and society at large. We will not attempt to deal with the possible decision needs of each class of user - such a discussion would require a book of its own. Instead we will concentrate on three aspects relevant to all groups of users, namely its profitability, liquidity and gearing. The topics will be discussed in terms of limited companies, but it should be realised that most of the points will be relevant when examining the accounts of other business entities.

Learning outcomes covered in this chapter

- Calculate and explain basic ratios

Syllabus content covered in this chapter

- Ratios: ROCE, gross and net profit margins, asset turnover, debtors collection and creditors time to pay, current and quick ratios, stock turnover, gearing.

1 RATIO ANALYSIS

KEY TERM

Ratio analysis is the calculation of ratios (eg profit margin) from a set of financial statements which is used for comparison with either early years or similar businesses to provide information for decision making.

Comparing different businesses

1.1 When ratio analysis is used to assess the relative strength of a particular business, by comparing its profitability and financial stability with another business, the two businesses should be largely similar.

- In size
- In their line of activities

1.2 If the businesses are not broadly similar in size or in what they do, then differences revealed by ratio analysis might merely arise as a natural consequence of the size difference, or the varying lines of business they operate in. We do not need ratios to tell us that one business is larger, or that two businesses operate in entirely different industries!

2 PROFIT MARGIN, ASSET TURNOVER AND RETURN ON CAPITAL EMPLOYED **Pilot Paper, May 2001**

Profit margin

KEY TERM

Profit margin. This is the ratio of profit to sales, and may also be called 'profit percentage' or 'profit to turnover ratio'. It is calculated as $\frac{\text{Net or gross profit}}{\text{Sales}} \times 100\%$

2.1 For example, if a company makes a profit of £20,000 on sales of £100,000 its profit percentage or profit margin is 20%. This also means that its costs are 80% of sales. A high profit margin indicates.

(a) **Either** costs are being kept well under control because if the ratio of costs:sales goes down, the profit margin will automatically go up. For example, if the costs:sales ratio changes from 80% to 75%, the profit margin will go up from 20% to 25%.

(b) **Or** sales prices are high. For example, if a company sells goods for £100,000 and makes a profit of £16,000 costs would be £84,000 and the profit margin is 16%. Now if the company can raise selling prices by 20% to £120,000 without affecting the volume of goods sold or their costs, profits would rise by the amount of revenue increase (£20,000) to £36,000 and the profit margin would also rise (from 16% to 30%).

Exam focus point

The May 2001 exam asked for a profit margin calculation in Section B.

Asset turnover

KEY TERM

Asset turnover. This is the ratio of sales in a year to the amount of net assets (capital) employed. It is calculated as $\frac{\text{Sales}}{\text{Net assets or capital employed}}$

2.2 For example, if a company has sales in 20X4 of £720,000 and has assets of £360,000, the asset turnover will be

$$\frac{£720,000}{£360,000} = 2 \text{ times.}$$

2.3 This means that for every £1 of assets employed, the company can generate sales turnover of £2 per annum. To utilise assets more efficiently, managers should try to create a higher volume of sales and so a higher asset turnover ratio. For example, suppose that our firm with assets of £360,000 can increase its sales turnover from £720,000 to £900,000 per annum. The asset turnover would improve to

$$\frac{£900,000}{£360,000} = 2.5 \text{ times.}$$

2.4 The significance of this improvement is that if a business can create more sales turnover from the same amount of assets it should make larger profits (because of the increase in sales) without having to increase the size of its investment.

Return On Capital Employed

KEY TERM

Return on capital employed (ROCE) is the amount of profit as a percentage of capital employed. It is calculated as $\frac{\text{Profit}}{\text{Capital employed or net assets}} \times 100\%$

2.5 If a company makes a profit of £30,000, we do not know how good or bad this profit is until we look at the amount of capital which has been invested to achieve the profit. £30,000 might be a good-sized profit for a small firm, but it would not be good enough for a 'giant' firm such as Marks and Spencer.

2.6 For this reason, it is helpful to measure performance by relating profits to the amount of capital employed, and because this seems to be the **only** satisfactory ratio or percentage which judges profits in relation to the size of the business, it is sometimes called the **primary ratio** in financial analysis.

Question 1

A business has the following results

Sales	£450,000
Profit	£100,000
Net assets	£400,000

Calculate:

(a) The profit margin
(b) Asset turnover
(c) Return on capital employed

Answer

(a) $\frac{£100,000}{£450,000} \times 100\% = 22.22\%$

(b) $\frac{£450,000}{£400,000} = 1.125$ times

(c) $\frac{100,000}{400,000} \times 100\% = 25\%$

Relationship between ratios

2.7 You may already have realised that there is a mathematical connection between return on capital employed, profit margin and asset turnover, since sales in the right-hand side of the equation below cancel out.

FORMULAS TO LEARN

$$\frac{\text{Profit}}{\text{Capital employed}} = \frac{\text{Profit}}{\text{Sales}} \times \frac{\text{Sales}}{\text{Capital employed}}$$

$$\text{ROCE} = \text{Profit margin} \times \text{Asset turnover}$$

2.8 This is important. If we accept that ROCE is the most important single measure of business performance, comparing profit with the amount of capital invested, we can go on to say that business performance is dependent on two separate 'subsidiary' factors, each of which contributes to ROCE.

(a) Profit margin.
(b) Asset turnover.

2.9 For this reason, just as ROCE is sometimes called the **primary ratio**, the profit margin and asset turnover ratios are sometimes called the **secondary ratios**.

2.10 The implications of this relationship must be understood. Suppose that a return on capital employed of 20% is thought to be a good level of business performance in the retail trade for electrical goods.

(a) Company A might decide to sell its products at a fairly high price and make a profit margin on sales of 10%. It would then need only an asset turnover of 2.0 times to achieve a ROCE of 20%:

20% = 10% × 2

(b) Company B might decide to cut its prices so that its profit margin is only 2½%. Provided that it can achieve an asset turnover of 8 times a year, attracting more customers with its lower prices, it will still make the desired ROCE:

20% = 2½% × 8

2.11 Company A might be a department store and company B a discount warehouse. Each will have a different selling price policy, but each, in its own way, can be effective in achieving a target ROCE. In this example, if we supposed that both companies had capital employed of £100,000 and a target return of 20% or £20,000.

(a) Company A would need annual sales of £200,000 to give a profit margin of 10% and an asset turnover of 2 times

$$\frac{£20,000}{£100,000} = \frac{£20,000}{£200,000} \times 2$$

(b) Company B would need annual sales of £800,000 to give a profit margin of only 2½% but an asset turnover of 8 times.

$$\frac{£20,000}{£100,000} = \frac{£20,000}{£800,000} \times 8$$

2.12 Clearly, a higher return on capital employed can be obtained by increasing the profit margin or the asset turnover ratio. The profit margin can be increased by reducing costs or by raising selling prices.

2.13 However, if selling prices are raised, it is likely that sales demand will fall, with the possible consequence that the asset turnover will also decline. If higher prices mean lower sales turnover, the increase in profit margin might be offset by the fall in asset turnover, so that total return on capital employed might not improve.

2.14 EXAMPLE: PROFIT MARGIN AND ASSET TURNOVER

Suppose that Swings and Roundabouts Ltd achieved the following results in 20X6.

Sales	£100,000
Profit	£5,000
Capital employed	£20,000

The company's management wish to decide whether to raise its selling prices. They think that if they do so, they can raise the profit margin to 10% and by introducing extra capital of £55,000, sales turnover would be £150,000.

Evaluate the decision in terms of the effect on ROCE, profit margin and asset turnover.

2.15 SOLUTION

Currently the ratios are

Profit margin (5/100)	5%
Asset turnover (100/20)	5 times
ROCE (5/20)	25%

With the proposed changes, the profit would be 10% × £150,000 = £15,000, and the asset turnover would be:

$$\frac{£150{,}000}{£(20{,}000+55{,}000)} = 2 \text{ times, so that the ratios would be}$$

Profit margin × Asset turnover	= ROCE
10% × 2 times	$= 20\% \left(\frac{£15{,}000}{£75{,}000}\right)$

In spite of increasing the profit margin and raising the total volume of sales, the extra assets required (£55,000) only raise total profits by £(15,000 – 5,000) = £10,000.

The return on capital employed falls from 25% to 20% because of the sharp fall in asset turnover from 5 times to 2 times.

Question 2

A trader has the following results.

	£
Sales	200,000
Profit	36,000
Capital employed	120,000

Fill in the blanks.

Profit margin = 0.18 ______________

Asset turnover = 0.3 ______________

ROCE = 30% ______________

Answer

Profit margin = $\frac{£36{,}000}{£200{,}000} = 18\%$

Asset turnover = $\frac{200{,}000}{120{,}000} = 1^2/_3$ times

ROCE = $\frac{36{,}000}{120{,}000} = 30\%$

Different definitions of 'profit' and 'capital employed

2.16 We have calculated Return on Capital Employed as a measure of how well a company is performing. What do we mean by 'return' and by capital employed?

> **KEY TERM**
>
> **Return** is a reward for investing in a business.
>
> **Capital employed** means the funds that finance a business.

2.17 The providers of finance to a business expect some return on their investment.

(a) Trade creditors and most other current liabilities merely expect to be paid what they are owed.

(b) A bank charges interest on overdrafts.

(c) Interest must be paid to the holders of loan stock and debentures.

(d) Preference shareholders expect a dividend at a fixed percentage rate of the nominal value of their shares.

(e) Ordinary shareholders also expect a dividend, and, any retained profits kept in the business also represent funds 'owned' or 'provided' by them.

2.18 So, when calculating return on capital employed, what measure of 'return' and what measure of 'capital employed' should be used?

Exam focus point

The examiner has stated that the measure of return should be net profit before tax and interest and the measure of capital employed should be share capital plus reserves (or capital plus reserves for a sole trader) plus any long term debt. So include debentures and mortgages but exclude any short term bank loans or overdrafts.

FORMULA TO LEARN

For a company, ROCE = $\dfrac{\text{Net profit before interest and tax}}{\text{Share capital + reserves + long term debt}}$

which is the same as, ROCE = $\dfrac{\text{Net profit before interest and tax}}{\text{Fixed assets plus net current assets}}$

2.19 EXAMPLE: ROCE

For example, suppose that Draught Ltd reports the following profit and loss account and balance sheet.

PROFIT AND LOSS ACCOUNT FOR 20X4 (EXTRACT)

	£
Profit before interest and tax	120,000
Interest	(20,000)
Profit before tax	100,000
Taxation	(40,000)
Profit after tax (earnings)	60,000
Ordinary dividend	(50,000)
Retained profits	10,000

BALANCE SHEET AT 31 DECEMBER 20X4

	£	£
Fixed assets: tangible assets		350,000
Current assets	400,000	
Less: current liabilities	(150,000)	
Net current assets		250,000
Total assets less current liabilities		600,000
Creditors: amounts falling due after more than one year:		
10% debenture loans		200,000
		400,000
Capital and reserves		
Called up share capital (ordinary shares of £1)		100,000
Profit and loss account		300,000
		400,000

2.20 SOLUTION

$$\text{ROCE} = \frac{\text{Profits before interest and tax}}{\text{Total assets less current liabilities}} \times 100\%$$

Where, total assets less current liabilities is equal to share capital plus reserves plus long term finance (ie the 10% debenture loan).

If assets financed by debt capital are included below the line, it is more appropriate to show profits before interest above the line because interest is the return on debt capital.

$$\frac{£120{,}000}{£600{,}000} \times 100\% = 20\%$$

Exam focus point: examination formula

The CIMA *Guidance Notes* 1997-98 for the *Financial Accounting Fundamentals* paper make the following statement with regard to ROCE.

'In the examination candidates may be required to calculate the return on capital employed using the formula:

Net profit before tax and interest/average capital employed

where average capital employed includes long-term finance, but does not include short-term finance such as bank overdrafts. As additional guidance where questions do not include any long-term finance, then any mention of interest payable can be assumed to relate to short-term finance. Where questions include both short-term and long-term finance, the Examiner will clarify the content of any figure for interest payable.'

KEY TERM

Average capital employed = capital employed at beginning of the accounting period + capital employed at the end of the accounting period ÷ 2

Question 3

Using the information in the last example for Draught Ltd, calculate ROCE.

Relevant figures as at 31 December 20X3 are as follows.

	£
10% debenture loans	200,000
Ordinary share capital	100,000
Profit and loss account	290,000
	590,000

Answer

Average capital employed = (590 + 600) ÷ 2 = £595,000

$$\text{ROCE} = \frac{120{,}000}{595{,}000} = 20.2\%$$

More profitability and asset turnover ratios

2.21 The profit:sales ratio and asset turnover ratio (assets:capital employed) can be analysed in more depth from information given in financial statements.

(a) Profitability can be analysed by measuring the ratio of various cost items to sales. For example:

FORMULAS TO LEARN

(i) $\frac{\text{cost of sales}}{\text{sales}}$ and $\frac{\text{gross profit}}{\text{sales}}$

(ii) $\frac{\text{distribution costs}}{\text{sales}}$

and

(iii) $\frac{\text{administrative expenses}}{\text{sales}}$

Changes in these ratios over time, from year to year, might indicate that a certain aspect of the business operations (eg cost of sales, distribution costs, administration expenses) are becoming too expensive and so squeezing profits.

(b) Asset turnover can be further analysed, taking fixed assets and working capital separately.

(i) The fixed asset turnover ratio is:

$$\frac{\text{Sales}}{\text{Fixed assets}}$$

(ii) Working capital ratios are described separately later in the chapter.

3 WORKING CAPITAL — Pilot Paper

KEY TERM

Working capital is the difference between current assets (mainly stocks, debtors and cash) and current liabilities (such as trade creditors and a bank overdraft).

3.1 Current assets are items which are either cash already, or which will soon lead to the receipt of cash. Stocks will be sold to customers and create debtors; and debtors will soon pay in cash for their purchases.

Current liabilities arc itcms which will soon have to be paid for with cash. Trade creditors will have to be paid and bank overdraft is usually regarded as a short-term borrowing which may need to be repaid fairly quickly (or on demand, ie immediately).

In balance sheets, the word 'current' is applied to stocks, debtors, short-term investments and cash (current assets) and amounts due for payment within one year's time (current liabilities).

Working capital and trading operations

3.2 Current assets and current liabilities are a necessary feature of a firm's trading operations. There is a repeated cycle of buying and selling which is carried on all the time. For example, suppose that on 1 April a firm has the following items.

	£
Stocks	3,000
Debtors	0
Cash	2,000
	5,000
Creditors	0
Working capital	5,000

3.3 It might sell all the stocks for £4,500, and at the same time obtain more stock from suppliers at a cost of £3,500. The balance sheet items would now be

	£
Stocks	3,500
Debtors	4,500
Cash	2,000
	10,000
Creditors	(3,500)
Working capital	6,500

(The increase in working capital to £6,500 from £5,000 is caused by the profit of £1,500 on the sale of the stocks.)

3.4 The debtors for £4,500 will eventually pay in cash and the creditors for £3,500 must also be paid. This would give us

	£
Stocks	3,500
Debtors	0
Cash (2,000 + 4,500 – 3,500)	3,000
	6,500
Creditors	0
Working capital	6,500

3.5 However, if the stocks are sold on credit for £5,500 and further purchases of stock costing £6,000 are made, the cycle of trading will continue as follows.

	£
Stocks	6,000
Debtors	5,500
Cash	3,000
	14,500
Creditors	(6,000)
Working capital (boosted by further profit of £2,000)	8,500

3.6 From this basic example you might be able to see that working capital items are part of a continuous flow of trading operations. Purchases add to stocks and creditors at the same time, creditors must be paid and debtors will pay for their goods. The cycle of operations always eventually comes back to cash receipts and cash payments.

The operating cycle or cash cycle

KEY TERM

The operating cycle (or cash cycle) is a term used to describe the time taken from the purchase of raw materials to the sale of finished goods.

3.7 A firm buys raw materials, probably on credit. The raw materials might be held for some time in stores before being issued to the production department and turned into an item of finished goods. The finished goods might be kept in a warehouse for some time before they are eventually sold to customers. By this time, the firm will probably have paid for the raw materials purchased. If customers buy the goods on credit, it will be some time before the cash from the sales is eventually received.

3.8 The cash cycle, or operating cycle, measures the period of time. Between the time cash is paid out for raw materials and the time cash is received in from debtors.

3.9 This cycle of repeating events is shown diagrammatically below.

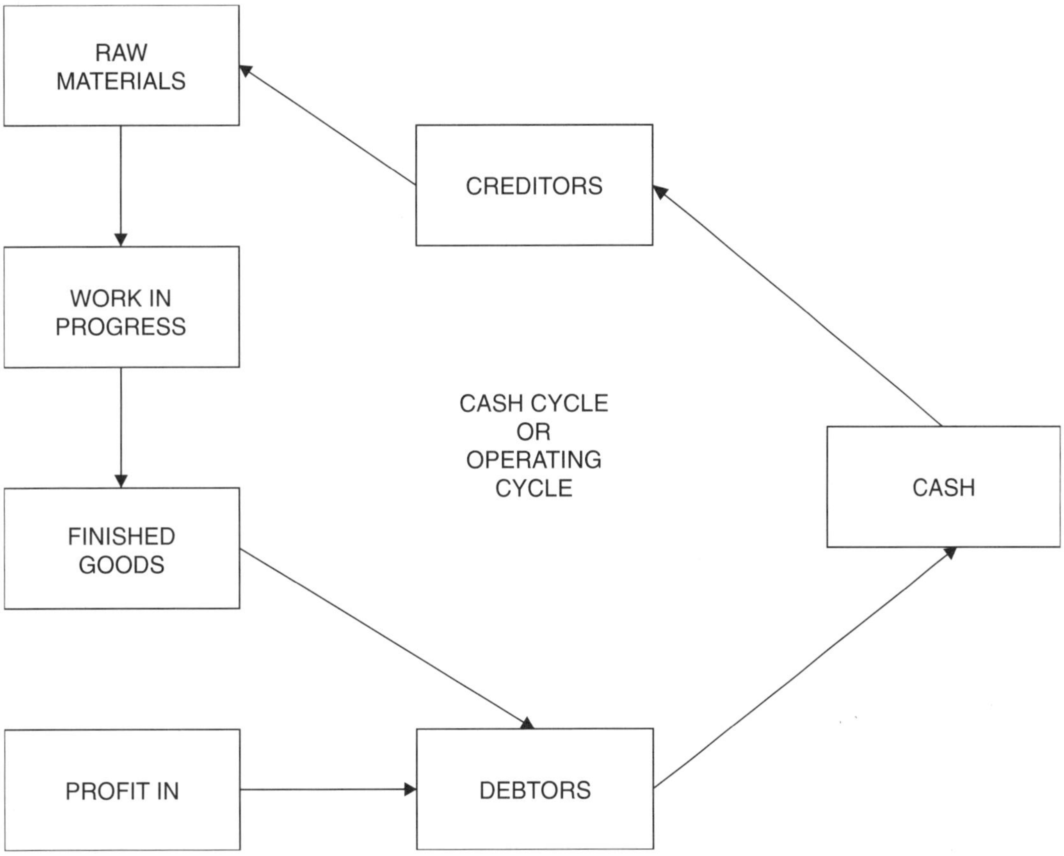

3.10 Suppose that a firm buys raw materials on 1½ months' credit, holds them in store for 1 month and then issues them to the production department. The production cycle is very short, but finished goods are held for 1 month before they are sold. Debtors take two months' credit. The cash cycle would be

	Months
Raw material stock turnover period	1.0
Less: credit taken from suppliers	(1.5)
Finished goods stock turnover period	1.0
Debtor's payment period	2.0
Cash cycle	2.5

There would be a gap of 2½ months between paying cash for raw materials and receiving cash (including profits) from debtors. A few dates might clarify this point. Suppose the firm purchases its raw materials on 1 January. The sequence of events would then be as follows.

	Date
Purchase of raw materials	1 Jan
Issue of materials to production (one month after purchase)	1 Feb
Payment made to suppliers (1½ months after purchase)	15 Feb
Sale of finished goods (one month after production begins)	1 Mar
Receipt of cash from debtors (two months after sale)	1 May

3.11 The cash cycle is the period of 2½ months from 15 February, when payment is made to suppliers, until 1 May, when cash is received from debtors.

Turnover periods

KEY TERM

A '**turnover**' period is an (average) length of time.

3.12 (a) In the case of stock turnover, it is the length of time an item of stock is held in stores before it is used.

(i) A raw materials stock turnover period is the length of time raw materials are held before being issued to the production department.

(ii) A work in progress turnover period is the length of time it takes to turn raw materials into finished goods in the factory.

(iii) A finished goods stock turnover period is the length of time that finished goods are held in a warehouse before they are sold.

(iv) When a firm buys goods and re-sells them at a profit, the stock turnover period is the time between their purchase and their resale.

(b) The debtors' turnover period, or debt collection period, is the length of the credit period taken by customers - it is the time between the sale of an item and the receipt of cash for the sale from the customer.

(c) Similarly, the creditors' turnover period, or period of credit taken from suppliers, is the length of time between the purchase of materials and the payment to suppliers.

Turnover periods can be calculated from information in a firm's profit and loss account and balance sheet.

FORMULAS TO LEARN

Stock turnover periods are calculated as follows.

(a) Raw materials: $\dfrac{\text{(Average) raw material stocks held}}{\text{Total raw material comsumed in one year}} \times 12 \text{ months}$

(b) Work in progress (the length of the production period):

$$\frac{\text{(Average) WIP}}{\text{Total cost of production in the year}} \times 12 \text{ months}$$

(c) Finished goods: $\dfrac{\text{(Average) stocks}}{\text{Total cost of goods sold in one year}} \times 12 \text{ months}$

(d) Stocks of items bought for re-sale:

$$\frac{\text{(Average) stocks}}{\text{Total (materials) cost of goods bought and sold in one year}} \times 12 \text{ months}$$

3.13 The word 'average' is put in brackets because although it is strictly correct to use average values, it is more common to use the value of stocks shown in a single balance sheet - at one point in time - to estimate the turnover periods. But if available use opening and closing balances divided by two.

3.14 EXAMPLE

A company buys goods costing £620,000 in one year and uses goods costing £600,000 in production (in regular monthly quantities) and the cost of material in stock at 1 January is £100,000.

3.15 SOLUTION

The stock turnover period could be calculated as:

$$\frac{£100{,}000}{£600{,}000} \times 12 \text{ months} = 2 \text{ months}$$

In other words, stocks are bought two months before they are used or sold.

Debt collection period

FORMULA TO LEARN

The debt collection period is calculated as:

$$\frac{\text{Average debtors}}{\text{Annual credit sales}} \times 12 \text{ months}$$

3.16 EXAMPLE

If a company sells goods for £1,200,000 per annum in regular monthly quantities, and if debtors in the balance sheet are £150,000.

3.17 SOLUTION

The debt collection period is

$$\frac{£150{,}000}{£1{,}200{,}000} \times 12 \text{ months} = 1.5 \text{ months}$$

In other words, debtors will pay for goods $1\frac{1}{2}$ months on average after the time of sale.

Credit period

FORMULA TO LEARN

The period of credit taken from suppliers is calculated as:

$$\frac{\text{Average trade creditors}}{\text{Total purchases in one year}} \times 12 \text{ months}$$

3.18 Notice that the creditors are compared with materials bought whereas for raw material stock turnover, raw material stocks are compared with materials used in production. This is a small, but very significant difference.

3.19 EXAMPLE

For example, if a company sells goods for £600,000 and makes a gross profit of 40% on sales, and if the amount of trade creditors in the balance sheet is £30,000.

3.20 SOLUTION

The period of credit taken from the suppliers is:

$$\frac{\pounds30,000}{(60\% \text{ of } \pounds600,000)} \times 12 \text{ months} = 1 \text{ month}$$

In other words, suppliers are paid in the month following the purchase of goods.

Question 4

Legion Ltd's 20X4 accounts show the following.

	£
Sales	360,000
Cost of goods sold	180,000
Stocks	30,000
Debtors	75,000
Trade creditors	45,000

Calculate the length of the cash cycle.

Answer

Stock turnover	*Debt collection period*	*Credit taken from suppliers*
$\frac{30,000}{180,000} \times 12$	$\frac{75,000}{360,000} \times 12$	$\frac{45,000}{180,000} \times 12$
= 2 months	= $2^1/2$ months	= 3 months

The cash cycle is

	Months
Stock turnover period	2.0
Credit taken from suppliers	(3.0)
Debt collection period	2.5
Cash cycle	1.5

In this example, Legion Ltd pays its suppliers one month after the stocks have been sold, since the stock turnover is two months but credit taken is three months.

Turnover periods and the total amount of working capital

3.21 If the stock turnover period gets longer or if the debt collection period gets longer, the total amount of stocks or of debtors will increase. Similarly, if the period of credit taken from the suppliers gets shorter, the amount of creditors will become smaller. The effect of these changes would be to increase the size of working capital (ignoring bank balances or overdrafts).

3.22 EXAMPLE

Suppose that a company has annual sales of £480,000 (in regular monthly quantities, all on credit) and a materials cost of sales of £300,000. (*Note.* A 'materials cost of sales' is the cost of materials in the cost of sales.)

(a) If the stock turnover period is 2 months, the debt collection period 1 month and the period of credit taken from suppliers is 2 months, the company's working capital (ignoring cash) would be

		£
Stocks	(2/12 × £300,000)	50,000
Debtors	(1/12 × £480,000)	40,000
		90,000
Creditors	(2/12 × £300,000)	(50,000)
		40,000

The cash cycle would be (2 + 1 – 2) = 1 month.

(b) Now if the stock turnover period is extended to 3 months and the debt collection period to 2 months, and if the payment period for purchases from suppliers is reduced to one month, the company's working capital (ignoring cash) would be

		£
Stocks	(3/12 × £300,000)	75,000
Debtors	(2/12 × £480,000)	80,000
		155,000
Creditors	(1/12 × £300,000)	(25,000)
		130,000

and the cash cycle would be (3 + 2 – 1) = 4 months.

3.23 If we ignore the possible effects on the bank balance or bank overdraft, (which are themselves included in working capital) it should be seen that a lengthening of the cash cycle will result in a larger volume of working capital.

3.24 If the volume of working capital required by a business varies with the length of the cash cycle, it is worth asking the question: 'Is there an ideal length of cash cycle and an ideal volume of working capital?'

3.25 Obviously, stocks, debtors and creditors should be managed efficiently.

(a) Stocks should be sufficiently large to meet the demand for stock items when they are needed, but they should not be allowed to become excessive.

(b) Debtors should be allowed a reasonable credit period, but overdue payments should be 'chased up', to obviate the risk of bad debts.

(c) Suppliers should be asked to allow a reasonable period of credit and the firm should make use of the credit periods offered by them.

4 LIQUIDITY

May 2001

KEY TERM

The word '**liquid**' means 'readily converted into cash' and a firm's **liquidity** is its ability to convert its assets into cash to meet all the demands for payments when they fall due.

4.1 The most liquid asset, of course, is cash itself (or a bank balance). The next most liquid assets are short-term investments (stocks and shares) because these can be sold quickly for cash should this be necessary.

4.2 Debtors are fairly liquid assets because they should be expected to pay their bills in the near future. Stocks are the least liquid current asset because they must first be sold (perhaps on credit) and the customers given a credit period in which to pay before they can be converted into cash.

4.3 Current liabilities are items which must be paid for in the near future. When payment becomes due, enough cash must be available. The managers of a business must therefore make sure that a regular supply of cash comes in (from current assets) at all times to meet the regular flow of payments it is necessary to provide for.

4.4 As the previous description of the cash cycle might suggest, the amount of current assets and current liabilities for any business will affect its liquidity. In other words, the volume of working capital helps us to judge the firm's ability to pay its bills.

The financing of working capital and business assets

4.5 EXAMPLE

BALANCE SHEET AS AT 31 DECEMBER 20X6

	£'000	£'000
Fixed assets		
Goodwill		50
Premises		700
Plant and machinery		300
		1,050
Current costs		
Stocks	99	
Debtors	50	
Cash in hand	1	
	150	
Current liabilities		
Bank overdraft	20	
Trade creditors	50	
Taxation due	30	
	100	
Net current assets (= working capital)		50
Total assets less current liabilities		1,100
Long-term liabilities		
Loan stock		200
		900
Capital and reserves		
Share capital		400
Reserves		500
		900

The **long-term funds** of the business are share capital and reserves of £900,000 and loan stock of £200,000, making £1,100,000 in total. These funds help to finance the business and we can calculate that these funds are being used as follows.

	£
To 'finance' goodwill	50,000
To finance premises	700,000
To finance plant and machinery	300,000
To finance working capital	50,000
	1,100,000

Working capital is therefore financed by the long-term funds of the business.

4.6 If a company has more current liabilities than current assets, it has **negative** working capital. This means that to some extent, current liabilities are helping to finance the fixed assets of the business. In the following balance sheet, working capital is negative (net current liabilities of £20,000).

BALANCE SHEET AS AT ....

	£	£
Fixed assets		220,000
Current assets	60,000	
Current liabilities	80,000	
Net current liabilities		(20,000)
Total assets less current liabilities		200,000
Capital and reserves		200,000

The fixed assets of £220,000 are financed by share capital and reserves (£200,000), but also by current liabilities (£20,000). Since current liabilities are debts which will soon have to be paid, the company is faced with more payments than it can find the cash from liquid assets to pay for. This means that the firm will have to

(a) Sell off some fixed assets to get the cash.

(b) Borrow money to overcome its cash flow problems, by offering any unmortgaged property as security for the borrowing.

(c) Be forced into 'bankruptcy' or 'liquidation' by the creditors who cannot be paid.

4.7 Clearly, a business must be able to pay its bills on time and this means that to have negative working capital would be financially unsound and dangerous. To be safe, a business should have current assets in excess of current liabilities, not just equality with current assets and current liabilities exactly the same amount.

4.8 The next question to ask then is whether there is an 'ideal' amount of working capital which it is prudent to have. In other words, is there an ideal relationship between the amount of current assets and the amount of current liabilities? Should a minimum proportion of current assets be financed by the long-term funds of a business?

4.9 These questions cannot be answered without a hard-and-fast rule, but the relative size of current assets and current liabilities are measured by so-called **liquidity ratios**.

Liquidity ratios

4.10 There are two common liquidity ratios.

(a) The current ratio or working capital ratio
(b) The quick ratio or acid test ratio

> **KEY TERM**
>
> The **current ratio** or **working capital ratio** is the ratio of current assets to current liabilities.

4.11 A 'prudent' current ratio is sometimes said to be 2:1. In other words, current assets should be twice the size of current liabilities. This is a rather simplistic view of the matter, because particular attention needs to be paid to certain matters.

(a) Bank overdrafts: these are technically repayable on demand, and therefore must be classified as current liabilities. However, many companies have semi-permanent overdrafts in which case the likelihood of their having to be repaid in the near future is remote. It would also often be relevant to know a company's overdraft limit - this may give a truer indication of liquidity than a current or quick ratio.

(b) Are the year-end figures typical of the year as a whole? This is particularly relevant in the case of seasonal businesses. For example, many large retail companies choose an accounting year end following soon after the January sales and their balance sheets show a higher level of cash and lower levels of stock and creditors than would be usual at any other time in the year.

4.12 In practice, many businesses operate with a much lower current ratio and in these cases, the best way to judge their liquidity would be to look at the current ratio at different dates over a period of time. If the trend is towards a lower current ratio, we would judge that the liquidity position is getting steadily worse.

4.13 For example, if the liquidity ratios of two firms A and B are as follows.

	1 Jan	*1 Apr*	*1 July*	*1 Oct*
Firm	A1.2 : 1	1.2 : 1	1.2 : 1	1.2 : 1
Firm	B1.3 : 1	1.2 : 1	1.1 : 1	1.0 : 1

we could say that firm A is maintaining a stable liquidity position, whereas firm B's liquidity is deteriorating. We would then begin to question firm B's continuing ability to pay its bills. A bank for instance, would need to think carefully before granting any request from firm B for an extended overdraft facility.

4.14 It is dangerous however to leap to conclusions when analysing ratios. As well as seasonal variations, it is possible that there is not so much overtrading as deliberately selling hard in order to build up business over time. What looks like a poor balance sheet in one year may develop later into a much bigger and better one.

4.15 **The quick ratio** is used when we take the view that stocks take a long time to get ready for sale, and then there may be some delay in getting them sold, so that stocks are not particularly liquid assets. If this is the case, a firm's liquidity depends more heavily on the amount of debtors, short-term investments and cash that it has to match its current liabilities.

> **KEY TERM**
>
> The quick ratio is the ratio of current assets **excluding stocks** to current liabilities.

4.16 A 'prudent' quick ratio is 1:1. In practice, many businesses have a lower quick ratio (eg 0.5:1), and the best way of judging a firm's liquidity would be to look at the trend in the quick ratio over a period of time. The quick ratio is also known as the **liquidity ratio** and as the **acid test ratio.**

Exam focus point

If asked to calculate and comment on liquidity ratios, do not make the common mistake of limiting the discussion to comments about the ideal ratios of 2:1 and 1:1 and the change since last year. To score well on such a question you also need to comment on the change in the component parts of working capital and on any outflow on fixed assets.

4.17 EXAMPLE: WORKING CAPITAL RATIOS

The cash balance of Wing Ltd has declined significantly over the last 12 months. The following financial information is provided.

		Year to 31 December	
		20X2	*20X3*
		£	£
Sales		573,000	643,000
Purchases of raw materials		215,000	264,000
Raw materials consumed		210,000	256,400
Cost of goods manufactured		435,000	515,000
Cost of goods sold		420,000	460,000
Debtors		97,100	121,500
Creditors		23,900	32,500
Stocks:	raw materials	22,400	30,000
	work in progress	29,000	34,300
	finished goods	70,000	125,000

All purchases and sales were made on credit.

Required

(a) Analyse the above information, which should include calculations of the cash operating cycle (the time lag between making payment to suppliers and collecting cash from customers) for 20X2 and 20X3.

(b) Prepare a brief report on the implications of the changes which have occurred between 20X2 and 20X3.

Notes

(a) Assume a 360 day year for the purpose of your calculations and that all transactions take place at an even rate.

(b) All calculations are to be made to the nearest day.

4.18 SOLUTION

(a) The information should be analysed in as many ways as possible, and you should not omit any important items. The relevant calculations would seem to be as follows.

(i)

	20X2	*20X3*
	£	£
Sales	573,000	643,000
Cost of goods sold	(420,000)	(460,000)
Gross profit	153,000	183,000
Gross profit percentage	26.7%	28.5%

(ii) Size of working capital and liquidity ratios, ignoring cash/bank overdrafts.

		£	£
Debtors		97,100	121,500
Stocks:	raw materials	22,400	30,000
	work in progress	29,000	34,300
	finished goods	70,000	125,000
		218,500	310,800
Creditors		(23,900)	(32,500)
Working capital (ignoring cash or overdraft)		194,600	278,300
Current ratio		$\frac{218,500}{23,900}$	$\frac{310,800}{32,500}$
		= 9.1:1	= 9.6:1

(iii) *Turnover periods*

	20X2	days	20X3	days
Raw materials in stock	$\frac{22,400}{210,000} \times 360 =$	38.4	$\frac{30,000}{256,400} \times 360 =$	42.1
Work in progress	$\frac{29,000}{435,000} \times 360 =$	24.0	$\frac{34,300}{515,000} \times 360 =$	23.9
Finished goods stock	$\frac{70,000}{420,000} \times 360 =$	60.0	$\frac{125,000}{460,000} \times 360 =$	97.8
Debtors' collection period	$\frac{97,100}{573,000} \times 360 =$	61.0	$\frac{121,500}{643,000} \times 360 =$	68.0
Creditors' payment period	$\frac{23,900}{215,000} \times 360 =$	(40.0)	$\frac{32,500}{264,000} \times 360 =$	(44.3)
Cash cycle		143.4		187.5

(b) Sales were about 12% higher in 20X3 than in 20X2 and the cost of sales was about 9% higher. The investments in stocks and debtors minus creditors rose from £194,600 to £278,300, ie by £83,700 or nearly 44%. This is completely out of proportion to the volume of increase in trade, which indicates that working capital turnover periods are not being properly controlled.

The increase in working capital of £83,700 means that the net cash receipts from profits in 20X3 were £83,700 less than they would have been if there had been no increase at all in stocks and debtors (less creditors) during 20X3. The company might therefore have an unnecessary bank overdraft, although we are not given enough information to comment on this point fully.

Current assets must be financed by a combination of long-term funds and current liabilities. Working capital (current assets minus current liabilities) is the amount of this finance provided by long-term funds. A large and unnecessary increase in working capital will mean that too many long-term funds are invested in current assets (and they are obviously being invested wastefully if trading operations can be sustained with less working capital). A current ratio (ignoring cash and bank overdraft) of over 9:1 would appear excessive, both in 20X2 and 20X3.

The causes of the increase in working capital in 20X3 are the increase in sales but mainly the increased length of turnover periods.

Raw materials stock turnover has risen from 38 to 42 days, although this increase was 'cancelled out' by an extension of the credit taken from suppliers, from 40 to 44 days. Debtors, already allowed 61 days to pay in 20X2, were allowed 68 days in 20X3 and this would seem to be an excessive length of time. The most serious change, however, is the increase in the finished goods stock turnover period from 60 days (2 months) to 98 days (over 3 months) and it is difficult to see an obvious reason why this should have occurred, although there may have been a temporary build-up at the end of 20X3 in preparation for a big sales drive.

Exam focus point

The May 2001 exam asked in Section B for a calculation of current ratio and debtor days and in Section C for a calculation of stock days

5 GEARING — May 2001

5.1 Companies are financed by different types of capital and each type expects a return in the form of interest or dividend.

KEY TERM

Gearing is a method of comparing how much of the long-term capital of a business is provided by equity (ordinary shares and reserves) and how much is provided by 'prior charge capital' investors who are entitled to interest or dividend before ordinary shareholders can have a dividend themselves.

FORMULA TO LEARN

The two most usual methods of measuring gearing are

(a) $$\frac{\text{Prior charge capital (long – term loans and preference shares)}}{\text{Equity (ordinary shares plus reserves)}} \times 100\%$$

(i) A business is low-geared if the gearing is less than 100%.
(ii) It is neutrally-geared if the gearing is exactly 100%.
(iii) It is high-geared if the gearing is more than 100%.

(b) $$\frac{\text{Prior charge capital (long – term loans and preference shares)}}{\text{Total long – term capital}} \times 100\%$$

5.2 A business is now low-geared if gearing is less than 50% (calculated under method (b)), neutrally-geared if gearing is exactly 50% and high-geared if it exceeds 50%.

5.3 Low gearing means that there is more equity finance in the business than there is prior charge capital. High gearing means the opposite - prior charge capital exceeds the amount of equity.

5.4 EXAMPLE

A numerical example might be helpful.

Draught Ltd, the company in paragraph 2.8, has a gearing of

$$\frac{\text{£200,000}}{\text{£400,000}} \quad \frac{\text{(debenture loans plus preference shares)}}{\text{(ordinary shares plus reserves)}} \times 100\% = 50\%$$

Why is gearing important?

5.5 Gearing can be important when a company wants to raise extra capital, because if its gearing is already too high, we might find that it is difficult to raise a loan. Would-be lenders might take the view that ordinary shareholders should provide a fair proportion of the total capital for the business and that at the moment they are not doing so, or they might be worried that profits are not sufficient to meet future interest payments.

When does gearing become excessive?

5.6 Unfortunately, there is no hard and fast answer to this question. The 'acceptable' level of gearing varies according to the country (eg average gearing is higher among companies in Japan than in Britain), the industry, and the size and status of the individual company within the industry. The more stable the company is, the 'safer' higher gearing should be.

5.7 The advantages of gearing (ie of using debt capital) are:

(a) Debt capital is cheaper.

(i) The reward (interest or preference dividend) is fixed permanently, and therefore diminishes in real terms if there is inflation. Ordinary shareholders, on the other hand, usually expect dividend growth.

(ii) The reward required by debt-holders is usually lower than that required by equity holders, because debt capital is often secured on company assets, whereas ordinary share capital is a more risky investment.

(iii) Payments of interest attract tax relief, whereas ordinary (or preference) dividends do not.

(b) Debt capital does not normally carry voting rights, but ordinary shares usually do. The issue of debt capital therefore leaves pre-existing voting rights unchanged.

(c) If profits are rising, and interest is fixed, ordinary shareholders will benefit from the growth in profits.

5.8 The main disadvantage of gearing is that if profits fall even slightly, the profit available to shareholders will fall at a greater rate.

Exam focus point

Calculation of a gearing ratio was in Section C of the May 2001 paper.

6 ITEMS IN COMPANY ACCOUNTS FORMATS

Question 5

You are given summarised results of an electrical engineering business, as follows.

PROFIT AND LOSS ACCOUNT

	Year ended 31.12.X7	Year ended 31.12.X6
	£'000	£'000
Turnover	60,000	50,000
Cost of sales	42,000	34,000
Gross profit	18,000	16,000
Operating expenses	15,500	13,000
	2,500	3,000
Interest payable	2,200	1,300
Profit before taxation	300	1,700
Taxation	350	600
(Loss) profit after taxation	(50)	1,100
Dividends	600	600
Transfer (from) to reserves	(650)	500

BALANCE SHEET

	£'000	£'000
Fixed assets		
Intangible	850	–
Tangible	12,000	11,000
	12,850	11,000
Current assets		
Stocks	14,000	13,000
Debtors	16,000	15,000
Bank and cash	500	500
	30,500	28,500
Creditors due within one year	24,000	20,000
Net current assets	6,500	8,500
Total assets less current liabilities	19,350	19,500
Creditors due after one year	6,000	5,500
	13,350	14,000
Capital and reserves		
Share capital	1,300	1,300
Share premium	3,300	3,300
Revaluation reserve	2,000	2,000
Profit and loss	6,750	7,400
	13,350	14,000

Required

(a) Prepare a table of the following 12 ratios, calculated for both years, clearly showing the figures used in the calculations.

Current ratio
Quick assets ratio
Stock turnover in days
Debtors turnover in days
Creditors turnover in days
Gross profit %
Net profit % (before taxation)
ROCE
Gearing

(b) Making full use of the information given in the question, of your table of ratios, and your common sense, comment on the apparent position of the business and on the actions of the management.

Answer

(a)	20X7	20X6
Current ratio	$\frac{30,500}{24,000} = 1.27$	$\frac{28,500}{20,000} = 1.43$

Quick assets ratio	$\frac{16,500}{24,000}$	= 0.69	$\frac{15,500}{20,000}$	= 0.78
Stock (number of days held)	$\frac{14,000}{42,000}$	× 365 = 122 days	$\frac{13,000}{34,000}$	× 365=140 days
Debtors (number of days outstanding	$\frac{16,000}{60,000}$	× 365 = 97 days	$\frac{15,000}{50,000}$	× 365=109 days
Creditors (number of days outstanding)	$\frac{24,000}{42,000}$	× 365 = 209 days	$\frac{20,000}{34,000}$	× 365=215 days
Gross profit	$\frac{18,000}{60,000}$	= 30%	$\frac{16,000}{50,000}$	= 32%
Net profit % (before taxation)	$\frac{300}{60,000}$	= 0.5%	$\frac{1,700}{50,000}$	= 3.4%
ROCE	$\frac{2,500}{19,350}$	= 13%	$\frac{3,000}{19,500}$	= 15%
Gearing	$\frac{6,000}{19,350}$	= 31%	$\frac{5,500}{19,500}$	= 28%

(b) Turnover has increased by 20%, but cost of sales has increased at a faster rate (23%) with the result that gross profit percentage has fallen by 2%. This trend may well be due to forces beyond the company's control such as the recession and the actions of suppliers and competitors.

Interest expense has increased significantly, and this is one of the main factors contributing to the after tax loss shown in 20X7. In view of the loss it was perhaps imprudent of the company to maintain the dividend at its 20X6 level although this may be a deliberate device to maintain shareholder confidence. Borrowing has increased, leading to a worsening of the gearing ratio.

As regards current assets, there is a welcome improvement in stock, debtors and creditors turnover which have all fallen. This is linked to a fall in the current and quick ratios neither of which, however, appears dangerously low.

An encouraging sign is that the company has invested in fixed assets which, it is to be hoped, will pay off in future years.

Question 6

Try to get hold of as many sets of published accounts as possible. Study them carefully to familiarise yourself with the format. Try to form your own opinions on how well the companies are doing.

As a morale booster you should repeat this exercise at later stages in your studies. You may be pleasantly surprised at the progress you make!

7 PLANNING YOUR ANSWERS

Exam focus point

Questions on interpreting company accounts generally call for discursive or 'wordy' answers, as do questions on internal and external audit. While you may feel like breathing a sigh of relief after all that number crunching, you should not be tempted to waffle. The best way to avoid going off the point is to prepare an answer plan. This has the advantage of making you think before you write and structure your answer logically.

7.1 The following approach may be adopted when preparing an answer plan.

(a) Read the question requirements.

(b) Skim through the question to see roughly what it is about.

(c) Read through the question carefully, underlining any key words.

(d) Set out the headings for the main parts of your answer. Leave space to insert points within the headings.

(e) Jot down points to make within the main sections, underlining points on which you wish to expand.

(f) Write your full answer.

Exam focus point

You should allow yourself the full time allocation for written answers, that is 1.8 minutes per mark. If, however, you run out of time, a clear answer plan with points in note form will earn you more marks than an introductory paragraph written out in full.

THE MAIN POINTS

You must learn these formulae, understand what they indicate and be able to explain what an increase or decrease means.

Current ratio	$\frac{\text{Current assets}}{\text{Current liabilities}}$
Quick assets (acid test) ratio	$\frac{\text{Current assets} - \text{stock}}{\text{Current liabilties}}$
Return on capital employed (ROCE)	$\frac{\text{Net profit before interest}}{\text{Total long} - \text{term capital}}$
Return on owner's equity (ROOE)	$\frac{\text{Profit after tax}}{\text{Share capital plus reserves}}$
Debtors turnover	$\frac{\text{Debtors}}{\text{Sales per day}}$, ie $\frac{\text{Debtor} \times 365}{\text{Sales}}$
Creditors turnover	$\frac{\text{Creditors}}{\text{Cost of sales per day}}$, ie $\frac{\text{Creditors}}{\text{Cost of sales}} \times 365$
Gross profit percentage	$\frac{\text{Gross profit}}{\text{Sales}}$
Net profit percentage	$\frac{\text{Net profit}}{\text{Sales}}$
Stock turnover	$\frac{\text{Average (or year} - \text{end) stock}}{\text{Cost of sales per day}}$, ie $\frac{\text{Stock} \times 365}{\text{Costof sales}}$

Chapter roundup

- The profit and loss account and balance sheet provide useful information about the condition of a business. Ratios can be calculated and trends identified so that different businesses can be compared or the performance of a business over time can be judged.
- The ratios which you need to be able to calculate for your examinations are as follows.
  - Return on capital employed
  - Gross profit percentage
  - Net profit percentage
  - Cost to sales ratios (eg cost of sales/sales, distribution costs/ sales, administrative expenses/sales)
  - Asset turnover
  - Debtors collection period
  - Creditors payment period
  - Current and quick ratios
  - Gearing
- Return on capital employed may be calculated in a number of ways. The examiner proposes to use the formula:

  $$\frac{\text{Net profit before tax and interest}}{\text{Average capital employed}}$$

  where average capital employed includes long-term, but not short-term finance.
- You also need to be able to interpret the ratios and suggest reasons for the results obtained.
- The interpretation of financial statements requires a large measure of common sense. For example:
  - you should not expect a firm of solicitors (say) to have substantial plant and machinery
  - you should not expect a chain of supermarkets to make many sales on credit or to turn over its (perishable) stock quickly
  - you should expect a business that 'piles 'em high and sells 'em cheap' to have a low gross profit margin
  - you should expect a more upmarket organisation to have higher selling and administrative costs, reflecting the level of service given to customers
- You should familiarise yourself with published accounts formats as much as possible both by exam question practice and if possible by looking at real life examples.

Quick quiz

1 A high profit margin will indicate?

A Effective cost control measures
B Increases in sales volume
C The sue of trade discounts to secure extra sales
D Increase in suppliers prices

2 Given opening stock £58,000, closing stock £62,000, opening creditors £15,000, closing creditors £25,000, payments to creditors £160,000. Calculate the rate of stock turnover.

A 2.74 times
B 2.58 times
C 2.66 times
D 2.76 times

3 A lengthening of the cash cycle will result in a smaller volume of working capital. True or false?

4 What does the 'quick ratio' measure?

A The rate of change of cash resources
B The speed with which debtors are collected
C The relationship between current assets (minus stock) and current liabilities
D The relationship between current assets and current liabilities

5 Capital gearing refers to?

A The relationship between ordinary shares and reserves
B The relationship between equity and preference shares
C A method of showing the relationship between prior charge capital and all forms of capital
D A method of explaining the risk of non payment of a dividend to the equity shareholders

Answers to quick quiz

1 A Correct.

B Sales volume increases do not necessarily mean high margins. High levels of sales of loss making profits would have the opposite effect.

C Trade discounts reduce invoiced prices and would tend to have the opposite effect.

D This would erode margins.

2 D Correct: purchases = £160,000 + £25,000 - £15,000 = £170,000

Cost of goods sold = £58,000 + £170,000 – £62,000 = £166,000

Average stock = £60,000, stock turnover = $\frac{£166,000}{£60,000}$ = 2.76 times

A If average stock is unobtainable, the use of average stock and purchases will give an acceptable answer.

B This is payments divided by closing stock.

C This is payments dividend by average stock.

3 False

4 C Correct, stock is excluded because it has to be sold to create a debtor balance.
A Incorrect.
B Incorrect, this is the debtor collection period.
D Incorrect, this is the current ratio.

5 C Correct, there is no single accepted definition but the key point is to compare outside borrowings with internally provided finance.

A Incorrect.

B Incorrect.

D The ordinary shareholders are always at risk, gearing is useful for the providers of debt capital as a measure of risk.

Now try the questions below from the Exam Question Bank

Number	Level	Marks	Time
65	Exam	15	27 mins
66	Exam	2	3 mins
67	Exam	2	3 mins

Question and answer bank

1 USERS OF ACCOUNTING INFORMATION

The Corporate Report identified many different user groups of accounting information. Identify those who might be interested in financial information about a large public company and describe their information needs. **15 Marks**

2 MCQ *3 mins*

Which of the following statements is true?

A Financial accountants provide historical information for internal use
B Financial accountants provide historical information for external use
C Financial accountants provide forward looking information for internal use
D Financial accountants provide forward looking information for external use **2 Marks**

3 PROFIT

A business receives and issues the following invoices and cash receipts and payments. There was no stock of goods for sale at either the beginning or end of the month.

	Invoice date	*Amount* £	*Date paid or received*
Purchases	8.9.X1	100	20.9.X1
	10.9.X1	200	2.10.X1
Sales	12.9.X1	200	25.9.X1
	30.9.X1	300	5.10.X1

Required

(a) The profit earned in September on a cash basis was:

Sales	£
Purchase	£
Profit	£

(b) The profit earned in September on an accruals basis was:

Sales	£
Purchase	£
Profit	£

5 Marks

4 DEFINITIONS

The observance of each of the following concepts is presumed in financial statements unless otherwise stated.

(a) Going concern
(b) Accruals
(c) Consistency
(d) Prudence

Required

Explain each of the above concepts giving examples of how each is observed in conventional financial statements. **15 Marks**

5 MCQ *3 mins*

Which basic accounting concept is being followed when a provision is made for bad and doubtful debts?

A Accruals
B Consistency
C Going concern
D Prudence **2 Marks**

6 ACCOUNTING BODIES *3 mins*

Write the full names of the following accounting bodies.

(i) FRC
(ii) FRRP
(iii) ASB **2 Marks**

7 THE ACCOUNTING EQUATION

Peter Reid decides he is going to open a bookshop called Easyread, which he does by investing £5,000 on 1 January 20X7. During the first month of Easyread's existence, the following transactions occur.

(a) Bookshelves are purchased for £1,800.
(b) Books are purchased for £2,000.
(c) Half of the books are sold for £1,500 cash.
(d) Peter draws £200 out of the business for himself.
(e) Peter's brother John loans £500 to the business.
(f) Carpets are purchased for £1,000 on credit (to be paid in two months time).
(g) A bulk order of books worth £400 is sold on credit (to be paid in one month's time) for £600.

Required

Write down the accounting equation after each transaction has occurred. **15 Marks**

8 MCQ *3 mins*

At 31 December 20X1, a business had net assets of £10,000. At 31 December 20X2 net assets had risen to £12,500. Profit for the year was £8,000 and no new capital was introduced. How much were drawings in the period.

A £2,500
B £3,000
C £5,500
D £10,500 **2 Marks**

9 PROFIT

At 1 January 20X4 a business had net assets of £15,000. By 31 December 20X4 it had:

	£
Buildings	4,000
Furniture	2,000
Bank overdraft	1,500
Debtors	3,500
Creditors	2,000
Proprietors capital	6,000

During the year the proprietor had introduced £1,000 of new capital and had drawings of £800. Calculate the profit for the year. **5 Marks**

10 FINANCIAL STATEMENTS

What is the difference between the balance sheet and the trading, profit and loss account? What is the difference between capital and revenue expenditure? Which of the following transaction is capital expenditure and which revenue expenditure?

(a) A bookseller buys a car for its director for £9,000.
(b) In the first year, the car is depreciated by £900.
(c) The business buys books for £1,500.
(d) The business builds an extension for £7,600.
(e) The original building is repainted, a job costing £1,200.
(f) A new sales assistant is taken on and his salary in the first year is £10,000. **10 Marks**

11 GROSS PROFIT *3 mins*

A business has prepared its draft profit and loss account which shows gross profit of £5,500 and net profit of £3,000. It is then realised that an invoice for £250 relating to cost of sales has been treated as an administration expense by mistake.

The correction of this error will **increase/decrease** gross profit by £______________ and **increase/decrease** net profit by £________________. **2 Marks**

12 MCQ *3 mins*

A business has spent £200 replacing worn out parts on a machine. How should this £200 be treated in the accounts and why?

A As revenue expenditure because it is repairing a fixed asset
B As capital expenditure because it is improving a fixed asset
C As revenue expenditure because it is likely to reoccur
D As capital expenditure because it is an small amount **2 Marks**

13 BUSINESS TRANSACTIONS

The following is a list of typical business transactions.

(a) The purchase of goods on credit.
(b) Allowance to credit customers upon the return of faulty goods.
(c) Refund from petty cash to an employee of an amount spend on entertaining a client.
(d) Credit card sales.

Required

For each transaction identify clearly

(i) The original document(s) for the data
(ii) The book of original entry for the transaction **10 Marks**

14 BEECHFIELD

Beechfield Ltd make use of a petty cash book as part of their book-keeping system. The following is a summary of the petty cash transactions for the month of November 20X9.

			£
November	1	Opening petty cash book float received from cashier	350
	2	Cleaning materials	5
	3	Postage stamps	10
	6	Envelopes	12
	8	Taxi fare	32
	10	Petrol for company car	17
	14	Typing paper	25
	15	Cleaning materials	4
	16	Bus fare	2
	20	Visitors' lunches	56
	21	Mops and brushes for cleaning	41
	23	Postage stamps	35
	27	Envelopes	12
	29	Visitors' lunches	30
	30	Photocopying paper	40

Required

Draw up the petty cash book for the month using analysis columns for stationery, cleaning, entertainment, travelling and postages. Show clearly the receipt of the amount necessary to restore the float and the balance brought forward for the start of the following month. Folio numbers are not required. **15 Marks**

15 FILL IN THE BLANKS *3 mins*

The sales book lists ______________________________.

The purchases book lists ______________________________.

The sales returns book lists ______________________________.

The purchases returns book lists ______________________________. **2 Marks**

16 J OCKEY *27 mins*

Mr J Ockey commenced trading as a wholesale stationer on 1 May 20X4 with a capital of £5,000 with which he opened a bank account for his business.

During May the following transactions took place.

May	1	Bought shop fittings and fixtures for cash form Store Fitments Ltd for £2,000
	2	Purchased goods on credit from Abel £650
	4	Sold goods on credit to Bruce £700
	9	Purchased goods on credit from Green £300
	11	Sold goods on credit to Hill £580
	13	Cash sales paid intact into bank £200
	16	Received cheque from Bruce in settlement of his account
	17	Purchased goods on credit from Kaye £800
	18	Sold goods on credit to Nailor £360
	19	Sent cheque to Abel in settlement of his account
	20	Paid rent by cheque £200
	21	Paid delivery expenses by cheque £50
	24	Received from Hill £200 on account
	30	Drew cheques for personal expenses £200 and assistant's wages £320
	31	Settled the account of Green

Required

(a) Record the foregoing in appropriate books of original entry. **5 Marks**

(b) Post the entries to the ledger accounts. **5 Marks**

(c) Post the entries to the sales and purchases ledger accounts. **5 Marks**

Total Marks = 15

Note. You are not required to complete any entries in personal accounts, nor are folio references required.

17 FILL IN THE BLANKS *3 mins*

____________________ are recorded in day books. The totals of day books are posted by double entry to ledger accounts in the ____________________ ____________________.

Individual invoice details in the day books are posted by single entry to accounts in the ____________________ ____________________. **2 Marks**

18 MCQ *3 mins*

An invoice for £18 received from a supplier is recorded as £81 in the purchases day book. When this error is corrected, it will affect:

A An account in the purchase ledger only
B Accounts in the nominal ledger only
C An account in the purchase ledger and accounts in the nominal ledger
D No accounts

2 Marks

19 HUBBLE *54 mins*

On 28.2.20X8, which is one month before the end of his financial year, the ledger accounts of A Hubble were as follows.

CASH

	£		£
Capital	9,500	Rent	2,750
Bank loan	3,000	Creditors	700
Sales	11,200	Interest	350
Debtors	400	Electricity	400
		Telephone	180
		Drawings	1,300

CAPITAL

	£		£
		Cash	9,500

BANK LOAN

	£		£
		Cash	3,000

SALES

	£		£
		Cash	11,200
		Debtors	4,600

DEBTORS

	£		£
Sales	4,600	Cash	400

RENT

	£		£
Cash	2,750		

PURCHASES

	£		£
Creditors	2,100		

CREDITORS

	£		£
Cash	700	Purchases	2,100

INTEREST

	£		£
Cash	350		

ELECTRICITY

	£		£
Cash	400		

TELEPHONE

	£		£
Cash	180		

DRAWINGS

	£		£
Cash	1,300		

During the last month of his financial year, A Hubble recorded the following transactions.

(a) He bought goods for £2,000, half for credit and half for cash.

(b) He paid the following amounts.

- (i) Interest £20
- (ii) Electricity £25
- (iii) Telephone £12

(c) He made sales of £3,500 of which £500 were for cash.

(d) He received £220 from debtors.

Required

(a) Post the transactions for March 20X8 into the ledger accounts. **15 Marks**

(b) Balance off the ledger accounts and draw up a trial balance. **8 Marks**

(c) Prepare a balance sheet as at 31.3.20X8 and a trading, profit and loss account for the year ended 31.3.20X8. **7 Marks**

Total Marks = 30

20 MCQ *3 mins*

The sales day book total for March of £250 was recorded in the nominal ledger as:

Cr Sales account
Cr Debtors account

At 31 December a trial balance was prepared. Would the trial balance balance?

A Yes
B No Credits would exceed debits by 250
C No Credits would exceed debits by £500
D No Debits would exceed credits by £250

2 Marks

21 TRIAL BALANCE *3 mins*

When a trial balance is prepared the clerk treats purchases of £3,000 as a credit balance. Credits exceed/are smaller than debits in the trial balance by £________________. **2 Marks**

22 RENT, RATES AND INSURANCE

From the information given below you are required:

(a) To calculate the charge to the profit and loss account for the year ended 30 June 20X6 in respect of rent, rates and insurance.

(b) To state the amount of accrual or prepayment for rent, rates and insurance as at 30 June 20X6.

The accruals and prepayments as at 30 June 20X5 were as follows.

	£
Rent accrued	2,000
Rates prepaid	1,500
Insurance prepaid	1,800

Payments made during the year ended 30 June 20X6 were as follows.

		£
20X5		
10 August	Rent, three months to 31 July 20X5	3,000
26 October	Insurance, one year to 31 October 20X6	6,000
2 November	Rates, six months to 31 March 20X6	3,500
12 December	Rent, four months to 30 November 20X5	4,000
20X6		
17 April	Rent, four months to 31 March 20X6	4,000
9 May	Rates, six months to 30 September 20X6	3,500

15 Marks

23 MCQ *3 mins*

During the year, £3,000 was paid to the electricity board. At the beginning of the year, £1,000 was owed, at the year end, £1,200 was owed.

What is the charge for electricity in the year's profit and loss account?

A £3,000
B £3,200
C £4,000
D £5,200

2 Marks

24 TRIAL BALANCE

Fred's trial balance included the following.

	£	£
Purchases	6,000	
Opening stock	400	
Carriage inwards	200	
Carriage outwards	150	
Sales		12,500

Closing stock cost £1,000, but it is slightly water damaged. Fred thinks that he can sell it for £1,100 but only if he spends £200 on repackaging it.

Gross profit is £______________. **5 Marks**

25 GEORGE *27 mins*

George is a wholesaler and the following information relates to his accounting year ending 30 September 20X2.

(a) Goods are sold on credit terms, but some cash sales are also transacted.

(b) At 1 October 20X1 George's trade debtors amounted to £30,000 against which he had set aside a provision for doubtful debts of 5%.

(c) On 15 January 20X2 George was informed the Fall Ltd had gone into liquidation, owing him £2,000. This debt was outstanding from the previous year.

(d) Cash sales during the year totalled £46,800, whilst credit sales amounted to £187,800.

(e) £182,500 was received from trade debtors.

(f) Settlement discounts allowed to credit customers were £5,300.

(g) Apart from Fall Ltd's bad debt, other certain bad debts amounted to £3,500.

(h) George intends to retain the provision for doubtful debts account at 5% of outstanding trade debtors as at the end of the year, and the necessary entry is to be made.

You are required to enter the above transactions in George's ledger accounts and (apart from the cash and bank and profit and loss accounts) balance off the accounts and bring down the balances as at 1 October 20X2. **15 Marks**

26 BAD AND DOUBTFUL DEBTS *3 mins*

At 1January 20X1, there was a provision for doubtful debts of £2,000. During the year, £1,000 of debts was written off, and £800 of bad debts was recovered. At 31 December 20X1, it was decided to adjust the bad debts provision to 10% of debtors which are £30,000.

What is the total bad debt expense for the year?

A £200
B £1,200
C £2,000
D £2,800

2 Marks

27 TRIAL BALANCE *3 mins*

When a trial balance was prepared, two ledger accounts were omitted.

Discounts received	£1,500
Discounts allowed	£1,000

The total of debits balances exceed/fall below the total of credit balances by £________________.

2 Marks

28 AFTER THE STOCK COUNT *27 mins*

After its end of year physical stock count and valuation, the accounts staff of Caveat Emptor Ltd have reached a valuation of £153,699 at cost for total stocks held as at the year end.

However, on checking the figures, the chief bookkeeper has come across the following additional facts.

(a) On one of the stock sheets, a sub-total value of £6,275 had been carried forward on to the next sheet as £6,725.

(b) 260 units of stock number 73113X which cost £0.60 each have been extended into the total value column at £6 each.

(c) The stock count includes £4,658 of goods bought on credit and still not paid for as at the year end.

(d) The stock count includes damaged goods which originally cost £2,885. These could be repaired at a cost of £921 and sold for £3,600.

(e) The stock count excludes 300 units of stock item 730052 which were sold to a customer Seesaft Ltd on a sale or return basis, at a price of £8 each. The original cost of the units was £5 each. Seesaft Ltd has not yet indicated to Caveat Emptor Ltd whether these goods have been accepted, or whether they will eventually be returned.

(f) The stock count includes 648 units of stock item 702422. These cost £7.30 each originally but because of dumping on the market by overseas suppliers, a price war has flared up and the unit price of the item has fallen to £6.50. The price reduction is expected to be temporary, lasting less than a year or so, although some observers of the market predicted that the change might be permanent. Caveat Emptor Ltd has already decided that if the price reduction last longer than six months, it will reduce its resale price of the item from £10.90 to about £10.

Required

Calculate the closing stock figure for inclusion in the annual accounts of Caveat Emptor Ltd, making whatever adjustments you consider necessary in view of items (a) to (f). Explain your treatment of each item. **15 Marks**

29 MCQ *3 mins*

Which two of the following statements are true?

(i) In times of inflation, FIFO will give you a higher profit than LIFO.
(ii) In times of inflation LIFO will give you a higher profit than FIFO.
(iii) FIFO matches revenue with up to date costs

A (i) and (iii)
B (i) and (iv)
C (ii) and (iii)
D (ii) and (iv) **2 Marks**

30 STOCK *3 mins*

These records were kept for a stock item in May.

May	1	100 units in stock at £10 each
	5	50 units bought at £10 each
	12	60 units sold
	20	20 units bought at £8 each
	29	80 units sold

The value of the stock at May 300:

(a) Using FIFO is £____________________.
(b) Using LIFO is £____________________. **2 Marks**

31 SPARKS *54 mins*

Sparks has been trading for a number of years as an electrical appliance retailer and repairer in premises which he rents at an annual rate of £1,500 payable in arrears. Balances appearing in his books at 1 January 20X1 were as follows.

	£	£
Capital account		1,808
Motorvan		1,200
Fixtures and fittings		806
Provision for depreciation on motor van		720
Provisions for depreciation on fixtures and fittings		250
Stock at cost		366
Debtors for credit sales		
Brown	160	
Blue	40	
Stripe	20	
		220
Cash at bank		672
Cash in hand		5
Loan from Flex		250
Creditors for supplies		
Live	143	
Negative	80	
Earth	73	
		296
Amount owing for electricity		45
Rates paid in advance		100

Although Sparks has three credit customers the majority of his sales and services are for cash, out of which he pays various expenses before banking the balance.

The following transactions took place during the first four months of 20X1.

	January	*February*	*March*	*April*
	£	£	£	£
Suppliers' invoices				
Live	468	570	390	602
Negative	-	87	103	64
Earth	692	-	187	-
Capital introduced		500		
Bankings of cash (from cash sales)	908	940	766	1,031
Expenditure out of cash sales before banking				
Drawings	130	120	160	150
Stationery	12	14	26	21
Travelling	6	10	11	13
Petrol and van repairs	19	22	37	26
Sundry expenses	5	4	7	3
Postage	12	10	15	19
Cleaner's wages	60	60	65	75
Goods invoiced to credit customers				
Brown	66	22	10	12
Blue	120	140	130	180
Stripe	44	38	20	48
Cheque payments (other than those to suppliers)				
Telephone	40	49	59	66
Electricity	62	47	20	106
Rates	-	-	220	-
Motor van (1 February 20X1)	-	800	-	-
Unbanked at the end of April	-	-	-	12

Sparks pays for goods by cheque one month after receipt of invoice, and receives a settlement discount of 15% from each supplier.

Credit customers also pay be cheque one month after receipt of invoice, and are given a settlement discount of 10% of the invoice price.

Required

(a) Write up the ledger accounts of Sparks for the four months to 30 April 20X1, and extract a trial balance after balancing off the accounts. **15 Marks**

(b) Prepare:

(i) trading and profit and loss accounts for the four months
(ii) a balance sheet on 30 April 20X1

after dealing with the following matters.

(i) The payment of £800 for a new motor van represents the balance paid to the garage after being granted a part-exchange value of £500 on the old van.

(ii) Depreciation is provided at the rate of 20% per annum on the cost of motor vans and at the rate of 10% on the cost of fixtures and fittings. No depreciation is to be provided in the period of disposal.

(iii) Interest on the loan from Flex is to be accrued at 10% per annum and credited to his account.

(iv) Amounts owing at 30 April 20X1 were electricity £22, and telephone £15. The payment for rates was for six months in advance from 1 March.

(v) Included in the payments for telephone was one of Sparks' private bills of £37 which is to be charged to him.

(vi) Stock at cost on 30 April 20X1 amounted to £390. **15 Marks**

Total Marks = 30

32 MCQ *3 mins*

During the year, a car was traded in for £3,000 against the cost (£10,000) of a new car. The old car had cost £8,000 and had a net book value at the time of trade in of £2,000.

The balance due on the new car was paid in cash and was debited to the cars account. No other entries were made.

What net adjustment is required to the cars account?

A Dr £10,000
B Dr £3,000
C Cr £8,000
D Cr £5,000 **2 Marks**

33 PROFIT ON DISPOSAL *3 mins*

On 31 March 20X9 a machine was sold which cost £20,000 on 1 May 20X5. The profit on disposal was £1,500. The depreciation policy is 20% pa straight line, with a full year being charged in year of acquisition and none in the year of sale. The year end is 31 December.

The sale proceeds were £________________. **2 Marks**

34 CAMFORD *27 mins*

The Treasurer of the Camford School Fund is attempting to reconcile the balance shown in the cash book with that appearing on the bank pass sheets. According to the cash book, the balance at the bank as at 31 May 20X2 was £1,900, whilst the bank pass sheets disclosed an overdrawn amount £470. Upon investigation, the treasurer identified the following discrepancies.

(a) A cheque paid to Summer Ltd for £340 had been entered in the cash book at £430. debit 90

(b) Cash paid into the bank for £100 had been entered in the cash book as £90. debit 10

(c) A transfer of £1,500 to the Midlands Savings Bank had not been entered in the cash book. credit 1500

(d) A receipt of £10 shown on the bank statement had not been entered in the cash book. debit 10

(e) Cheques drawn amounting to £40 had not been paid into the bank. timing

(f) The cash book balance had been incorrectly brought down at 1 June 20X1 as a debit balance of £1,200 instead of a debit balance of £1,100.

(g) Bank charges of £20 do not appear in the cash book.

(h) Receipts of £900 paid into the bank on 31 May 20X2 do not appear on the bank pass sheets until 1 June 20X2.

(i) A standing order payment of £30 had not been entered in the cash book.

(j) A cheque for £50 previously received and paid into the bank had been returned by the subscriber's bank marked 'account closed'.

(k) The bank received a direct debit of £100 from an anonymous subscriber.

(l) Cheques paid into the bank had been incorrectly totalled. The total amount should have been £170 instead of £150.

You are required to draw up a bank reconciliation statement as at 31 May 20X2. **15 Marks**

35 MCQ *3 mins*

A debit entry in the cash book will have which effect on the level of a bank overdraft and a bank balance?

	Bank overdraft	*Bank balance*
A	Increase	Increase
B	Decrease	Decrease
C	Increase	Decrease
D	Decrease	Increase

2 Marks

36 BANK RECONCILIATIONS *3 mins*

When preparing a bank reconciliation, it is realised that:

(i) There are unpresented cheques of £3,000.
(ii) There are unrecorded lodgements of £2,500
(iii) Bank charges of £35 have not been recorded in the cash book.
(iv) A cheque written out to pay a supplier £39 was entered in the cash book as £93.

The necessary adjustment to the cash book is a debit/credit of £____________. **2 Marks**

37 P & CO *18 mins*

P & Co maintain a sales ledger control account within the nominal ledger. At 30 November 20X0, the total of the list of individual balances extracted from the sales ledger was £15,800, which did not agree with the balance on the sales ledger control account. An examination of the books revealed the following information, which can be used to reconcile the sales ledger and the sales ledger control account.

(i) The credit balance of £420 in Ahmed's purchase ledger account had been set off against his account in the sales ledger, but no entries had been made in the sales and purchase ledger control accounts.

(ii) The personal account of Mahmood was undercast by £90.

(iii) Yasmin's balance of (debit) £780 had been omitted from the list of balances.

(iv) Thomas' personal account balance of £240 had been removed from the sales ledger as a bad debt, but no entry had been made in the sales ledger control account.

(v) The January total of £8,900 in the sales daybook had been posted as £9,800.

(vi) A credit note to Charles for £1,000, plus VAT of £300, had been posted to the sales ledger control account as £1,300 and to Charles' personal account as £1,000.

(vii) The total on the credit side of Edward's personal account had been overcast by £125.

Required

(a) Prepare the journal entries, where appropriate, to correct these errors. (Note: You are *not* required to give narrative descriptions for the journal entries.) **3 Marks**

(b) Prepare an amended total of the balances extracted from the sales ledger. **4 Marks**

(c) Prepare the sales ledger control account, showing the opening balance *before* these errors had been corrected and the closing balance *after* they have been corrected. **3 Marks**

Total Marks = 10

38 CONTROL ACCOUNTS *3 mins*

When reconciling the creditors control account to the list of balances, it was discovered than an invoice received from a supplier for £72 had been recorded in the purchases day book as £27.

What adjustment is necessary to the control account and the list of balances?

	Control account	*List of balances*
A	Debit £45	Add £45
B	Credit £45	Add £45
C	Debit £45	Subtract £45
D	Credit £45	Subtract £45

2 Marks

39 SALES DAY BOOK *3 mins*

The sales day book has been undercast by £50, and an invoice for £20 has been entered into the sales day book twice.

The necessary adjustment to the debtors control account is £_________________ debit/credit.

2 Marks

40 HYPER

The following extracts are taken from Hyper Ltd's accounts for the quarter ended 30 June 20X1.

	£
Debtors balance, 1 April 20X1	40,000
Creditors balance, 1 April 20X1	22,000
VAT creditor, 1 April 20X1	4,100

Transactions during the quarter were as follows.

	£
Invoiced sales, including VAT	141,000
Purchases on credit, including VAT	84,600
Payments made for credit purchases	92,700
Receipts from debtors	128,300
Payment to VAT creditor	4,100

The rate of VAT during the quarter was 17.5% and this rate applied to all purchases and sales.

Required

Prepare the ledger account entries to record these transactions. **15 Marks**

41 MCQ *3 mins*

Which of the following is *not* a valid reason for adding 17.5% VAT on the goods sold by a business?

A A business is not registered for VAT.
B The customer is not registered for VAT.
C The business made sales of exempt products.
D The business made sales of zero-rated products. **2 Marks**

42 VAT *3 mins*

In its first period of trading a business has charged VAT of £12,000 on its credit sales and £2,000 on its cash sales. VAT suffered on credit purchases is £3,000 and on cash expenses and purchases is £1,500. The amount owed to Customs & Excise is £______________. **2 Marks**

43 PAYROLL *27 mins*

As at 1 November 20X3, the following balances existed in the ledger of Payroll Ltd.

	£
Creditors	800
Bad debts provision	450
Wages control	38
PAYE income tax deductions	35
National Insurance contributions liability	44

During the year ended 31 October 20X4 the following transactions occurred.

	£
Gross wages earned	2,000
Cash paid to suppliers	5,400
Discounts received	100
Debtors and creditors accounts set off against each other and settled by contra	700
Sales on credit	12,000
Purchases on credit	6,000
Cash received from customers	11,800
Discounts allowed	300
Bad debts written off against the provision	200
Bad debts previously written off now recovered in cash	50
Increase in the bad debts provision charged to profit and loss account	100
Net wages paid in cash	1,330
PAYE income tax deducted from employees' wages	407
National Insurance contributions deducted from employees' wages	260
National Insurance contributions, employer's contribution	290
Cash paid to Inland Revenue for:	
PAYE income tax deductions	400
Employer's and employees' National Insurance contributions	546
Debtors at 31 October 20X4 amounted to £1,000	

There were no cash sales or cash purchases during the year.

You are required to write up the following accounts in the company's ledger for the year ended 31 October 20X4.

(a) Creditors
(b) Debtors
(c) Provision for doubtful debts
(d) Wages control
(e) PAYE income tax deductions
(f) National Insurance contributions liability **15 Marks**

44 MCQ *3 mins*

Gross payroll cost recorded in the profit and loss account is:

A Gross pay paid to employees plus employers National Insurance contributions and any employers pension contributions.

B Net pay paid to employees' plus employer's National Insurance contributions and any employer's pension contributions.

C Gross pay paid to employees plus employer's and employees' National Insurance contributions.

D Net pay paid to employees plus employer's and employees' National Insurance contributions.

2 Marks

45 PAYE AND NIC *3 mins*

The double entry to record PAYE and employees' National Insurance contributions is:

DEBIT ______________________________

CREDIT ______________________________ **2 Marks**

46 BRENDA BAILEY *27 mins*

The following trial balance has been extracted from the accounts of Brenda Bailey, a sole trader.

BRENDA BAILEY
TRIAL BALANCE AS AT 30 JUNE 20X9

	Dr	*Cr*
	£	£
Sales		427,726
Purchases	302,419	
Carriage inwards	476	
Carriage outwards	829	
Wages and salaries	64,210	
Rent and rates	12,466	
Heat and light	4,757	
Stock at 1 July 20X8	15,310	
Drawings	21,600	
Equipment at cost	102,000	
Motor vehicles at cost	43,270	
Provision for depreciation		
Equipment		22,250
Motor vehicles		8,920
Debtors	50,633	
Creditors		41,792
Bank		3,295
Sundry expenses	8,426	
Cash	477	
Capital		122,890
	626,873	626,873

The following information as at 30 June 20X9 is also available.

(a) £350 is owing for heat and light.

(b) £620 has been prepaid for rent and rates.

(c) Depreciation is to be provided for the year as follows.

Equipment - 10% on cost
Motor vehicles- 20% on cost

(d) Stock at the close of business was valued at £16,480.

Required

Prepare Brenda Bailey's trading and profit and loss account for the year ended 30 June 20X9 and her balance sheet at that date. **15 Marks**

47 SUSPENSE ACCOUNT *3 mins*

When a trial balance was prepared, a suspense account was opened. It was discovered that the only error that had been made was to record £350 of discounts received on the wrong side of the trial balance.

What is the journal to correct this error?

A	Dr	Discounts received	£350
	Cr	Suspense	£350
B	Dr	Suspense	£350
	Cr	Discounts received	£350
C	Dr	Discounts received	£700
	Cr	Suspense	£700
D	Dr	Suspense	£700
	Cr	Discounts received	£700

2 Marks

48 MCQ *3 mins*

Materials used to repair some machinery have been treated as purchases in the draft account. Correcting this error will have what effect on gross profit and net assets?

	Gross profit	*Net assets*
A	Increase	No change
B	Increase	Increase
C	Decrease	Decrease
D	No change	Increase

2 Marks

49 GILTAN GOLF CLUB *36 mins*

The treasurer of the Giltan Golf Club has prepared the following receipts and payments account for the year ended 31 March 20X8.

	£			£
Balance at 1 April 20X7	682	Functions		305
Subscriptions	2,930	Repairs		146
Functions	367	Telephone		67
Sale of land	1,600	Extensions to clubhouse		600
Bank interest	60	Furniture		135
Bequest	255	Heat and light		115
Sundry income	46	Salary and wages		2,066
		Sundry expenses		104
		Balance c/d:		
		Bank	2,300	
		Cash	102	
				2,402
	5,940			5,940

The treasurer has supplied the following additional information.

(a) Subscriptions received included £65 which had been in arrears at 31 March 20X7 and £35 which had been paid for the year commencing 1 April 20X8.

(b) Land sold had been valued in the club's books at cost £500.

(c) Accrued expenses:

	31 March 20X7	*31 March 20X8*
	£	£
Heat and light	32	40
Wages	12	14
Telephone	14	10
	58	64

(d) Depreciation is to be charged on the original cost of assets appearing in the books at 31 March 20X8 as follows.

Buildings	5 per cent
Fixtures and fittings	10 per cent
Furniture	20 per cent

(e) The following balances are from the club's books at 31 March 20X7.

	£
Land at cost	4,000
Buildings at cost	3,200
Buildings provision for depreciation	860
Fixtures and fittings at cost	470
Fixtures and fittings provision for depreciation	82
Furniture at cost	380
Furniture provision for depreciation	164
Subscriptions in arrears (including £15 from a lapsed member who had emigrated)	80
Subscriptions in advance	30
Accrued expenses	58
Bank	600
Cash	82
Accumulated fund	7,618

Required

Prepare an income and expenditure account for the year ended 31 March 20X8. **20 Marks**

50 MCQ *3 mins*

At 1 January 20X4 a club had £500 of subscriptions received in advance and 10 members still owed £20 each for their year's subscription. At 31 December £600 had been received in advance for next year and £180 was owed by members. During the year £1,200 was received from members.

The amount credited to the income and expenditure account for the year to 31.12.X4 was:

A £480
B £1,080
C £1,200
D £1,920 **2 Marks**

51 SUBSCRIPTIONS *3 mins*

At the beginning of the year, a club had subscriptions in arrears of £50 and subscriptions received in advance of £80. At the end of the year, subscriptions in arrears were £100, and subscriptions received in advance were £60. Subscriptions received in the year were £2,060.

(a) The figure for subscriptions in an income and expenditure account would be £____________.

(b) The figure for subscriptions in a receipts and payments record would be £____________. **2 Marks**

52 HIGHTON *36 mins*

A Highton is in business as a general retailer. He does not keep a full set of accounting records. However it has been possible to extract the following details from the few records that are available.

		1 April 20X1	*31 March 20X2*
		£	£
Freehold land and buildings at cost		10,000	10,000
Motor vehicle (cost £3,000)		2,250	
Stock, at cost		3,500	4,000
Trade debtors		500	1,000
Prepayments:	motor vehicle expenses	200	300
	property insurance	50	100
Cash at bank		550	950
Cash in hand		100	450
Loan from Highton's father		10,000	
Trade creditors		1,500	1,800
Accruals:	electricity	200	400
	motor vehicle expenses	200	100

Extract from a rough cash book for the year to 31 March 20X2

	£
Receipts	
Cash sales	80,400
Payments	£
Cash purchases	17,000
Drawings	7,000
General shop expenses	100
Telephone	100
Wages	3,000

Extract from the bank pass sheets for the year to 31 March 20X2

	£
Receipts	
Cash banked	52,850
Cheques from trade debtors	8,750
	£
Payments	
Cheques to suppliers	47,200
Loan repayment (including interest)	10,100
Electricity	400
Motor vehicle expenses	1,000
Property insurance	150
Rates	300
Telephone	300
Drawings	1,750

Note. Depreciation is to be provided on the motor vehicle at a rate of 25% per annum on cost.

You are required to prepare a trading and profit and loss account for the year to 31 March 20X2, and a balance sheet as at that date. **20 Marks**

53 MCQ *3 mins*

At 1 January 20X1 creditors were owed £10,000, by 31 December 20X1 they were owed £8,000. In the year, debtors and creditors contras were £3,500, and £350 of debit balances were transferred to debtors, credit purchases were £60,000 and £2,500 of discounts were received.

What was paid to suppliers during the year?

A £55,650
B £56,000
C £56,350
D £58,000 **2 Marks**

54 OPENING STOCK *3 mins*

During the year, all sales were made at a gross profit margin of 10%. Sales were £25,500, purchases were £22,000 and closing stock was £5,000.

Opening stock was £___________. **2 Marks**

55 EXCEL *54 mins*

The following balances were extracted from the accounting records of Excel Ltd, a car hire and taxi service company in respect of the year ended 30th November 20X5.

	£
Motor cars	111,200
Depreciation - motor cars to 30th November 20X4	46,320
Revenue from business operations	510,500
Ordinary shares - 200,000 of £1 each, allotted and fully paid	200,000
Retained profits at 30th November 20X4	127,200
Drivers' wages and expenses	245,200
Motor vehicle expenses	
Licence and insurance	7,500
Repairs etc.	35,460
Petrol and oil	45,310
Trade debtors	62,530
Administration expenses	30,460
Advertising expenses	12,540
Directors' remuneration	40,000
12% Debentures issued 1st September 20X5	
(interest payable January and July)	120,000
Interim dividend on ordinary shares	12,000
Freehold premises at cost	420,000
Stock at 30th November 20X4	
Petrol and oil	1,200
Vehicle spares	700
Share premium	40,000
Cash at bank	19,920

Additional information relevant to the year ended 30th November 20X5 is as follows.

(a) Trade debtors include bad debts of £890. In addition, it is considered necessary to make a provision for doubtful debts of 3% of debtors.

(b) The following expenses were outstanding at 30th November 20X5.

	£
Advertising	800
Auditor's fee	2,000
Repairs	1,450

(c) Prepayments in respect of licences and insurance amounted to £1,500.

(d) Stocks at 30th November 20X5 were

	£
Petrol and oil	1,640
Vehicle spares	3,170

(e) All the motor vehicles were bought after 1st December 20X1. The depreciation of the vehicles is provided from the date of purchase to the date of sale at the rate of 25% per annum on the straight line method. The motor vehicles figure is made up as follows.

	£
Cost to 30th November 20X4	85,200
Additions - 1 September 20X5	32,000
Sale proceeds 1 September 20X5 (cost £24,000 on 1 December 20X2)	6,000

(f) A final ordinary share dividend of 12p per share is proposed for the year ended 30th November 20X5.

Required

(a) Prepare the profit and loss appropriation accounts for the year ended 30 November 20X5.
15 Marks

(b) Prepare the balance sheet as on the above date. **15 Marks**

Total Marks = 30

56 MCQ *3 mins*

Which of these transactions would *not* increase a company's retained profit for the year?

A Revaluation of a freehold factory from £140,000 to £250,000.
B Receipt of £5,000 from a debtor previously written off.
C Receive discounts of £1,000 from a supplier.
D Sell for £6,000 a car which cost £10,000 and has depreciated by £4,500. **2 Marks**

57 RETAINED PROFIT *3 mins*

A company has profit before tax of £140,000. The tax charge for the year is £25,000 and £15,000 is to be transferred to a fixed asset reserve. A final dividend of 5p per ordinary share is proposed. In the year these dividends were paid:

	£
Last year's final dividend on 375,000 25p ordinary shares	15,000
This year's interim dividend on 375,000 25p ordinary shares	10,000
This year's interim dividend on 100,000 6% preference shares	3,000

The retained profit for the year is £____________. **2 Marks**

58 PEAKEWAR *54 mins*

Peakewar Ltd, a manufacturing and trading company, has extracted the following trial balance from its ledgers on 31 October 20X9.

	Debit	*Credit*
	£'000	£'000
Premises at cost	200	
Plant and equipment at cost	180	
Vehicles at cost	64	
Accumulated depreciation at 1 November 20X8		
Premises		32
Plant and equipment		102
Vehicles		24
Ordinary shares (£1 each)		150
Share premium		50
Profit and loss reserve		283
Stocks: direct materials (1 November 20X8)	12	
work in progress (1 November 20X8)	8	
finished goods	16	
Purchases of direct materials	164	
Sales		671
Production overhead incurred	104	
Selling overhead	26	
Administration overhead	49	
Trade debtors and creditors	46	28
PAYE creditor		13
VAT creditor		28
Cash in hand	3	
Balance at bank	329	
Direct manufacturing wages	180	
	1,381	1,381

The following information is also relevant.

(a) On 1 November 20X8 the company sold a piece of plant for £6,000. It had originally cost the company £20,000 on 1 November 20X5. The proceeds from the sale were recorded as a credit to the sales account and a debit to the bank account.

(b) The company provides for depreciation using the following rates.

Premises	4% per annum on cost
Plant and equipment	20% per annum on cost
Vehicles	25% per annum reducing balance

The depreciation of premises and plant and equipment is treated as a manufacturing overhead, the depreciation of vehicles is apportioned 50% to manufacturing overhead, 25% to selling overhead and 25% to administration overhead.

No entries have yet been made for depreciation in respect of the year ended 31 October 20X9.

(c) Closing stocks of raw materials on 31 October 20X9 were valued at cost as £14,000 but some of these items had been in stock for ten years and had never been used. These items had an original cost of £3,000 but it was believed that their only value was as scrap for which £1,000 would be realised.

(d) Closing work in progress on 31 October 20X9 was valued at £17,000.

	£
Direct labour	8,000
Direct materials	5,000
Production overhead	4,000

(e) Unfortunately, the closing finished goods stock could not be counted until 3 November 20X9 when it had a total production cost of £13,000. The following transactions took place during the three days after the company's year end but before the stock-take.

Sales to customers	£5,000 at selling price
Returns by customers	£1,250 at selling price
Work in progress completed	£2,000 at total production cost

The company priced the goods sold to/returned by customers during this period using a mark-up of 25% on total production cost.

Required

(a) Record the disposal of plant in the plant disposal account in the ledger of the company, showing clearly any profit/loss on disposal. **3 Marks**

(b) Prepare the manufacturing, trading and profit and loss account of the company for the year ended 31 October 20X9. **10 Marks**

(c) Prepare the balance sheet of the company at 31 October 20X9. **10 Marks**

(d) Explain the basis of your valuation of raw material, work in progress and finished goods stock on 31 October 20X9, relating your answer to stock valuation theory as appropriate. **7 Marks**

Total Marks = 30

59 B LTD *36 mins*

The draft financial statements for B Ltd are set out below.

B LTD: PROFIT AND LOSS ACCOUNT EXTRACT FOR THE YEAR ENDED 30 SEPTEMBER 20X1

	£'000
Turnover	600
Cost of sales	(410)
Gross profit	190
Profit on sale of fixed asset	10
	200
Depreciation	(30)
Operating expenses	(70)
Interest	(15)
Dividends	(50)
Retained profit	35

B LTD: BALANCE SHEETS AS AT 30 SEPTEMBER

	20X1		20X0	
	£'000	£'000	£'000	£'000
Fixed assets (see note)		450		520
Current assets				
Stock	65		50	
Debtors	80		30	
Bank and cash	30		15	
	175		95	
Current liabilities				
Creditors	60		20	
Dividends	50		35	
	110		55	
		65		40
		515		560
Long-term liability				
Loan		(20)		(100)
		495		460
Share capital		400		400
Profit and loss account		95		60
		495		460

Note. B Ltd purchased fixed assets for £40,000 during the year ended 30 September 20X1.

Required

(a) Prepare a cash-flow statement for B Ltd for the year ended 30 September 20X1. The format need not comply with the accounting standard. **10 Marks**

(b) Discuss whether a cash-flow statement is more important than a profit and loss account to users of accounts. **10 Marks**

Total Marks = 20

60 MCQ *3 mins*

A business had net cash flow from operating activities of £80,000, and these results:

	£
Operating profit	23,000
Depreciation	4,000
Loss on sale of fixed assets	22,000
Decrease in stock	13,000
Increase in creditors	10,000

What was the change in debtors?

A No change
B Decrease of £8,000
C Increase of £18,000
D Decrease of £5,000

2 Marks

61 CASH FLOW *3 mins*

Which two of the following would cause net cash flow from operating activities in the cash flow statement to be bigger than operating profit in the profit and loss account.

(i) An increase in stocks of raw materials
(ii) A decrease in stocks of finished goods
(iii) A profit on the sale of a fixed asset
(iv) A loss on the sale of a fixed asset

2 Marks

62 WEAKNESSES *27 mins*

The managing director of H plc read a newspaper report of a fraud with had recently come to the attention of the police. The perpetrators had sent invoices to several thousand companies. These requested payment for an entry in a trade directory.

The directory did not, however, exist. The newspaper report claimed that approximately 700 companies had paid £2,000 each for an entry in this alleged directory. H plc's managing director asked whether the company had received one of these invoices. It was discovered that H plc was one of the companies which had paid the £2,000 charge. The reason for this payment was investigated.

H plc's accounting system was recently computerised. All invoices are keyed straight into a standard accounting package. The company's accounting department is short staffed and so the default settings on the package have been set to minimise the amount of clerical effort required to process transactions. If, for example, an invoice is received from a new supplier, the program will automatically allocate an account number and open an account in the purchase ledger. At the end of every month, the program calculates the amount which is due to each creditor; a cheque for each creditor is automatically printed out for the total of all of the invoices from that creditor input during the month. When the system was first installed, the accountant used to review creditors' accounts prior to the cheque run as a check that the system was not being abused. This review was, however, discontinued because of pressure of work and because there were too many invoices to review properly.

The managing director was most disturbed by this description of the purchases system and decided that it was in urgent need of improvement. The company's accountant was ordered to redesign the system. The accountant was authorised to employ additional staff if the extra expense could be justified.

Required

(a) Describe three weaknesses in H plc's existing purchases system. **6 Marks**

(b) How should the purchases and creditors system should be reorganised? **9 Marks**

Total Marks = 15

63 MCQ *3 mins*

When external auditors perform an audit of a limited company their main objective is:

A To help management's decision making process

B To advise existing and potential investors

C Find and expose system weaknesses

D State their opinion on the financial statements **2 Marks**

64 CONTROLS *3 mins*

Which two of the following are detect controls?

(i) Bank reconciliations

(ii) Reconciliation of asset register to physical assets

(iii) Matching invoices to goods received notes prior to payment

(iv) Matching wages calculations to clock cards prior to payment **2 Marks**

65 A AND B *27 mins*

Business A and Business B are both engaged in retailing, but seem to take a different approach to this trade according to the information available. This information consists of a table of ratios, shown below.

Ratio	*Business A*	*Business B*
Current ratio	2:1	1.5:1
Quick assets (acid test) ratio	1.7:1	0.7:1
Return on capital employed (ROCE)	20%	17%
Return on owner's equity (ROOE)	30%	18%
Debtors turnover	63 days	21 days
Creditors turnover	50 days	45 days
Gross profit percentage	40%	15%
Net profit percentage	10%	10%
Stock turnover	52 days	25 days

Required

(a) Explain briefly how each ratio is calculated. **7 Marks**

(b) Describe what this information indicates about the differences in approach between the two businesses. If one of them prides itself on personal service and one of them on competitive prices, which do you think is which and why? **8 Marks**

Total Marks = 15

66 MCQ *3 mins*

A company has a gross profit margin of 10% and an asset turnover of 3 times a year.

What is the return on capital employed?

A 3.33%
B 7%
C 13%
D 30% **2 Marks**

67 WORKING CAPITAL *3 mins*

A company has sales of £420,000 spread evenly over the year. All sales are on credit with a debt collection period of 2 months. Cost of sales are £240,000 and the stock turnover period is 1 month, the company gets on average 45 days credit from its suppliers.

The company's working capital (excluding cash) is £______________.

The cash cycle is ______________ months. **2 Marks**

1 USERS OF ACCOUNTING INFORMATION

The people who might be interested in financial information about a large public company may be classified as follows.

(a) *Managers of the company.* These are people appointed by the company's owners to supervise the day-to-day activities of the company. They need information about the company's financial situation as it is currently and as it is expected to be in the future. This is to enable them to manage the business efficiently and to take effective control and planning decisions.

(b) *Shareholders of the company*, ie the company's owners. These will want to assess how effectively management is performing its stewardship function. They will want to know how profitably management is running the company's operations and how much profit they can afford to withdraw from the business for their own use.

(c) *Trade contacts*, including suppliers who provide goods to the company on credit and customers who purchase the goods or services provided by the company. *Suppliers* will want to know about the company's ability to pay its debts, *customers* need to know that the company is a secure source of supply and is in no danger of having to close down.

(d) *Providers of finance to the company.* These might include a bank which permits the company to operate an overdraft, or provides longer-term finance by granting a loan. The bank will want to ensure that the company is able to keep up with interest payments, and eventually to repay the amounts advanced.

(e) *Government and its agencies such as the Inland Revenue*, who will want to know about business profits in order to assess the tax payable by the company, or to prepare statistics.

(f) *Employees*, will want to know if they have secure futures with the organisation.

2 MCQ

B.

3 PROFIT

(a) The profit earned in September on a cash basis was:

	£
Sales	200
Purchases	(100)
Profit	100

(b) The profit earned in September on an accruals basis was:

	£
Sales	500
Purchases	(300)
Profit	200

4 DEFINITIONS

(a) The *going concern* concept is the assumption that, when preparing accounts, the business will continue trading for the foreseeable future, without closing down or even running down its activities to a significant extent.

If a business is to be closed down, for example, then any stock on hand will have to be valued at the amount they will realise in a forced sale. But if the business is regarded as a going concern, then the value of any unsold stock at the end of an accounting period will be carried forward to the next period and will eventually be matched against income earned in that subsequent period.

(b) The *accruals concept* is that, when profit is being calculated, revenue earned must be matched against the expenditure incurred in earning it. For example, suppose you were calculating profit for the year ended 31 December 20X8 and had got as far as working out that gross profit was £12,000. To calculate net profit, expenses must be deducted - suppose rent paid in 20X8 was £700. Then only that part of the £700 relating to 20X8 should be deducted from the gross profit. If £200 was actually a prepayment for rent in 20X9, then that £200 must be matched against next year's income, not against the £12,000 for 20X8.

(c) The *consistency concept* states that in preparing accounts consistency should be observed in two respects.

(i) Similar items within a single set of accounts should be given similar accounting treatments.

(ii) The same treatment should be applied from one period to another in accounting for similar items. This enables valid comparisons to be made from one period to the next.

For example, suppose a business owns a fleet of cars. Then the consistency concept rules that each car should be depreciated in the same way (by whatever method the business deems most appropriate) and once that depreciation policy has been set, it should be applied consistently from one year to the next.

A business can change its accounting methods, but it should explain clearly why it is doing so, and it should show the effects of the change on the profits for the relevant year in its financial statements.

(d) The *prudence concept* is that where alternative procedures, or alternative valuations, are possible, the one selected should be the one which gives the most cautious presentation of the business's financial position or results. For example, stocks should be stated in the balance sheet at the lower of cost or net realisable value rather than their selling price: to value the stock at selling price would be to anticipate making a profit before the profit had been earned, and would not be 'prudent'.

The other aspect of the prudence concept is that where a loss is foreseen, it should be anticipated and taken into account immediately. If a business purchases stock for £1,200 but because of a sudden slump in the market only £900 is likely to be realised when the stock is sold, the prudence concept dictates that the stock should be valued at £900. It is not enough to wait until the stock is sold, and then recognise the £300 loss. It must be recognised as soon as it is foreseen.

and guarantees.

5 MCQ

D.

Making a provision for bad and doubtful debts follows the prudence concept, ie recognising a potential loss.

6 ACCOUNTING BODIES

(i) Financial Reporting Council
(ii) Financial Reporting Review Panel
(iii) Accounting Standards Board

7 THE ACCOUNTING EQUATION

Transaction	*Assets*		=	*Capital*		+	*Liabilities*	
		£			£			£
Start of business	Cash	5,000	=		5,000	+		0
(a)	Cash	3,200	=		5,000	+		0
	Shelves	1,800						
		5,000						
(b)	Cash	1,200	=		5,000	+		0
	Shelves	1,800						
	Books	2,000						
		5,000						
(c)	Cash	2,700	=		5,000	+		0
	Shelves	1,800		Profit	500			
	Books	1,000						
		5,500			5,500			
(d)	Cash	2,500	=		5,000	+		0
	Shelves	1,800		Profit	500			
	Books	1,000		Drawings	(200)			
		5,300			5,300			
(e)	Cash	3,000	=		5,000	+	Loan	500
	Shelves	1,800		Profit	500			
	Books	1,000		Drawings	(200)			
		5,800			5,300			500
(f)	Cash	3,000	=		5,000	+	Loan	500
	Shelves	1,800		Profit	500		Creditor	1,000
	Books	1,000		Drawings	(200)			
	Carpets	1,000			5,300			1,500
		6,800						
(g)	Cash	3,000	=		5,000	+	Loan	500
	Shelves	1,800		Profit	700		Creditor	1,000
	Books	600		Drawings	(200)			
	Carpets	1,000			5,500			1,500
	Debtor	600						
		7,000						

8 MCQ

C.

P = I + D – C

800 = 2,500 + D + 0

⇒ D = £5,500

9 PROFIT

Net assets at 31.12.X4 = £4,000 + £2,000 – £1,500 + £3,500 – £2,000 = £6,000 (which is of course equal to capital)

So, the decrease in net assets is £7,000.

P = I + D – C

P = –£7,000 +£800 – £1,000

P = –£7,200

ie, a loss of £7,200

10 FINANCIAL STATEMENTS

A balance sheet is a 'snapshot' of the financial position of a business. It is a statement of the liabilities, assets and capital of the business at a given moment in time. It is basically the same as the accounting equation, but written out in more detail.

The trading profit and loss account is not a static picture like the balance sheet, but is a record of income generated and expenditure incurred over the relevant accounting period.

Capital expenditure is expenditure which results in the acquisition of fixed assets (or an improvement in their earning capacity). It is not charged as an expense in the trading, profit and loss account.

Revenue expenditure is any other expenditure such as purchase of goods and expenses incurred to keep the business running (for example repairs, wages, electricity and so on). It is accounted for in the trading, profit and loss account.

Capital expenditure: (a), (d)
Revenue expenditure: (b), (c), (e), (f) (Note that the value of the transactions is irrelevant.)

11 GROSS PROFIT

Decrease gross profit by £250

No effect on net profit.

This £250 must be 'moved up' from the profit and loss account to the trading account. This reduces gross profit and has no effect on net profit.

12 MCQ

A correct.
B incorrect, this is repairs not improvement
C incorrect, reoccurrence is not important
D incorrect, the fact it is such a small amount is more likely to justify its treatment as a revenue item

13 BUSINESS TRANSACTIONS

(a) *Purchase of goods on credit*

(i) The supplier's invoice would be the original document.
(ii) The original entry would be made in the purchase day book.

(b) *Allowances to credit customers on the return of faulty goods*

(i) The usual documentation is a credit note. Occasionally, however, a customer may himself issue a debit note.

(ii) The book of original entry would be the sales returns day book.

(c) *Petty cash reimbursement*

(i) The original documents for the data would be receipts and a petty cash voucher.
(ii) The transaction would be entered in the petty cash book.

(d) *Credit card sale*

(i) The original document would be the credit card sales voucher or, strictly speaking, a copy of it.

(ii) The original entry would be made in the cash book. This is because a credit card sale is like a cash sale as far as the retailer is concerned. The credit card company pays immediately, or very soon after the transaction has taken place. There is no need to set up a debtor.

14 BEECHFIELD

(a) PETTY CASH BOOK

Receipts	Date	Narrative	Total	Stationery	Cleaning	Enter-tainment	Travel	Postages
£	20X9		£	£	£	£	£	£
	Nov							
350	1	Cash						
	2	Materials	5		5			
	3	Stamps	10					10
	6	Envelopes	12	12				
	8	Taxi fare	32				32	
	10	Petrol	17				17	
	14	Typing paper	25	25				
	15	Materials	4		4			
	16	Bus fare	2				2	
	20	Visitors' lunch	56			56		
	21	Mops and brushes	41		41			
	23	Stamps	35					35
	27	Envelopes	12	12				
	29	Visitors' lunches	30			30		
	30	Photocopying pape	40	40				
			321	89	50	86	51	45
321	30	Cash						
	30	Balance c/d	350					
671			671					
	Dec							
350	1	Balance b/d						

15 FILL IN THE BLANKS

The sales book lists **all invoices sent to customers**.

The purchases book lists **all invoices received from suppliers**.

The sales returns book lists **all credit notes sent to customers**.

The purchases returns book lists **all credit notes received from suppliers**.

16 J OCKEY

(a) The relevant books of prime entry are the cash book, the sales day book, the purchase day book.

CASH BOOK (RECEIPTS)

Date	Narrative	Total	Capital	Sales	Debtors
		£	£	£	£
May 1	Capital	5,000	5,000		
May 13	Sales	200		200	
May 16	Bruce	700			700
May 24	Hill	200			200
		6,100	5,000	200	900

CASH BOOK (PAYMENTS)

Date	*Narrative*	*Total*	*Fixtures and fittings*	*Creditors*	*Rent*	*Delivery expenses*	*Drawings*	*Wages*
May		£	£	£	£	£	£	£
1	Store Fitments Ltd	2,000	2,000					
19	Abel	650		650				
20	Rent	200			200			
21	Delivery expenses	50				50		
30	Drawings	200					200	
30	Wages	320						320
31	Green	300		300				
		3,720	2,000	950	200	50	200	320

SALES DAY BOOK

Date	*Customer*	*Amount*
		£
May 4	Bruce	700
May 11	Hill	580
Mat 18	Nailor	360
		1,640

PURCHASE DAY BOOK

Date	*Customer*	*Amount*
		£
May 2	Abel	650
May 9	Green	300
May 17	Kaye	800
		1,750

(b) and (c)

The relevant ledger accounts are for cash, sales, purchases, creditors, debtors, capital, fixtures and fittings, rent, delivery expenses, drawings and wages. Because this is not the end of the accounting period, balances on sales and expense accounts are not transferred to P & L but are simply carried down to be continued in the next month.

CASH ACCOUNT

	£		£
May receipts	6,100	May payments	3,720
		Balance c/d	2,380
	6,100		6,100

SALES ACCOUNT

	£		£
Balance c/d	1,840	Cash	200
		Debtors	1,640
	1,840		1,840

PURCHASES ACCOUNT

	£		£
Creditors	1,750	Balance c/d	1,750

DEBTORS ACCOUNT

	£		£
Sales	1,640	Cash	900
		Balance c/d	740
	1,640		1,640

CREDITORS ACCOUNT

	£		£
Cash	950	Purchases	1,750
Balance c/d	800		
	1,750		1,750

CAPITAL ACCOUNT

	£		£
Balance c/d	5,000	Cash	5,000

FIXTURES AND FITTINGS ACCOUNT

	£		£
Cash	2,000	Balance c/d	2,000

RENT ACCOUNT

	£		£
Cash	200	Balance c/d	200

DELIVERY EXPENSES ACCOUNT

	£		£
Cash	50	Balance c/d	50

DRAWINGS ACCOUNT

	£		£
Cash	200	Balance c/d	200

WAGES ACCOUNT

	£		£
Cash	320	Balance c/d	320

Sales ledger

BRUCE

	£		£
SDB	700	Cash book	700

HILL

	£		£
SDB	580	Cash book	580

NAILOR

	£		£
SDB	360		

Purchase ledger

ABLE

	£		£
Cash book	650	PDB	650

HILL

	£		£
Cash book	300	PDB	300

KAYE

	£		£
		PDB	800

17 **FILL IN THE BLANKS**

Source documents are recorded in day books. The totals of day books are posted by double entry to ledger accounts in the **nominal ledger.**

Individual invoice details in the day books are posted by single entry to accounts in the **personal ledgers.**

18 MCQ

C is correct. This error affects the total posted to the purchases account and the creditors accounts in the nominal ledger, and it affects the amount posted to the suppliers account in the purchase ledger.

19 HUBBLE

Rather than write out the ledger accounts all over again, the question may be answered as follows.

(a) The postings necessary for each transaction are

		£	£
DEBIT	Purchases	2,000	
CREDIT	Cash		1,000
CREDIT	Creditors		1,000
DEBIT	Interest	20	
CREDIT	Cash		20
DEBIT	Electricity	25	
CREDIT	Cash		25
DEBIT	Telephone	12	
CREDIT	Cash		12
DEBIT	Cash	500	
DEBIT	Debtors	3,000	
CREDIT	Sales		3,500
DEBIT	Cash	220	
CREDIT	Debtors		220

(b) Once these have been posted and the accounts balanced off, the trial balance is

Account	*Dr* £	Cr £
Cash	18,083	
Capital		9,500
Bank loan		3,000
Sales		19,300
Debtors	6,980	
Rent	2,750	
Purchases	4,100	
Creditors		2,400
Interest	370	
Electricity	425	
Telephone	192	
Drawings	1,300	
	34,200	34,200

(*Note.* If you are not confident of your arithmetic, you may find it safer to write out and balance off all the ledger accounts individually.)

PROFIT AND LOSS (LEDGER) ACCOUNT

	£		£
Rent	2,750	Sales	19,300
Purchases	4,100		
Interest	370		
Electricity	425		
Telephone	192		
Balance (net profit taken to balance sheet)	11,463		
	19,300		19,300

(c) A HUBBLE BALANCE SHEET AS AT 31 MARCH 20X8

	£	£
Assets		
Cash	18,083	
Debtors	6,980	
	25,063	
Current liabilities		
Creditors	(2,400)	
		22,663
Long-term liabilities		
Loan		(3,000)
		19,663
Capital		
Capital as at 1.4.20X7		9,500
Add profit for year		11,463
Less drawings		(1,300)
Capital as at 31.3.20X8		19,663

A HUBBLE
TRADING, PROFIT AND LOSS ACCOUNT
FOR THE YEAR ENDED 31 MARCH 20X8

	£	£
Sales		19,300
Less cost of sales		4,100
Gross profit		15,200
Less other expenses		
Rent	2,750	
Interest	370	
Electricity	425	
Telephone	192	
		3,737
Net profit		11,463

20 MCQ

C is correct. The clerk has done two credits of £250, and no debit, so credits will exceed debits by £500.

21 TRIAL BALANCE

Purchases should be a debit balance so credits will exceed debits by £3,000.

22 RENT, RATES AND INSURANCE

(a) *Rent for the year ending 30 June 20X6*

	£
1 July 20X5 to 31 July 20X5 = £3,000/3	1,000
1 August 20X5 to 30 November 20X5	4,000
1 December 20X5 to 31 March 20X6	4,000
Accrued, 1 April 20X6 to 30 June 20X6 = 3/4 × £4,000	3,000
Charge to profit and loss for year ending 30 June 20X6	12,000

Rates for the year ending 30 June 20X6

	£	£
Rates prepaid last year, relating to this year		1,500
1 October 20X5 to 31 March 20X6		3,500
1 April 20X6 to 30 September 20X6	3,500	
Less prepaid July to September (3/6)	1,750	
April to June 20X6		1,750
Charge to profit and loss for year ending 30 June 20X6		6,750

Insurance for the year ending 30 June 20X6

	£	£
Insurance prepaid last year, relating to this year		1,800
1 November 20X5 to 31 October 20X6	6,000	
Less prepaid July to October (4/12)	2,000	
		4,000
Charge to profit and loss for year ending 30 June 20X6		5,800

(b) The accrual or prepayment for each expense can be summarised from the workings in part (a).

As at 30 June 20X6	£
Rent accrued	3,000
Rates prepaid	1,750
Insurance prepaid	2,000

23 MCQ

B.

ELECTRICITY EXPENSE ACCOUNT

	£		£
Cash	3,000	B/d	1,000
C/d	1,200	Profit and loss	3,200
	4,200		4,200
		B/d	1,200

24 TRIAL BALANCE

Gross profit is £6,800.

	£	£
Sales		12,500
Less cost of sales		
Opening stock	400	
Purchases	6,000	
Carriage inwards	200	
	6,600	
Closing stock £(1,100 – 200)	(900)	
		(5,700)
Gross profit		6,800

25 GEORGE

DEBTORS ACCOUNT

		£			£
1.10.X1	Balance b/f (b)	30,000	15.1.X2	Bad debts-Fall Ltd (c)	2,000
30.9.X2	Sales (d)	187,800	30.9.X2	Cash (e)	182,500
				Discounts allowed (f)	5,300
				Bad debts (g)	3,500
				Balance c/d	24,500
		217,800			217,800
1.10.X2	Balance b/d	24,500			

SALES ACCOUNT

		£			£
30.9.X2	Trading P & L a/c	234,600	30.9.X2	Cash (d)	46,800
				Debtors (d)	187,800
		234,600			234,600

BAD DEBTS ACCOUNT

		£			£
15.1.X2	Debtors-Fall Ltd (c)	2,000	30.9.X2	Trading P & L a/c	5,500
30.9.X2	Debtors (g)	3,500			
		5,500			5,500

PROVISION FOR DOUBTFUL DEBTS ACCOUNT

		£			£
30.9.X2	Balance c/d (h)		1.10.X1	Balance b/f (b)	
	5% × £24,500	1,225		5% × £30,000	1,500
	Trading P & L a/c - reduction in provision	275			
		1,500			1,500
			1.10.X2	Balance b/d	1,225

DISCOUNTS ALLOWED ACCOUNT

		£			£
30.9.X2	Debtors	5,300	30.9.X2	Trading P & L a/c	5,300

CASH ACCOUNT (EXTRACT)

		£
30.9.X2	Debtors	182,500
	Sales	46,800

TRADING PROFIT AND LOSS ACCOUNT (EXTRACT)

		£			£
30.9.X2	Bad debts	5,500	30.9.X2	Sales	234,600
	Discounts allowed	5,300		Provision for doubtful debts	275

26 BAD AND DOUBTFUL DEBTS

B.

PROVISION

	£		£
		B/d	2,000
C/d	3,000	Bad debts expense	1,000
	3,000		3,000

BAD DEBTS EXPENSE

	£		£
Debtors	1,000	Cash	800
Increase in provision	1,000	Profit and loss	1,200
	2,000		2,000

27 TRIAL BALANCE

We have 'missed' income (and thus a credit balance) of £1,500 and an expense (and thus a debit balance) of £1,000. Thus debit balances will exceed credit balances by £500.

28 AFTER THE STOCK COUNT

		Adjustment	
		Add to stock value	Subtract from stock value
Item	*Explanation*	£	£
(a)	The sub-total error has over-valued stocks by £(6,725 – 6,275)		450
(b)	This arithmetical error has over-valued the stock item by £(6 – 0.6) per unit for 260 units		1,404
(c)	Goods in stock should be included in the valuation regardless of whether or not they have been paid for yet		
(d)	Cost £2,885. Net realisable value £(3,600 – 921) = £2,679. The stock should be valued at the lower of cost and NRV. Since NRV is lower, the original valuation of stocks (at cost) will be reduced by £(2,885 – 2,679)		206
(e)	Stocks issued on sale or return and not yet accepted by the customer should be included in the stock valuation and valued at the lower of cost and NRV, here at £5 each (cost)	1,500	
(f)	The cost (£7.30) is below the current and foreseeable selling price (£10 or more) which is assumed to be the NRV of the item. Since, the current valuation is at the lower of cost and NRV no change in valuation is necessary	-	-
		1,500	2,060

	£	£
Original valuation of stocks, at cost		153,699
Adjustments and corrections:		
to increase valuation	1,500	
to decrease valuation	(2,060)	
		(560)
Valuation of stocks for the annual accounts		153,139

29 MCQ

B. (i) and (iv) are correct.

Under LIFO, stock is the oldest receipts, so cost of sales is at current (higher) prices which reduces profit.

30 STOCK

FIFO is £260, LIFO is £300.

Under FIFO

	Units		*Value* £
May 1	100	@ £10	1,000
May 5	50	@ £10	500
Balance	150	@ £10	1,500
May 12	(60)	@ £10	(600)
Balance	90	@ £10	900
May 20	20	@ £8	160
Balance	110	@ £8	1,060
May 29	(80)	@ £10	(800)
	30		260

Under LIFO

	Units		*Value* £
May 1	100	@ £10	1,000
May 5	50	@ £10	500
Balance	150	@ £10	1,500
May 12	(60)	@ £10	(600)
Balance	90	@ £10	900
May 20	20	@ £8	160
Balance	110	@ £8	1,060
May 29	(20)	@ £8	(160)
	(60)	@ £10	(600)
	30		300

31 SPARKS

(a) Check the balances on your ledger accounts with the trial balance shown below.

	Debit £	*Credit* £
Cash book		
Bank (note below) (W1)	1,703	
Cash (unbanked at end of period) (W2)	12	
Nominal ledger		
Drawings	560	
Postage and stationery	129	
Travelling expenses	40	
Motor expenses	104	
Cleaning expenses	260	
Sundry expenses	19	
Telephone	214	
Electricity	190	
Motor vans	2,000	
Rates	320	
Fixtures and fittings	806	
Capital		2,308
Purchases	3,163	
Discounts received		419
Credit sales		830
Cash sales		4,764
Discount allowed	81	
Provision for depreciation:		
motor van		720
fixtures and fittings		250
Stock at 1 January 20X1	366	
Loan – Flex		250
Sales ledger		
Brown	12	
Blue	180	
Stripe	48	
Purchase ledger		
Live		602
Negative		64
Earth		
	10,207	10,207

Workings

1 *Cash at bank*

	£
Opening balance	672
Bankings of cash (908+940+766+1,031)	3,645
Capital introduced	500
Received from customers	
90% × (160+66+22+10+40+120+140+130+20+44+38+20) = 90% of 810	729
	5,546
Less cheque payments (telephone, electricity, rates, van)	(1,469)
Payments to suppliers	
85% × (143+468+570+390+80+87+103+73+692+187) = 85% × 2,793	(2,374)
Closing balance	1,703

2 *Cash in hand*

	£		£
Balance b/d	5	Bank	3,645
∴ Sales	4,764	Drawings	560
		Stationery	73
		Travel	40
		Petrol and van	104
		Sundry	19
		Postage	56
		Cleaner	260
		Balance c/d	12
	4,769		4,769

(b) (i) SPARKS - TRADING AND PROFIT AND LOSS ACCOUNT FOR THE FOUR MONTHS ENDED 30 APRIL 20X1

	£	£	£
Sales			5,594
Opening stock		366	
Purchases		3,163	
		3,529	
Closing stock		390	
			3,139
Gross profit			2,455
Discount received			419
Profit on sale of motor van			20
			2,894
Rent (W1)		500	
Rates (W2)		174	
Electricity		212	
Telephone (W3)		192	
Motor expenses		104	
Travelling		40	
Postage and stationery		129	
Cleaning		260	
Sundry expenses		19	
Depreciation (W4)			
Motor van	65		
Fixtures and fittings	27		
		92	
Discount allowed		81	
Loan interest (W5)		8	
			1,811
Net profit			1,083

Workings

1 Rent: 4/12 × £1,500 = £500; Accrual of £500 at 30 April

2 Rates: £100 + 2/6 × £220 = £174; Prepayment of £146 at 30 April

3 Telephone: £214 + £15 - £37 = £192

4 Depreciation: Motor van: 20% × £1,300 × 3/12 = £65
Fixtures: 10% × £806 × 4/12 = £27

5 Loan interest: 10% × £250 × 4/12 = £8

(ii) SPARKS - BALANCE SHEET AS AT 30 APRIL 20X2

	Cost	*Dep'n*	
	£	£	£
Fixed assets			
Motor van	1,300	65	1,235
Fixtures and fittings	806	277	529
	2,106	342	1,764
Current assets			
Stock at cost		390	
Debtors		240	
Payments in advance		146	
Cash at bank		1,703	
Cash in hand		12	
		2,491	
Current liabilities			
Trade creditors	666		
Accrued expenses	537		
		1,203	
			1,288
			3,052
Loan account: Flex			258
			2,794
Capital account			£
Balance at 1 January			1,808
Capital introduced			500
Profit for the four months			1,083
			3,391
Less drawings			597
			2,794

32 MCQ

D is correct.

Have debited cars		£7,000	
Should	Credit cars	£8,000	} ie Debit £2,000
	Debit cars	£10,000	

⇒ net adjustment is credit cars £5,000

33 PROFIT ON DISPOSAL

Sales proceeds were £5,500.

31.7.X5

	£
Cost	20,000
Depreciation y/e 31.12.X5 to y/e 31.12.X8	16,000
NBV at date of sale	4,000
Profit on disposal	1,500
⇒ Sale proceeds	5,500

34 CAMFORD

The first step is to correct the errors in the cash book.

CASH BOOK

	£		£
Uncorrected balance b/f	1,900	Transfer to Midlands Savings	
Transposition error (a)	90	Bank - previously omitted (c)	1,500
Cash lodgement understated (b)	10	Error in bringing down balance at 1.6.X1 (f)	100
Sundry receipt omitted (d)	10	Bank charges (g)	20
Subscription credited directly (k)	100	Standing order (i)	30
		Subscriptions - cheque returned (j)	50
		Corrected balance c/d	410
	2,110		2,110
Corrected balance b/d	410		

BANK RECONCILIATION STATEMENT AS AT 31 MAY 20X2

	£	£	
Balance shown by bank statement		470	o/d
Unpresented cheques (e)		40	
		510	o/d
Outstanding lodgements (h)	900		
Error on bank statement (l)	20		
		920	
Balance shown in cash account		410	

35 MCQ

D is correct.

When cash is received by a business a debit entry is made in the cash book. A receipt of cash decreases an overdraft and increases a bank balance.

36 BANK RECONCILIATIONS

Debit £19.

Unpresented cheques and increased lodgements are timing differences so no adjustments is necessary.

The bank charges need a credit to cash of £35.

The transposition errors needs a debit to cash £54, ie a net debit of £19.

37 P&CO

(a) JOURNAL ENTRIES

		£ DR	£ CR
Error (i)	Purchase ledger control - Ahmed	420	
	Sales ledger control - Ahmed		420
Error (iv)	Bad debts - Sales ledger control - Thomas	240	
	Sales ledger control - Thomas		240
Error (v)	Sales	900	
	Sales ledger control		900

(b) BALANCES EXTRACTED FROM THE SALES LEDGER

		+	–	
		£	£	£
Total before corrections for errors				15,800
Error (ii)	Mahmood	90		
Error (iii)	Yasmin	780		
Error (vi)	Charles		300	
Error (vii)	Edward	125		
		995	300	695
				16,495

(c) CONTROL ACCOUNT

SALES LEDGER CONTROL ACCOUNT

	£			£
Balance b/f	18,055	Error (i)	Ahmed	420
		Error (iv)	Thomas	240
		Error (v)	Sales daybook total	900
				1,560
		Balance c/f		16,495
	18,055			18,055

38 CONTROL ACCOUNTS

B.

This affects both the total which was posted to the control account and the individual posting to the purchase ledger.

39 SALES DAY BOOK

Debit £30.

For the undercast	debit £50
For the invoice entered invoice	credit £20
A net debit of	£30

40 HYPER

Initial workings

1 Invoiced sales excluding VAT = $\frac{£141,000}{117.5} \times 100 = £120,000 \therefore \text{VAT} = £21,000$

2 Purchases excluding VAT = $\frac{£84,600}{117.5} \times 100 = £72,000 \therefore \text{VAT} = £12,600$

DEBTORS

	£		£
Balance b/f	40,000	Bank	128,300
Sales and VAT creditor	141,000	Balance c/f	52,700
	181,000		181,000

CREDITORS

	£		£
Bank	92,700	Balance b/f	22,000
Balance c/f	13,900	Purchases and VAT creditor	84,600
	106,600		106,600

VAT CREDITOR

	£		£
Creditors (W2)	12,600	Balance b/f	4,100
Bank	4,100	Debtors (W1)	21,000
Balance c/f	8,400		
	25,100		25,100

SALES

	£		£
		Debtors (W1)	120,000

PURCHASES

	£		£
Creditors (W2)	72,000		

BANK ACCOUNT (EXTRACT)

	£		£
Debtors	128,300	Creditors	92,700
		VAT creditor	4,100

41 VAT

B is correct.

The others are all valid reasons for not adding VAT on sales invoices.

42 VAT

£9,500

VAT CREDITOR

	£		£
Creditors	3,000	Debtors	12,000
Cash	1,500	Cash	2,000
C/d	9,500		
	14,000		14,000
		B/d	9,500

43 PAYROLL

(a)

CREDITORS

	£		£
Cash	5,400	Balance b/f	800
Discounts received	100	Purchases	6,000
Debtors - contra	700		
Balance c/d	600		
	6,800		6,800
		Balance b/d	600

(b) DEBTORS

	£		£
Balance b/d (bal. fig.)	2,000	Creditors - contra	700
Sales	12,000	Cash	11,800
		Discounts allowed	300
		Bad debts	200
		Balance c/d	1,000
	14,000		14,000
Balance b/d	1,000		

(c) PROVISION FOR DOUBTFUL DEBTS

	£		£
Debtors	200	Balance b/f	450
Balance c/d	400	Cash - bad debt recovered	50
		P&L a/c: increase in provision	100
	600		600
		Balance b/d	400

(d) WAGES CONTROL

	£		£
Bank	1,330	Balance b/f	38
PAYE control	407	Wages expense a/c - gross wages	2,000
NIC control	260		
Balance c/d	41		
	2,038		2,038
		Balance b/d	41

(e) PAYE CONTROL

	£		£
Cash	400	Balance b/f	35
Balance c/d	42	Wages control	407
	442		442
		Balance b/d	42

(f) NIC CONTROL

	£		£
Cash	546	Balance b/f	44
Balance c/d	48	Wages control - employees	260
		Wages expense a/c - employer	290
	594		594
		Balance b/d	48

44 MCQ

A.

45 PAYE AND NIC

Debit	Wages control account (total deductions)
Credit	PAYE control account (PAYE)
Credit	NIC control account (NIC)

46 BRENDA BAILEY

TRADING AND PROFIT AND LOSS ACCOUNT
FOR THE YEAR ENDED 30 JUNE 20X9

	£	£
Sales		427,726
Opening stock	15,310	
Purchases	302,419	
Carriage inwards	476	
	318,205	
Less closing stock	16,480	
Cost of sales		301,725
Gross profit		126,001
Carriage outwards	829	
Wages and salaries	64,210	
Rent and rates (12,466 – 620)	11,846	
Heat and light (4,757 + 350)	5,107	
Depreciation - equipment	10,200	
- motor vehicles	8,654	
Sundry expenses	8,426	
		109,272
Net profit for the year		16,729

BRENDA BAILEY
BALANCE SHEET AS AT 30 JUNE 20X9

	Cost £	*Dep'n* £	*Net book value* £
Fixed assets			
Equipment	102,000	32,450	69,550
Motor vehicles	43,270	17,574	25,696
	145,270	50,024	95,246
Current assets			
Stock		16,480	
Debtors		50,633	
Prepayments		620	
Cash		477	
		68,210	
Current liabilities			
Bank overdraft		3,295	
Creditors		41,792	
Accruals		350	
		45,437	
Net current assets			22,773
			118,019
Capital			
Balance at 1 July 20X8			122,890
Add profit for the year			16,729
			139,619
Less drawings			21,600
Balance at 30 June 20X9			118,019

47 SUSPENSE ACCOUNT

D is correct.

Discounts received are income and thus, a credit balance. Recording them as a debit will have made debits in the trial balance exceed credits by £700, ie the suspense account balance is a credit of £700. So the correction is debit suspense £700, and credit discounts received £700.

48 MCQ

A is correct.

The correction will increase expenses and reduce purchases. Thus gross profit will increase and net assets not change.

49 GILTAN GOLF CLUB

> *Tutorial note.* In this problem, there is no bar trading account to deal with. The expenses of the functions should be netted off against the income from the functions. Subscriptions for the year consist of total cash received from subscriptions (£2,930) minus the cash received which relates to arrears from the previous year (£65) and payments in advance for the next year (£35), plus arrears for the current year (£30).

The income of the previous year (to 31 March 20X7) included £15 owed as subscriptions in arrears by the member who has now emigrated. This £15, added to income last year, must now be deducted as an expense in the current year to even things out.

Where there are accrued expenses, brief workings are shown to indicate how the expenditure for the year is calculated.

The bequest of £255 to the club should be added directly to the accumulated fund. It is not a part of the regular income and expenditure of the club, and so should be excluded from the income and expenditure account.

The surplus on the sale of the land (£1,600 – £500) should be added directly to the accumulated fund, since the fixed asset has not been subject to depreciation charges in the past.

INCOME AND EXPENDITURE ACCOUNT
FOR THE YEAR ENDED 31 MARCH 20X8

	£	£
Income		
Subscriptions £(2,930 – 65 – 35 + 30 – 15)		2,845
Functions: income	367	
less expenses	305	
		62
Bank interest received		60
Sundry income		46
		3,013
Expenditure		
Repairs	146	
Telephone £(67 – 14 + 10)	63	
Heat and light £(115 – 32 + 40)	123	
Salary and wages £(2,066 + 14 – 12)	2,068	
Sundry expenses	104	
Depreciation		
Buildings (5% × £3,800)	190	
Fixtures and fittings (10% × £470)	47	
Furniture (20% × £515)	103	
		2,844
Surplus transferred to accumulated fund		169

50 MCQ

B £1,080.

SUBSCRIPTIONS ACCOUNT

	£		£
Arrears b/f	200	Prepaids b/f	500
Income and expenditure a/c (balance)	1,080	Bank/cash	1,200
Prepaid c/f	600	Arrears c/f	180
	1,880		1,880

51

The figure for subscriptions in an income and expenditure account would be £2,130.

SUBSCRIPTIONS ACCOUNT

	£		£
Arrears b/f	50	Prepaid b/f	80
Income and expenditure a/c (balance)	2,130	Cash	2,060
Prepaid c/f	60	Arrears c/f	100
	2,240		2,240

The figure for subscriptions in a receipts and payments account would be £2,060.

52 HIGHTON

TRADING PROFIT AND LOSS ACCOUNT
FOR THE YEAR ENDED 31 MARCH 20X2

	£	£
Sales: cash	80,400	
credit (W1)	9,250	
		89,650
Cost of sales		
Opening stock	3,500	
Purchases: cash	17,000	
credit (W2)	47,500	
	68,000	
Less closing stock	4,000	
		64,000
Gross profit		25,650
Expenses		
Depreciation of motor vehicle (25% × £3,000)	750	
Motor vehicle expenses (W3)	800	
Property insurance £(50 + 150 – 100)	100	
Loan interest	100	
Electricity £(400 + 400 – 200)	600	
General shop expenses	100	
Telephone £(100 + 300)	400	
Wages	3,000	
Rates	300	
		6,150
Net profit		19,500

BALANCE SHEET AS AT 31 MARCH 20X2

	£	£
Fixed assets		
Freehold land and buildings at cost		10,000
Motor vehicle: cost	3,000	
accumulated depreciation	1,500	
		1,500
		11,500
Current assets		
Stock	4,000	
Trade debtors	1,000	
Prepayments	400	
Cash at bank	950	
Cash in hand	450	
	6,800	
Current liabilities		
Trade creditors	1,800	
Accruals	500	
	2,300	
Net current assets		4,500
		16,000

	£	£
Proprietor's capital		
At 1 April 20X1 (W4)*		5,250
Net profit for the year	19,500	
Less drawings £(7,000 + 1,750)	8,750	
Profit retained in business		10,750
		16,000

*The opening capital could be inserted as a balancing figure, W4 is included merely to prove the figure.

Workings

1 DEBTORS CONTROL ACCOUNT

	£		£
Opening balance	500	Bank	8,750
∴ Credit sales	9,250	Closing balance	1,000
	9,750		9,750

2 CREDITORS CONTROL ACCOUNT

	£		£
Bank	47,200	Opening balance	1,500
Closing balance	1,800	∴ Credit purchases	47,500
	49,000		49,000

3 MOTOR VEHICLE EXPENSES

	£		£
Prepayment b/f	200	Accrual b/f	200
Bank	1,000	∴ P & L account	800
Accrual b/f	100	Prepayment c/f	300
	1,300		1,300

4 PROPRIETOR'S CAPITAL AT 1 APRIL 20X1

	£	£
Assets		
Freehold land and buildings	10,000	
Motor vehicle	2,250	
Stock	3,500	
Debtors and prepayments	750	
Cash at bank and in hand	650	
		17,150
Liabilities		
Loan	10,000	
Creditors and accruals	1,900	
		11,900
		5,250

53 MCQ

C is correct.

SUBSCRIPTIONS ACCOUNT

	£		£
Contra	3,500	B/d	10,000
Discounts received	2,500	Transfers to debtors	350
Cash (balance)	56,350	Purchases	60,000
C/d	8,000		
	70,350		70,350

54 OPENING STOCK

Opening stock was £5,500.

	£	£
Sales (100%)		25,000
Opening stock (balance)	5,500	
Purchases	22,000	
Less closing stock	(5,000)	
Cost of sales (25,000 – 2,500) or 90%		(22,500)
Gross profit (10%)		2,500

55 EXCEL

(a) EXCEL LIMITED
PROFIT AND LOSS ACCOUNT
FOR THE YEAR ENDED 30 NOVEMBER 20X5

	£	£
Revenue		510,500
Less loss on vehicle disposal		1,500
		509,000
Less expenses		
Wages and expenses	245,200	
Licences and insurance	6,000	
Repairs	34,440	
Petrol and oil	44,870	
Administration expenses	30,460	
Advertising expenses	13,340	
Directors' remuneration	40,000	
Bad debts	890	
Provision for doubtful debts	1,849	
Auditor's fees	2,000	
Debenture interest	3,600	
Depreciation	21,800	
		444,449
		64,551
Appropriations		
Interim share dividend	12,000	
Final proposal dividend	24,000	
		36,000
Retained profit		28,551
Retained profit 30/11/X4		127,200
Retained profit 30/11/X5		155,751

(b) EXCEL LIMITED
BALANCE SHEET AS AT 30 NOVEMBER 20X5

	Cost	*Depreciation*	*NBV*
Fixed assets	£	£	£
Premises	420,000	-	420,000
Vehicles	93,200	51,620	41,580
	513,200	51,620	461,580
Current assets			
Stocks: petrol and oil	1,640		
spares	3,170		
		4,810	
Debtors	61,640		
Provision for doubtful debts	(1,849)		
		59,791	
Prepayments		1,500	
Cash		19,920	
		86,021	

	£	£
Creditors: amounts falling due within one year:		
Debenture interest	3,600	
Final share dividend	24,000	
Advertising accrual	800	
Auditors fee	2,000	
Repairs	1,450	
	31,850	
Net current assets		54,171
Total assets less current liabilities		515,751
Creditors: amounts falling due after more than one year		
12% debentures		(120,000)
		395,751
Capital and reserves		
Shares (200,000 at £1, fully paid)		200,000
Share premium		40,000
Profit and loss account		155,751
		395,751

Workings

1 Provision for doubtful debts

Provision = 3% × £(62,530 – 890) = £1,849

2 *Accounting treatment for stocks*

Because of the nature of the business, it is difficult to come to a 'cost of sales' figure for Excel Ltd. Consequently no attempt has been made to arrive at a gross profit figure. Stocks figures have therefore been incorporated into the relevant expense figures as follows.

	Petrol and oil	*Vehicle spares (repairs)*
	£	£
Charge shown in list of balances	45,310	35,460
Add opening stock	1,200	700
	46,510	36,160
Less closing stock	1,640	3,170
Charge to P & L account	44,870	32,990 *

* There is also a repairs accrual of £1,450, so the P & L charge for repairs is £32,990 + £1,450 = £34,440

3 Motor vehicles and depreciation

The motor vehicles figure of £111,200 is incorrect, as it has been made up incorrectly. The sales proceeds should not be shown in the motor vehicles account, but the £24,000 original cost disposed of should be. Journal entries to correct these errors are:

		£	£
DEBIT	Motor vehicles	6,000	
CREDIT	Motor vehicles disposals		6,000
DEBIT	Motor vehicle disposals	24,000	
CREDIT	Motor vehicles		24,000

In addition, depreciation in respect of the vehicle disposed of should be debited to depreciation account, and credited to disposals account (25% × £24,000 × 2.75 years = £16,500). Also, depreciation for the year should be calculated on the motor vehicles account balance.

The effect of all these adjustments is:

MOTOR VEHICLES

	£		£
Balance b/f	85,200	Sale proceeds	6,000
Additions	32,000	Disposals	24,000
Sales proceeds correction	6,000	Balance c/f	93,200
	123,200		123,200

DISPOSALS

	£		£
Motor vehicles	24,000	Sale proceeds	6,000
		Depreciation	16,500
		P & L account	1,500
	24,000		24,000

DEPRECIATION

	£		£
Disposals	16,500	Balance b/f	46,320
Balance c/f	51,620	P & L account	21,800 *
	68,120		68,120

		£
* £85,200 × 25% × 9/12	=	15,975
£93,200 × 25% × 3/12	=	5,825
		21,800

4 *Debenture interest*

Accrued debenture interest = 12% × £120,000 × 3 months
= £3,600

56 MCQ

A.

'Profit' on revaluation must be credited to a revaluation reserve, not to retained profits for the year.

57 RETAINED PROFIT

£65,250

	£
Profit before tax	140,000
Tax	(25,000)
Reserves	(15,000)
This years final dividend (5p × 375,000)	(18,750)
This years preference dividend (100,000 × 6%)	(6,000)
Retained profit for the year	65,250

58 PEAKEWAR

(a) PLANT DISPOSAL ACCOUNT

	£'000		£'000
Plant at cost	20	Sales proceeds	6
		Depreciation *	12
		Loss on disposal to manufacturing account	2
	20		20

* Annual depreciation on plant = £20,000 × 20% = £4,000

∴ Cumulative depreciation since 19X5 = 3 years × £4,000 = £12,000

(b) PEAKEWAR LIMITED
MANUFACTURING TRADING AND PROFIT AND LOSS ACCOUNT
FOR THE YEAR ENDED 31 OCTOBER 20X9

	£'000	£'000
Direct materials		
Opening stock	12.0	
Purchases	164.0	
	176.0	
Closing stock (note (I))	(12.0)	
		164.0
Direct manufacturing wages		180.0
		344.0
Production overhead		
Overhead incurred	104.0	
Depreciation: premises (£200,000 × 4%)	8.0	
plant and equipment (note (ii))	32.0	
vehicles (note (iii))	5.0	
Loss on disposal of plant (from part (a))	2.0	
		151.0
		495.0
Work in progress		
Opening stock	8.0	
Closing stock	17.0	
		(9.0)
Production cost of goods completed c/d		486.0
Sales (note (iv))		665.0
Cost of sales		
Opening stock of finished goods	16.0	
Production cost of goods completed b/d	486.0	
	502.0	
Closing stock of finished goods (note (v))	(14.0)	
		488.0
Gross profit		177.0
Selling overhead: incurred	26.0	
Depreciation of vehicles (note (iii))	2.5	
		28.5
Administration overhead: incurred	49.0	
Depreciation of vehicles (note (iii))	2.5	
		51.5
Net profit		97.0

(c) PEAKEWAR LIMITED
BALANCE SHEET AS AT 31 OCTOBER 20X9

		Cost	Depreciation	Net
		£'000	£'000	£'000
Fixed assets				
Premises		200	40	160
Plant and equipment (note (vi))		160	122	38
Vehicles		64	34	30
		424	196	228
Current assets				
Stocks:	direct materials (note (i))	12		
		17		
	finished goods (note (v))	14		
			43	
Trade debtors			46	
Balance at bank			329	
Cash in hand			3	
			421	
Current liabilities				
Trade creditors			28	
PAYE creditor			13	
VAT creditor			28	
			69	
Net current assets				352
				580
Financed by				
Ordinary £1 shares				150
Share premium				50
Profit and loss reserve (283 + 97)				380
				580

Notes

(i) See part (d) of this solution.

(ii) Depreciation of plant and equipment

	£'000
Plant and equipment at cost as per trial balance	180
Less cost of plant sold	20
	160
Depreciation at 20%	32

(iii) Depreciation of vehicles

	£'000
Vehicles at cost	64
Less accumulated depreciation at 1 November 20X8	24
Net book value at 1 November 20X8	40
25% reducing balance depreciation	10

Apportioned:	£'000
manufacturing overhead 50%	5.0
selling overhead 25%	2.5
administration overhead 25%	2.5

(iv) *Sales value for the year*

	£'000
Sales as per trial balance	671
Less proceeds of plant sale incorrectly credited to sales account	6
	665

(v) Finished goods closing stock valuation

	£'000	£'000
Value as at 3 November 20X9		13
Add back net sales to customers since year end		
Sales at selling price	5.00	
Less returns at selling price	(1.25)	
Net sales at selling price	3.75	
Deduct profit mark-up (25/125)	(0.75)	
Net sales at cost		3
		16
Less production completed since year end		(2)
		14

(vi) *Plant and equipment*

	Cost	*Depreciation*	*Net*
	£'000	£'000	£'000
Balances at 1 November 20X8	180	102	78
Sale of plant	(20)	(12)	(8)
	160	90	70
Depreciation for year	-	32	32
	160	122	38

(d) *Raw materials stocks*

Stocks should be valued at the lower of cost and net realisable value. The items which have been in stock for ten years now have a net realisable value of £1,000 which is lower than the cost of £3,000. These items should therefore be valued at £1,000 and the total value of stock must be reduced accordingly.

	£'000
Raw material stock at cost	14
Less stock written down to net realisable value (3 – 1)	2
	12

Finished goods

The workings in note (v) were carried out to determine the cost of finished goods stock held at the balance sheet date. Since the sales values include a profit margin this must be removed to deduce the cost price of the stock.

59 B LTD

(a) **B LTD: cash-flow statement for the year ended 30 September 20X1**

	£'000	£'000
Operating activities - see workings		95
Sale of fixed assets - see workings		90
Interest		(15)
Purchase of fixed asset		(40)
Dividends		(35)
Repayment of loan		(80)
		15
Opening bank and cash	15	
Closing bank and cash	30	
Increase in cash		15

Workings

	£'000
Operating activities	
Operating profit (35 + 50 + 15)	100
Adjustment for non-cash-flow items	
Profit on sale of fixed asset	(10)
Depreciation	30
	120
Adjustment for working capital	
Stock	(15)
Debtors	(50)
Creditors	40
	95
Sale of fixed assets	
Net book value (520 + 40 – 30 – 450)	80
Profit on sale	10
Proceeds on sale	90

(b) A cash-flow statement (CFS) helps users to assess the liquidity, solvency and financial adaptability of an entity. The liquidity of an entity is revealed by the change in the bank/cash balances between the beginning and end of the period. The solvency of an entity, and whether it is a going concern, may be assessed by using the historical cash flow to forecast future cash flows. The financial adaptability of an entity is its ability to use its cash to meet changes in its business environment.

A CFS is easier to understand than the accruals-based concept of profit and loss account, since it simply records the receipt and payment of cash, and is therefore likely to be more important to the user of accounts than the more complex profit and loss account.

A CFS is more objective than accruals-based financial statements and it is less capable of manipulation. Users are therefore likely to place greater importance on this statement than the more subjective profit and loss account.

Cash is the life-blood of a business and it is, therefore, vital that users of accounts assess cash flow when appraising a business. The CFS shows how finance is raised and where this is invested in the business. It thus provides a link between the profit and loss account and the balance sheet.

Cash flow provides a basis for determining the amount of dividends to pay, and this is of interest to the users of accounts; similarly, cash flow is useful in valuing a business, which is also of interest to users.

Cash flow from operations is a measure of the 'quality' of the profit: the more closely cash approximates to profit, then the higher the quality.

However, although CFS is conceptually easier to understand than a profit and loss account, the information it gives may be less easy to interpret. An increase in profit gives a positive message; a decrease in profit gives a negative message. Such a direct correlation does not apply tot he CFS. Cash may increase, but this may be as a result of selling all the fixed assets; it may decrease, although this may be the result of buying fixed assets which will yield long-term advantages.

The CFS focuses on cash, not working capital, and thus there may be a temporary decrease/increase in cash depending on whether a large debtor has paid or stock has been built up.

The pattern of cash flows may be erratic and these are not smoothed out by the accruals policy as used in the profit and loss account. The CFS is not, therefore, a measure of economic performance.

Thus the profit and loss account and the CFS are both relevant to the users of accounts and neither should be used in isolation.

60 MCQ

B.

	£
Operating profit	23,000
Add depreciation	4,000
Add loss on sale of fixed assets	22,000
Add decrease in stock	13,000
Add increase in creditors	10,000
	72,000
Total cash inflow	80,000
Thus change in debtors produced cash inflow of	8,000

∴ a **decrease** in debtors

61 CASH FLOW

(ii) and (iv) are added to operating profit to get cash flow from operating activities.

62 WEAKNESSES

> *Tutorial note.* This is a 'problem' question. You should have resisted the temptation to write all you know about purchases systems.

(a) Weaknesses in H plc's existing purchase system are as follows.

(i) Invoices are not approved before they are input. This could lead to the creation of fictitious liabilities.

(ii) New supplier accounts are opened automatically as a result of keying in an invoice without approval from a responsible official. It would thus be possible to create fictitious accounts.

(iii) Cheque payments for creditors' balances are issued without scrutiny of the account and approval. The could lead to inaccuracy in the account or the name of the supplier.

(b) The purchases and creditors system should be reorganised as follows.

(i) Purchase invoices should only be input after they have been approved by the relevant department/official who should check them to orders and goods received notes.

(ii) New suppliers' accounts should only be opened with written approval from a responsible official. An audit report of new accounts opened in a particular period (eg a month) should be produced and reviewed.

(iii) The batching of invoices and cash payments will allow batch totals to be agreed to output totals.

(iv) Creditor accounts should be reconciled to suppliers' statements on a regular basis.

(v) Cheque payments should not be made without approval linked to a review of the relevant invoices.

63 MCQ

D is correct.

Remember that the external audit report is addressed to shareholders and states their opinion on the financial statements.

64 CONTROLS

(i) and (ii) are detect controls.

(iii) and (iv) are prevent controls.

65 A AND B

> *Tutorial note.* You are not required to discuss the ratios, this will only waste precious time which could be devoted to part (b), the interpretation question.

(a) (i) *Current ratio*

$$\frac{\text{Current assets}}{\text{Current liabilities}}$$

(ii) *Quick assets (acid test) ratio*

$$\frac{\text{Current assets - stock}}{\text{Current liabilities}}$$

(iii) *Return on capital employed (ROCE)*

$$\frac{\text{Net profit before interest}}{\text{Total long-term capital}}$$

(iv) *Return on owner's equity (ROOE)*

$$\frac{\text{Profit after tax}}{\text{Share capital plus reserves}}$$

(v) *Debtors turnover*

$$\frac{\text{Debtors}}{\text{Sales per day}}, \text{ ie } \frac{\text{Debtors} \times 365}{\text{Sales}}$$

(vi) *Creditors turnover*

$$\frac{\text{Creditors}}{\text{Cost of sales per day}} \text{ ie } \frac{\text{Creditors}}{\text{Cost of sales}} \times 365$$

(vii) *Gross profit percentage*

$$\frac{\text{Gross profit}}{\text{Sales}}$$

(viii) *Net profit percentage*

$$\frac{\text{Net profit}}{\text{Sales}}$$

(ix) *Stock turnover*

$$\frac{\text{Average (or year-end) stock}}{\text{Cost of sales per day}}, \text{ ie } \frac{\text{Stock} \times 365}{\text{Cost of sales}}$$

(b) (i) *Profitability*

A has a much higher gross profit margin than B. It may be assumed that B concentrates on volume, while A has a higher mark-up, because it serves a smaller clientele which is prepared to pay higher prices.

Turning to the net profit margin, this is the same for both businesses, reflecting the fact that the more exclusive business will have relatively higher operating costs.

(ii) *Liquidity*

The current and quick assets ratios both show that A has a higher working capital requirement than B. Comparing the current and quick ratios, B has high stocks relative to liabilities (0.8:1), compared with A (0.3:1). It may be inferred from this that A has significantly higher debtors. This reflects the fact that a more 'upmarket' retailer is far more likely to give extended credit to its more exclusive, and richer customers. The latter is also reflected in the higher debtors collection period. Stock moves more slowly in A than in B, perhaps reflecting the less conventional nature of the products sold.

(iii) *Efficiency and gearing*

ROCE is slightly higher for A than for B indicating more efficient use of assets (perhaps less store space is needed to display the products on sale). ROOE is significantly higher for A, suggesting that A has high long-term borrowings at an interest rate below 20%. B on the other hand probably has low long term borrowings, since ROCE and ROOE are about the same. Alternatively B's long term borrowings may be at an interest rate close to 18%.

(iv) *Summary*

Accounting ratios cannot tell us everything about an organisation. In particular, they give no definite information on the size of A relative to B. However, even without this background information, the lower margins and faster stock turnover of B would suggest a high sales volume at low prices, while A clearly sells more slowly at a higher mark-up, suggesting a niche rather than a mass market.

66 MCQ

D is correct.

ROCE = Profit margin × Asset turnover

30% = 10% × 3

67 WORKING CAPITAL

The company's working capital (excluding cash) is £60,000.

The cash cycle is one and a half months.

	£
Stocks ($^1/_{12}$ × £240,000)	20,000
Debtors ($^2/_{12}$ × £420,000)	70,000
Less creditors ($^{1.5}/_{12}$ × £240,000	(30,000)
Working capital	60,000

Cash cycle is 1 + 2 – 1.5 = 1.5 months.

Index

> **Note: Key Terms** and their page references are given in **bold**

REVIEW FORM & FREE PRIZE DRAW

All original review forms from the entire BPP range, completed with genuine comments, will be entered into one of two draws on 31 January 2002 and 31 July 2002. The names on the first four forms picked out on each occasion will be sent a cheque for £50.

Name: ______________________ **Address:** ______________________

____

How have you used this Text?
(Tick one box only)

- ☐ Self study (book only)
- ☐ On a course: college (please state)________
- ☐ With 'correspondence' package
- ☐ Other ________

Why did you decide to purchase this Text?
(Tick one box only)

- ☐ Have used BPP Texts in the past
- ☐ Recommendation by friend/colleague
- ☐ Recommendation by a lecturer at college
- ☐ Saw advertising
- ☐ Other ________

During the past six months do you recall seeing/receiving any of the following?
(Tick as many boxes as are relevant)

- ☐ Our advertisement in CIMA *Insider*
- ☐ Our advertisement in *Financial Management*
- ☐ Our advertisement in *Pass*
- ☐ Our brochure with a letter through the post
- ☐ Our website www.bpp.com

Which (if any) aspects of our advertising do you find useful?
(Tick as many boxes as are relevant)

- ☐ Prices and publication dates of new editions
- ☐ Information on product content
- ☐ Facility to order books off-the-page
- ☐ None of the above

Which BPP products have you used?

Text ☐ **Kit** ☐ **Passcard** ☐ **MCQ cards** ☐ **Tape** ☐ **Video** ☐

How did you/will you take the exam for this paper (Tick one box only)

Written exam ☐ Computer based assessment ☐

Your ratings, comments and suggestions would be appreciated on the following areas

	Very useful	*Useful*	*Not useful*
Introductory section (Key study steps, personal study)	☐	☐	☐
Chapter introductions	☐	☐	☐
Key terms	☐	☐	☐
Quality of explanations	☐	☐	☐
Case examples and other examples	☐	☐	☐
Questions and answers in each chapter	☐	☐	☐
Chapter roundups	☐	☐	☐
Quick quizzes	☐	☐	☐
Exam focus points	☐	☐	☐
Question bank	☐	☐	☐
Answer bank	☐	☐	☐
Index	☐	☐	☐
Icons	☐	☐	☐
Mind maps	☐	☐	☐

	Excellent	*Good*	*Adequate*	*Poor*
Overall opinion of this Study Text	☐	☐	☐	☐

Do you intend to continue using BPP products? ☐ Yes ☐ No

Please note any further comments and suggestions/errors on the reverse of this page. The BPP author of this edition can be e-mailed at: janiceross@bpp.com

Please return this form to: Alison McHugh, CIMA Range Manager, BPP Publishing Ltd, FREEPOST, London, W12 8BR

REVIEW FORM & FREE PRIZE DRAW (continued)

Please note any further comments and suggestions/errors below.

FREE PRIZE DRAW RULES

1 Closing date for 31 January 2002 draw is 31 December 2001. Closing date for 31 July 2002 draw is 30 June 2002.

2 Restricted to entries with UK and Eire addresses only. BPP employees, their families and business associates are excluded.

3 No purchase necessary. Entry forms are available upon request from BPP Publishing. No more than one entry per title, per person. Draw restricted to persons aged 16 and over.

4 Winners will be notified by post and receive their cheques not later than 6 weeks after the relevant draw date.

5 The decision of the promoter in all matters is final and binding. No correspondence will be entered into.

See overleaf for information on other
BPP products and how to order

Mr/Mrs/Ms (Full name)

Daytime delivery address

Postcode

Daytime Tel | Email | Date of exam (month/year)

CIMA Order

To BPP Publishing Ltd, Aldine Place, London W12 8AW
Tel: 020 8740 2211. Fax: 020 8740 1184
www.bpp.com Email publishing@bpp.com
Order online www.bpp.com

	7/01 Texts	1/01 Kits	1/01 Passcards	9/00 Tapes	7/00 Videos	8/01 i-Pass		7/01 MCQ cards
FOUNDATION								
1 Financial Accounting Fundamentals	£20.95 ☐	£10.95 ☐	£5.95 ☐	£12.95 ☐	£25.95 ☐	£24.95 ☐		£5.95 ☐
2 Management Accounting Fundamentals	£20.95 ☐	£10.95 ☐	£5.95 ☐	£12.95 ☐	£25.95 ☐	£24.95 ☐		£5.95 ☐
3A Economics for Business	£20.95 ☐	£10.95 ☐	£5.95 ☐	£12.95 ☐	£25.95 ☐	£24.95 ☐		£5.95 ☐
3B Business Law	£20.95 ☐	£10.95 ☐	£5.95 ☐	£12.95 ☐	£25.95 ☐	£24.95 ☐		£5.95 ☐
3C Business Mathematics	£20.95 ☐	£10.95 ☐	£5.95 ☐	£12.95 ☐	£25.95 ☐	£24.95 ☐		£5.95 ☐
INTERMEDIATE						1/02 i-Pass	1/02 i-Learn	
4 Finance	£20.95 ☐	£10.95 ☐	£5.95 ☐	£12.95 ☐	£25.95 ☐	£29.95 ☐	£19.95 ☐	£5.95 ☐
5 Business Tax (FA 2001)	£20.95 ☐ (9/01)	£10.95 ☐	£5.95 ☐	£12.95 ☐	£25.95 ☐	£29.95 ☐	£19.95 ☐	£5.95 ☐
6 Financial Accounting	£20.95 ☐	£10.95 ☐	£5.95 ☐	£12.95 ☐	£25.95 ☐	£29.95 ☐	£19.95 ☐	
6I Financial Accounting International	£20.95 ☐	£10.95 ☐						
7 Financial Reporting	£20.95 ☐	£10.95 ☐	£5.95 ☐	£12.95 ☐	£25.95 ☐	£29.95 ☐	£19.95 ☐	
7I Financial Reporting International	£20.95 ☐	£10.95 ☐						
8 Management Accounting - Performance Management	£20.95 ☐	£10.95 ☐	£5.95 ☐	£12.95 ☐	£25.95 ☐	£29.95 ☐	£19.95 ☐	£5.95 ☐
9 Management Accounting - Decision Making	£20.95 ☐	£10.95 ☐	£5.95 ☐	£12.95 ☐	£25.95 ☐	£29.95 ☐	£19.95 ☐	£5.95 ☐
10 Systems and Project Management	£20.95 ☐	£10.95 ☐	£5.95 ☐	£12.95 ☐	£25.95 ☐	£29.95 ☐	£19.95 ☐	
11 Organisational Management	£20.95 ☐	£10.95 ☐	£5.95 ☐	£12.95 ☐	£25.95 ☐	£29.95 ☐	£19.95 ☐	
FINAL								
12 Management Accounting - Business Strategy	£20.95 ☐	£10.95 ☐	£5.95 ☐	£12.95 ☐	£25.95 ☐			
13 Management Accounting - Financial Strategy	£20.95 ☐	£10.95 ☐	£5.95 ☐	£12.95 ☐	£25.95 ☐			
14 Management Accounting - Information Strategy	£20.95 ☐	£10.95 ☐	£5.95 ☐	£12.95 ☐	£25.95 ☐			
15 Case Study				£12.95 ☐	£25.95 ☐			
(1) Workbook	£20.95 ☐							
(2) Toolkit for 11/01 exam: available 9/01		£19.95 ☐						
(3) Toolkit for 5/02 exam: available 3/02		£19.95 ☐						

Total ☐

POSTAGE & PACKING

Study Texts

	First	Each extra	
UK	£3.00	£2.00	£
Europe***	£5.00	£4.00	£
Rest of world	£20.00	£10.00	£

Kits/Passcards/Success Tapes

	First	Each extra	
UK	£2.00	£1.00	£
Europe***	£2.50	£1.00	£
Rest of world	£15.00	£8.00	£

Breakthrough Videos

	First	Each extra	
UK	£2.00	£2.00	
Europe***	£2.00	£2.00	£
Rest of world	£20.00	£10.00	£
MCQ cards	£1.00	£1.00	£
			£

Grand Total (Cheques to *BPP Publishing*) I enclose a cheque for (incl. Postage) £

Or charge to Access/Visa/Switch

Card Number

Expiry date Start Date

Issue Number (Switch Only)

Signature

We aim to deliver to all UK addresses inside 5 working days. A signature will be required. Orders to all EU addresses should be delivered within 6 working days. All other orders to overseas addresses should be